WILLIAM ALMON WHEELER

William Almon Wheeler. Brady-Handy Collection, Library of Congress.

William Almon Wheeler

Political Star of the North Country

Herbert C. Hallas

excelsior editions

State University of New York Press
Albany, New York

Published by State University of New York Press, Albany

© 2013 State University of New York

All rights reserved

Printed in the United States of America

No part of this book may be used or reproduced in any manner whatsoever without written permission. No part of this book may be stored in a retrieval system or transmitted in any form or by any means including electronic, electrostatic, magnetic tape, mechanical, photocopying, recording, or otherwise without the prior permission in writing of the publisher.

Excelsior Editions is an imprint of State University of New York Press

For information, contact State University of New York Press, Albany, NY
www.sunypress.edu

Production by Dana Foote
Marketing by Fran Keneston

Library of Congress Cataloging-in-Publication Data

Hallas, Herbert C., 1937-
William Almon Wheeler : political star of the north country / Herbert C. Hallas.
pages cm
Includes bibliographical references and index.
ISBN 978-1-4384-4812-1 (pbk. : alk. paper) 1. Wheeler, William A. (William Almon), 1819–1887. 2. Vice-Presidents—United States—Biography. 3. Legislators—United States—Biography. 4. United States. Congress. House—Biography. 5. United States—Politics and government—1877–1881. 6. United States—Politics and government—1869–1877. 7. New York (State)—Politics and government—1865–1950. 8. New York (State)—Politics and government—1775–1865. 9. Malone (N.Y.)—Biography. I. Title.
E664.W57.H35 2013
328.73'092--dc23
[B]

2012044465

10 9 8 7 6 5 4 3 2 1

To

Barbara Hallas

and

Alan G. Friedman

(1937–2007)

Contents

Illustrations

ACKNOWLEDGMENTS

To WRITE THIS BOOK, I needed the help of many people. First and foremost, I am indebted to James T. Otten, whose scholarly research about Wheeler paved the way for my work. I am also grateful to David M. Jordan for his perceptive biography of Roscoe Conkling, one of Wheeler's archrivals, and to Ari Hoogenboom for his insightful writing about Wheeler's presidential running mate, Rutherford B. Hayes.

There are many historians, librarians, curators, and archivists who provided valuable assistance to me and several of them deserve special mention, including: Edward Knoblauch, New York History Net; Loretta Ebert and Barbara Massago, New York State Library; Jim Folts and Bill Gorman, New York State Archives; Paul Carnahan, Vermont Historical Society; Eileen Meyer Sklar, Presbyterian Historical Society; Nan J. Card, Rutherford B. Hayes Presidential Center; Amy E. Burton, U.S. Senate Curator's Office; Felicia Wivchar, Office of Art and Archives for the U.S. House of Representatives; Sylvia J. Bugbee, Bailey/Howe Library of the University of Vermont; and Sarah Hartwell, Rauner Special Collections Library of Dartmouth College.

I also received special help from people working in Wheeler's hometown, Malone, New York. For their important assistance I offer thanks to Cheryl Learned, Ted Mills, and Susan Tobias at the Franklin County Historical and Museum Society, and to Dick Murphy, Lynn Dufort, and Bob Hutchins at the Malone Lodge of Elks.

I owe a special debt to three members of my family. I thank my brother, Henry C. Hallas, for his continuous encouragement and invaluable help in locating information for me about Wheeler's role in the establishment of the state Adirondack

Park. I also thank my cousin, James H. Hallas, for his enthusiastic support and wise counsel based on his many successful writing and publishing experiences. And I thank my son, Edmond P. Hallas, for sharing his extensive knowledge of philosophy and theology with me in order to assist me in evaluating the impact Calvinism had on Wheeler's life.

This book is dedicated to my late friend, Alan G. Friedman, and to my wife, Barbara Hallas. Alan was truly a one-of-a-kind guy. He was the only person I knew who was familiar with every forgotten nineteenth-century political figure I might bring up in conversation and enjoyed talking knowledgeably about them. Alan's steadfast interest in all my Wheeler anecdotes and research spurred me on when the going got rough.

Barbara has been a twenty-four-hour-a-day help to me. As I slogged my way along researching Wheeler's life, she was always there for me to discuss the latest "news of the day" or "political problem of the moment"—provided I first answered her question: What century are we in? She accompanied me on many journeys to Malone and other towns in the North Country without complaint even though I knew how uncomfortable the sight of too many trees could be to this self-styled Queens girl. Barbara read and reread this biography through all its various stages offering solid criticism and superb proofreading along the way. No author could ask for any more caring and loving support than that. Thanks, Barb.

Introduction

"So this is where the elephants come to die!" According to local legend, that is how New York's Republican governor and vice president, Nelson A. Rockefeller, described Malone, New York, "The Star of the North," when he made a campaign stop there in the 1960s. Located more than two hundred miles north of Albany, close to the Canadian border, Malone is the county seat of Franklin County and the only home William Almon Wheeler ever had.

A lawyer, state legislator, bank executive, and railroad president by the time he was thirty-five, Wheeler's life is an American success story. Overcoming a poverty-stricken childhood in a remote, sparsely populated county in New York's North Country, William Wheeler, nicknamed Bill, became a nationally known political figure during the Gilded Age. He served five terms in Congress where he marshaled political support for the nation's fledgling transcontinental railroad system and negotiated an end to a racial civil war in Louisiana, before becoming the nineteenth vice president of the United States.

Wheeler was a distinguished looking man of medium height who enjoyed wearing popular fashions of his day, such as the dashing Inverness or Ulster overcoat, a large loose coat with a cape affixed to the collar. He had a light complexion and a muscular build. When people shook his hand, they felt magnetism in his touch and were impressed by his commanding mien. However, as a Washington columnist wrote about Wheeler, "He don't claw you and rub your left shoulder blade and invite you to ask him favors he will never bestow."[1]

Wheeler talked in a sharp, rugged way and had a quick wit. He disdained empty formalities and ceremonies. According to one columnist, Bill's mouth "would seem a little grim in expression, were it not smoothed out by a pair of the kindest eyes in the world" and a smile that "lights his entire countenance."[2]

His kind eyes and smile could be deceiving because he was one of the most powerful political figures ever to operate in the North Country. His enemies described him as ruthless and autocratic.[3]

An avid outdoorsman, Wheeler loved the beauty of nature and the therapeutic effect it could have on him.[4] As a congressman, he supported the creation of Yellowstone Park and as a state official, he was instrumental in the creation of both the Adirondack Park and the Niagara Falls State Park. Particularly fond of fishing, he would travel annually up country, into the Adirondacks, to fish with members of the Saranac Navigation Company, the name he gave to a small group of his closest friends.[5] He would also take fishing vacations with his wife in the White Mountains where they would stay at the Twin Mountain House in Bretton Woods, New Hampshire.[6] Bill's fishing prowess became so well known in Washington, newspapers began to rib him as "the piscatorial Mr. Wheeler."[7]

In addition to fishing in the mountains, Wheeler's other joy was singing. He had a clear bass voice and loved to sing gospel music, folk songs, and Presbyterian hymns whenever he could. On Sunday mornings when he was in Washington, he could be found singing during services at his church, the New York Avenue Presbyterian Church. At other times, he would sing duets with his wife in the parlor after supper or would join the Hayes family and cabinet members for a hymn sing in the upstairs library at the White House.[8]

Described as a "cultivated man" by a noted U.S. historian, Wheeler proudly displayed a leather-bound, steel-engraved illustrated set of Shakespeare's works in his library in Malone.[9] Bill's letters and speeches are laced with quotes not only from Shakespeare but also from poets such as Wordsworth, Tennyson, Milton, Whittier, and Pope. Latin phrases and sayings pepper his writing.[10]

A consummate political realist, Wheeler was greatly influenced by the Protestant theology of John Calvin that Bill's ancestors had brought with them from England in the seventeenth century. His great-great-great-great-great grandfather, Thomas Wheeler of Cranefield, England, arrived on the ship *Defiance* in New England on October 3, 1635, with his wife and six children on board. They were part of a wave of Puritans that flooded the Massachusetts Bay Colony with settlers who carried with them a fervent desire to purify the Church of England of the Roman Catholic practices to which the Anglican establishment clung.[11]

Following internal religious strife in Concord, Massachusetts, where they lived for nine years, Thomas Wheeler and his family moved to the Black Rock section of Fairfield, Connecticut, where they prospered. Within one generation, the Wheelers became one of the richest families in the Connecticut Colony.[12]

Bill Wheeler revered his Puritan ancestry and believed that the Puritans were "the foundation stone of the greatest political edifice of the world—the United States of America."[13] He first learned about Calvin and the Puritans from his father, Almon Wheeler, which is where William Almon Wheeler's story begins.

1
Tragedy in Malone

☆

Twenty-two-year-old Almon Wheeler came to the frontier town of Malone, New York, in 1812 with his teenage bride, Eliza, and a head full of dreams. He wanted to buy some land, build a home, start a family, and become a lawyer.[1]

Almon had been born in Fairfield, Vermont, a town named for his father's birthplace in Connecticut, on October 1, 1789, four months and a day after George Washington had been inaugurated president.[2] When he was eighteen, he had enrolled in the University of Vermont but had dropped out before graduating to head west with other Vermonters who were looking for new opportunities.[3] Before he left the Green Mountain state for Malone, he married seventeen-year-old Eliza Woodward of Castleton, Vermont.[4] She was a strong woman with keen black eyes and a commanding figure. People who knew her were impressed by her firm character and strong convictions. They said she "never swerved a hair when her mind was fully made up."[5]

When Almon and Eliza first arrived, Malone was barely ten years old. It was the county seat for Franklin County, which had been created in 1808.[6] Bordering Canada on the north, Franklin County lies between Clinton County and Lake Champlain on the east and St. Lawrence County on the west. The landscape of the central and southern sections of Franklin County is dominated by the Adirondack Mountains. Malone is in the northern part of the county, forty miles north of Saranac Lake, and about fifty miles east of Plattsburgh.

Within a year after the Wheelers settled in Malone, Almon put his dreams into action. He borrowed money and purchased a half-acre lot on Elm Street and built a home.[7] He also convinced the Franklin County court to suspend its rules for the admission of attorneys and swear him in as a lawyer without requiring him to study law with an attorney for the requisite number of years.[8]

Almon had not practiced law very long before life in the North Country was disrupted by war. Congress declared war on Great Britain on June 18, 1812. As hostilities broke out all along the Canadian border in the opening rounds of the War of 1812, Eliza gave birth to the couple's first child, Jane, in 1813.[9]

A year later, in September 1814, Almon answered a call for military help that had been sent to Malone from Plattsburgh. Volunteers were urgently needed to help the U.S. Army stop a powerful force of British veterans from advancing down Lake Champlain from Canada and cutting off the New England states from the rest of the Union. Almon took up arms and fought as a volunteer at the battle of Plattsburgh.[10] The battle was a turning point in the war, which officially came to an end a few months later with the signing of the Treaty of Ghent on December 24, 1814.[11]

The end of the war brought joy to the Wheeler household in Malone and a second child, Sarah Fidelia, born on November 27, 1815.[12] The conclusion of the war also brought Almon a legal rival. He was Asa Hascall, a twenty-nine-year-old Vermont native who had been studying law in Essex County before he came to Malone.[13]

Hascall was politically well connected with the faction of the Democratic-Republican Party, which was led by Governor DeWitt Clinton. In 1818, Governor Clinton appointed Hascall to be Franklin County district attorney, a post he would hold, except for two years, until 1846.[14] Hascall was popular with Malone voters who elected him town supervisor in seventeen consecutive elections beginning in 1818.[15] He was a political powerhouse in Franklin County and was destined to play an important role in the fate of the Wheeler family, particularly in the life of Eliza and Almon's third child, William Almon Wheeler, who was born on June 30, 1819, one month after Walt Whitman was born on Long Island, and one month before Herman Melville was born in New York City.[16]

Bill Wheeler's father now had a wife and three children to support and a large mortgage on his house to pay. He began to dabble in local Democratic-Republican politics in order to find a way to earn additional revenue and generate legal business. His political activities soon paid off. In 1820, Almon was appointed Malone postmaster.[17]

Eliza and Almon's family grew up in a religious household. They regularly attended Congregational Church services, which were conducted by the Reverend

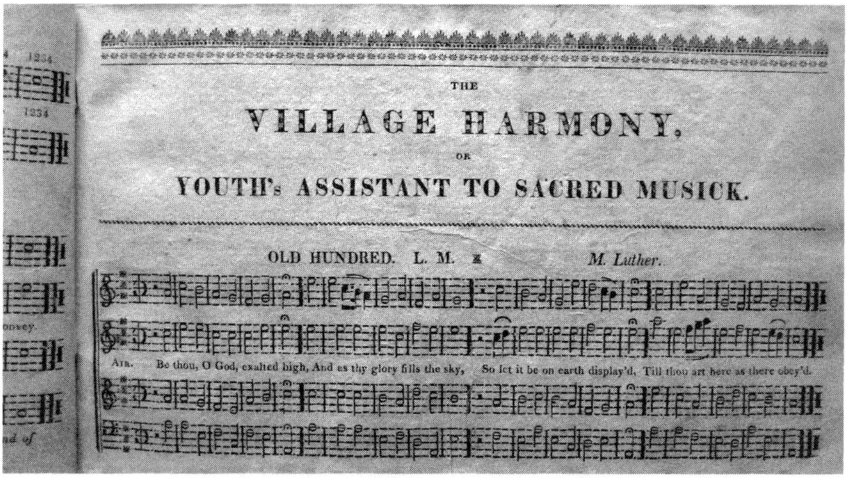

The Village Harmony songbook. Courtesy of the Franklin County Historical and Museum Society.

Ashbel Parmelee who had come from Vermont to Malone in 1809. He served as pastor of the church for the next thirty-six years.[18] Almon was also an officer in the Franklin County Bible Society and a Mason in the same lodge as the Reverend Parmelee.[19] When Bill was four years old, a Congregational Church Sunday School was organized and his parents saw to it that Bill rarely missed a class.[20]

Religion also permeated the Wheeler home in the form of music. Bill's father owned a songbook, *The Village Harmony: or Youth's Assistant to Sacred Music*. It contained sheet music, words to psalms, and sacred music that was popular in the early nineteenth century. An introduction to the book included instructions about how to read music and also had lessons for tuning the voice.[21] Because of the musical instruction Bill received from his parents and older sisters at home, he developed into a fine singer.

When Bill Wheeler's family was not praying or singing, they were concerned about paying their bills and putting food on the table. In the 1820s, nothing sounded better to promote economic growth and development in Malone and the North Country than a canal. The opening of the Champlain Canal in 1823 created an all-water route from Lake Champlain to New York City that cut the dependence of the North Country's agricultural and lumbering interests on Quebec as a market. Goods that previously had to go north to Canada could now be sent south to New York City. As an added benefit, the door to more and cheaper imports was flung wide open.[22]

Across the North Country, there was vigorous agitation for an east–west canal to be built from Lake Champlain to the St. Lawrence River.[23] In 1824, the legislature subsidized the design of a proposed 133-mile route that went from Ogdensburg in St. Lawrence County on the St. Lawrence River, east through Malone in Franklin County, on to the Chazy River in Champlain, and from there to Lake Champlain.[24]

Boston financial interests joined North Country canal advocates in promoting a canal from Ogdensburg to Lake Champlain. Their vision was to win commerce for Boston from the Great Lakes. Some saw the port of Ogdensburg on the St. Lawrence River as the destination point from Boston because at that time, Ogdensburg was the foot of sloop and steam transportation from Lake Ontario. With the help of canals from Boston to Lake Champlain and another around Niagara Falls (the Welland Canal was in the planning stages), Boston would be able to access the commerce of all of the Great Lakes.[25]

Because of the high costs and the difficult geographic obstacles canal builders had to face, none of the plans for canals from Lake Champlain to Ogdensburg moved beyond the drawing boards. The dream of a Boston–North Country–Great Lakes transportation system would have to await the coming of the railroad and the maturation of young Bill Wheeler.

Bill was six years old when his father became a major legal figure in one of the most notorious criminal trials that had ever been held to date in the North Country. Almon agreed to defend Stephen Videtoe, the first murderer brought to trial in Franklin County.[26] Following an investigation by District Attorney Hascall, Videtoe had been arrested and charged with murdering his fiancée, Fanny Mosley. A tailor by trade and pregnant at the time of her murder, she had been living with Videtoe and his family in their two-room house in Fort Covington where she was found shot to death on her bed, two days before her wedding. Videtoe denied shooting Fanny and proclaimed his innocence.[27]

The trial became the center of attention in the North County. For five long days, Hascall and Almon fought it out in the courtroom. When they rested their cases, a jury took fifteen minutes to find Videtoe guilty. He was sentenced to be hanged in a field a half-mile away from the Wheeler home on Elm Street. One eyewitness said that six- to eight thousand people witnessed the hanging.[28] As a result of his vigorous defense of Videtoe, Almon won the respect and admiration of the North Country bar in general, and District Attorney Hascall in particular. Two years later, he would show his high regard for Almon's character by helping Almon's son Bill, and his family, when they really needed it. However, before that happened, another crime took place almost three hundred miles west of Malone that set in motion political events that would also greatly influence Bill Wheeler's future.

Luther Bradish. Brady-Handy Collection, Library of Congress.

In 1826, a Mason named William Morgan of Batavia, New York, published an expose of the secrets and rituals of Freemasonry. Suddenly, Morgan disappeared. Wild rumors had it that he had been taken out on a boat on the Niagara River and murdered by Masons to protect their order. People began to say that Morgan's killers would never be brought to justice because the prosecutors and judges were Masons. Morgan's disappearance and the resultant public outcry led to what some historians have called "the first mass movement in American history." Soon, what had begun as a campaign to protest the undue influence of Masons on governmental affairs, turned into a political crusade and the Anti-Masonic Party was born. Its main goal was to make sure that no Mason would be elected to public office. Masons by the score renounced their affiliations. Churches were torn asunder in the excitement and preachers thundered from the pulpit against the Masons. Before the year was out, the existence of the Masonic lodges in Malone and nearby Chateaugay was being threatened.[29]

Astute politicians such as Thurlow Weed, Millard Fillmore, Francis Granger, William Seward, and Franklin County's own Luther Bradish, correctly saw the political potential of the anti-Masonic fervor that was sweeping east across New York State and began to make plans to use it to win political power. In 1826, Luther Bradish, one of the absentee owners of land in the Town of Moira, which lay directly west of Malone, relocated his home to a farm there. He became a leader of the anti-Masonic movement in the North Country and began to make plans to run for the assembly from Franklin County.[30] He would become one of the most popular and influential political leaders in New York State. Bradish's success prepared political leaders across the state to accept leadership from a Franklin County man who lived miles away from the urban centers of power and influence.

The Wheeler household was shaken by the power and fury of the anti-Masonic movement. Almon had been an early member of the Masonic lodge in Malone. Many of his fellow lawyers, friends, and clients were Masons. However shaken the Wheelers were by the social and political ramifications of the anti-Masonic movement, nothing prepared them for the family disaster that happened next. On January 5, 1827, thirty-seven-year-old Almon Wheeler suddenly became ill and died.[31]

His wife Eliza was thirty-three. Almon left her no money to support their three children: Jane, age fourteen; Sarah Fidelia, age eleven; and William Almon, age seven. The home on Elm Street was mortgaged heavily and Eliza did not know how she was going to pay the bills and raise her children.[32] She worried about what would happen to her children without a father and without money, especially her youngest child, seven-year-old Bill.

2

The Making of a "Cultivated" Man

☆

Eliza Wheeler was devastated emotionally and financially by Almon's death but she found the strength, energy, and commitment to keep the family together in their home on Elm Street and help her children grow up in a warm and loving environment. Eliza was determined to see to it that Bill got a good education and that their home would not be taken from them by creditors.[1]

Two prominent men in Malone stepped forward to help Eliza raise Bill. The Reverend Ashbel Parmelee, pastor of the Congregational Church in Malone, and Asa Hascall, the prominent county public figure, became Bill's substitute fathers—they were his role models and mentors.

Parmelee immersed Bill in Calvinism and taught him an uncompromising moral code. However narrow and intolerant the pastor's Calvinist theology may have seemed to others, Bill venerated Parmelee's character. His strength of conviction, acts of personal kindness, candor, and profound sense of civic duty greatly influenced the development of Bill's philosophy of life.[2]

In retirement, Wheeler wrote how much he was moved as a child by Parmelee's sermons, delivered from a pulpit shaped like the gun turret of the USS *Monitor,* ten feet above the congregation. As Wheeler put it, Parmelee "hurled the hot shot of the divine law into the rebellious hosts of the 'adversary of souls' at close range, with the fuse cut short."[3]

Ashbel Parmelee. Courtesy of the Franklin County Historical and Museum Society.

By his example, Hascall showed Bill how to be a successful businessman, active citizen, and public servant, all in one life. In Hascall, Bill saw up close what it was like to be a lawyer, trustee of a church, founder of an educational academy, town supervisor, county district attorney, state assemblyman, justice of the peace, candidate for the state senate and Congress, real estate agent, and president of an insurance company.[4] Hascall encouraged Bill to follow in his footsteps, showed him how to do it, and gave him help to do it.

To make ends meet, Eliza and her daughters hired themselves out to do housework. Bill earned what he could by doing chores and odd jobs for neighbors. One winter, a friend of the family gave them all the fallen timber they could find on a lot he owned about a mile north of the Wheeler home. Single-handedly, Bill cut the timber, loaded it on a hand sled, pulled it home, and cut the wood up into stove-length pieces. When he was done, there was enough wood to supply the family for a year.[5]

Bill wore full-cloth pants in the winter and linen pants in the summer. Twice a year, Eliza would buy a pair of pants for Bill from "Aunt" Nabby Hawley, a woman who would make the rounds of Malone selling clothes she had made, door to door. On Sundays, Bill wore bleached white pants to church. He polished his shoes with blackening taken from the bottom of a kettle that hung on the crane in the fireplace using a wet cloth with molasses on it.[6]

Eliza sent Bill to grade school where he excelled in mathematics. During recess, when the boys played soldiers, Bill liked to stand in the ranks and give orders to the boy who played captain. Bill was a lively, jolly, and happy youngster and adults trusted him. Sometimes he was given tasks seldom given to any person under twenty-five.[7]

When Bill was in fifth grade, Eliza became alarmed because family income began to tighten up. But thanks to a suggestion most likely made by Hascall, a founder and trustee of Franklin Academy, the new high school that was about to open in Malone, Eliza came up with an additional way to earn money. When the school opened in December 1831, she provided room and board to incoming students.[8] She and her daughters performed the housework and Bill chopped wood and hauled water.[9] When it was Bill's turn to go to high school, he worked his way through Franklin Academy, probably with an assist from Hascall.[10]

During Bill's grade school years, the Democrats dominated New York State. Martin Van Buren was their undisputed leader and in the North Country, Silas Wright of Canton in St. Lawrence County, was Van Buren's right-hand man. The Democratic organization built by these two men was so formidable, their opponents dubbed it the *Albany Regency*. Thanks to the vote-getting power of the Regency, Andrew Jackson had been elected president twice by the time Bill completed seventh grade.[11]

In Franklin County during this period of time, anti-Masonic rhetoric reached fever pitch. On February 12, 1829, the *Malone Telegraph* denounced the Masons as "a barbarous system of deception, fraud, folly, wickedness, tyranny, and vengeance." Mass meetings were held demanding an investigation of the order.[12] As a result, the Masonic lodges in Malone and Chateaugay were forced to close their doors, not to reopen them again for decades.[13]

Downstate, a young political genius named Thurlow Weed began harnessing anti-Masonic sentiment for use against the Regency.[14] In Franklin County, Luther Bradish stepped forward as an Anti-Mason to defeat the Democrats for a seat in the assembly in three straight elections beginning in 1828.[15] The Anti-Masons became the Regency's leading opponents but Weed and Bradish knew that simple opposition to a secret order was too slim a base on which to build a successful political party.[16]

In high school, Bill became more conscious of political parties. He noticed that a majority of the Anti-Masons in Franklin County were making new allegiances and broadening their party's base. Their counterparts in other parts of the state did the same thing and in 1834, a new political party to oppose the Regency was created. It adopted the name Whig. At first, the Whigs were no match for the Regency, which reached the pinnacle of its power in 1836. Martin Van Buren became the first man from New York to be elected president and the Democrats were in solid control of the state government in Albany. However, the Whigs were on the rise.[17]

Bill's mentor, Asa Hascall, joined the Whigs, as did Luther Bradish. The Whigs won every election for the assembly in Franklin County while Bill was in high school. In his senior year, Bradish was made Speaker.[18] As far as Bill could tell, the Whigs were clearly the ascendant power in Franklin County and had excellent prospects to win over the entire state of New York, as well as the nation.

Few of Bill's friends at school liked to talk about politics but railroads were another matter. Ever since Boston financial interests had begun promoting the idea of winning commerce for Boston from the Great Lakes by using railroads rather than canals, entrepreneurs in the North Country caught railroad fever—it seemed like everyone in Malone wanted to talk about railroads. The most commonly discussed route for a railroad from Boston to take in order to tap trade from the Great Lakes was across New Hampshire, Vermont, and New York to the port of Ogdensburg on the St. Lawrence River.[19]

By making its own connection with Lake Ontario, Boston interests hoped to outwit the New York City competition, which was using the Erie Canal and the Hudson River to carry its trade from the Great Lakes. Once the Welland Canal connecting Lake Ontario with Lake Erie west of Niagara Falls was large enough, the Boston promoters counted on boats carrying Great Lakes produce to scornfully sail by Buffalo and Oswego where the New York canals began, and travel down the St. Lawrence River to Ogdensburg, where Boston railroads would stand ready to receive their cargo.[20]

Railroad entrepreneurs organized railroad conventions in Vermont and in northern New York in 1830 to promote interest in the line to Boston.[21] Mass meetings were held in Ogdensburg and Malone, the midway point between Ogdensburg and the port of Plattsburgh on Lake Champlain. Boston financiers attended the meetings but were not impressed enough to invest their money in the project and decided, for the time being, to continue using a transportation system based on dirt and corduroy roads. Eventually, the idea of building one trunk railroad line from Boston to Ogdensburg was abandoned because of the size and cost of the project. Instead, it would be broken down into segments. One segment consisted of a rail line between Ogdensburg and the vicinity of Plattsburgh on Lake Champlain.[22] Mountain grades persuaded promoters of this line to change the eastern terminus from Plattsburgh to Rouses Point, which had relatively easier grades to cross.[23] In addition, railroad planners could see that making a subsequent rail connection to Boston across Lake Champlain would be easier from Rouses Point than from Plattsburgh.

In 1836, the New York legislature incorporated a Lake Champlain and Ogdensburg railroad company but its promoters were not able to raise enough capital and the venture failed. Two years later, during Bill's senior year in high school, another railroad convention was held in Malone and the project was revived. The legislature appropriated money for a survey and routes were mapped out but a bill proposing that the state build the road as a public work did not pass.[24]

Talk about building a railroad in the North Country connecting Ogdensburg to Lake Champlain sputtered, stalled, and came to an end as the effects of the Panic of 1837 swept through Boston and the North Country. Agricultural prices collapsed and farmers in Franklin County staggered. The nation began to experience one of the most severe depressions in American history. Banks and businesses failed by the hundreds, factories closed and unemployment mounted.[25]

Money began to dry up in Malone and it looked like Eliza's dream of sending Bill to the University of Vermont (UVM) in Burlington after he graduated from Franklin Academy might shatter. However, a financial angel, probably named Asa Hascall, loaned Bill enough money to enable him to enroll in the Class of 1842 at UVM in the fall of 1838.[26]

UVM was one of the most respected institutions of higher learning in New England.[27] While Bill was a student there, its president was John Wheeler, a Congregational minister who urged his students to follow a path of religious and political moderation.[28] UVM was the first American college to establish an English Literature Department.[29] From it, Bill acquired a life-long appreciation of English literature, which often found its way into Bill's subsequent political discourse and enhanced his reputation as a cultivated man.

At UVM, Bill came under the influence of philosophy professor James Marsh, a former president of the college. Marsh was an evangelical Christian who impressed on Bill a belief that the self can be realized only in and through communities. According to Marsh, what enables individuals to realize themselves as individuals, is their role within a group.[30]

Marsh is credited with being an inspiration for the American Transcendental movement of the 1830s and 1840s.[31] He trained Bill in what was known as the *Burlington philosophy,* which stressed the importance of rigorous introspection and analysis. Vermont Transcendentalism was fundamentally conservative. Marsh taught Bill about the importance of preserving institutions, not reinventing, debunking, or ignoring them.[32] These sentiments struck a comforting chord with Bill. His own pastor in Malone, Ashbel Parmelee, stressed the same themes. At the time Boston Transcendentalism was repudiating it, Marsh and Parmelee clung to the Calvinist belief that the moral depravity of human beings can never be eradicated in this world.[33] As an impressionable underclassman, Bill mulled all of these ideas.

Important as his classroom learning at UVM was to Bill, he learned the most important practical skill in his life outside the classroom. After classes, Bill learned how to use parliamentary procedure as a tool to determine the fate of proposed legislation, control debate, and run a meeting fairly and smoothly. On Saturday nights, literary and debating societies lit up the UVM campus with their programs. This was where Bill and his fellow students learned to use their wits in political campaigning, debating, literary composition, and satire.[34] It was at these meetings that Bill also learned that the best students, the ones who succeeded in winning praise from their classmates for a job well done, were the ones who were the most skilled in using the rules of parliamentary procedure.

Bill decided that he, too, would become proficient in the use of parliamentary law and began to study the rules. He subsequently acquired a superb command of parliamentary procedure and used it to unlock the doors to the inner circles of political power in Albany and Washington.

At UVM, Bill's horizons were not only broadened intellectually, but also socially. For the first time in his life, he met students who lived outside of Franklin County. Most of them came from Vermont and other towns throughout New York State and New England.[35]

One of Bill's best friends during his freshman year was Henry J. Raymond, a junior from Lima in Livingston County. After graduation, Raymond had a spectacular career in journalism and politics. He founded the *New York Times,* was named Speaker of the assembly, was elected lieutenant governor, and became chairman of the Republican National Committee.[36] Another UVM alumnus who remained

University of Vermont. Detroit Publishing Company Collection, Library of Congress.

close to the Burlington campus and whose path would frequently cross Bill's in the years to come, was J. Gregory Smith of the Class of 1838. Smith became president of two railroads, the Vermont Central first and then, the Northern Pacific.[37]

Day-to-day life on the campus in Burlington was not an easy one for Bill. In fact, at times it was extremely difficult. He had no money and had to do extra work to pay for his tuition, books, room and board. The economy had not recovered from the Panic of 1837 and money continued to be scarce. For one trying period of six weeks, Bill's only food was bread and water. To make matters worse, his eyes began to bother him and his mother wrote him about how difficult it was for her to make ends meet in Malone. He seriously wondered how long he could continue on as a student at UVM.[38]

During the summer term of his sophomore year, Bill turned twenty-one and all the weight of becoming an adult came crashing down on his shoulders. He discussed his financial future with Asa Hascall. He offered to allow Bill to study law with him in his office but he warned Bill that unlike his father, it could take Bill as long as seven years of study before he could be admitted to the bar.[39] Bill discussed the matter with his mother and decided to begin his legal education with Hascall immediately and not return to UVM.[40]

As Bill looked up and down the dirt road that ran through Malone to Ogdensburg in the west and Lake Champlain in the east, he felt a greater sense of community than he had ever felt before. He also had a more cosmopolitan outlook than most of his peers who had not gone to college. Bill was eligible to vote now and he thought about where he would stand politically.

While he had been away at college, the Whigs had wrestled control of New York State away from the Democrats. In 1838, William Seward had been elected governor with Luther Bradish as lieutenant governor, and the Whigs won control of the assembly. The following year, the Whigs won a majority of seats in the state senate and controlled both houses of the legislature. Bill thought that Asa Hascall's advice was right. Becoming a Whig would be good politics for him.

The economy continued to sour but Bill had the kind of confidence in himself that only a twenty-one-year-old can have. He knew he could take the measure of any man and that he could make a financial success out of himself. All he needed was a chance. But he had to wonder, as he looked up and down Malone's dreary Main Street, would he be able to find that chance, way up there, on the Canadian border, in Franklin County?

3

Love and the New District Attorney

☆

Malone had never seen anything like it before. Neither had Franklin County, New York State, or the nation. The Whigs had launched one of the most colorful presidential campaigns in American history—the log cabin, hard cider campaign of 1840.[1] Thurlow Weed had engineered the nomination of William Henry Harrison of Ohio, the man who had claimed a decisive victory over the Indians at the Battle of Tippecanoe, to run as a Whig for president against the Democratic incumbent, Martin Van Buren. To appeal to the South, the Whigs named John Tyler of Virginia for vice president. In New York, the Whig team of Governor Seward and Lieutenant Governor Bradish ran for reelection. In newspaper articles, Democrats attacked Harrison by saying that he was the kind of man who would be happy to spend the rest of his days in a log cabin with a barrel of hard cider. In response, the Whigs made log cabins and cider barrels their party's campaign symbols.[2]

There were log-cabin handkerchiefs, log-cabin sunbonnets, log-cabin buttons, log-cabin teacups, log-cabin plates, Tippecanoe tobacco, Tippecanoe shaving soap, and Old Cabin Whiskey (produced by the E.C. Booz distillery of Philadelphia). Every town in Franklin County had its own Tippecanoe Club and Malone had a Tippecanoe Choir, which sang campaign songs that usually included the refrain, "For Tippecanoe and Tyler Too."[3]

As a young Whig campaign worker, Bill probably helped organize the massive July 4 Whig campaign rally, which was held in Malone. Processions came from all over the county, most of them accompanied by bands. About three- to four thousand people attended. Some of the cavalcades were one-half to a mile long and each one featured log cabins on wagons drawn by four to six horses draped with campaign regalia. Live raccoons scurried around inside the cabins or on the roofs. Some wagons had large canoes emblazoned with flags and the names of the Whig candidates. The contingent from Bangor had a sixty-four-foot high liberty pole on one of its wagons. Booming cannons greeted each division as it pulled into town. The day was filled with speeches and dinner was served on Arsenal Green.[4] Bill's first political campaign as a voter got off to a rousing start, as did his career.

Bill began studying law and doing legal work in Asa Hascall's law office. Some of the work involved helping Hascall earn generous real estate commissions as a land agent for John Oliver of Baltimore, Maryland. He owned more than ten thousand acres in Bombay, a town in Franklin County located about twenty miles northwest of Malone, on the St. Lawrence County line.[5]

As Malone town supervisor, Hascall arranged for Bill to be appointed town clerk, his first public office. Harking back to that time in later years, Bill said that at that critical point in his life, the $30-a-year salary was "of more value to me than the thousands I have since attained."[6]

Hascall also used his influence to secure a teaching position for Bill in the district schools for $10 a month. On cold days in December, Bill would often have to get up early and walk through falling snow to teach in surrounding towns where he would board in log houses with "shrunken roof boards." Looking through them before falling asleep at night, Bill said he became "literally a star gazer."[7]

After the votes were tallied following the November election, Bill savored a major Whig victory. His new political allies, Seward and Bradish, were going back to Albany to lead the state, and Harrison and Tyler were heading to Washington to lead the nation. However, within a month of his inauguration, Harrison died of pneumonia and Tyler became the nation's first vice president to accede to the presidency on the death of a president. From that moment on, the phrase used to describe the vice presidency, an office one heartbeat away from the Presidency, took on a more significant meaning for Bill. Before he turned forty-six, two more vice presidents would become president when the chief executive died in office.

Politics, the law, and public service were heady stuff for Bill but they paled when he began thinking about Mary King. He met her on his first day as a teacher when she marched up to his desk and gave him her name. Bill was twenty-one and she was thirteen, the eldest daughter of William King, one of the most successful businessmen in Malone.[8]

Wheeler's home. Courtesy of the Franklin County Historical and Museum Society.

He had come to Malone from Keene, New Hampshire in 1831 and had opened a tannery as well as a boot and shoe shop. Business was so good, he and his two sons expanded the store to include the sale of general merchandise and began to invest in farms and lumbering operations.[9]

Mary was a pretty girl with a bright and inquiring mind. As she blossomed into a young woman, her cultivated and refined nature appealed to Bill and he fell in love with her. On September 17, 1845, a month after Mary's eighteenth birthday, Bill and Mary got married.[10] As a wedding gift, Bill's father-in-law gave the young couple a "modest fortune."[11]

Not to be outdone, Hascall also gave a wedding gift to Bill and Mary. Hascall arranged to have Bill appointed town superintendent of schools and also recommended that the court admit Bill to the bar so he could practice law on his own.[12]

As a new attorney, Bill took on some of the real estate work that Hascall did not have time to handle because of poor health. One of Bill's first clients was the son of one of Hascall's clients, John Oliver of Maryland. The son was trying to sell a large tract of land he owned in Dickinson, a town about fifteen miles west of

Malone, and he offered Bill a large commission if he could find a buyer for him and arrange for a speedy sale. Bill did just that and used the commission to build a handsome brick house on the Wheeler family lot on Elm Street—the same house he and his family would live in for the rest of his life.[13]

While Bill was busy falling in love with Mary, the Democrats were busy winning elections. In 1844, Democrat James K. Polk defeated Whig Henry Clay for president and Democrat Silas Wright defeated Whig Millard Fillmore for governor.[14]

Eight months after Bill and Mary's wedding, Congress declared war on Mexico and a national debate concerning slavery erupted. One of the critical issues that emerged concerned whether slavery should be allowed to exist in any new territory acquired by the United States from Mexico.[15]

The debate in the North Country was particularly heated and politically complex. Democratic Congressman Preston King from Ogdensburg in St. Lawrence County, was one of the leaders of a group of northern Democrats who attempted to block the expansion of slavery into territory taken from Mexico by proposing what became known as the *Wilmot Proviso*. Despite support from northern Whigs, the measure died in the Senate.[16]

Bill had been raised to believe that slavery was an evil institution. His mentor, the Reverend Ashbel Parmelee, was the most prominent member of the Franklin County Anti-Slavery Society, which had been founded in 1829, when Bill was ten years old, and two years after the last slaves in New York State were freed.[17] However, Parmelee did not support William Lloyd Garrison's strident demands for immediate abolition. He was a "warm abolitionist" with one foot in the gradual abolition camp and the other in the colonization camp.[18]

As Parmelee probably explained to Bill, immediate abolition would tear the fabric of the nation apart. Southern slave owners would not accept it and war and secession would be the result. A moderate approach similar to New York's twenty-eight-year plan of gradual abolition would be more acceptable to more people, which would make war and secession extremely unlikely.

Important as national issues involving the war with Mexico and the expansion of slavery might have been to the Whigs and Democrats in Franklin County, the number one subject on the lips of county politicians in 1846 was the health of Franklin County's longtime district attorney and Whig political leader, Asa Hascall. He was sixty years old and had become incapacitated from a prolonged sickness. In Franklin County, he had been a giant on the political stage for the past twenty-eight years.

With Hascall out of the political picture, ambitious Whigs and Democrats saw opportunities for gain and debated strategy. However, Hascall had his own plan and put it into operation as soon as he felt strong enough. One day, in the fall of 1846, he called Bill into his office and asked if he would be interested in succeeding Hascall as district attorney if he resigned. Bill jumped at the chance and Hascall smoothed the way for the twenty-seven-year old to be appointed district attorney in October when Hascall resigned.[19]

A month later, the voters adopted a new state constitution that changed the way in which district attorneys would be chosen. Instead of being appointed by the governor, district attorneys would now be elected by the voters. For Bill, that meant that in 1847, when Hascall's term expired, if Bill wanted to keep the job of district attorney, he would have to win the Whig nomination and the November election.[20] The new constitution also abolished the Court of Common Pleas and created a new Franklin County Court.[21]

Immediately after settling in to his new office, Bill began to lay plans for winning the upcoming election. So did the Democrats. Incumbent Democratic Common Pleas Court Judge Henry B. Smith, a former merchant and lumber manufacturer from Chateaugay, no longer had a court to preside over. Someone new had an opportunity to become judge of the new County Court.[22]

As Bill surveyed the Whig political scene, he was appalled by what he saw. Whigs were preparing to politically rip each other's throats out. After sweeping Democratic victories in 1842 and 1844 sent Franklin County's most celebrated Whig, Luther Bradish of Moira, packing for a new home in New York City, some Whigs blamed Seward and Weed. They singled out Seward's controversial antislavery views as one reason for defeat and urged Whigs to adopt the more conservative views of Millard Fillmore instead. Their hottest fire was directed at Weed. They did not like the heavy-handed way he ran the party and called him the *Dictator*. Some of the most bitter critics began a campaign to dethrone Weed and Seward and promote Fillmore.[23]

Bill admired Seward and Weed but wanted to avoid intra-party warfare, which could only damage him on his maiden voyage for elective public office. He wondered how he could court Whigs for the nomination and avoid being forced to take sides in the brewing Whig civil war. Fortunately for Bill, forces at work within the Democratic Party enabled him to cut a deal, side step local Whig turmoil, and win the election.

In 1847, the fiery and outspoken Flanders brothers led Democrats in Franklin County. The older brother was thirty-two-year-old Joseph Flanders, a well-respected lawyer known for his intellect and knowledge of constitutional law. He had been a delegate to the 1846 convention that revised the state constitution. The younger brother was twenty-seven-year-old Francis Flanders, a former assemblyman and hard-hitting editor of the Democratic newspaper, the *Franklin Gazette*.[24]

Thurlow Weed. Brady-Handy Collection, Library of Congress.

Since 1843, the Democrats had won more elections in Franklin County than the Whigs.[25] Even in 1846 when the Whigs won back control of the state government, the Democrats had run well in the North Country. Democrat Sidney Lawrence of Moira defeated both the Whig and the Liberty party candidates for a seat in Congress from Bill's congressional district by garnering 53 percent of the vote.[26]

The popularity of Democrats in Franklin County was largely due to the influence of Democrat Silas Wright of neighboring St. Lawrence County. A kingpin in the Albany Regency and known as the *Cato of the American Senate,* after the Roman whose incorruptible honesty caused him to oppose Caesar, Wright was an ardent opponent of the expansion of slavery and supported the Wilmot Proviso.[27] He led a wing of the Democratic Party, which was seething with anger because President Polk and his supporters in Congress had opposed the Proviso. Polk Democrats nicknamed this wing the *Barnburners* because they were willing to destroy the Democratic Party in order to eliminate slavery, much like the fabled farmer who had senselessly burned down his barn to rid it of rats. The Barnburners nicknamed their opponents *Hunkers* because they hankered or hungered for public office and spoils.[28]

In 1846, Hunkers sabotaged Wright's bid to be reelected governor and Whigs won control of the state.[29] With renewed vigor, the Barnburners began work to nominate Wright for President in 1848.[30] Suddenly, on August 27, 1847, two hours after suffering a stroke at his home in Canton, Wright died. Barnburners blamed Hunkers for breaking Wright's heart by treacherously cutting him on election day and began referring to Hunkers as *Silas Wright's assassins.* Barnburners vowed to take revenge at the polls in November by refusing to support Hunker-backed candidates.[31]

In Franklin County, Democrats were evenly split between Barnburners and Hunkers.[32] The party leadership reflected that split. Francis Flanders was a Barnburner and his brother Joseph was a Hunker.[33] Aware of the danger to their party's chances at the polls in the upcoming election for district attorney and county judge, they made a deal with the Whigs. On election day, there would be no Hunker-backed candidate, no Barnburner candidate, no Fillmore Whig candidate, and no Seward-Weed Whig candidate. Bill would run for district attorney and Joseph Flanders would run for county judge on one nonpartisan "fusion" or "union" ticket. To an inquisitive general public, party spokesmen explained that it was logical and good for the county that the choice of district attorney and county judge in the first election of its kind in state history should be made without drawing party lines. Bill heaved a sigh of relief and on election day cruised unopposed to his first election victory.[34]

After the election, Bill expanded his private legal practice. He brought law student Horace A. Taylor into his law office to study law with him and help him with his legal work.[35] Business had picked up ever since Bill had taken over Hascall's real estate work in Bombay for the Olivers.[36]

Bill also became the St. Regis Mohawk Indian agent for New York State. The Mohawks lived in Akwesasne, a six-square-mile Indian reservation bordering the northwest corner of Franklin County on the St. Lawrence River. Shortly after beginning work as Indian agent, which involved distributing a state annuity to the tribe and advising the tribe about state governmental matters, a religious controversy broke out on the reservation. Bill discussed the situation with Millard Fillmore, who was state comptroller at the time and responsible for distribution of annuity payments. He admonished Bill to keep his hands off any and all such disputes, which he did.[37]

On January 4, 1848, Congressman Preston King of Ogdensburg reintroduced the Wilmot Proviso in the House reigniting a national debate over slavery and exacerbating the split in the Democratic Party.[38] That summer, Barnburners walked out of the Democratic National Convention in Baltimore and formed the Free Soil Party, a new national party committed to "free soil" in the western territories.[39] Adopting the motto, "Free Soil, free speech, free labor, and free men," the party nominated Martin Van Buren to run for president.[40] In Bill's congressional district, incumbent Sidney Lawrence deserted the Democrats and ran for Congress as the Free Soil candidate.[41] Thurlow Weed papered over many of the differences of opinion within the Whig party at its national convention and helped Mexican War hero Zachary Taylor win the presidential nomination. To appease the conservative Whigs, Millard Fillmore was nominated for vice president.[42]

In the 1848 election, Taylor and the Fillmore Whigs swept to victory. Whigs routed the fractured Democrats in New York State taking the governor's office and both houses of the legislature making possible the subsequent election of Whig William Seward to the U.S. Senate.[43] In the race for Congress in Bill's district, Whig John R. Thurman of Warren County won even though he polled only 42 percent of the vote. Free Soiler Lawrence siphoned off 26 percent of the vote from Democrat William Hedding who won 32 percent.[44]

In Franklin County, all eyes were on the contest for the county's seat in the assembly because railroad fever was racing across the North Country once again and state legislative action was required. Whig George B. R. Grove, a seventy-year-old businessman from Fort Covington, won election to the post he previously held when he was initially elected to represent Franklin County as a Clinton-Federalist in 1823, the first year the county was made into an assembly district.[45] Younger Whigs were concerned that he had been out of touch with the New York political scene too long and was too old to be aggressive enough to win legislation the railroad desperately needed for it to have a chance to boom financially.

On May 14, 1845, the New York legislature had chartered a railroad corporation, the Northern Railroad Company, to construct and run a railroad from Lake Champlain to Ogdensburg.[46] Within months, Boston investors swooped in to control the road, which they saw as the last link in a transportation chain that would enable Boston to win commerce from the Great Lakes away from New York City. Boston financier T. P. Chandler was named president and five members of the board of directors were from Boston, including Abbott Lawrence, a founder of the New England textile industry.[47]

By March 1848, construction began simultaneously in the west at Ogdensburg and in the east at Rouses Point. The road was graded and rails were spiked down on hemlock ties.[48] In six months, the engine Chateaugay pulled a single wooden-benched car regularly between Rouses Point and Mooers Forks, sixteen miles to the west.[49]

Few followed the construction of the railroad more closely than the new Franklin County district attorney and his father-in-law, William King, who had just built the first potato starch factory in Franklin County and added it to the number of businesses he owned.[50] Both men saw how important a Great Lakes–Boston rail link could be to the economy of the North Country. With Malone at the midway point between the Ogdensburg and Rouses Point section of the road, they were in a position with other Malone businessmen to make a financial killing.

However, Lake Champlain stood in their way. From the beginning, its waters had broken the route from Boston to the Great Lakes and had haunted the plans of promoters. Shipping goods across Lake Champlain from railroad to railroad was far more cumbersome than on the Hudson River where canal boats from the Erie Canal easily crossed the river to the Greenbush railroad terminal. To be able to compete for Great Lakes commerce, Lake Champlain had to be bridged. The distance between West Alburg, Vermont, and Rouses Point, New York, was only 3,880 feet and the water was fairly shallow. But, bridging Lake Champlain required legislative permission from Vermont and New York.[51] The matter would be taken up in the upcoming 1849 session of the legislature.

Newly elected Assemblyman Grove left for Albany and proposals to bridge the Lake were introduced in the legislature where war immediately broke out. Shipping interests on Lake Champlain opposed a drawbridge as an obstruction to navigation. Ports like Plattsburgh, Whitehall, and Burlington joined in to oppose any bridging that might take business away from them. Troy and New York City businesses were particularly alarmed and vocal in their opposition. They did not want to lose any of their Erie Canal business to Boston and also opposed a drawbridge.[52]

A bill passed the assembly authorizing the construction of a bridge but it lost in the state senate by a tie vote.[53] Grove returned to Malone empty-handed. Civic leaders and business interests were deeply disappointed and some blamed Grove.

Bill's father-in-law and Bill's friends began to look at the thirty-year-old district attorney with new eyes. He knew parliamentary procedure backward and forward. Maybe, they thought, he could succeed in Albany where Grove had failed.

4

"Here Lies an Honest Man"

Bill warmed to the idea of moving up in politics by running for the assembly. To free up time to do that, he agreed to share some of his office space with a new lawyer in town, Horace Meriam.[1] Suddenly, in July 1849 all Bill's political plans had to be put on hold. A devastating forest fire broke out in Bombay, which completely disrupted Bill's real estate work for the Olivers. The fire destroyed crops and homes of hundreds of farmers living on Irish Ridge who had purchased their property from the land company of the Olivers. Thousands of acres were burned and families were left destitute, unable to make their mortgage payments to the Olivers. Bill took the catastrophe personally and he immediately headed out to Bombay to meet with each and every burned-out family. Sometimes the roads were not passable and he had to travel by foot. Bill promised the families that he would do everything in his power to save their property from foreclosure if they would agree to start anew and not give up. Returning to Malone, he convinced the Olivers to abate the interest payments that had come due until the farmers could get back on their feet. Most of them were Irish Democrats and they told Bill they would not forget what he had done for them.[2]

Meanwhile, on the political front, tension between Fillmore Whigs and Seward-Weed Whigs continued to rise. In the legislature, Fillmore Whigs mounted an unsuccessful challenge to Seward's candidacy for election to his first six-year term in the U.S. Senate. In Washington, following Fillmore's inauguration as vice president, Whig party boss Weed fought with Fillmore for President Taylor's ear about federal patronage appointments. In response, the vice president fought back and began organizing Whig committees loyal to him in every school district in New York State.[3] In Franklin County, the Fillmore and Seward-Weed Whig factions stepped back from the party unrest momentarily to nominate Bill Wheeler to run for the assembly in the upcoming November election.[4]

Meanwhile, Free Soiler, Hunker, and Barnburner Democrats continued their feud over the extension of slavery into the territories. Free Soilers renewed their demands for passage of the Wilmot Proviso. One of the leaders of the Hunkers in the U.S. Senate, Daniel S. Dickinson of Binghamton, known as *Scripture Dick* because of his penchant for using quotations from the Bible, countered by proposing legislation calling for people in the territories to vote on whether they desired slavery, a policy that became known as *popular sovereignty*.[5] Anxious to avoid a repeat of the election disaster that befell them in 1848, warring Democrats across the state agreed to a truce and in 1849 nominated coalition tickets consisting of Hunkers, Barnburners, and Free Soilers.[6] In Franklin County, the Democrats nominated Free Soiler William Weed, a two-term town supervisor of Belmont, to run against Wheeler for the assembly.[7]

On the campaign trail, the New York Democrats cautiously stressed party unity and agreed that opinions on the issue of slavery should not be a test of allegiance to the Democratic Party.[8] Trying not to offend anyone, Democrats in Franklin County ran a relatively positive campaign emphasizing Weed's years of governmental experience compared to the newly elected district attorney's inexperience.

In contrast, the Wheeler Whigs went into attack mode describing Weed and the Democrats as "discordant spirits striving for one common objective—public plunder." Furthermore, they had faces "as animated as slippery cheese" and could be heard shouting "hurrah for the mongrel, log-rolling, truck-and-dicker, spoils ticket."[9]

It was a very close election. Democrats outpolled Whigs by a small margin statewide and won four of the eight state races.[10] In Franklin County, Wheeler defeated Weed by 198 votes.[11] The Whig press rejoiced in Wheeler's victory declaring that it was "enough to stir a fever in the blood of age." In fact, the editor was so excited by the win, he wrote that he "never felt more like sending up a pious ejaculation" in his entire life![12]

When Bill analyzed the returns, he found that he won because of the support he was given by the Irish farmers in the Democratic stronghold of Bombay. If they had not remembered to thank him for helping them in their hour of need by voting as a bloc for him, Bill's budding political career might have very well come to a crashing halt.[13] Instead, he began packing his bags for Albany where he would make his debut on the state political stage in January. Because the Democrats had won control of the assembly by two votes, however, Bill knew that he would have to play a minor role.[14]

Construction of a railroad line traversing the North Country from Lake Champlain to the St. Lawrence River was progressing rapidly. Northern Railroad trains were running west from Rouses Point to Ellenburg, in Clinton County, a distance of thirty miles. Four locomotives were busy hauling gravel, earth, iron, and lumber for use in construction of the line. However, because of the winter weather, no more rails would be laid until the following spring when they were expected to reach Chateaugay in Franklin County, thirteen miles east of Malone.[15] In Vermont, the Rutland Railroad announced new service from Burlington to Boston. Newspaper headlines screamed, "The Atlantic and Lake Champlain United!"[16]

As a minority member in the Democratically controlled assembly, Bill did not have the votes in this session to win permission for the Northern Railroad to bridge Lake Champlain. Nevertheless, he looked forward to spreading his political wings for the first time outside Franklin County. Bill took rooms at Stanwix Hall in Albany in time to attend the opening session of the legislature on New Year's Day 1850.[17]

His first task was to identify the forces that had been blocking the building of the railroad drawbridge across Lake Champlain for so many years. He learned that the major sources of opposition came from the southern and middle parts of the state.[18] Their ringleaders were from Troy and Plattsburgh. Troy opposed the bridge because it did not want to lose any of its Erie Canal shipping business to a rival.[19] Plattsburgh's opposition was a case of sour grapes. The terminus of the Northern Railroad had been fixed at Rouses Point, not Plattsburgh. Business interests in Plattsburgh called the proposed bridge a "vile and oppressive measure."[20] They rounded up captains and boatmen who plied the lake to argue that a bridge would obstruct the channel at Rouses Point and destroy navigation between New York State and Canada.[21] Citing shipping statistics, they asserted that if the bridge were built, the Champlain Canal would lose 25 percent of its revenue.[22]

The freshman legislator from Malone countered the obstruction-of-navigation argument by pointing out that when the proposed drawbridge was open, there would be a sixty-foot opening for lake traffic to use without difficulty. As proof that railroad drawbridges did not hinder water transportation, Bill referred lawmakers to the successful use of drawbridges over Boston Harbor.[23]

Bill urged his fellow legislators to look beyond parochial economic interests and consider how the Lake Champlain bridge could benefit consumers and businesspeople throughout the state. He argued that bridging Lake Champlain would promote competition between carriers, which would lead to a wider selection of goods becoming available at the lowest prices.[24]

As persuasive as Bill's arguments were, he had no political clout. He was a newcomer to Albany's ways—an unknown Whig swimming in a session of the assembly controlled by Democrats. Until Bill made a name for himself and the Whigs regained control of the assembly, he would not have a chance to utilize his considerable political skills to move any levers of power to get a bridging bill passed. He accepted his lot and began work to establish a credible reputation for himself that he could use in the next session when the Whigs might retake the majority in the assembly.

Bill captured the attention of the state's legislative press corps by introducing legislation calling for the peaceful annexation of Canada. All of a sudden, his name began popping up in Democratic and Whig newspapers across the state.[25] He also introduced bills involving jury selection and encroachments on public highways.[26]

Bill made his biggest legislative splash by promoting bills to overhaul the state legal code. In debate over the measures, he gained statewide notoriety. The proposed change was the brainchild of David Dudley Field, a prominent legal reformer who had been working since 1841 to update New York State's legal system. He proposed greatly simplifying the rules of legal procedure in order to merge the courts of law and equity.[27] Field proposed a radically new design of the system of civil procedure, which obliterated the distinctions between the forms of action and between legal and equitable suits, so that all the rights of the parties in litigation could be determined in one action, instead of dividing them up into different suits.[28]

Prominent members of the New York State bar rose to defend their way of doing business and opposed Field's reforms. Many of them were legislators and they organized an effort to kill the new Code. In response, Edwards W. Fiske, an assemblyman from Brooklyn, issued a broadside attacking the entire legal profession for its hostility to the proposals. Wheeler rose to defend his profession and support adoption of the Code. He argued that the profession "must bow before the omnipotent sway of the spirit of progress." Wheeler pledged to work to get the Code passed and urged every lawyer who was a legislator "to work for the perfection of the system and not the destruction of it." Then, with a smile, Wheeler added that if his opponents outlived him, they should write on his tombstone, "God works wonders, now and then—Here lies a lawyer, an honest man!"[29]

Wheeler's outspoken support for Field's Code was heralded in newspapers across the state and he won a reputation in the legislature as an honest and forthright lawmaker. His fellow legislators rewarded him by electing him to a prominent committee formed to investigate fraud in the building and enlarging of the Erie Canal.[30]

When the initial projection of $12.42 million to enlarge and improve the Erie Canal mushroomed to $30 million, and the time required to complete the work went from twelve years to twenty-seven years, the public had demanded a legislative investigation. The first round of investigations was completed in 1847. Wheeler's committee worked on the second round, which culminated in a 332-page report that found fraud in the allocation of contracts to "friends, acquaintances, and neighbors," forged vouchers for reimbursement of materials, padded payrolls, and stolen materials.[31]

After the session was over, the thirty-year-old assemblyman from Malone returned home, emboldened by his first political foray into Albany.[32] He had made a statewide name for himself as an intelligent political operative with high moral standards and a fine-tuned sense of humor.

As one of the leading businesspeople in the North Country, Wheeler's father-in-law, William King, was also encouraged by what his son-in-law had accomplished in one term in Albany and envisioned a great political future for him—a future that could very well make Malone the "Star of the North," and make businessmen like himself rich.

Because of its central location on the railroad line between the port of Ogdensburg on the St. Lawrence River in the west and Rouses Point on Lake Champlain in the east, Malone had a chance to prosper more than other communities on the line if the line could achieve direct rail access to the Boston market. For this to happen, the New York legislature would have to grant the Northern Railroad permission to bridge Lake Champlain at Rouses Point. That would become one of Wheeler's missions in Albany—if he could win reelection to the assembly.

Signaling his intention to run for reelection, Wheeler resigned his position as Franklin County district attorney. He used his influence to have Whig Governor Hamilton Fish appoint Ashbel B. Parmelee, the son of Wheeler's spiritual mentor, the Reverend Ashbel Parmelee, to take his place.[33] To help his son-in-law firm up his political base, King opened King's Hall where Wheeler and his allies could hold political meetings and rallies. King's Hall was a large room with a stage and benches that could seat four hundred people. For the rest of his political life, Wheeler would have free use of King's Hall to stage political events.[34]

Next, Wheeler and his father-in-law encouraged a movement to incorporate the village of Malone. They knew that those who had political control of the village would also have control over how land in the village might be developed for railroad purposes.[35]

At the same time he was making political plans, Wheeler was also nervously watching events unfold in Washington where the bitter sectional debate continued over whether slavery should be allowed in the territory just acquired from Mexico by war. The heat generated by the debate between proslavery interests in the South and antislavery forces in the North carried the country dangerously close to disunion and civil war.[36]

Wheeler's Whig Party in Congress fractured into warring factions over whether to resolve the dispute by adopting legislation, which became known as the Compromise of 1850. While in Albany, Bill learned from the Malone newspapers that Kentucky Whig Henry Clay had introduced a series of measures in the Senate as a compromise to the "Territorial Slavery" question and that President Taylor threatened to veto them if they became law.[37] Massachusetts Whig Daniel Webster stunned Northern antislavery Whigs by endorsing the Compromise and vowing that he could never support the Wilmot Proviso.[38]

New York Whig Seward adamantly opposed the Compromise because it strengthened the Fugitive Slave Law and made it possible for slavery to be introduced in the new territories. In a speech to the Senate, he affirmed the Wilmot Proviso and said in response to charges that it was unconstitutional, "there is a higher law than the Constitution." The speech made Seward into the principal antislavery voice in the Senate.[39]

By the time Wheeler had packed his bags in Albany and returned home to Malone in April, he was solidly in Seward's camp.[40] Bill was also confident that even if Congress passed the Compromise measures, President Taylor would veto them.[41]

In July, a stage coach passenger from Montreal brought shocking news to Malone that thoroughly upset Bill's sense of political well-being and seriously threatened to derail his plans for reelection.

5

"Old Hunkerism" Is Dead

☆

The stagecoach brought the shocking news to Malone that President Taylor had suddenly died on July 9, 1850, after an attack of gastroenteritis. Vice President Fillmore would now become President Fillmore.[1]

For the second time in Bill's life, and in the life of the Republic, the vice president would succeed to the presidency because of the president's death. But what was even more important to Bill at this time was the shift in power in Washington from the Seward-Weed Whigs to the Fillmore Whigs. Ever since Fillmore had been elected vice president, Wheeler's political allies, Seward and Weed, had been conducting an open, merciless war against Fillmore Whigs because they considered Fillmore to be Seward's chief rival for the presidency and Weed's chief rival for control of the Whig party in New York.[2] Suddenly, with Taylor's death, Fillmore Whigs in the North Country had their man poised to begin work as president in the White House. As a Seward-Weed Whig, Wheeler saw dark clouds beginning to form over his political future.

To stop Bill from winning a second one-year term as an assemblyman in the fall elections of 1850, the Democrats nominated a popular, up-and-coming young Democrat, thirty-three-year-old George S. Adams, clerk of the Franklin County Board of Supervisors. Like Wheeler, Adams was a lawyer and was from Malone.[3]

Bill knew that if the Democrats in Franklin County remained united behind Adams, and if the Fillmore Whigs punished Wheeler for supporting Weed and

Seward by staying home on election day or voting for Adams, Wheeler could lose the election. He was in deep political trouble and worried about his future.

Meanwhile in Washington, President Fillmore threw his support behind passage of the Compromise of 1850 legislation and when Congress enacted the Compromise bills, he quickly signed them into law. Weed and Seward were rocked back on their heels but continued their efforts to thwart Fillmore's next steps. Weed was convinced that Fillmore Whigs planned to gain control of the upcoming New York Whig convention, which had been called to open in Syracuse on September 26, 1850, to nominate candidates for governor and other state offices. Once in control, Weed expected that the Fillmore faction would seek vindication of Fillmore's role in the passage of the Compromise legislation and would also rebuke all Whigs who opposed the Compromise, particularly Weed and Seward. They sent out a call for help to their Whig allies across the state.[4]

Wheeler answered the call. He got himself elected to be the Franklin County delegate to the Whig state convention. His election was unanimous.[5]

Weed had done his work well and his men, not Fillmore's, controlled the convention. When Wheeler arrived in Syracuse, Weed tabbed him to help direct the convention's work. Silver-gray-haired Francis Granger of Canandaigua, a friend of Fillmore's, was appointed chairman of the convention, which went on to nominate Washington Hunt of Lockport for governor. From the floor of the convention, Wheeler helped direct Weed-Seward delegates to defeat resolutions extolling Fillmore and not mentioning Seward; and passing measures denouncing slavery and eulogizing Seward. The Fillmore Whigs were furious. Granger abruptly threw down the gavel and walked out of the convention in protest with all the other Fillmore delegates.[6]

Granger's long silver-gray hair seemed to stand out like a mane as he walked up the aisle and out the door. Weed labeled the group the *Silver Grays*. They met a month later in Utica and endorsed a platform backing Fillmore and the Compromise of 1850. Some Silver Grays decided to back Democrats in the fall election rather than support Weed-Seward Whigs.[7] This weighed heavily on Wheeler as he prepared to run for a second term in the state assembly against Democrat George S. Adams.

Wheeler kicked off the campaign by spotlighting his "unsullied reputation for honesty" and his "enviable standing in the legal profession." He denied that there was a split in the party and described the convention walkout by the Silver Grays as merely "the action of a few disaffected individuals."[8]

The heavy guns of Wheeler's campaign took aim at the twin evils of the Compromise of 1850—the Fugitive Slave Law and the rejection of the Wilmot Proviso. He demanded that the legislature replace Democrat U.S. Senator Dickinson, one of the architects of the Compromise, when his term expired during the upcoming legislative session.[9] The Wheeler Whigs lambasted Dickinson as a man who had "prostrated himself at the feet of Southern slavery" and denounced Adams as a "Dickinson Hunker" who favored the extension of slavery into the territories, and supported the Fugitive Slave Law.[10]

The Democrats struck back with a vengeance by reminding voters that Whigs in Washington were responsible for the Fugitive Slave Law—Whig congressmen had voted for it and Whig President Fillmore had signed it. Calling Wheeler a *hypocrite*, the Democrats said he was "too slippery to be trusted" because in the past he had "expressed contempt" for the Wilmot Proviso and its supporters by once describing the Proviso as "the ____ humbug."[11]

Wheeler answered the Democratic attack by labeling the Fugitive Slave Law "an outrage upon the principles of justice and humanity." He was particularly incensed that the law denied fugitive slaves the right to a trial by jury. He said, "I would not deny to the black man, where his liberty, his happiness, his all is at stake, that right which our laws accord to the white man, whose only offense is the smallest larceny." Wheeler also declared that it was the "solemn duty" of Congress to exclude slavery from the territories. Because Dickinson supported passage of the Fugitive Slave Law and opposed exclusion of slavery from the territories, Wheeler said Dickinson should not be reelected to the U.S. Senate.[12]

On November 5, the voters went to the polls. After the ballots were tallied, the Whig press crowed, "We have met the enemy and they are ours," "Old Hunkerism is forever dead in Franklin County."[13] Wheeler had defeated Adams by 134 votes, winning 1,696 to 1,562. However, the Democratic state ticket had swept to victory in Franklin County. For governor, the Democrat Horatio Seymour carried Franklin County by 111 votes over the Whig Hunt. By defeating Hunt 1,711 to 1,600, Seymour polled fifteen more votes than Wheeler had polled—the election was a great deal closer than the jubilation of the Whig press would lead people to think.[14]

In what the Whigs described as a *hard-fought battle,* Wheeler won a majority of the votes in every town in Franklin County except Burke, Chateaugay, Fort Covington, Moira, and Westville. According to the *Palladium,* although "many of our Free Soil opponents" voted for Wheeler,[15] Adams lost primarily because he tried to campaign on one side of the street as a Free Soiler, and on the other side of the street as a Hunker. The Democrats "furnished the weapons of their own demolition."[16]

The Democrats saw the election differently. They acknowledged that Adams was "severely injured" by a split in Democratic ranks but they said the biggest reason Wheeler won was because of the "old game of Whig deception and fraud." Democrats accused the Whigs of printing split tickets "so exactly like the

Democratic tickets" no one could tell the difference unless they examined them very closely. As proof of this, the Democrats pointed to election returns in Chateaugay where the Democrat Seymour won by 167 votes but Adams only won by 133 votes.[17] Until 1890, each party supplied and distributed its own ballots.[18] The Whig printer admitted printing split tickets using the same ink and paper that the Democratic printer used but he explained that he had done so because the Democrats had put in an order for them. Furthermore, Wheeler Whigs added, Democrats put the split tickets in the ballot box, Whigs did not.[19]

Bill's 1850 campaign was a true test of his political mettle. He ran at a time in the United States when racial prejudice ran deep. Racial stereotypes, crude jokes, and insulting images were pervasive throughout the culture. Wheeler's position in the campaign that fugitive blacks should be entitled to the right to a trial by jury and that slavery should be restricted, was a distinct minority view. It ran up against an intense northern prejudice against blacks, which Democrats constantly exploited.[20]

By winning, Wheeler consolidated his influence with the state Whig leaders. His victory in Franklin County at the same time the Democratic state ticket was sweeping the field there, proved that Wheeler was not a flash in the pan. In Albany, Whig party boss Thurlow Weed was overjoyed with the election returns that showed his party had regained control of the assembly. He immediately began lining up capable men he could trust for leadership positions. The newly elected thirty-one-year-old assemblyman from Malone jumped to the top of Weed's list and he began to lay the groundwork to make Bill the Whig leader of the assembly and chairman of the powerful Ways and Means Committee.[21]

Weed wasn't the only person overjoyed with the election results. Business interests, investors, and dairy farmers in the North Country sensed that with Bill's influence in Albany and Whig control of the executive and legislatives branches, their dream of creating a direct, continuous rail connection, across Lake Champlain to the Boston markets was about to become a reality.

Prior to the election, the Northern Railroad laid rails along the 118-mile line from Rouses Point in the east to Ogdensburg in the west. The press trumpeted each step of the way. On June 1 the first westward-bound passenger train from Rouses Point reached Chateaugay. Press reports were glowing. They described the locomotive, named the Chateaugay, as a "most beautiful machine, shining with new paint—the brass work looking as bright as the old-fashioned andirons on the hearth of a good housewife."[22]

On September 19, the first passenger train from Rouses Point reached Malone. A cannon was fired to mark the event. North Country promoters hailed a "new era in the history and prosperity of Northern New York" and proclaimed "Excelsior!"[23]

The next day, the engine Chateaugay pulled bright yellow passenger coaches the entire 118-mile length of the line from Rouses Point to Ogdensburg. There was no telegraph so bonfires all along the route announced the progress of the train. As the train pulled into Ogdensburg, flags were waved, city bells rang out, bands played, and a cannon was fired. People waved banners and paraded through the streets as music played. A free supper was served and speeches were given. The evening was capped with a fireworks display.[24]

The initial runs by the Northern were not without incident. One train was forced to come to a screeching halt because there were cows on the track. The engineer frightened them away by puffing steam and blowing his whistle. All seemed clear and just as the train started up again, a cow that had hidden between two large piles of wood, saw daylight between the tender and the baggage car, made a bold dash for it and got jammed, throwing the train off the rails.[25] No one was injured but later Wheeler was heard to quip, "trains run safer without the engine."[26]

Malicious human beings also created travel hazards. One afternoon as the train was traveling east, three people were seen putting rails and chairs across the tracks. The train stopped and passengers chased the villains. One was caught but the others escaped. The Northern offered a $100 reward for the detection and conviction of anyone found guilty of willfully placing obstructions on the track—state criminal law called for a five-year prison sentence.[27]

The Northern Railroad ran milk, mail, passenger, and freight trains but it was its butter train that made railroad history. The line was the first to build and operate refrigerator cars.

Jonas Wilder of Rouses Point was the father of the refrigerator cars, which were built by the line in its Ogdensburg shops. He used a regular boxcar, put in another floor, roof, and wall, and then filled the space between the two with sawdust for insulation. On July 1, 1851, the "icebox on wheels" carried eight tons of northern New York State butter to Boston. Farmers who shipped this butter made a handsome profit and soon the butter train became famous. It ran from Ogdensburg to Rouses Point every Monday. The shipments of butter reached Boston after first being transported by boat across Lake Champlain early Wednesday morning in perfect condition.[28]

The coming of the Northern Railroad helped make business boom in the North Country. As farmers began to be paid cash for their crops, the North Country's barter system of purchase and exchange gave way to a cash system.[29] Some property values in Ogdensburg increased 500 percent and the value of farmlands along the line almost doubled. The Northern spent lavishly on company buildings including wharves, docks, and piers on both ends of the line. In Ogdensburg, a forty-two-bin grain elevator was built with each bin having a capacity of twelve tons of wheat.[30]

Entrepreneurs in Malone, the geographic center of the line, such as Bill's father-in-law, William King, and his friend, Samuel C. Wead, a wealthy lumberman, retailer, and banker, could see this was only the beginning.[31] They knew that one of the keys to even greater financial opportunities for everyone was a railroad bridge across Lake Champlain that would provide a continuous rail connection from the North Country to Boston, and eventually New York City. If freight did not have to be unloaded from the cars on one side of the lake, put on boats for transport across the lake, and then reloaded onto different cars on the other side of the lake, transportation charges could be substantially lowered, which in turn could substantially increase everyone's profit margin.

King, Wead, and other businessmen ratcheted up the pressure on Wheeler to deliver them a railroad bridge across Lake Champlain. Based on the measure of the men he had taken during his first term in Albany, Bill thought he could do it and he dreamed of the great wealth he might generate for his family, friends, and neighbors, if he played his cards right.

6

A "Mere Act of Justice"

★

On New Year's Day 1851 Bill left Malone for Albany.[1] Because of the brilliance he had shown Whig party managers during his first term in the assembly, Bill had received support to become Speaker this time around but he knew Whig party boss Weed wanted Bill's University of Vermont classmate and future founder of the *New York Times,* Henry J. Raymond, to be Speaker.[2] Therefore, Bill disavowed any interest in the Speakership and threw his support to Raymond.[3] Weed rewarded the thirty-one-year-old lawyer from Malone by arranging to have Raymond appoint him to be chairman of the powerful Ways and Means Committee and be Whig leader of the assembly.[4] As such, Bill was in a position to control the flow of all proposed legislation that involved spending or borrowing state money—a most influential position indeed.

There were several major issues scheduled to come before the legislature in 1851. First and foremost was the election of a U.S. Senator. The term of Democratic incumbent, Daniel S. Dickinson, would expire on March 4 and the Whig legislative majority members had the votes to name their own man, if they could agree on who he should be. Fillmore Whigs backed James Watson Webb, owner of New York City's *Courier and Enquirer,* the organ of the Silver Grays, to succeed Dickinson. Seward-Weed Whigs favored outgoing Governor Hamilton Fish.[5]

The second major issue concerned a plank in the Whig platform that called for a $9 million enlargement of the Erie Canal. The proposal was extremely controversial. Democratic legislators challenged the constitutionality of the measure

Henry J. Raymond. Brady-Handy Collection, Library of Congress.

and some Whigs opposed it because the enlargement would not directly benefit their districts.[6]

To win passage of his bill authorizing the Northern Railroad to build a bridge across Lake Champlain, Wheeler planned to use his skills as a superb parliamentarian and his power as chairman of the Ways and Means Committee to bargain with the other Whig leaders. Bill would trade his support for getting Fish elected to the U.S. Senate and the Enlargement bill passed, in exchange for passage of his Bridge bill.

As legislators began jockeying for position in anticipation of the U.S. Senate election, Wheeler was busy supporting a massive North Country lobbying campaign to apply pressure on the politicians in Albany to pass the Bridge bill. Responding to a call signed by Bill's father-in-law, William King, his friend, Samuel C. Wead, and nine other Malone businessmen, five thousand people from St. Lawrence, Franklin, and Clinton counties took advantage of the offer of free transportation from the Northern and assembled in Malone on January 16. They passed pro-Bridge bill resolutions and two thousand people signed a thirty-six-foot long memorial addressed to the legislature calling for the bridge to be built.[7]

Two months later, a second pro-bridge rally drew more than ten thousand people to Ogdensburg.[8]

Opponents to the Bridge bill were not asleep at the switch. They organized Montreal businessmen to oppose the Bridge bill on the grounds that a railroad bridge across Lake Champlain would threaten their livelihoods because it would cut off their use of the St. Lawrence River–Chambly Canal route to Burlington and points south on Lake Champlain, including the Champlain Canal. Whigs in Troy attacked the Bridge bill by calling the Northern Railroad a *voracious monster*, which was determined to devour the canal revenues of the state.[9]

Bridge supporters countered by calling their opponents *Lake Monopoly* men who were demanding that all business in the vicinity of the lake pay tribute to the Erie and Champlain canals.[10]

While the furor over the Bridge bill mounted outside the legislature, passions concerning the election of a U.S. Senator were rising inside the legislature. Fillmore Whigs refused to allow a vote on the matter until resolutions were passed endorsing the Compromise of 1850 and President Fillmore. Seward-Weed Whigs refused to do so and a stalemate set in that lasted six weeks.[11]

Using his parliamentary procedure skills and his position as the Whig leader of the assembly, Wheeler ultimately outmaneuvered the Fillmore Whigs and forced a vote in the assembly, which Fish won. The state senate followed suit and on March 19, 1851, Hamilton Fish was duly elected to be the next U.S. Senator from New York. Whig party boss Weed was grateful to Bill and the *Albany Evening Journal* heaped praise on Wheeler for delivering the election to Fish.[12]

The first step in Bill's two-step strategy to get his Bridge bill passed had been accomplished. The second step, securing approval of a $9 million enlargement of the Erie Canal, was going to be more difficult.

As chairman of the committee through which the Enlargement bill had to go before it could reach the floor of the assembly, Bill made it clear that unless the Erie Canal interests supported his Bridge bill, the Enlargement bill would not see the light of day.

Pro-Erie Canal Whigs in the senate buckled under Wheeler's pressure and on April 4 they passed his Bridge bill.[13] In the assembly, Bill wrenched the Bridge bill out of the control of the unfriendly Railroad Committee and had it referred by Speaker Raymond to a Select Committee dominated by pro-bridge Whigs led by himself. He promptly and favorably reported the Bridge bill out to the full assembly.[14]

Things were looking good for passage of the Bridge bill in the assembly when suddenly twelve Democratic state senators resigned to stop the progress of the Canal Enlargement bill and the legislature was forced to adjourn on April 14 because of a lack of a quorum in both houses. The governor called a special election to fill the senate vacancies and a special session of the legislature was called to begin on June 10.[15]

As the regular session came to a close, Wheeler kept the pressure on. He refused to sign the Whig Legislative Address, which reiterated Whig demands for the $9 million enlargement of the Erie Canal.[16] His refusal captured Weed's attention and he agreed to move more aggressively behind passage of the Bridge bill—a proposal Wheeler referred to as a "mere act of justice" for the North Country.[17]

Within days of the opening of the special session, Weed kept his bargain with Wheeler. At the appointed hour when the state senate was scheduled to vote on the Bridge bill and the Canal Enlargement bill, Weed stood outside the senate chamber lobbying senators to vote for both bills. With additional help from Wheeler's new ally in the senate, wealthy New York City merchant Edwin D. Morgan, the Canal Enlargement bill passed and, despite some resistance from senators representing Troy and Plattsburgh, the Bridge bill also passed.[18] Its fate was now in the hands of the assembly where Wheeler again took direct charge of it.

Assembly debate on the Bridge bill's merits began on June 26. No matter how vigorously Wheeler pushed and argued, he was unable to persuade the assembly to pass it. His opponents had convinced the majority that a railroad drawbridge across Lake Champlain that only left a space of seventy feet between piers would obstruct so many vessels going north and south on the Lake that the state would lose a significant amount of sorely needed revenue from the Champlain Canal.[19]

On June 28, two days before his thirty-second birthday, Bill dramatically shifted gears and introduced a substitute bill from his Select Committee on the bridge. Declaring that "this was the age of compromise," Wheeler put a new Bridge bill in front of the assembly, which did not call for a permanent railroad drawbridge over the lake.[20] Instead, the new Bridge bill authorized construction of a floating bridge designed by the renowned railroad engineer, Henry R. Campbell.[21]

The floating bridge actually amounted to a large ferry. The bridge would have two piers with a three-hundred-foot-long slip extending from the bank into the lake, and then a space of two hundred and fifty feet across the middle of the lake, and then two more piers with a three-hundred-foot slip between them. The railroad cars would be run onto a three-hundred-foot-long ferry laid with railroad tracks that would transport the cars across the lake during the navigation season. For winter crossings, the ferry would be moved into the two-hundred-and-fifty-foot open channel, and temporary tracks laid over the frozen water in the slips.[22]

Wheeler's substitute Bridge bill caught his opponents completely off guard because it took their persuasive obstruction-of-the-lake argument off the table. Bill's call for a vote on his new bill was greeted with demands that voting be delayed until the substitute bill was printed so that it could be studied. Wheeler said such requests were "sheer hypocrisy" and demanded that the substitute bill "sink or swim" on its own merits. Waving a special drawing illustrating the floating bridge, Bill called for an immediate vote.[23] The substitute Bridge bill passed the assembly 70 to 21 and on July 1 the senate also passed it, giving Bill a day-late thirty-second birthday present he could happily bring back with him to Malone.[24]

The state press hailed Bill's "hard fought and great victory" as an astonishing triumph over the rich and powerful lobby that had been arrayed against him from Troy and Montreal.[25] Back home in Franklin County, Whigs passed resolutions heralding Bill as an "able and unfaltering champion" for his work.[26]

In anticipation of increased rail traffic, entrepreneurs in the North Country sprang into action and began building a new stone depot in Malone. On September 1, the first passenger train crossed Lake Champlain on the bridge, and three days later, the first freight train from Boston did the same.[27]

As Bill basked in glory at his home in Malone in the fall of 1851, he thought about his personal priorities. When he was rubbing shoulders with legislators in Albany, he experienced firsthand how important money was to success in politics and government. Two of Bill's closest friends in the legislature were affluent men from New York City. Speaker Henry J. Raymond was a journalist who was well connected with many financially well-to-do investors.[28] State Senator Edwin D. Morgan was a wealthy merchant, banker, and broker.[29] Their wealth helped smooth the way for them in political circles. Bill wanted the same thing for himself and began to focus on making money.

Toward that end, he made a business alliance with one of the most prominent and outspoken Democrats in the North Country, Joseph R. Flanders, and formed a new three-man law firm with him. Flanders was completing a four-year term as Franklin County Judge and he had recently quarreled politically with his brother, Francis D. Flanders, the Franklin County Democratic party leader, over what direction the party should take.[30] Horace A. Taylor was the third member of the new firm. He had been admitted to the bar earlier in the year after having worked as Wheeler's law clerk.[31] Flanders, Wheeler, and Taylor opened its doors for business on January 8, 1852.[32]

With his law firm's business in capable hands, Wheeler made a bold move into the banking world. During the summer of 1851, forty investors from the North Country and Vermont, led by Bill's father-in-law William King, and his business friend, Samuel C. Wead, organized the Bank of Malone, the first truly commercial bank to do business in Franklin County.[33] Wead was elected president of the bank and Wheeler was asked if he was interested in becoming the bank's chief executive officer.[34] He agreed and took the banking title *cashier*. The bank transacted its business in a "banking room" in Wheeler's law offices until construction of a new stone bank building could be completed across the street. Wheeler opened the Bank of Malone for business on September 15 with $100,000 in capital resources.[35] The bank building was completed on November 20 and by the following spring, the Bank of Malone was issuing its own bills and its resources had grown to more than a quarter of a million dollars as the railroad boom continued to grow in the North Country.[36]

At the same time Bill was organizing his new law firm and supervising the opening of the Bank of Malone, he made the most dramatic and significant business decision of his young life—he became a railroad man. On October 9, 1851, the Northern Railroad took steps to issue a second series of bonds to borrow money to complete additional construction and operate an ever-expanding line. About two months later, the Northern granted a mortgage to Wheeler and to two other men, one from New York and the other from Boston. The three men had agreed to serve as trustees for the buyers of the second issue of bonds. Bill was named chairman of this three-man board. Wheeler's law partner, Flanders, helped draw up the necessary legal documents and notarized Wheeler's signature on them.[37]

In February 1852 the Northern had thirty locomotives, all of which were named for the lakes, rivers, and towns of the North Country. The railroad employed fifty-seven men as mechanics on both ends of the line to keep the trains running.[38] As chairman of the board of trustees, Wheeler helped influence the board of directors to locate the Northern's machine shops, engine house, and business depot in Malone, the geographic center of the line between Rouses Point and Ogdensburg.[39] According to Wheeler's business plan, all the Northern's locomotives, passenger coaches, and freight cars would be made at these facilities where one hundred and fifty men would be employed.[40]

The small, one-story building in the center is the Bank of Malone as it appeared in the 1850s. Courtesy of the Franklin County Historical and Museum Society.

In March 1853 the Northern Railroad organized the Northern Transportation Corporation, a wholly owned subsidiary. It purchased waterfront property in Chicago with dockage and grain-handling facilities there and in Ogdensburg. Using the St. Lawrence River, the Welland Canal and the Great Lakes, the Northern's boats shipped twenty thousand tons of merchandise west and thirty thousand tons east in its first year. The company also ferried freight cars from Ogdensburg across the St. Lawrence River to Prescott, Canada, where connection was made with the Canadian rail network.[41]

As the Northern Railroad continued to expand its operations east and west, its business center in Malone flourished and Wheeler took financial advantage of it. With the election of his father-in-law as the first president of the newly formed Village of Malone,[42] Bill became one of the first to know where the best railroad-related business opportunities could be found. When Boston investors organized the Malone Sandstone Company, a new building materials company, which also owned a sandstone quarry near Malone, Wheeler became a member of the company's board of directors and its president.[43]

The Northern kept acquiring more real and personal property and on April 7, 1854, it gave another mortgage to Wheeler's board of trustees.[44] Four months later, the Northern defaulted on the interest payments due on its second mortgage bonds.[45]

Wheeler's board of trustees immediately got into a serious argument about what the legal consequences of the default should be. Bill demanded that the Northern deed all its property, fuel, and shop stock over to his board. The other two trustees disagreed with Bill and argued that although the board did have a legal right to own the property, the trustees were required to pay the railroad company for it out of the future earnings of the railroad.[46] The dispute boiled over into the spring of 1855. In the summer, Wheeler sued the other two trustees to resolve the disagreement. The Supreme Court of New York ruled in Wheeler's favor and enjoined the trustees from paying out any money for any purpose except for the Northern's operating expenses and the interest on the bonds.[47]

In February 1856 Wheeler's board sued the railroad company to foreclose on the second mortgage and on October 21, 1856, the railroad was sold to the thirty-seven-year-old Wheeler and the other two trustees, in trust for the benefit of the bondholders.[48] The sale wiped out all of the railroad company's capital stock and the railroad became the property of the second mortgage bondholders.[49] As a result of the sale, Wheeler as chairman of the board of trustees, was authorized to operate the railroad and be paid for his services.[50] All business funds of the railroad were collected and deposited in Wheeler's Bank of Malone and Wheeler was authorized to sign all the railroad checks.[51]

By the time all the dust from the railroad's financial troubles had settled, thirty-seven-year-old Bill Wheeler's financial future was secure. His legal, banking, railroading, and investment income had made him a wealthy man in the North Country. Bill was now free to turn his attention back to politics and government.

7

"Grinding" It Out in Albany

☆

DURING THE 1850s, Wheeler's Whig Party gradually disintegrated and the modern Republican Party (GOP) emerged. In Franklin County, Bill energetically became the number one Republican and one of the party's leading champions in the North Country.

From Malone, Bill applauded Seward's role in denying President Fillmore the nomination for a full four-year term at the Whig national convention in June 1852. Wheeler was unable to forgive Fillmore for signing the Fugitive Slave Act and understood why Seward Whigs castigated Fillmore as a traitor to freedom, principle and party.[1]

As Bill experienced the issues in the early 1850s, the slavery question was not the only matter tearing at the fabric of the Whig Party and American life. A surge in Irish immigration led to a rise of anti-Catholicism and nativism. Politically, the Democratic Party was becoming the Irishman's party. Some of Bill's Whig allies were horrified by the surge in Irish Democratic political strength and talked of changing the law so that it would take twenty-one years for naturalization.[2]

In July 1854 the nativist Order of the Star Spangled Banner held a convention in New York City with delegates from thirteen states to create a new political party. They fixed secret rituals and pledged never to vote for any foreign-born or Roman Catholic candidate for office. Politically they named themselves the American Party but because of their practice when questioned about their secrets of saying, "I know nothing," they were called *Know-Nothings*.[3]

During the summer, membership of the Know-Nothings soared. In the North Country, local Know-Nothing organizations sprang up everywhere. Some of Wheeler's close Whig associates joined.[4] Know-Nothings became the rage of the day. Vendors sold Know-Nothing Candy, Know-Nothing Tea, and Know-Nothing Toothpicks.[5]

At this time in 1854, it seemed likely that the Catholic or immigrant question might replace the slavery question as the foremost issue in U.S. politics.[6] However, as Bill watched the popularity of the Know-Nothings grow phenomenally in Franklin County, his number one issue continued to be the prevention of the spread of slavery. There were practical political reasons for steering clear of the Know-Nothings. When Bill ran for the assembly, he owed his election to support from Irish voters who usually voted Democratic. Courting the Irish vote was smart politics as far as Bill was concerned. He noticed that Seward agreed with him. When Seward was the Whig governor, he had encouraged Irish support by advocating that public funds be appropriated to aid Catholic schools.[7]

As Fillmore Whigs began gravitating toward the Know-Nothing Party,[8] passage of the Kansas-Nebraska Act, which became law on May 30, 1854, jolted Wheeler and the antislavery forces into greater political activity.[9]

The law called for repeal of the Missouri Compromise and opened the Territories of Kansas and Nebraska to slavery.[10] New antislavery groups began organizing throughout the North taking the name *Republican*.[11] Bill and other Seward-Weed Whigs were attracted to this new party.[12]

The first meeting in northern New York to form a new Republican Party was held on February 2, 1855, in Philadelphia, Jefferson County, the next county west of St. Lawrence County on the St. Lawrence River.[13] Seven months later, on September 26, 1855, the New York Republican Party was born at a convention in Syracuse, which selected a state GOP ticket to run in the upcoming November election. Ogdensburg's Preston King headed up the ticket as the GOP candidate for secretary of state.[14]

Bill sprang into action and organized the first Republican campaign in Franklin County. He put together a slate of candidates to run against the Know-Nothings and the Democrats.[15] Even more significantly, Bill hired twenty-two-year-old Patrick H. Shields to work as his full-time political deputy. Born in Ireland, Shields was put on the Northern Railroad's payroll as a baggage master and given a room in Wheeler's Elm Street residence to live in.[16]

After the election and the votes were counted statewide, the Know-Nothings defeated the Republicans by ten thousand votes. Two factions of the Democrats came in third and fourth respectively.[17] The Know-Nothings also swept to victory in Franklin County taking all the county offices by four hundred votes.[18]

State Republican leaders were disappointed on the one hand, but encouraged on the other by the fact that their new party had done well in its first election by defeating both Democratic factions.[19] In addition, Bill's work in Franklin County was pointed to with pride. Preston King, the GOP candidate for secretary of state, came in first in Franklin County by 177 votes.[20] Wheeler and other leading Republicans in New York immediately began planning for greater success in 1856.[21]

Dramatic news from Washington and Kansas at the end of May 1856 further strengthened Republican prospects. In Washington, a South Carolina congressman beat Massachusetts Senator Charles Sumner, a national antislavery leader, senseless on the floor of the Senate chamber. The brutal attack firmed up the Republican argument that the South would use force to defend slavery. In Kansas, this perception was further reinforced. Pro-slavery combatants invaded the antislavery town of Lawrence. They burned down homes, a hotel, and a newspaper office, killing one person in the process.[22]

A convention of New York State Republicans met in Syracuse on the last few days of May and chose delegates to represent the party at the upcoming 1856 GOP national convention in Philadelphia. Bill Wheeler was one of the men chosen. With Bill's support, the convention also passed resolutions expressing sympathy for the suffering of the pioneers in Kansas fighting for the Free State cause and recommending that every town and city in New York organize a committee to provide aid and education to the orphan children in Kansas.[23]

Bill was appalled by the wave of violence going on in what Republicans began calling *bleeding Kansas*. He attended a Republican mass meeting in Chicago that addressed the suffering in Kansas. After the meeting, Bill made several large financial contributions to aid "our hunted and oppressed brethren in Kansas." In a subsequent letter to the *Chicago Tribune,* Bill wrote, "It is well that the slave power has thrown off its mask. It now stands revealed in all its naked, hideous deformity."[24]

In June, Bill arrived in Philadelphia for the opening of the first GOP national convention. He was one of six hundred delegates present representing all the northern states, the border slave states of Delaware, Maryland, Virginia, and Kentucky, and the District of Columbia.[25] His friends from his assembly days, Henry J. Raymond and Edwin D. Morgan, were in attendance with him. Raymond would be the keynote speaker and Morgan, already the party's state GOP chairman, would be elected the party's first national chairman.[26]

The convention nominated former U.S. Senator and famous explorer John C. Fremont of California for president after Seward chose to withdraw as a candidate before the balloting began. Bill listened to supporters of Abraham Lincoln of Illinois pitch him for the vice presidential nomination but ended up voting for the eventual winner, New Jersey's William L. Dayton.[27]

Bill returned home after the convention and warmly supported Fremont in his bid for the presidency against Democrat James Buchanan and Fillmore, who ran as the Know-Nothing candidate.[28] Buchanan won the election but Fremont took New York by eighty thousand votes. West and north of Albany, every elected congressman and nearly every assemblyman was a Republican.[29]

A sharp, national economic crisis dampened Bill's political exuberance in 1857. In August, an insurance company failed in New York, which triggered the Panic of 1857. Within months, foreclosures, bankruptcies, and unemployment spread across the northeast. The country slipped into a severe depression that lasted more than two years.[30]

Creditors began circling around the Northern Railroad demanding payment and eventually brought foreclosure proceedings against the corporation.[31] Wheeler decided that the best thing he could do for himself and the railroad financially was to get back into the state legislature. The 1857 GOP state convention had appointed him to the Republican State Committee[32] and he used his party influence and business connections to garner the GOP nomination to run for the state senate in the 1857 election. His senate district encompassed Franklin County and St. Lawrence County.[33]

During the ensuing election campaign, the Panic of 1857 replaced bleeding Kansas as the primary issue in the minds of the voters. The Democrats and the Know-Nothings blamed Republican extravagance for the hard times.[34] In response to Bill's appeal to Morgan on the state GOP committee for help, he sent Bill funds to help his campaign for the state senate.[35] When the votes were counted, the Democrats won the statewide offices that were up for grabs but Bill won election to a two-year term in the state senate by 3,478 votes.[36] He was the first man to win election by carrying Franklin County as a Republican candidate, without any other party backing.[37]

The newly elected state senator from Malone's assignment to the Banks Committee and the Public Expenditures Committee was overshadowed by his appointment to the senate's powerful *Grinding Committee*, the popular name for the Committee on Local General Orders. The Grinding Committee weeded out what it considered petty and frivolous bills and determined which ones would come before the senate for action. If legislation did not get the green light from Bill's Grinding Committee, it would be highly unlikely that it would ever have a chance to become law.[38]

One of the first bills drafted by Wheeler concerned the future of his Northern Railroad. He introduced a bill to authorize the formation of a railroad corporation to take the place of the Northern, which had recently been forced to dissolve by creditors. The bill provided that the new corporation have the power to mortgage its property.[39] To further aid the cause of railroaders such as himself, from his position on the Banking Committee, Bill also introduced a bill to repeal the law prohibiting corporations from claiming usury as a defense in legal actions brought against them by creditors. Wheeler's Northern Railroad was not mentioned by name but the *New York Times* observed that Wheeler's bill was a way to protect railroads from having to pay for reckless borrowing or indifferent spending, and being forced into eventual bankruptcy.[40]

On another front, Bill brandished his reputation for honesty by introducing legislation designed to prevent illegal voting throughout the state. Wheeler's measure established a new system for the registration of voters.[41]

Bill's work in the state senate prompted GOP state and national chairman, Edwin D. Morgan, to urge Wheeler to come to Washington for an upcoming meeting of Republican leaders that had been called to ensure the success of the Republican party in the upcoming 1860 election. Wheeler turned Morgan down explaining that his senate duties prevented him from going.[42]

In the fall of 1858, the Republicans nominated Morgan for governor and he won election in November by 17,440 votes.[43] Because of Wheeler's talent as a parliamentarian and his friendship with Morgan, Wheeler's star in the senate rose even higher. At the beginning of the second year of his senate term in 1859, Bill was elected president pro tempore of the senate, an extraordinary honor for a freshman senator.[44]

Aside from killing proposals from canal interests on the Canal Committee to increase taxes on railroads, and to investigate charges of corruption in connection with the passage of the Albany Bridge bill, Wheeler spent the remainder of his term in the senate earning a new reputation as a fair, efficient, and knowledgeable presiding officer.[45]

This reputation would follow Wheeler for the rest of his political career and serve him well. When the 1859 GOP state convention met in Wieting Hall in Syracuse on September 7, 1859, to name a slate of candidates to run in the November state election, Bill was chosen president of the convention over James W. Nye, popular chairman of New York City's Metropolitan Board of Police.[46]

In his speech to the convention following his election, Wheeler told the delegates that the coming election would be a "preparatory drill" for the "great contest of 1860." With a nod toward the ambition of his GOP ally, Seward, to run as the 1860 GOP candidate for president, Wheeler reminded the delegates that the nation's Republicans would be looking to New York for leadership about who to nominate for president. Next Bill trained his guns on the South and attacked it for trying to take over the federal government in order to protect slavery in the Territories and repeal laws prohibiting the slave trade. To rousing applause, Wheeler thundered that in fighting against such demands, there could be "no middle ground, no compromise."[47]

About a month after the convention completed its business, almost as if he had been waiting for such a no compromise cue, John Brown and a band of eighteen men attacked and captured the U.S. armory in Harper's Ferry, Virginia, as part of his plan to instigate a slave rebellion.[48]

Wheeler was as shocked by Brown's raid as was Seward, Weed, and other New York Republican leaders. Through his newspaper, Weed said that Brown and his men "justly deserve universal condemnation." Seward denounced Brown's actions and tried to reassure voters that the Republican Party was one of moderation.[49] Wheeler was forced to explain that his call for *no middle ground, no compromise* was in no way a call for violence.

In the 1859 election, Republicans won six of the nine statewide offices on the ballot. This was the last substantive appearance of the Know-Nothings in New York electoral politics and most of the Know-Nothings subsequently joined the Republican Party. In Franklin County, the entire GOP county ticket was elected after the Know-Nothings withdrew from the contest before the votes were cast.[50]

As New Year's Eve 1860 drew near, forty-year-old Bill Wheeler reflected on his personal life and political future. His income stream had grown to the point where he was able to hire thirty-year-old Margaret Chambers as his family's live-in housekeeper and servant.[51] With about $350,000 in resources, his Bank of Malone was sound and his job secure.[52] Thanks to legislation he had sponsored in his recent term in the state senate, he was orchestrating a corporate reorganization of the Northern Railroad, which was proceeding as planned. The name of the line would be changed to the Ogdensburg Railroad and it would soon be possible for passengers to leave Malone at 5 a.m. and reach Albany the same day, and New York City or Boston the next morning.[53]

Bill was the acknowledged leader of a vibrant Republican organization in Franklin County and a person with a sterling reputation in state Republican circles. However, his dreams went beyond serving Franklin County and the North Country in Albany. National events stirred his blood and he decided to run for Congress. To free up more time to mount a campaign, he dissolved his law partnership with Flanders and Taylor. Flanders returned to the regular Democratic fold and reunited with his brother Francis. Taylor formed a partnership with Albert Hobbs, a former Know-Nothing assemblyman.[54]

Wheeler lived in the Sixteenth Congressional District, which consisted of Franklin, Clinton, and Essex Counties.[55] In 1858, he had brokered an agreement with the other county GOP leaders that the next nominee for Congress from the

Sixteenth Congressional District would be from Franklin County.[56] Given Bill's control over the Republican Party machinery in Franklin County, he knew that the nomination would be his for the asking and as the 1860 election approached, Wheeler prepared himself to make a bid for the national political stage.

8

A Pen "Dipped in Gall"

☆

HISTORIANS HAVE DESCRIBED the 1860 election as "the most momentous in American history," and as a Republican candidate for Congress and one of the party's most influential leaders in the North Country, Wheeler played an essential role in it.[1] He expected a donnybrook with the Flanders brothers and he didn't have long to wait before they fired a broadside.

In February, the brothers painted Wheeler and the Republicans as dangerous radicals who were intent on destroying the unity of the nation. They declared that the Republicans should call their party by its true name, the *Abolition Party*. The Wheeler press replied that Bill and the Republicans were not "crazy-headed abolitionists" or "hare-brained fanatics" and that the Republicans would not disturb slavery where it existed.[2]

In addition to being troubled by the Flanders brothers, Wheeler was troubled by the ethics of New York Republican boss, Thurlow Weed, who was trying to ram through the legislature a bill granting himself a railroad franchise in New York City to finance Seward's campaign for president.[3] Even though Bill was a Seward man through and through and had Weed to thank for much of his political and financial success, Bill believed that Weed's demand for a railroad franchise to finance a campaign was not in the public interest and smacked of dishonesty. He urged Governor Morgan to veto the bill. Bill wrote, "If the New York Railroads can be brought within the pale of common honesty, or *slaughtered by your veto,* we will 'thank God and take courage.'"[4]

Membership certificate awarded to those who marched in the Wide Awake Club to support the 1860 Lincoln-Hamlin ticket. In Franklin County, members also marched in support of Wheeler's first run for Congress. The uniformed figure on the left carries a staff and a lantern, and the figure on the right holds a burning torch. Library of Congress.

News from Chicago in May that Abraham Lincoln of Illinois had outmaneuvered Seward and Weed to win the presidential nomination surprised Bill but it did not change his plans to run for Congress.[5] The Sixteenth Congressional District nominating convention would be coming up in September and Bill spent the summer organizing his campaign.

As heirs to the Whig hurrah-type of campaign, the national Republicans planned to rely on local uniformed marching clubs, the Wide Awakes, to provide noise, spectacle, and an opportunity for voter participation.[6] In early July, Wheeler and the Republicans called a meeting to form a local Wide Awake club.[7] Members would carry lighted pitch torches about two feet long and two inches in diameter and wear black oilskin caps and capes to protect them from dripping pitch and sparks. For special effects, each man would have several Roman candles to discharge as he marched behind the Malone Coronet Band.[8]

Not to be outdone, the Flanders brothers organized a Democratic marching club to support their candidate for president, Stephen A. Douglas.[9] Their uniforms were orange and they were called the *Little Giants*.[10]

Toward the end of July, Bill staged a massive Republican campaign rally in Malone. A Wide Awake contingent from Ogdensburg arrived by train with their martial band, torches, and banners. They marched to King's Hall where Wheeler welcomed them. Soon King's Hall was filled to capacity and Wheeler had to move everyone to the railroad freight depot. But that wasn't large enough either so the rally had to be held outdoors. To the delight of the crowd, a piece of one of the thousands of rails split by Lincoln thirty years previously was held up by a member of the Malone GOP Campaign Club. Wheeler was next on the program. In a two-hour speech he attacked Douglas and his doctrine of "squatter sovereignty." When Bill was done, darkness had settled in and the Wide Awakes formed for a torchlight procession. As the bands played, the Wide Awakes marched up and down Malone streets, shooting off Roman candles on the way. Rockets were set off from the roofs of business buildings whose windows were lighted up with colored lanterns. The streets were ablaze with light and cheer after cheer for the Republicans went up. The Ogdensburg Wide Awakes left for home at 1:30 a.m.[11]

In August, a few days before the Franklin County Republican convention was to meet to select delegates to the Sixteenth Congressional District nominating convention, a second campaign rally was held in Brushton for Republicans in the towns west and north of Malone. A crowd in the thousands appeared. Fifteen train carloads of people came from Malone. Several companies of Wide Awakes assembled. Bill gave his two-hour stump speech arguing against the extension of slavery into the territories and attacking Douglas for trying to make Kansas a slave state and himself president. A torchlight procession followed by fireworks concluded the rally.[12]

After the Franklin County GOP convention unanimously endorsed him to be nominated for Congress at the upcoming Sixteenth Congressional District convention, Wheeler wrote Morgan for campaign help. Bill wanted Morgan, who was poised to be renominated to run for governor, to send "the best speakers" to Malone for the campaign in the fall. Wheeler's selling point to Morgan was the central position Malone played on the railroad line between Clinton and St. Lawrence Counties. In the letter, Bill admitted to Morgan that he was concerned about embarking again "upon the stormy sea of politics" but would be "radiant with joy" to run on a ticket with Morgan, a man Wheeler said "could afford to do right, and trust the people."[13]

A week before the Sixteenth Congressional District nominating convention, Morgan delivered two of his best speakers to help Wheeler's campaign. Horace

Greeley, editor of the *New York Tribune,* came up to speak at the Franklin County fair and Governor Salmon Chase of Ohio came to speak at a campaign rally attended by almost twenty thousand people in Plattsburgh.[14]

On September 19, three delegates each, from Franklin, Clinton, and Essex Counties, met at the Cumberland Hotel in Plattsburgh and unanimously nominated Wheeler to run for Congress as a Republican in the Sixteenth district.[15] When he arrived back home in Malone a crowd of supporters led by the Malone Wide Awakes marched to Wheeler's house to honor and cheer him. Bill invited them all inside for "a handsome entertainment" that lasted about an hour.[16]

Newspaper endorsements from around the state quickly poured in. They praised Wheeler's "reputation for integrity and independence" and his "thorough knowledge of parliamentary proceedings." Weed's newspaper emphasized Bill's "statesmanship" and his skill as a debater. The *New York Evening Post* touted Wheeler's "great ability as a parliamentarian" and said he was "one of the purest and clearest-headed of our public men."[17]

To run against Wheeler, the Democrats nominated Augustus C. Hand, a fifty-seven-year-old State Supreme Court judge and former congressman from Elizabethtown in Essex County.[18]

The Flanders brothers wasted no time in going after Wheeler and they hit him where it hurt the most—his integrity. They charged Wheeler with using his "business, corporate and moneyed" interests to promote himself politically. The Flanders brothers intimated that Wheeler operated his railroad and bank as patronage mills for his Republican cronies. With Bill's political deputy, Patrick Shields, on the railroad's payroll as baggage master, it was difficult for Wheeler to refute the charges—but answer them he did. Bill pointed out to the voters that he hired Democrats as well as Republicans to work for his business enterprises. Chief among the Democrats employed by Wheeler was Joseph Flanders, who until recently had been hired to work as legal counsel for the bank and the railroad. In addition, there were any number of Democrats currently working for the railroad as clerks, roadmasters, foremen, and agents.[19]

Even though the charges by the Flanders brothers were basically rooted in the same moral and ethical high ground he himself had stood on when he had attacked Weed for wanting a railroad franchise to finance his political ambitions, Wheeler dismissed them as personal abuse and wanton and unprovoked assaults. Wheeler's integrity was his political strong suit and he fiercely protected it. Within the coming year, the Flanders brothers would pay a high price for their attack on Wheeler and their strident Democratic partisanship.

Wheeler hit the campaign trail with the Wide Awakes and addressed large crowds in Peru, Clinton County, and Ticonderoga, Essex County.[20] In response, the Flanders brothers stoked the coals of racism by calling the Wide Awakes, "nigger-skins" and denouncing their processions as "ridiculous performances" and "disgusting to candid and sensible people."[21]

On November 6, 1860, the voters went to the polls. On election night, Wheeler remained at election headquarters in King's Hall until 3 a.m. tallying the results with his party regulars. The totals showed that Wheeler won 58 percent of the vote, garnering 10,571 votes to Hand's 7,427 votes. In each of the three counties making up the Sixteenth Congressional District, Wheeler ran ahead of the other statewide Republican winners, Lincoln and Morgan. The *Palladium* crowed that every man in King's Hall that night "seemed determined to shout himself hoarse" with joy.[22]

Republican elation soon gave way to anxiety. Many southerners refused to accept the election of Republicans like Lincoln and Wheeler because they were committed to stopping the spread of slavery. By February 1, 1861, seven southern states seceded from the Union and formed a new government, the Confederate States of America.[23]

Wheeler was aghast at the reaction to secession by many New York Democratic leaders. Former Democratic Governor and party leader Horatio Seymour argued that the southern states should be allowed to leave the Union peacefully.[24] New York City Democratic Mayor Fernando Wood proposed that the City should also secede and free itself from the "foreign power" in Albany that "plundered" the city through unfair taxes.[25]

In Franklin County, the Flanders brothers joined the Democratic chorus, which sympathized with southern secession.[26] In response, the Wheeler Republican press stated threateningly, "Punish the traitors. Demand unqualified obedience to the law."[27]

Bill had been elected to the Thirty-seventh Congress and its first session would not begin until July 4. Nevertheless, he packed his bags at the end of February and went to Washington to attend Lincoln's inauguration in March and talk to him about securing some federal jobs for Bill's supporters in his congressional district. Bill saw what Lincoln looked like for the first time when the two men attended the same Sunday services at the New York Avenue Presbyterian Church. Years later, Bill wrote that he was struck by the great kindness, determination, and political shrewdness he saw in Lincoln's face.[28]

Bill wasn't the only man in Washington who wanted to see the president about federal jobs. Wheeler said the city was thronged with people "hungering and thirsty for them." He went to the White House several times but could not get in to see Lincoln because, as a newcomer to the federal political scene, he kept being put at the end of the long lines at the door. One day he ran into Orlando Kellogg, an ex-congressman from Essex County, in the corridor of the Willard Hotel where they both were staying. Bill knew Kellogg because of legal work they had done together in the past. Wheeler told Kellogg of his problems in getting in to see Lincoln. Kellogg said he had served in Congress with Lincoln and could get Bill an appointment to see him. The next morning, Wheeler and Kellogg went to the White House despite the fact that a cabinet meeting would be in session. Kellogg prevailed upon the White House doorkeeper to inform Lincoln that he was at the door and wanted to tell Lincoln "the story of the stuttering justice." Lincoln interrupted the cabinet meeting to have Kellogg ushered in to tell his story. Lincoln convulsed with laughter and subsequently agreed to see Wheeler the next morning at an appointed time that he wrote on a card and gave to Kellogg. This was to be the first of several face-to-face meetings Wheeler would have with Lincoln.[29]

War broke out between North and South in April after Fort Sumter was attacked by Confederate forces. Lincoln issued a call for seventy-five thousand troops and suspended the writ of habeas corpus, the guarantee of a person's right to appear before a judge before being imprisoned. Although the suspension was confined to a narrowly defined emergency area between Washington and Philadelphia,[30] and Wheeler's hometown of Malone was more than four hundred miles north of this area, six months later the suspension would have a devastating effect on Wheeler's chief Democratic foes, the Flanders brothers.

To meet Lincoln's call for troops, the New York legislature authorized the raising of thirty thousand volunteers.[31] Congressman-elect Wheeler became one of the North Country's most fervent recruiters. As president of the newly reorganized railroad, now called the Ogdensburg Railroad, Wheeler informed the commander of the militiamen in the North Country that he could use the railroad free of charge for military purposes. When the first company of volunteers from Ogdensburg stopped for dinner in Malone on the way to Albany by train, the men were cheered by crowds of people, bells were rung, and cannons fired. Wheeler was called for and he gave a speech to the company, which "quickened the pulses of patriotism."[32]

Bill put a large American flag up on the side of his Elm Street home and donated $1,000 to start a fund to provide support for the families of volunteers. He rallied the leading businessmen in Franklin County to agree to continue the salaries of their clerks if they volunteered to serve in the military. A large landowner, James H. Titus, further agreed to deed any volunteer in his employ forty acres of land when he returned from service.[33]

The first regiments raised in the North Country included the Sixteenth Regiment with men from St. Lawrence and Franklin Counties. The volunteers were business and professional men, farmers and skilled artisans. They were mostly young men in their early twenties or younger. In Malone, Joel Seaver, editor of the *Palladium,* raised eighty-one men to form one company as part of the Sixteenth Regiment and was the company's captain. Frederick F. Wead, son of the president of the Bank of Malone, Samuel C. Wead, was the company's first lieutenant. The men in the Sixteenth Regiment wore distinctive straw hats, which attracted a great deal of attention wherever the men marched.[34]

Wheeler organized a Union Meeting at the Congregational church for men from all political parties who were in favor of preserving the federal Union. American flags were draped all over the church and the Malone Band accompanied several choirs who sang patriotic music. Bill gave a major speech supporting the war effort and announced that four other prominent businessmen had joined him to form a committee to solicit funds to aid the families of volunteers.[35]

Bill's wife, Mary King Wheeler, was elected president of a new organization of women who had come together to support the war. At their first meeting, more than one hundred women attended and in three days they sewed more than one hundred undergarments for the Malone volunteers to use. Within another month, they completed sewing eighty Havelocks, white kepi covers with a long tail draping over the wearer's neck and shoulders to ward off sunstroke, for the volunteers. In addition, Mary Wheeler's women gathered a supply of needles, buttons, and woolen socks for the troops.[36]

The Flanders brothers rallied Democrats to snort and sneer at all the preparations for war and expressions of patriotism that were bubbling up all around them. To protest the call to arms, Francis Flanders resigned his commission as colonel of one of the militia regiments.[37] Within a week of his resignation, he publicly mocked the forty-one-year-old Wheeler's failure to enlist by writing in the *Gazette,* that given the "fervent patriotism" sweeping the area, it appeared "a little strange" that there were no volunteers "from the elite of our population." That same week, the Flanders brothers called for formal recognition of the Confederate States of America.[38]

The Flanders brothers saved their most caustic attack on Wheeler and Lincoln for the week that Bill left on a special train for the first session of the Thirty-seventh Congress in Washington. Joseph and Francis Flanders charged that the Lincoln Republicans had precipitated the Civil War in order to whip up war fever so that they could maintain the Republican Party in power. With a generous nod to Lincoln's suspension of the writ of habeas corpus, the Flanders brothers warned that Lincoln and his Republicans were determined to carry out a policy of "military despotism." According to the Flanders brothers, the Republicans in Washington were using unnecessary calls for the defense of the nation's capital and preservation of the Union to accustom the people to the loss of their liberties. The Flanders brothers predicted, "These wretches will turn upon us, and with vulture rapacity, prey upon the life-blood of the people."[39]

The *Palladium* responded saying that the Flanders brothers were writing with a pen "dipped in gall" and that their words sounded like "the ravings of a madman."[40] Within four months, the words of the Flanders brothers would become a self-fulfilling prophecy for each of them.

9

An Early-Morning Knock on the Door

☆

Wheeler was one of one hundred and two Republicans elected to the House of Representatives of the Thirty-seventh Congress. There were also forty-four Democrats, twenty-one Unionists and seven others from a scattering of parties.[1]

Bill would be working with a number of Republican heavyweights in the House, including Roscoe Conkling of Utica, future U.S. senator and party boss of New York State; Reuben Fenton of Chautauqua County, future two-term New York governor and U.S. senator; Thaddeus Stevens of Pennsylvania, leader of the Radical wing of the party; and Schuyler Colfax of Indiana, future vice president. Sitting across the aisle from Wheeler were several notable Democrats, including Albany's Erastus Corning, founder and president of the New York Central Railroad, and Clement L. Vallandigham of Ohio, leader of the antiwar or Copperhead wing of the Democratic Party.[2]

To Bill's extreme embarrassment and alarm, on July 4, the very day he was sworn in as a House member,[3] two hundred men with guns raised a Confederate flag in Burke, the next town east of Malone on Wheeler's railroad line. The men threatened to shoot anyone who tried to tear it down. When news of the flag raising got back to Malone, a large group of men were recruited from the railroad's machine shops to board the next train for Burke and haul the flag down. While the railroad men waited for the eastbound train, Francis Flanders sent word by horseback to the rebel sympathizers that trouble was headed their way from Malone and to avoid bloodshed, they should lower the flag. As the train from Malone arrived in sight of the Burke station, the pole and flag were seen to fall. A subsequent search located the flag hidden in a drainpipe.[4]

In Washington on the following day, Wheeler listened while the House clerk read President Lincoln's message to Congress about his war measures.[5] As a lawyer who had endured severe criticism from the Flanders brothers for supporting Lincoln's efforts to preserve the Union and opposing the extension of slavery into the territories, Wheeler listened intently to what Lincoln had to say about his recent suspension of the writ of habeas corpus.

Lincoln said he felt it was his duty to arrest individuals he "might deem dangerous to the public safety." The president assured the House that he was exercising this authority "very sparingly" and was aware of his critics who were arguing that his action was illegal because under the Constitution, only Congress had the power to suspend habeas corpus. Lincoln disputed this and stated that the Constitution is silent as to whether the Congress or the president is vested with this power. He said the provision in the Constitution for suspension of the writ of habeas corpus, Article One, Section Nine, was "plainly made for a dangerous emergency" and that the framers could have hardly intended that the danger should be allowed to run its course until Congress should be called together, the very assembling of which might be prevented by those fomenting the "dangerous emergency."[6]

Wheeler was appointed by the Speaker to chair the House Committee on Expenditures in the War Department and serve on the Committee on the Territories.[7] Much of his work in the first session involved voting the straight Republican Party line in support of Lincoln's prosecution of the war and a measure calling for the death penalty or fine and imprisonment for those convicted of treason against the United States.[8]

On the floor of the House, it did not take long for Bill to establish a reputation among his colleagues as an agile parliamentarian. He used motions to postpone debate on a bill in order to obtain permission to speak about it, and he was quite facile at making motions to reconsider a vote and to table his motion to reconsider, in the same breath.[9] Bill also used his wit and sense of humor to keep fellow House members on their toes. Once during a contentious debate on a bill calling for the licensing of attorneys and defining the word *lawyer,* Bill offered an amendment to an amendment that read, "No member of Congress shall make a set speech upon any other subject than that directly before the House without a special license for which he shall pay the sum of fifty dollars."[10]

Back up in the North Country, the Flanders brothers kept up their assault on Wheeler by accusing him of voting blindly as a pawn of the controversial abolitionist, Republican Congressman Owen Lovejoy of Illinois.[11]

Toward the end of July, Lincoln ordered thirty thousand Union troops to attack Richmond, Virginia, the new Confederate capital, and capture the city. It is not known if Bill rode in any of the carriages that made up a parade of congressmen, socialites, and curiosity seekers who, carrying their picnic lunches, accompanied the troops. However, after Confederate forces repulsed the attack at Bull Run, causing the Union troops and the panicked spectators to flee back to Washington, Wheeler did seek out the soldiers from the North Country's Sixteenth Regiment and filed a report for the *Palladium* reassuring readers that no one from Malone was wounded or injured.[12]

The Flanders brothers had a different take on the Union disaster at Bull Run. They said that it was the result of a continuing plot by the "black Republicans" to revive "war fever." Joseph and Francis Flanders raged against what they saw as a "mad and wicked war" and urged the public to "demand peace" because "ruin is staring us in the face."[13]

On August 6, the last day of the first session of the Thirty-seventh Congress, Wheeler voted to pass a Confiscation Act, which called for the seizure of all property used to aid the Southern rebellion.[14] Before heading home to Malone to await the start of the second session, which was scheduled to begin on December 2, Wheeler visited the troops from his hometown who were camped near Alexandria and gave the men a barrel of tobacco and a box of pipes to smoke it.[15]

On Bill's return to the North Country, he immediately picked up where he had left off rallying men to volunteer for the army and generating public support for Lincoln and the Union. Bill organized another open-air Union Meeting near the railroad station in Malone and arranged for prominent Republican speakers to come from St. Lawrence County, among them, Calvin T. Hulburd, lawyer, businessman, and farmer from Brasher Falls. To honor Wheeler's war work, the major troop depot in Ogdensburg where North Country volunteers were trained and processed for duty was named Camp Wheeler.[16]

Wheeler also fired a shot across the bow of the Flanders brothers. The *Palladium* warned them that newspapers who criticize the government during war should not be granted freedom of the press or speech because such criticism encourages the Southern rebels. From the Wheeler Republican point of view, during war, there had to be a limit on the First Amendment rights of freedom of the press and speech.[17]

The warning fell on deaf ears. Joseph and Francis Flanders were passionate about their views and confident that the First Amendment of the Constitution would protect their right to criticize the government. On October 22, five days after they learned that Wheeler was scheduled to present an American flag to a new regiment of volunteers in Ogdensburg, the Flanders brothers found out how wrong they were to have faith in First Amendment protection. At about 7 a.m., as

William H. Seward. Library of Congress.

both Joseph and Francis Flanders were eating breakfast with their families, they heard a knock on their doors. U.S. marshals had arrived with orders signed by Secretary of State Seward to have them arrested![18]

They were taken by train to Fort Lafayette, the military prison lying in the Narrows between Staten Island and Brooklyn, and incarcerated. About a week later they were transferred to Fort Warren in Boston Harbor. Agents of Seward offered to free them if they signed an oath of allegiance prescribed by the Lincoln administration. They agreed to sign an oath of loyalty to the U.S. Constitution but refused to sign an oath to support the Lincoln government. The Flanders brothers contended that the Lincoln government had illegally arrested them and had unconstitutionally deprived them of their freedom to oppose it. They remained behind bars in a military prison for four months.[19] On February 22, 1862, the Flanders brothers signed a promise not to give aid and comfort to the enemy. The next day, they were set free.[20]

The four months in prison may not have dampened the fiery spirits of the Flanders brothers but their arrest had a chilling effect on Franklin County Democrats. They were unable to elect an assemblyman from Franklin County for the rest of the nineteenth century.[21]

The historical record is not clear about Wheeler's role in the arrest of the Flanders brothers. He certainly had a motive to have them arrested. They had attacked his integrity, impugned his courage, and charged him with being part of a Republican conspiracy to keep his party in office by lying about Southern threats to national security. In addition, they were involved with the Confederate flag-raising incident in Burke and it was reported that federal officials had intercepted a letter from Francis's wife to Jefferson Davis.[22]

On top of all this, it is not difficult to imagine Wheeler feeling he had to do something when panic of invasion swept through Washington following the Union defeat at Bull Run. Bill fervently believed in the cause of preserving the Union and the Flanders brothers in Malone were a tempting target. He had the opportunity and the means to effect their arrest. Wheeler was in Washington during the months of March, July, and August. As a congressman, he had talked with Lincoln and was a longtime political ally of Seward.

There is also the possibility that the arrest of the Flanders brothers, in a small town near the Canadian border, was a trial balloon launched by the Lincoln administration to gauge public reaction to the arrest and military imprisonment of Democrats for antiwar activity undertaken far away from the actual fields of battle. If that were so, surely Lincoln and Seward would have consulted with the Republican congressman from the district in which the Flanders brothers lived. Whether Lincoln and Seward talked with Wheeler or not, on August 8, 1862, shortly after the release of the Flanders brothers, Lincoln issued a nationwide suspension of the writ of habeas corpus and used military prisons to incarcerate prisoners.[23]

In Franklin County, when news that Lincoln Republicans in Washington had arrested the county leaders of the Democratic party for their antiwar views and locked them away in a military prison without a hearing before a judge, Republicans began to regard their congressman in a new light. From now on, they were more cautious about what they said publicly about him. Wheeler's grip on the Republican Party in Franklin County tightened.

Some party members in the county began to whisper that he was acting like an autocrat who would not hesitate to use unsavory political methods to get exactly what he wanted. Bill's grip tightened even further. Soon, no Republican in Franklin County could run for office or become a delegate to a party convention without Wheeler's blessing.[24]

On November 26, 1861, with the Flanders brothers behind bars in the federal military prison in Boston Harbor, Bill and his wife Mary left Malone by train for Washington.[25] The second session of the Thirty-seventh Congress was scheduled to open on December 2 and the Wheelers were eager to get settled before it began.

10

Suddenly, a "Junior Partner"

☆

No sooner had the Wheelers arrived in Washington than Bill had a dustup with Secretary of War Edwin M. Stanton over a military appointment Wheeler wanted for one of his old boyhood and longtime political friends, Major John A. Sabin. At Bill's request, first made in July 1861, President Lincoln had appointed Sabin to the post of army paymaster and sent the order to Stanton. Months went by and Sabin heard nothing from Stanton about the appointment. Wheeler complained to Stanton about the delay and he told Wheeler that Sabin would have to wait his turn, even if it took all winter. Bill argued that Sabin shouldn't have to wait to be mustered in to duty because he had been appointed by the commander-in-chief. Stanton would not budge and snapped at Bill, "You have my answer. No argument!"

Writing later about the incident, Bill said he was "provoked" by Stanton's "insolence of office" and marched over to the White House that evening to speak with Lincoln about the matter. Taking a copy of Sabin's appointment letter signed by Lincoln with him, Bill met with Lincoln who was dressed in a long calico dressing gown with leather slippers and homemade blue wool socks. He was sitting in a rocking chair with his legs stretched across the office table.

When Lincoln asked what Wheeler wanted, Bill told him he had come to find out from him who was the paramount power in the government: the president or the secretary of war. Lincoln said *he* was and inquired why Bill asked. When Wheeler explained what had happened concerning the Sabin appointment,

Edwin M. Stanton. Brady-Handy Collection, Library of Congress.

Lincoln took the appointment letter from Wheeler and wrote on it that Sabin should be appointed *at once*, underlining the words twice, and signed the letter. Bill took it to Stanton the next morning. He was furious and charged Wheeler with interfering with the secretary of war's work and using "undue persistence."

Undaunted, Bill told Stanton he would come back the following morning for the paperwork mustering Sabin in as paymaster. When Wheeler arrived the next morning, Stanton handed him the order in a rage and said he hoped he would not hear about the matter ever again.

That evening, Bill was at a reception for the new Speaker of the House and Stanton was present. Wheeler went over to him, shook his hand, and said nothing about their recent exchange. From that point on, according to Wheeler, Stanton never refused anything Bill asked for.[1]

Congressman Wheeler worked hard for his constituents. He made sure the troops from the North Country were paid on time, helped an inventor renew his patent for a portable saw mill, and aided a War of 1812 widow to get her pension.[2]

During the second session, Wheeler voted for a number of bills that had a significant impact on the nation's financial, transportation, and educational systems. Bill lent his support to the call for a uniform bankruptcy law, which brought him into close contact with Roscoe Conkling, the House's expert on bankruptcy laws—it would be the first of many times their political paths would cross and one of the few times that they would agree with each other.[3] Wheeler also voted for a bill to aid in the construction of a railroad and telegraph line from the Missouri River to the Pacific Ocean—the nation's first transcontinental railroad, the Union and Central Pacific Railroad.[4] In addition, he voted for a bill that granted each state thirty thousand acres of federal land for each congressman a state sent to Washington. According to the measure, when the states sold the land, the proceeds were to be used to establish colleges for agriculture and the mechanical arts. Over the coming years, these funds were used by states to fund sixty-nine land grant colleges.[5]

In his first term as a congressman, Bill fought against unnecessary government spending. He opposed a bill providing for a temporary government for the Territory of Arizona, which was to be formed from the western part of the existing Territory of New Mexico. He was against the measure because he felt there were not enough people living in the area to justify the cost of creating a new government for them. Quoting from census records he brought with him to the floor of the House, he said there were only 2,401 white men, 21 blacks, and 4,004 Indians in Arizona. Bill argued that if a territorial government were to be established, money to pay for it would be "ground out between the upper and nether mill-stones of taxation." He stated that if the bill were passed, requests for appropriations for capital buildings, surveys, roads, and other projects would pour into Congress, year after year. Wheeler also predicted that "mercenary whites" would start a large-scale Indian war to cover their "piracy upon the Treasury." Bill tried to postpone the bill, and then table it, but it passed over his objections.[6]

Slavery and emancipation were the most controversial subjects Wheeler dealt with during the second session. The fact that two competing factions of the New York Republican Party sought his support made matters doubly difficult for him. The Conservatives, led by Seward, Weed, and Raymond, put the pressure on him from one side to support their agenda. They were worried about the negative impact that emancipation would have on New York voters and opposed immediate abolition arguing that Lincoln's war aim should be the preservation of the Union—the war should not be turned into a crusade against slavery.[7] The Radicals, led by Greeley and Congressman Reuben Fenton of Chautauqua County, put pressure on him from the other side. They demanded immediate abolition and full civil liberties for the freedmen.[8]

At first, Wheeler hewed the Conservative line. He voted for a resolution that declared that it was no part of a soldier's duty to capture or return fugitive slaves.[9] Resisting pressure to vote for immediate abolition, Bill would only endorse gradual emancipation.[10] However, in April he began to change his mind and moved toward the Radical camp by voting to abolish slavery in the District of Columbia.[11] Two months later, he voted to abolish slavery in the Territories.[12] On June 18, 1862, he voted to free slaves owned by rebels "engaged in or abetting the existing rebellion against the government of the United States."[13]

Midway through the second session, just as Bill was beginning to hit his stride as a freshman congressman, he received some devastating political news. The Republican-controlled New York legislature had reapportioned him out of office! Using the population figures from the 1860 census, the legislature drew new congressional district lines for the state, as it was constitutionally mandated to do every ten years. Bill had been elected from a district composed of Franklin, Clinton, and Essex Counties. If the legislature had left the lines of this district alone, Wheeler would have been a favorite to win reelection in 1862 because he would have been running as an incumbent. Instead, the lawmakers in Albany abolished the district and created a new, safe, Republican district, the Seventeenth Congressional District, by attaching Franklin County to the heavily Republican St. Lawrence County. The lines of this new district mirrored those of a Franklin-St. Lawrence County state senate district that had been in place since 1846.[14]

Because St. Lawrence County was three times the size of Franklin County, Republicans from St. Lawrence County would have the voting power to name the party's candidate for Congress. At the upcoming Republican Seventeenth Congressional District nominating convention, St. Lawrence County would have nine votes, three from each assembly district in the county, and Franklin County, with one assembly district, would have only three votes.[15] Bill knew he would not be renominated because popular St. Lawrence Republican assemblyman, Calvin T.

Hulburd, was interested in running for Congress and at convention time, he would have the support of all nine St. Lawrence County votes. Bill had no choice but to bow to the inevitable and plan for the future. The *Palladium* praised the new Franklin-St. Lawrence County congressional district because it was "contiguous and compact" and noted that the "interests of the counties are closely woven." The paper added that it was confident that St. Lawrence County would "deal magnanimously with her junior partner."[16]

The best the congressman from St. Lawrence County's junior partner could hope for politically at this juncture was to keep his name before the voters in St. Lawrence County, make as many new political allies as he could there, and broker a deal with St. Lawrence County GOP leaders for the congressional nomination at some time in the future. During the break between the second and third sessions of Congress and the days running up to the 1862 fall elections, Bill began laying the groundwork to do those things and to stage a comeback.

On July 29 he attended a meeting of the War Committee of the Seventeenth State Senatorial District, which was held in North Potsdam, a community in St. Lawrence County. The major item on the agenda called for the recommendation of a new commander for the 106th Volunteer Regiment to Governor Morgan. Wheeler favored the appointment of Captain N. Martin Curtis from St. Lawrence County. Other committee members opposed Curtis and wanted to make no recommendation. Bill outmaneuvered them and by a vote of 13 to 3, made some new allies in St. Lawrence County by winning the post for Curtis. At the same meeting, Bill made additional friends by supporting the appointment of six men to work as military recruiters.[17] Later in the summer, Bill continued his quest to make allies in St. Lawrence County by successfully importuning Governor Morgan to replace several Democratic office holders in the county with Wheeler Republicans.[18]

In August, Wheeler decided to keep his name in front of the voters in his new congressional district by taking his Radical stance on slavery into St. Lawrence County. At a meeting of the War Committee of the Seventeenth State Senatorial District, Bill rammed through a series of resolutions calling for Lincoln to immediately issue an emancipation proclamation using his powers as commander-in-chief. One of the resolutions said, "The welfare of the country, the lives of loyal soldiers, and happiness of loyal families all over the free states demand the proclamation. The whole civilized world will applaud the proclamation of emancipation." The resolutions were adopted unanimously.[19]

In September, Bill rejoiced when he read that Lincoln had issued an Emancipation Proclamation that would take effect on January 1, 1863.[20] The *Palladium* described the Emancipation Proclamation as "the most important document ever issued in the land since the 4th of July, 1776." Echoing Wheeler's sentiments, the paper declared, "Slavery has evoked and sustained this terrible rebellion and slavery must die."[21]

The 1862 Republican nominating conventions were also held in September. Assemblyman Hulburd was unanimously nominated to run for Congress in the new Franklin-St. Lawrence congressional district, as Bill expected. He put on a happy face for the public stating that he did not want to run again, and in any event, because St. Lawrence County was the larger member of the new district, it was entitled to the nomination. Bill added that he and his friends were "content" with Hulburd's nomination given his legislative experience as an assemblyman.[22]

At the GOP state convention, the Radicals were in the ascendance and when Governor Morgan declined to run for a third term, they nominated abolitionist General James S. Wadsworth of Geneseo County for governor.[23] The Democrats nominated former Governor Horatio Seymour, an advocate of states' rights from Utica. Critical of Lincoln's management of the war, the Democratic platform denounced "the illegal, unconstitutional and arbitrary arrests" of New Yorkers by his administration and insisted on liberty of speech and freedom of the press.[24]

The Democrats made the loss of civil liberties the centerpiece of their campaign and turned the election, for Wheeler, into a referendum on the propriety of the arrest of the Flanders brothers. Bill campaigned vigorously for Wadsworth and Hulburd, arguing that the key question in the election was whether New York would continue to prosecute the war "with vigor and energy; or whether it shall turn its guns against the government and the country." At a campaign rally organized by Wheeler in Malone, Henry J. Raymond forcefully restated Wheeler's theme. Raymond said that "all sympathizers with treason" in the North are also supporters of Seymour and the Democrats.[25]

When the votes were counted, Hulburd garnered 67 percent of the vote and won by more than six thousand votes. Wadsworth along with the entire GOP county ticket swept to victory in Franklin County. However, Wadsworth lost statewide to Seymour by more than ten thousand votes.[26] As Wheeler analyzed the returns, he was naturally disappointed by the Democratic win for governor but was pleased by the GOP showing in Franklin County because it vindicated the decision to have the Flanders brothers arrested.

Hulburd was the congressman-elect following the election but his term would not begin until the Thirty-eighth Congress convened on December 7, 1863—thirteen months after the election! Congressman Wheeler would continue in office as a lame duck until the third session of the Thirty-seventh Congress adjourned on March 3, 1863.[27]

Wheeler hadn't been back at work in Congress for much more than a month before he was asked to help halt what has been called "one of the most blatant official episodes of anti-Semitism in 19th century American history."[28] He refused.

At issue was General Ulysses S. Grant's infamous General Order No. 11, which expelled Jews, "as a class," from Kentucky, Tennessee, and Mississippi. Grant issued the order on December 17, 1862, as part of his campaign to curb the frenzied black market in Southern cotton, which he was convinced was organized "mostly by Jews and other unprincipled traders." In response to enforcement of the order, Jewish leaders organized protest rallies in St. Louis, Cincinnati, and Louisville. Telegrams poured in to Lincoln from Chicago, New York, and Philadelphia. Jewish merchants traveled to Washington and conferred with their representatives in Congress.[29]

Republicans and Democrats in Washington stepped forward together to roll back Grant's order. Influential Jewish Republican Adolphus Solomons and John A. Gurley, Republican congressman from Cincinnati, met with the Jewish merchants. Antiwar Democratic Congressman George H. Pendleton of Ohio introduced a resolution condemning Grant's order and the president, as commander-in-chief, because the order was "tyrannical and cruel" and "illegal and unjust."[30]

Support for Pendleton's resolution crossed party lines. However much Wheeler may have detested Grant's sweeping assault on religious freedom, Bill could not bring himself to support a Democratic-sponsored attack on the Lincoln administration's handling of the war. Wheeler voted with fifty-five others to table the measure—fifty-three voted against tabling it.[31] As Congress debated the issue, Jewish leaders met with Lincoln and convinced him to order Grant to revoke General Order No. 11.[32]

Before the third session adjourned, there were two other significant, war-related measures that crossed Wheeler's desk. The first was legislation providing for a draft. Bill voted for it and the measure easily passed the House, 115 to 49.[33] By mid-July, 2,757 men were drafted in Franklin and St. Lawrence Counties without incident. However, there were major draft riots in New York City and Troy.[34]

The second significant proposal coming before Wheeler concerned the legality of Lincoln's suspension of habeas corpus. Antiwar Democrats and civil libertarians had stepped up their charges that, according to the Constitution, only Congress had the authority to suspend the privilege of the writ of habeas corpus and Lincoln's acts doing so were illegal. Lincoln argued that he was acting legally because he had inherent authority to suspend habeas corpus as commander-in-chief during war and rebellion. By the time Wheeler was asked to vote on legislation dealing with this matter, thousands of civilians had been arrested and put in prison without being given a chance to go before a judge and argue the legality of their incarceration.[35]

On March 2, the second to last day of the third session, the Habeas Corpus Act of 1863 came before the House for a vote. It legalized all of Lincoln's habeas corpus suspensions and authorized future suspensions for the rest of the war. With images of the Flanders brothers in his head, Bill voted for the measure, which passed 99 to 45.[36]

After the Thirty-seventh Congress finished its business and went out of existence, and Bill and Mary were back home in Malone, it was time for Wheeler to regroup, firm up his political base of operations in the North Country, and pay closer attention to his banking and railroad interests. Major business decisions were looming and Conservatives and Radicals were imploring him to seek statewide office.

11

A Sporting Gentleman Gets the Itch

By the summer of 1863, Bill Wheeler had been in the banking business for almost twelve years and the railroad business for almost ten years. During that time, he had become a wealthy man by North Country standards. In August, the Wheeler family became even wealthier when Bill's well-to-do father-in-law, seventy-year-old William King, died and Mary Wheeler inherited a share of his estate.[1]

Since Bill began managing the railroad, first named the Northern Railroad in 1845 and then the Ogdensburg Railroad in 1858, his control of the line had been under constant attack by Boston investors and managers of the Vermont Central Railroad. Prompted by Bill's fellow UVM alumnus, J. Gregory Smith, the Vermont Central stepped up pressure to seize management of the line from Wheeler in the fall of 1863.

Bill answered the threat by laying plans to reorganize and reincorporate the line for a second time. To devote more time to this work, Bill eased himself out of banking. He gave up day-to-day management of the Bank of Malone and became its vice president.[2] Then, in 1865, four months after overseeing the conversion of the bank into a national bank with the new name, the National Bank of Malone, Wheeler resigned as vice president and turned to railroad concerns.[3]

Using his political influence, Bill succeeded in having the legislature pass a law giving the Ogdensburg Railroad permission to reincorporate.[4] On June 10, 1864, the holders of the second mortgage bonds of the Ogdensburg Railroad organized the Ogdensburg and Lake Champlain Railroad Company at a meeting in Malone. They elected Wheeler president of the new corporation and installed him as a director on a thirteen-man board, which was dominated by nine directors from Boston.[5]

When Wheeler sought judicial permission to transfer the property of the Ogdensburg Railroad to the new Ogdensburg and Lake Champlain Railroad, he ran into legal difficulties from competing Boston and Vermont financial interests. The transfer was delayed and Wheeler's role as manager was challenged. Instead of continuing to fight to maintain control of the line, Bill accepted an offer to settle the dispute, which received judicial approval. In exchange for stepping down as president and director, Wheeler was paid his salary until the end of the year and was given a guarantee that a new, spacious passenger station would be erected in Malone.[6] In addition, the settlement allowed Wheeler to continue serving as a trustee of more than a million dollars worth of second mortgage bonds.[7] Within a year, the new passenger station was completed and opened for business. When the last brick was laid on the new station, considered by some to be one of the finest railway stations in New York State at that time, the workers sent up a long, loud "hurrah" and were treated to an oyster supper.[8]

Bill was legally ousted by the stockholders as president and director of the railroad at a meeting in July 1865, the same month he had to pack to go to Hanover, New Hampshire, to be awarded an honorary master of arts degree at the Dartmouth commencement exercises.[9] They were held in the College Church on July 20. Bill sat on stage with Dartmouth alumnus, Salmon P. Chase, Chief Justice of the U.S. Supreme Court, and the other honorary degree recipients who included Frederick Smyth, the newly elected governor of New Hampshire. After Bill was awarded his master's degree, he attended the annual Dartmouth alumni dinner at the Dartmouth Hotel where Chase gave a "spirited" speech advocating full black suffrage. The evening's festivities were topped off by music provided by Gilmore's Band from Boston.[10] It was a day the forty-six-year-old college dropout from Malone would never forget.

Wheeler's retirement from banking and railroading allowed him to spend more time doing what he loved best—fishing. In May of every year, Bill and five or six of his closest political and business friends would head out into the woods and lakes of the Adirondacks, the *Great Southern Wilderness* as they called the area, to fish for trout, commune with nature, and plot political and business strategy. They fancied themselves "sporting gentlemen" and called themselves the *Saranac*

This open camp at Raquette Lake is typical of the shelters used by Wheeler and the members of his Saranac Navigation Company when they went on their annual fishing expeditions. Detroit Publishing Company Collection, Library of Congress.

Navigation Company. They would be gone for one or two weeks at a time. Often, the Company would spend the first night at Martin's Hotel at the foot of Lower Saranac Lake or at Bartlett's Hotel between the Lower and Upper Saranacs, before moving on to other favorite fishing spots on Tupper Lake, Raquette Lake, and Blue Mountain Lake.

The men had no predetermined route and let Bill decide where he thought the fishing would be the best. As one member of the Saranac Navigation Company put it, "Wherever the spirit taketh Bill, thither shall we go, if it be among things possible." In a single day, the anglers might catch fifteen trout weighing from one-half to three pounds each. Sometimes, they would rendezvous with other "sporting gentlemen" from downstate, such as John Adams Appleton, one of the owners of the preeminent publishing house, D. Appleton & Company of New York, or George Dawson, influential editor of the *Albany Evening Journal*.[11] Over the coming decades, Bill would not allow political or business matters to interfere with his time fishing, if he could possibly help it. As a result, his fishing prowess

Blue Mountain Lake from Blue Mountain in the Adirondacks. Detroit Publishing Company Collection, Library of Congress.

and interest in the sport would often be the subject of both friendly and hostile press commentary in the years to come.

As state Republicans began jockeying for position in the upcoming 1864 elections for governor and president, party rivalry between Radicals and Conservatives heated up. Both factions agreed that a war Democrat should replace Hannibal Hamlin as Lincoln's vice president at the national convention in June. The Radicals, led by Horace Greeley, had a majority of the New York delegates and supported Daniel S. Dickinson of Binghamton. However, the Conservatives, led by Weed, Seward, Raymond, and Morgan, favored the eventual winner, Andrew Johnson, war governor of Tennessee. Wheeler had friends in both factions and endorsed neither Dickinson nor Johnson but subsequently let it be known that he had misgivings about Johnson.[12]

Wheeler was named to be a delegate to the GOP state convention in September, which nominated Radical five-term Congressman Reuben Fenton for governor to run against the incumbent Democrat, Horatio Seymour.[13] A few weeks later, Hulburd was nominated by the Franklin and St. Lawrence County Republicans to run for a second term in Congress.[14]

As Bill looked forward to campaigning in the fall with Greeley in Franklin County for the Lincoln-Fenton ticket, he studied the new voting regulations that had been put in place by a Republican-dominated legislature. It had amended the state constitution to allow soldiers in the field to vote by proxy—they had not been allowed to do that in the 1862 gubernatorial election, which had been won by Seymour and the Democrats.[15]

Bill could see the possibilities for voting fraud because under the new proxy voting system, soldiers in the field were supposed to mail their ballots to electors in the county where the soldiers had enlisted. The electors were then supposed to cast these ballots for the soldiers on election day. Wheeler learned that Democrats were conspiring to vote dead and missing soldiers and alerted his election officials to be on the lookout. Wheeler's informants told him shortly before election day that some seven hundred bogus votes had been shipped into St. Lawrence County. Bill also learned that voting agents from New York appointed by Governor Seymour had been arrested and charged with using dead and missing soldiers' names on absentee ballots packed in dry goods boxes and shipped to New York and Albany from Baltimore, Washington, and Harper's Ferry.[16]

Wheeler's efforts to prevent voting fraud by Democrats was a complete success. Not surprisingly, given Bill's control over the election machinery in Franklin County, there were no investigations of bogus votes being cast for Republicans! The vote of New York soldiers statewide was decisive and Lincoln, Fenton, Hulburd, and the entire state GOP ticket carried the state.[17]

On the first Monday afternoon in April 1865, Wheeler was startled to hear bells ringing at the Court House and at Franklin Academy. He learned that they were ringing to celebrate the news that had just come in by telegraph to Malone that Richmond had fallen to Union troops. The next day, all the stores closed, a cannon fired, dozens of steam whistles blew from the railroad steam shops, and all the bells in the village rang for more than an hour. In the evening, Bill joined the mass of people who gathered in the village streets to listen to the Malone Coronet Band play patriotic music and watch a fireworks display.[18]

A week later, Lee surrendered but Bill's joy was dashed by subsequent news that Lincoln had been assassinated. On the day of Lincoln's funeral in Washington, businesses closed in Malone and Bill attended religious services at his church. Bells tolled for a half hour before the service and a gun was fired every half hour from sunrise to sunset. A salute of twenty-one guns was fired at noon.[19]

With President Johnson now in the White House, Wheeler felt pressure once again from both Radicals and Conservatives for his support. Conservatives Weed, Seward, and Raymond courted Johnson's favor and encouraged his Reconstruction policies, which left the granting of black suffrage up to the state legislatures of the individual Southern states. According to Johnson, only white men should be allowed to vote for the members of the new legislatures.[20] Radicals, such as Horace Greeley, favored immediate enfranchisement of blacks to enable them to have a voice in the legislatures that would be reorganizing their state governments. Where the New York Republican Party would stand on this matter would be decided at the upcoming 1865 GOP state convention, which was scheduled to meet in Syracuse in September.[21]

Wheeler was elected to be a delegate to the convention and was named one of the convention's vice presidents. He was also appointed to the resolutions committee, which would deal with whether the 1865 party platform should call for immediate black suffrage in the Southern states or endorse President Johnson's policies.[22]

Despite Wheeler's desire to promote black voting rights, the Conservatives prevailed. The committee passed resolutions that recognized Johnson as "a man of ability and patriotism and integrity" and commended his policy of Reconstruction. The convention adopted the resolutions unanimously. The concerns of New York Radicals for advancing black suffrage would have to wait for another day and another forum.[23]

As spring came to the North Country in 1866, Bill got the itch to run for Congress again. However, Hulburd showed no sign he was willing to give up his seat. A unified St. Lawrence County Republican Party meant that Hulburd could have the congressional nomination as long as he wanted it. But rumors that Abel Godard of DeKalb, the state senator representing St. Lawrence and Franklin Counties, was up to his neck in corruption, gave Bill the opening that he needed to split the Republican ranks in St. Lawrence County. Godard was an ally of Hulburd. The state senator's chief accuser was General Edwin A. Merritt of Potsdam, a thirty-eight-year-old respected Republican with political ambition.[24]

At the Republican Seventeenth Congressional District convention held at L. H. Dunton's Hotel in Stockholm Depot on August 23, the delegates agreed that in exchange for Wheeler's support for Hulburd to run for a third time, Bill would be granted the nomination to run for the next two Congresses, the Forty-first and Forty-second. This meant that Wheeler would be running for Congress in the 1868 election. He had two more years to prepare for it.[25]

In the meantime, while Wheeler was firming up his congressional future, the Conservatives in his party were laying plans to hold back a rising tide of Radicalism. In Washington, Weed, Seward, and Raymond began organizing a new political party consisting of conservative Republicans and Democrats who supported President Johnson's Reconstruction policies that, among other things, denied blacks immediate suffrage and full civil equality. As a first step toward forming a

Edwin D. Morgan. Brady-Handy Collection, Library of Congress.

new party, the three men orchestrated a call for a National Union Convention to meet in Philadelphia in August 1866.[26]

From the North Country, Wheeler threw cold water on the project. He told Morgan there was "no sympathy" for a new party in either Franklin or St. Lawrence Counties. Wheeler declared that the new party would interfere with the "march to human equality," one of the "legitimate results" of the Civil War that had been ordained by "Providence." Not said to Morgan, was another reason Wheeler was not eager to support the president. Bill had learned that Johnson was threatening to remove Hiram Dunn, one of Bill's political friends, as Collector of the

Champlain District. If that happened, a significant source of Wheeler's patronage appointments would dry up.[27]

Conservatives were also concerned about the rising power of Radicals in New York State. Governor Fenton, the popular Radical chieftain, wanted to run for a second term in 1866 and had his eyes on seizing control of the party from Conservative Thurlow Weed.[28] In a letter labeled *Personal and Confidential*, Morgan suggested to Wheeler that he run for governor to stop Fenton and Radicalism in New York.[29]

Wheeler was flattered by Morgan's support but Bill preferred to use his resources for his anticipated run for Congress in two years. However, he did allow his name to be put forward for lieutenant-governor as a replacement for the incumbent, Thomas G. Alvord of Syracuse. Wheeler's opponent for the nomination was General Stewart L. Woodford, a thirty-year-old graduate of Columbia from Brooklyn. A man of brilliant oratorical ability, Woodford had been working as an assistant U.S. attorney when the Civil War broke out. He resigned and raised a company of men to march off to fight for the Union cause. During the war, Woodford subsequently rose to command the black 103rd Infantry Regiment and was the first Union military commander of Charleston, South Carolina, and Savannah, Georgia. At the GOP state convention, he had the support of the entire New York and Brooklyn delegations and was also the second choice of the delegates from western New York, whose first choice was Alvord. Sensing that Woodford was going to win the nomination, Wheeler withdrew his name.[30]

Ten years later, the Wheeler-Woodford rivalry would resume over a bigger prize—the nomination for vice president of the United States—and Woodford would withdraw in favor of Wheeler. But in September 1866, Wheeler was content to applaud the Fenton-Woodford ticket and prepare for the coming campaign.

12

"True to Our Trust, True to Ourselves, and True to Truth"

In the months leading up to the 1866 election, voters were riveted by debate over issues concerning black civil rights. Southern states adopted "Black Codes" to bind newly freed slaves to the land. In Washington, President Johnson fought with Congress over Reconstruction. He vetoed measures designed to ensure rights for blacks including the Civil Rights Act and legislation seeking to enlarge the scope of the Freedmen's Bureau. Congress overrode Johnson's vetoes and also adopted the Fourteenth Amendment, which was submitted to the states for ratification. Debate about the merits of the amendment's definition of national citizenship, guarantee of equal protection of the law and due process of law, ran hot and heavy.[1]

In New York State, the principles of congressional Reconstruction and the Fourteenth Amendment became the major planks of the state GOP platform for 1866.[2] Radicals also favored calling a state constitutional convention to reform the state constitution. New York's existing constitution, which had been effect since 1846, required that the voting public be asked at least once every twenty years if they wanted to call a constitutional convention. This question would be on the ballot in November.[3] The most dramatic and most controversial change to the constitution sought by Radicals was one providing for equal suffrage for black men.

According to the existing state constitution, every "man of color" had to own at least $250 worth of property in order to vote. This property qualification meant that all but a few of New York's black men were ineligible to vote. Since it did not apply to white men, their eligibility to vote was not restricted by it.[4] Wheeler believed that this was very wrong and vigorously supported equal voting rights for black men.

Bill believed that the political rights of blacks in the South had to be guaranteed in order to prevent Southern whites from passing laws to reenslave blacks. Wheeler agreed with the Radicals that it was up to the Northern states, like New York, which still discriminated against blacks at the polls, to set an example for the South to follow and set the stage for equal suffrage to be granted everywhere. There was a second, practical political reason why Wheeler wanted to grant black men impartial suffrage. If Republicans were able to eliminate the $250 property qualification, eleven thousand additional black men in New York would have the vote and the bulk of the new black votes would be cast in New York and Brooklyn—Democratic strongholds.[5]

In the fall, Wheeler vigorously campaigned in favor of the Fenton-Woodford ticket and the call for a state constitutional convention. Bill traveled throughout Franklin County with Woodford and the ex–vice president and former U.S. Senator Hannibal Hamlin of Maine. Bill endorsed the *Palladium*'s description of the upcoming election as "A great battle in the interest of liberty, progress and enduring Union on the one side, and treason, anarchy and misrule on the other." Wheeler spoke nightly to large audiences and as the *Palladium* put it, "When he speaks, the people listen and believe."[6]

As election day approached, Wheeler met in his office with his key political operatives in every school district to lay plans to get out the full Union vote. Bill achieved outstanding results. For example, soon after the polls opened, a procession of fifteen to twenty carriages containing every voter in one of Malone's school districts drove down Main Street. The carriages were preceded by wagons pulled by double teams of horses, which carried a large U.S. flag and a banner that read, "Traitors Defeated In Battle Shall Not Rule By Ballot." The procession halted at the courthouse where the men marched in a solid body to the polls to vote for calling a constitutional convention and for "Fenton—Freedom and equal rights for all men."[7]

When the votes were counted, the Republican Radicals swept to victory in the nation, the state, and Franklin County. Fenton was elected governor and the GOP controlled both houses of the legislature ensuring that a Republican would be elected to represent New York in the U.S. Senate when Ira Harris's term expired on March 3, 1867. The new U.S. senator would be Congressman Roscoe Conkling of Utica. Voters also voted in favor of calling a state constitutional convention, 352,854 to 256,364.[8]

Wheeler's carte de visite.

In March, the legislature passed a law providing for a constitutional convention to assemble in Albany on June 4. There would be 160 delegates—four from each senatorial district and thirty-two from the state at-large. Each major political party guaranteed itself the election of sixteen of the thirty-two at-large seats. The law gave voters the opportunity to vote for four delegates from their senatorial districts but they could only vote for sixteen of the at-large delegates. This meant that in the special election set for April 23, if Republicans voted for Republican candidates, and Democrats voted for Democratic candidates, all thirty-two at-large nominees would win.[9]

Two weeks before the special election, a Republican state convention was held in Syracuse to nominate the party's at-large candidates. Widely regarded as one of the party's most dignified and respected members, Wheeler won one of the sixteen at-large nominations. Other prominent Republicans chosen included: William M. Evarts, future defense attorney for President Johnson during his impeachment trial and subsequently his attorney general and secretary of state under President Hayes; George Opdyke, mayor of New York City during the Civil War; George W. Curtis, editorial writer for *Harper's Weekly* and *Harper's Monthly;* Horace Greeley, founder and editor of the *New York Tribune;* U.S. Senator Ira Harris; and State Senator Charles J. Folger, future chief justice of the New York Court of Appeals and U.S. secretary of the treasury under President Arthur.[10]

As expected, the voter turnout for the special election in the North Country was very low. Farmers were busy preparing for spring planting and many decided not to vote.[11] In the election statewide, ninety-seven Republicans won to sixty-three Democrats. Wheeler garnered 153,124 votes.[12]

Once the votes were tabulated, a contest broke out over who should be elected president of the convention. The candidates included Wheeler, Lieutenant Governor Thomas G. Alvord, U.S. Senator Harris, and State Senator Folger. Publicly, Bill took the standard nineteenth-century "the office should seek the man" line, claiming that he would "not rob the position of its dignity and honor" by seeking it for himself. Wheeler stated that he would not make a deal with anyone to get the post because if he did, he would "embarrass his freedom of action and impair his usefulness." Bill was only speaking for himself, and again, in the nineteenth-century political tradition, he was not speaking for his many friends who were working hard to secure the nomination for him. They convinced the *New York Evening Post* to tout Wheeler for the job on the grounds that he was not heavily involved with any Republican faction—and in addition, the *Post* said it liked Bill because he was "a gentleman of fine personal character" and when he was a state senator, he "charmed everyone."[13]

Several days before the convention was to convene, Bill went down to Albany to meet with his political allies and map out strategy. He checked into No. 7 Park Place, avoiding the Delavan House where many of the delegates and most of the press were staying.[14] Under the heading, *occupation*, on the official roll of delegates, Wheeler set himself distinctly apart from the other delegates by listing himself as "Gentleman." Almost one hundred delegates designated themselves as "Lawyer." Other common occupations listed were "Merchant," "Farmer," "Surveyor," "Clergyman," "Author," and "Editor."[15]

On June 2 and 3, the Republicans met in caucus to select their candidate for president and organize themselves. With the support of Fenton Radicals, Wheeler emerged as the first choice of the GOP caucus defeating Alvord, Harris, and Folger.[16] At the caucus, Bill also secured Republican backing to have his friend from Malone, Hiram T. French, named doorkeeper, one of the paid officers of the convention.[17]

At 11 a.m. on June 4, the convention was called to order. The delegates were sworn in but before anyone could nominate someone for president of the convention, James Brooks of New York City, Democratic congressman and editor of the *New York Daily Express,* jumped to his feet and brought the normal order of the proceedings to a halt. He castigated the Republicans for meeting elsewhere to pick the president and said he was "apprehended with fear" that a man chosen in that way by the majority would not "respect the views of the minority." When Brooks was done, the floor was opened for nominations for convention president. The Republicans promptly nominated Wheeler and the Democrats nominated several of their party's prominent men including: Erastus Corning, former congressman from Albany; Samuel J. Tilden, Democratic state chairman from New York City; and Henry C. Murphy, former mayor of Brooklyn and ambassador to the Netherlands under President Buchanan. When the votes were counted, Wheeler was the winner with one hundred. Murphy was the second highest vote getter with nine. The rest of the votes were scattered among other candidates. U.S. Senator Harris and Murphy escorted Wheeler to the chair where he gave an opening speech that set the tone for the convention.[18]

Bill issued a clarion call for equal black suffrage and described the convention's work in religious terms. He said the spirit of New York State, "the Commonwealth of the world, Empire in name and Empire in fact," rested on "free, equal, conscious, intelligent and enfranchised manhood." Wheeler told the delegates that fostering such "manhood" was the "highest civil duty" that "patriotic statesmen" could be engaged in. Bill insisted that "every man" of "whatever race or color," no matter how "poor, helpless or lowly he may be," was entitled to have the right to vote. According to Wheeler, the "God of Nations" was leading the delegates on a "mission" of "destiny" and the convention had a duty to seek "the highest attainable points of enlightened Christian civilization." Bill concluded by exhorting the delegates to be "true to our trust, true to ourselves, and true to truth."[19]

The delegates were still buzzing about Wheeler's speech as they returned to their hotels when shocking news about a murder in the reception room of the Stanwix Hotel swept across Albany. L. Harris Hiscock, a Radical assemblyman from Syracuse and a delegate, was shot and killed by George W. Cole, a highly successful timber dealer, also from Syracuse. They were friends before the war and when Cole left home to serve in the cavalry, he asked Hiscock to take care of his wife. While Cole was away, he came to believe that Hiscock had "seduced and ravished" her. Even though almost three years had passed since Cole had come home from the war as a brevet major general and had apparently become friends with Hiscock again, Cole traveled to Albany to murder him. Cole walked up to Hiscock while he was talking with friends and without saying a word, drew a pistol and shot Hiscock in the face. The ball entered just below the right eye and lodged in Hiscock's brain. He died within an hour. Cole made no effort to escape, was arrested and taken to prison.[20]

The delegates were in an uproar over the murder and the convention was postponed for a week. This gave Wheeler time to work on his committee assignments. He appointed Horace Greeley to chair the Suffrage Committee, which would handle all the controversial proposals concerning equal suffrage. It was expected that Wheeler would appoint Republicans to chair all the other committees but he surprised everyone by naming Democrats to chair four important committees and on one of these, he appointed a Democratic majority to work with the Democratic chair.[21]

Under the rules of the convention, Wheeler had the power to "preserve order and decorum" and decide all questions of order subject to appeal to the convention. Bill often had to remind speakers what they could or could not do according to parliamentary law. Republican and Democratic delegates quickly learned to respect Wheeler's mastery of the rules of parliamentary procedure.[22]

The convention dealt with a myriad of significant subjects but all eyes were on Greeley's Suffrage Committee. It held hearings for a week and a half on a number of proposals concerning voting rights before issuing its reports. The Republican majority report proposed to strike out all references to race and color in the constitution's suffrage clause. In a minority report, the Democrats urged that no change be made to the 1846 property requirement for black men.[23]

Henry C. Murphy, Democratic leader from Brooklyn, argued that black voting was "morally and socially" wrong. To show how wrong it was, Murphy played a "scientific" race card. He submitted a "craniological" analysis he said proved the existence of inferior (black) and superior (white) breeds of men. According to Murphy, giving black men the right to vote would lead to social equality, race mixing, and the downfall of civilization.[24]

Martin I. Townsend of Troy led the Republican defense of equal suffrage by stating that he too opposed social equality and intermarriage but that political equality did not have anything to do with social equality. Other Republicans picked up on this theme and argued that granting political rights would make race mixing less likely because it would grant black men "a sense of dignity," obviating any potential desire by blacks to "intermingle" the races. In addition, Republicans argued that race was not referred to in connection with voting requirements until New York's 1821 constitution was adopted.[25]

The article granting black men equal voting rights was adopted by the convention in August. Wheeler influenced the *Palladium* to print the measure on its front page and endorse its passage with the argument that a property qualification for blacks was "partial, unjust and undemocratic."[26] In response, the Democratic press in New York City opposed equal suffrage for blacks by attacking black morality and stirring up fears of miscegenation. The *World* stated that the Republican Radicals' real motive for supporting equal suffrage was to do in New York what the national government was trying to do in the South—secure "perpetual Republican majorities" at the polls by enfranchising black men.[27]

As the summer waned and the early fall election returns came in from other states, some Republicans began to have doubts about the timing of putting equal suffrage for blacks before the New York State voters. In Connecticut and Ohio, Radical Republicans favored equal suffrage for blacks and they suffered defeat at the polls. Radical Republicans lost political ground in Vermont, Maine, and California for the same reason.[28]

In September, the Republicans caucused to discuss timing issues. Some agreed with Greeley and argued that the convention should move boldly forward and put the new suffrage amendment on the ballot in the fall. They put the blame for the Republican losses in other states on "extremists," lack of national leadership by President Johnson, and local issues such as liquor prohibition in Maine.[29] Wheeler disagreed. He sensed that the voting public was losing enthusiasm for equal voting rights for blacks and that if the amendment were put on the ballot in November, it would be defeated. Wheeler did not want to lose the chance of winning equal voting rights for blacks because of poor timing. Bill thought that voting on the suffrage amendment should be delayed until its chances for success were improved. He urged his fellow GOP delegates to adjourn the convention until after the elections. After sharp debate, the majority in the caucus voted to finish the constitution by October 10 and submit it to the electorate in the November elections. However, a week later, the Republicans did an about face and voted to follow Wheeler's advice instead. The delegates voted 78 to 40 to adjourn until after the fall election. Of the 78 votes to adjourn, 74 were Republicans. All 40 votes not to adjourn were Democrats—to them, equal voting rights for blacks was a good issue to have on the ballot.[30] The election results proved that Wheeler's political barometer was correct. The Democrats won every state office, control of the assembly, and nearly won control of the state senate.[31]

After the election, Wheeler called the convention to order once again and by January 1868 it completed its work by adopting three amendments to the constitution.[32] One provided for equal suffrage for blacks, another outlined a new, uniform method of assessment and taxation, and a third revamped the judiciary branch.[33]

In February, Wheeler brought his gavel down for the last time to adjourn the convention, *sine die.* He flattered the delegates in his closing remarks for their "uniform confidence and toleration," which he said made his job an "easy accomplishment" and Bill wished them "a life of usefulness, prosperity and happiness."[34]

Wheeler received bipartisan praise from the delegates for his work as president. Democrat James Brooks, the delegate from New York City who was an early critic of the choice of Wheeler to be president at the onset of the convention, offered a resolution thanking Bill for his work and complimenting him for putting a "padlock on his mind" in order to be impartial. Republicans and Democrats voiced their support for the resolution by saying that Wheeler displayed a "conscientious sense of justice to the minority" and was "our teacher of parliamentary law." The resolution passed unanimously.[35]

The press was equally impressed by the Gentleman from Malone's performance as president of the convention. The Albany *Evening Journal* concluded its praise of Wheeler by saying, "No man in the State has warmer friends, or more deserves them."[36] In *Harper's Weekly,* Curtis credited Bill for the "high tone of the assembly" and lauded Wheeler for his "simple dignity of manner and accurate knowledge of parliamentary law."[37]

New York lawmakers delayed the vote on the proposed amendments to the constitution until November 1869. In the voting, a majority of New Yorkers strongly agreed with banners such as those at Tammany Hall in New York City that read, "No Suffrage Nor Negro Equality! White Man's Government for White Men! White Men Shall Rule America!"[38] Equal suffrage for blacks lost 282,403 to 249,802. The taxation amendment was also defeated; however, the judiciary amendment passed.[39] The suffrage restriction on black men would not be removed until the Fifteenth Amendment to the U.S. Constitution was adopted in 1870.[40]

Bill was very disappointed by the rejection of equal suffrage for blacks but as soon as the convention adjourned in February 1868, he began working to fulfill the recent prediction made about him by the *Palladium.* The paper had said that in light of Wheeler's outstanding work as president of the convention, he would be called to "higher honors and fields of wider fame." To Bill at the age of forty-eight, there was no higher honor than being able to serve his district, state and nation as a congressman. He immediately began organizing his political friends in Franklin and St. Lawrence Counties to secure the 1868 GOP nomination to run for the Forty-first Congress.[41]

13

"Ho! For California"

☆

As Wheeler surveyed the political scene from his house on Elm Street in Malone during the spring of 1868, he watched several Republican dramas unfold that would set the stage for his bid to win the congressional nomination in the summer. The first involved U.S. Senator Roscoe Conkling and Governor Reuben E. Fenton. They were warily circling each other as they organized their forces to win control of the GOP in New York State and pick up Thurlow Weed's mantle as Republican Party boss. Fenton had his eyes set on running for vice president with Grant in the fall elections. The state GOP convention to name delegates to the May 20 national convention recommended Fenton to be named Grant's running mate.[1] Conkling was bitterly opposed to Fenton's candidacy.[2]

The second drama was taking place in Washington where, in February, the House impeached President Johnson on eleven charges, including allegations that he had violated several federal laws and had attempted to bring disgrace and ridicule on Congress. By the end of March, Johnson's trial on the charges in the Senate was underway.[3]

Wheeler was mum about Fenton's political ambition but boldly predicted that Grant would win in Bill's congressional district by eight thousand votes. He heartily disliked Johnson and described him as "the great Apostate" in a letter to U.S. Senator Morgan. Concerning the trial in the Senate, Wheeler wrote that it was "fortunate that the demands of justice and party are in common" and cautioned against "any unnecessary delay" in the proceedings.[4]

In May, "the great Apostate" was acquitted by a vote of 35 to 19, one vote short of the necessary two-thirds to convict. Less than a week after the Senate began voting on the charges against Johnson, the GOP national convention opened in Chicago where Grant was unanimously nominated for president on the first ballot. However, the real battle at the convention was for the vice presidential nomination. Fenton and ten other candidates vied for the nomination in a wide-open race. Conkling sought to undermine Fenton wherever he could. After the first ballot, Senator Benjamin Wade of Ohio led. He was followed by Fenton, Massachusetts Senator Henry Wilson, Speaker of the House Schuyler Colfax of Indiana, Maine Senator Hannibal Hamlin, and six other candidates. After six ballots, Fenton lost to Colfax 541 to 69.[5] The Democrats nominated former New York Governor Horatio Seymour for president and former Republican, General Francis P. Blair of Missouri, for vice president.[6]

Bill followed the GOP contest for vice president in the press but avoided taking sides in the Fenton-Conkling rivalry, preferring to devote his resources toward winning his own race for the Republican nomination for Congress. He had been assured by his St. Lawrence County allies that "it was Franklin County's turn" to have the nomination and that the understanding would be good for the Forty-first and Forty-second Congresses. However, the three-term incumbent, Calvin T. Hulburd, had not yet announced he would be retiring from Congress when his current term expired on March 3, 1869.[7]

The GOP Seventeenth Congressional District nominating convention would not be held until August, about a month and a half after the GOP state convention, where a candidate for governor would be nominated. Hulburd and his friends in St. Lawrence County had plenty of time to change their minds about whose turn it was for the congressional nomination. Wheeler went to work to make sure no one changed their minds. In June, on the day Bill and his Saranac Navigation Company returned from a two-week fishing trip to the Saranac Lakes, the Republican press in the North Country turned the political spotlight on Wheeler.[8] The newspapers in Malone and Potsdam touted Bill for governor. They said he would be an excellent candidate because he had "no enemies" and was wealthy enough to put him "above the temptation of gain"—the "destructive pit" that some St. Lawrence County Republicans had recently fallen into. By resurrecting the bribery charges that had led to the recent civil war in the county party ranks, the press gave Wheeler an opening to review the pledges of support he had from his St. Lawrence County allies for his return to Congress. The stories also gave Bill excellent publicity with the voting public. He modestly denied any interest in the gubernatorial nomination but it was clear to readers that the office of governor was seeking Wheeler![9]

As though Wheeler had orchestrated his own press coverage, a week later newspapers in Malone, Ogdensburg, and Canton reminded readers that an agreement had been made that the GOP's nominee for Congress should come from Franklin County and that Wheeler was "the first choice" of a majority of the party in the district.[10]

The GOP convention for the Seventeenth Congressional District was held at L. H. Dunton's Hotel in Stockholm Depot on August 20. The delegates unanimously nominated Wheeler and passed a resolution declaring that Bill was "unassailable—politically, morally and socially." The *Palladium* crowed that Wheeler's name was "a tower of strength—a synonym for integrity, for patriotism and unselfish devotion to the public weal." Downstate, the *Albany Journal* said the delegates "reflected honor upon themselves" by nominating Wheeler—"a zealous, faithful and eloquent advocate of righteous principles."[11] In response, the Democrats in the Seventeenth Congressional District nominated William H. Wallace, a wealthy lawyer from Potsdam, to run against Wheeler.[12]

Bill wasted no time getting the Republican campaign off and running. He sparked the formation of uniformed, torch-bearing marching organizations in North Country towns to add glamour and excitement to the Grant and Wheeler campaign. The groups were called *Tanners' Clubs* because Grant had been a tanner.[13] Bill set up a hectic speaking tour for himself, which would take him to almost every major community in the district. Bill also influenced his party to offer a twenty-five- by fifteen-foot American flag as a prize to the town in Franklin County that had the largest increase in Republican votes cast since the last election in 1867. Wheeler secured the endorsement of the Union Soldiers' and Sailors' Committee for the congressional district and brought Massachusetts Senator Wilson into the district to campaign with him.[14]

In a savage campaign, Wheeler Republicans charged the Democrats with treason and waved *the bloody shirt* of war. The tempestuous issue of Southern Reconstruction dominated the Grant and Wheeler offensive. The Democrats countered by calling for amnesty for former Confederates and restoration of Southern states. Black suffrage, the Democrats argued, was a matter for the states to deal with, not the national government.[15] The Democrats also used racial demagoguery to appeal to voters. One Democratic editor described the election as a "fight for white supremacy" and predicted that "there will be such an outpouring of nigger blood and such a hanging of Radicals to sour the apple trees as was never known since the world emerged from chaos."[16]

The heat got so hot between the parties that violence broke out at the final GOP campaign rally in Chateaugay where Wheeler was the headline speaker. The Tanners' Club of Malone took the train east and marched through Chateaugay's streets before filing into the hall where Bill was scheduled to speak. As they lined up outside to gain entrance and find seats, stones, and brickbats rained down on them cutting their heads and faces. The county sheriff made several arrests. Wheeler was inside and was not injured.[17]

On November 3, when the votes were counted, Wheeler won 70.8 percent of the vote defeating Wallace 15,262 to 6,284.[18] Statewide, the Republicans did not fare as well. Seymour defeated Grant by ten thousand votes and the Democrats captured the governor's office by almost twenty-eight thousand votes.[19]

When the Forty-first Congress organized on March 4, 1869, there were 136 Republicans, 61 Democrats and one Conservative. Thirteen members had not been elected yet and there were twenty-four seats assigned to states that had not been readmitted to the Union.[20] Among those sworn in with Bill were two New England men who became his close political friends, Luke P. Poland of Vermont and George F. Hoar of Massachusetts, and future President James A. Garfield of Ohio.[21]

James G. Blaine of Maine was elected Speaker with Bill's support and vote.[22] Blaine held Wheeler in high regard. He admired Bill's intelligence and success in the worlds of banking, the law, and especially railroads.[23] Blaine appointed Wheeler chairman of the Pacific Railroad Committee and a member of the Committee on Expenditures in the Treasury Department.[24]

Wheeler respected Blaine's popularity in the House but Bill had doubts about Blaine's ability as a parliamentarian. This was Blaine's first term as Speaker and Bill was quick to notice that Blaine would often contradict himself in his rulings. If a congressman challenged one of the Speaker's rulings, Bill was dismayed when Blaine would audaciously bully the challenger to back off by insisting that every Speaker before him had ruled the way Blaine had ruled. Wheeler clipped Blaine's rulings from the pages of the *Congressional Globe* and glued them onto the appropriate pages of the *Digest of Rules of the House of Representatives*. In the margin, Bill wrote notes about each key ruling and kept this book in his desk on the floor of the House for instant use if Blaine ever ruled against him. Blaine learned about Bill's annotated version of the House Rules and was very uncomfortable about it. As a result, Blaine and Wheeler never collided on any significant parliamentary point—Blaine knew he was up against one of the best parliamentarians in Washington.[25]

As chairman of the House Pacific Railroad Committee, Wheeler held the keys to the future of the nation's budding railroad empire that was promising to become the most extensive railroad network in the world. In his role as committee chairman, Bill was poised to play a key role in promoting a vast expansion of the transcontinental railroad system. Bill, along with most of the members of his

James G. Blaine. Brady-Handy Collection, Library of Congress.

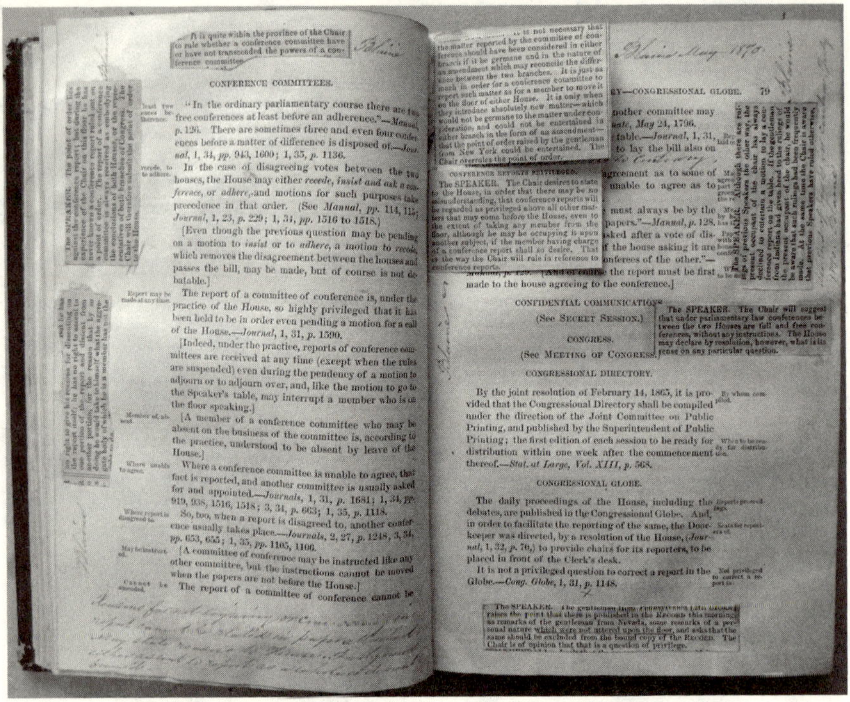

Wheeler's annotated *Digest of Rules of the House of Representatives.* Courtesy of the Franklin County Historical and Museum Society.

generation, was convinced that the railroad would serve as the foundation for the development of the nation's resources and the establishment of a national market involving mass production and mass consumption.[26]

The construction of the country's first transcontinental railroad, the Union Pacific and Central Pacific Railroad, was nearing completion as Bill organized his Pacific Railroad Committee in the spring of 1869.[27] Sitting on Bill's desk in the House was a report from the Senate Committee on Pacific Railroads favoring two additional transcontinental lines—one for the Northern states and one for the Southern states. The Northern Pacific was proposed to run from Lake Superior to Puget Sound and the Southern Pacific was to run from Arkansas, along the thirty-fifth parallel, to San Diego and San Francisco.[28]

Bill's committee began work preparing its own railroad legislation calling for additional transcontinental lines. One measure that had Bill's support drew the attention of a railroad lobbyist who had come to Washington to buy the bill through the House. When Bill learned about this scheme his Calvinist blood boiled. He sent for the man and heatedly upbraided him for even thinking that Bill's vote could be purchased. He warned the lobbyist that if Bill heard a single trustworthy whisper of any attempt by the lobbyist to bribe a single member of the House, he would himself kill the bill. However, the congressman from Malone assured the lobbyist that if he left Washington, Bill would see to it that the legislation passed on its own merits. In shock, the lobbyist took the next train out of Washington. After the bill subsequently passed, the railroad that had employed the lobbyist offered Bill $100,000 of its stock as a testimonial of its appreciation but Wheeler indignantly refused the offer.[29]

The first session of the Forty-first Congress was short and Bill's committee did not complete work on any important railroad legislation before the session adjourned on April 10. Four weeks later, back home in Malone, Bill was thrilled to read the news that the first train to carry passengers across the continent had arrived in Sacramento, California, from its starting point in Springfield, Massachusetts.[30]

Wheeler knew that as chairman of the House Pacific Railroad Committee, he had an obligation to make at least one cross-country railroad trip himself and made plans for it. But first, he had to answer the call of the "South Woods" and his Saranac Navigation Company. Bill and his key political advisers gathered their fishing tackle, guns, and provisions and headed south into the Adirondacks for their "annual exodus."[31] They resumed their friendly competition for an imaginary championship belt to be awarded to the man who caught the largest trout. Bill usually came home wearing the belt and this year was no exception. The lakes were filled with trout. The Company caught so many that they packed forty trout into a box filled with ice and wild moss and sent it back to the *Palladium*'s offices. The fish weighed from one-quarter pound to eleven pounds each.[32] When Wheeler's fishing party emerged out of the Adirondacks and returned home, the press reported that the men were looking "tough and healthy."[33]

These were flush times for the Wheeler household. Bill had decided to go back into banking and had been elected director of the National Bank of Malone.[34] He sought and received investment advice from his friend, former Governor and U.S. Senator Morgan.[35] Wheeler's income swelled to such an extent that he was able to employ two full-time domestic servants to live in his home along with his wife, Mary, and his sister, Fidelia. One of his servants, Margaret Chambers, had served as his live-in housekeeper before the outbreak of the Civil War. The other servant was a twenty-eight-year-old Canadian immigrant, Harriett Morrow, who had been hired to help Chambers after Wheeler had been reelected to Congress.[36]

In early September, the press crowed, "Ho! For California," to herald news that the Wheelers and two other couples from the North Country had boarded a

Malone's Main Street in 1870. Courtesy of the Franklin County Historical and Museum Society.

transcontinental train in New York City and were on their way to San Francisco. The trip was designed to give the new chairman of the House Pacific Railroad Committee firsthand knowledge of the importance of rail transportation to the destiny of the nation but there was an additional reason for Bill's trip west. He wanted to see the wild beauty of Yosemite Valley's impressive waterfalls, cliffs, and unusual rock formations. It was likely that articles he had read in Boston and New York newspapers by the Unitarian minister and lecturer, Thomas Starr King, and by Horace Greeley, had first stimulated Bill's interest in the grandeur of the Yosemite Valley. In addition, photographs taken of Yosemite by Carleton E. Watkins, which had been on display in New York galleries, also must have caught Wheeler's eye.[37]

It was also at this time that the use of government to protect the beauty of nature from the ravages of unbridled commercial development captured Wheeler's attention. In 1864, Bill's former Republican colleagues in Congress had passed a law granting more than 36,000 acres of the Yosemite Valley to the state of California in order to preserve Yosemite's monumental scenery for recreational purposes. This legislation was the first instance of a central government anywhere in the world doing such a thing.[38] After visiting Yosemite Valley, the significance of the government's role to protect scenic values for the people as a whole to enjoy would make a lasting impression on Wheeler. Years later, Bill would play an instrumental role in New York State's efforts to preserve the scenery of the Adirondacks and Niagara Falls.

After four days on the train, the Wheeler party arrived in Chicago. Bill's reputation as chairman of the House Pacific Railroad committee did not go unnoticed by the Chicago newspapers who trumpeted his arrival by describing him as "an experienced railroad man and statesman of eminent general ability."[39] Following a brief stopover in the Windy City, Bill's party got back on the train for San Francisco and arrived there on September 23. They checked in to the Lick House, a sumptuous 164-room hotel known as the finest hotel west of the Mississippi.[40]

James Lick, one of the richest men in California, had built the Lick House. Bill had to have been dazzled by the hotel dining room, which was a replica of one Lick had visited at the Palace of Versailles in Paris in 1825. Sunlight poured in through the stained-, ground-, and cut-glass ceiling by day and two great gas-burning chandeliers lighted the room by night. Nine-by-twelve-foot French plate-glass mirrors decorated the corners of the hall.[41]

Bill and his party toured the city and were "happily surprised" by what they saw.[42] After a tour of Yosemite Valley and more sightseeing in and around San Francisco, the Wheeler party boarded a train and headed back east to the North Country. In his moments alone on the train, Bill had a great deal to think about. The second session of the Forty-first Congress would open on December 6. He knew that for the first time as chairman of a House committee, he would be reporting out several pieces of significant railroad legislation that would provide for two additional transcontinental railroad lines as well as the expansion of several other railroad lines.

Wheeler was aware that his railroad bills would face substantial opposition, not only from most of the House Democrats, but also from a number of House Republicans who represented districts that were currently being served by the first transcontinental line, the Union and Central Pacific. One of the major goals of these Republicans was to protect the Union and Central Pacific from additional transcontinental competition.

The Northern Pacific Railroad, a second transcontinental line, would compete with the Union and Central Pacific for business if Congress passed legislation enabling it to be built. As chairman of the House Pacific Railroad committee, Bill was poised to report such a bill out for House action early in the second session. On the train ride home from California, he began to plot his strategy for getting it passed.

14

Spreading "Law, Order, Population, Industry and Wealth"

★

The Northern Pacific Railroad was the brainchild of Josiah Perham. Born in Maine, Josiah promoted railroad excursions throughout the East from his offices in Boston. Perham long dreamed of building a railroad from Maine to the Pacific. In 1864, with the help of Congressman Thaddeus Stevens of Pennsylvania, he obtained a federal charter from Congress for the Northern Pacific Railroad Company to build a rail line from Lake Superior to Puget Sound.[1]

Perham touted the Northern Pacific as the most practical route to the Pacific because it was the shortest, had no deserts to cross, and had plenty of water, timber, and stone that could be used for its construction. According to Perham, with Puget Sound as the road's western terminus, it would be the most direct and closest route to the markets of Russia, China, and Japan.[2]

The 1864 legislation granting the charter awarded the Northern Pacific forty-seven million acres of land and authorized it to issue $100 million in stock. However, the line was prohibited from raising money to construct the road by issuing bonds and mortgaging the land grant to secure the bonds. This restriction, coupled with the refusal of Congress to award the company a subsidy as it had done for the Union and Central Pacific railroads, made it impossible for Perham to start construction. Deeply in debt, Perham sold the Northern Pacific to a group of eastern financiers. They elected J. Gregory Smith to be the Northern Pacific's new president.[3]

Smith had been the Civil War governor of Vermont and one year before he was elected president of the Northern Pacific, he and business interests connected with the Vermont Central Railroad had engineered Bill Wheeler's ouster as president of the Ogdensburg and Lake Champlain Railroad. As the new president of the Northern Pacific, Smith bombarded Congress with requests for subsidies so that construction of the road might begin and prevent its demise. Congress continued to say no. Under the influence of friends of the Union and Central Pacific railroads who were hostile to construction of a rival, second line to the Pacific, and growing public sentiment against any kind of additional federal financial aid to railroads in the West, bills to enable the construction of the Northern Pacific never passed. Because of its inability to raise enough money, it began to look like the company would never be able to build its line and the whole enterprise was headed for a fatal disaster.[4]

When Wheeler returned to Washington from Malone in December for the second session of the Forty-first Congress, he emerged as the Northern Pacific's white knight, riding forward to save the road from extinction. By stoutheartedly overcoming hostile opposition to it in the House, he masterfully won passage of legislation that enabled the construction of the nation's first northern transcontinental railroad.

On January 25, 1870, in order to save the Northern Pacific from impending doom, Wheeler introduced legislation authorizing the company to issue bonds for the construction of the road and to secure them by mortgages. The bill was referred to the Commerce Committee where it was bottled up.[5] Meanwhile, the Senate passed a bill similar to Wheeler's. It was referred to his Committee on the Pacific Railroad and he reported it out on May 5. Before Bill could begin explaining the proposal's merits, he was hit with a storm of opposition but the congressman from Malone stiffened and refused to allow any interruptions. Bill said he would not yield to anyone until he was finished with his remarks.[6]

Bill began by describing the Northern Pacific as a "second continental enterprise" designed "to unite by iron bands the Great Lakes with Puget Sound and the Pacific Ocean." His voice rang out saying, "The locomotive is the 'open sesame' to over half a million square miles of territory alternating in prairie and pine forests and teeming with coal, iron, gold, silver and copper, the sure elements of national wealth." Wheeler continued, "It is now the home of the Indian, the buffalo, the elk and the antelope" and "wholly inaccessible, unproductive and dead property to the United States." Bill thundered that the Northern Pacific was "the sole agency by which we can spread law, order, population, industry and wealth" over this area and he urged the House to pass his bill, which would enable the line finally to be built.[7]

Wheeler reassured the House that he was "an intimate acquaintance" of Smith, the new president of the Northern Pacific. Of Smith, Bill said he was "the embodiment of New England pluck and enterprise." Wheeler promised the House that if it gave Smith "the sinews of war," he would "push on, defying all natural obstacles, subjugating mountains and plains to the dominion of the rail."[8]

When Wheeler was finished, he yielded the floor to Republican John B. Hawley, a lawyer from Illinois who vehemently opposed the bill. He stated that he would be offering an amendment that would restrict the sale of railroad land to actual settlers, at a price of not more than $2.50 an acre. In addition, Hawley said his amendment would limit all sales to not more than 160 acres. The congressman from Illinois described the land grant to the Northern Pacific as a "vast empire" and he argued that railroads should be stopped from "swallowing up the public lands" and using them for "speculation."[9]

When Hawley sat down, there was a flurry of activity designed to stop Wheeler's bill dead in its tracks. There were multiple calls for roll call votes on motions to table the bill, to adjourn, to reconsider the bill, to appeal each and every ruling by the Speaker, and to adjourn again, and so on. Wheeler beat back all these attempts to delay the bill to death but as the day wore on, he eventually agreed to adjourn the House and let the bill go over to another day.[10]

That day was May 25. When Wheeler took the floor to press passage of his Northern Pacific bill, he said that it was his understanding that twenty-four of the bill's opponents had prepared amendments to prevent the bill's passage. Using House rules to his advantage, Wheeler gave opponents only one hour of time to prepare and debate their amendments. Shocked, one congressman jumped up and exclaimed, "That would be little over two minutes to each gentleman!" Wheeler ignored the interruption and said he did not care how long opponents took to argue about their amendments but that he was giving everyone notice, that in one hour, he was taking the floor back and demanding a vote on his bill.[11]

Opponents of the bill rose to amend it and renew their objections, many of which had already been placed in the record. Some of the most caustic remarks came from congressmen from Kansas, Illinois, and Indiana.

Sidney Clarke, Republican from Kansas, ripped into Wheeler's bill by saying that it "opens the door to a career of robbery and public plunder, heretofore unknown in the history of the country!" As Clarke saw it, giving away millions of acres of public land to the Northern Pacific without rights to actual settlers was "a most wicked, unjustifiable proceeding." The Kansas congressman concluded, saying that Wheeler's bill was a "sham and a cheat" and an "insult to the intelligence of the American people."[12]

Hawley from Illinois agreed with Clarke. Hawley said that if Wheeler's bill were passed without restrictions, Congress would be delivering the people who lived along the railroad line "bound hand and foot" over "to this monster monopoly." To Hawley, Wheeler's bill was "a bold and naked swindle."[13]

The opposition from Illinois was bipartisan. Hawley's Democratic colleague, John M. Crebs, also a lawyer, put a slightly different spin to his objections. Crebs argued that the land grants to the Northern Pacific were so large, they were "dangerous to the very existence of government." As Crebs analyzed Wheeler's bill, he said it would place the land that would be opened up for development by the Northern Pacific "in the control of a soulless corporation" and put "the hardy pioneer entirely at its mercy."[14]

To William Williams, a Republican banker and lawyer from Indiana, Wheeler's bill should be defeated for the simple reason that the Northern Pacific was a "bastard monopoly." Williams stated that the Northern Pacific's representatives "throng the lobbies of Congress every session crying, Give!, Give!, Give!, until their rapacious maws are filled with the plunder of the people's substance."[15]

Many congressmen defended Wheeler's bill. Its strongest support came from Thomas W. Ferry, Republican from Michigan. He pointed out that fear of competition to the Union and Central Pacific railroads was behind most of the virulent rhetoric opposing it. Ferry said the Union and Central Pacific was afraid of losing business to the Northern Pacific if it were built. Ferry argued, "We need competing routes across the continent. These roads are national highways and competition is the surest, most permanent mode of keeping down freight rates and passenger fares."[16]

When the hour was up, Wheeler rose to close debate. He began by charging one of the measure's staunchest opponents, Clarke from Kansas, with being a flip-flopper on aid to the Northern Pacific. Bill offered up several of Clarke's previous speeches to the House as evidence that Clarke supported aid to the Northern Pacific when it helped Kansas and opposed aid when it did not. Wheeler and Clarke nearly came to blows when the congressman from Kansas challenged Bill by crying out, "Not at all!" Bill shot back, "Directly. Let the House and the country be the judge!"[17]

Wheeler urged the House to use "calm judgment" and consider the Northern Pacific bill as they would "any business proposition." Warning his colleagues not to be "deluded" by a "delusive cry against gigantic corporations," Bill reminded them that Congress always has the power to amend a bill at any time and that it was "preposterous" to believe Congress would ever permit a "huge swindle" or fraud to be undertaken.[18]

Wheeler debunked the idea of restricting the sale of railroad land to settlers at $2.50 an acre because instead of preventing speculation, he said such a restriction would encourage it. According to Wheeler, the price restriction would encourage speculators, masked as settlers, to buy up land in advance of the construction of the line and then sell it at a profit later to genuine settlers who wished to live near the railroad.[19]

In closing, Wheeler urged the House to vote every amendment down and pass the bill as his committee had proposed it. Bill made a special appeal for support from southern congressmen by declaring that "it is only a question of time" before a Northern Pacific and a Southern Pacific railroad would be built and that he supported legislation to build them both, in the name of "common equity."[20]

When Wheeler was done and he sat down, opponents to his Northern Pacific bill tried to amend it again, nine more times. All nine amendments were voted down and Wheeler's bill to enable the construction of the nation's first northern transcontinental railroad passed 107 to 85.[21]

Much of the Northern Pacific's route would follow the 1804 to 1806 trail blazed by the famed explorers, Meriwether Lewis and William Clark. Beginning in Duluth, Minnesota on Lake Superior, the line would terminate in Tacoma, Washington on Puget Sound—a true "Northwest Passage." Along the way it would pass through what would become the cities of Fargo and Bismarck, North Dakota, and Billings and Butte, Montana.[22]

During the second session, Wheeler brought out several other railroad bills from his Pacific Railroad Committee. Among them was a proposal granting the Utah Central Railroad a thirty-six-mile long right of way through Utah Territory. The right of way extended from the junction of the Union Pacific and Central Pacific railroads at Ogden City, to Salt Lake City, thereby connecting the territory's most populated city with the transcontinental line. In support of the bill, Wheeler argued that the line would promote the development of the Territories and strengthen the military presence in that part of the nation.[23]

However, his most potent argument played to the deep-seated anti-Mormon bias that was prevalent in the House. For years, the nation's newspapers had been luridly discussing the Mormon practice of polygamy. Antagonism to it was so great, Congress had passed an antipolygamy law aimed solely at Utah in 1862.[24] Wheeler said that the most important reason for passage of the bill was the impact it would have on the Mormons and their church in Utah, which he described as the "crowning disgrace of American civilization." According to Wheeler, it was the isolation of Utah that allowed the Mormon Church to "rear its degrading, abhorrent, lustful head." Bill said that the revelations of Joseph Smith and Brigham Young, which have "so long held the deluded masses" in an "iron grasp" will be powerless to resist "the revelations that the iron horse" will bring to Utah. Wheeler stated, "The gospel of Mormon must give way to the gospel of steam." Referring to Mormonism as "this damnable heresy" and "a plague spot upon our body politic" that must be destroyed, Wheeler moved passage of the bill. It passed easily.[25]

The second session of the Forty-first Congress adjourned on July 15. Because the third session would not open until December 5, Bill returned home to the North Country. He wanted the voters to send him back to Washington as a member of the Forty-second Congress, which opened the following March. This meant that between the second and third sessions, he had to organize his political forces to secure the nomination and win the 1870 election.

15

"Common Justice" for the South

Wheeler did not expect to have any difficulty winning renomination to Congress for a second straight term. The political deal between Republicans in St. Lawrence and Franklin Counties called for the nominee for Congress to come from Franklin County for two Congresses in a row—the Forty-first and the Forty-second.[1] In addition, Wheeler's chief political rival for the nomination from St. Lawrence County, former three-term Congressman Calvin T. Hulburd of Brasher Falls, was no longer a threat to Bill's renomination because in the fall of 1869, Hulburd had taken a lucrative federal job overseeing the construction of the new post office in New York City.[2] Nevertheless, Bill paid attention to every political detail and left nothing to chance.

The Republican convention for the Seventeenth Congressional District was held at noon in the office of Benjamin G. Baldwin at Potsdam Junction on September 2. To ensure that his support from St. Lawrence County did not waver, Wheeler made an unprecedented personal appearance at the convention. Of the nine delegates assembled in Baldwin's office, six were from St. Lawrence County and three were from Franklin County. Before the vote was taken, Wheeler gave a brief speech. He was the convention's unanimous choice. The press in the Seventeenth Congressional District said that Bill would be "a tower of strength to the local ticket." The *Albany Journal* hailed Wheeler's nomination by calling it a "wise and proper thing" and reminding voters that in all the years Wheeler had been in public life, "he has never betrayed a trust or made an enemy."[3]

Less than a week after Bill's nomination, the state GOP convention met in Saratoga Springs to nominate a governor. It turned into a political brawl between allies of U.S. Senator Roscoe Conkling and those of U.S. Senator Reuben Fenton for control of the state party. When the convention opened, Conkling used his influence in Washington over federal patronage to defeat Fenton's bid to become president of the convention by successfully backing George William Curtis, the reform-minded editor of *Harper's Weekly,* for the post. Then, Conkling successfully backed former General Stewart L. Woodford of Brooklyn, a man reportedly favored by President Grant, for governor. In the subsequent balloting for seats on the GOP state committee, Conkling won more than two-thirds of them and installed Alonzo B. Cornell as Republican state chairman. For the next eleven years, Conkling would be the virtual dictator of the New York State GOP and a man Wheeler had to be extremely wary of as he traveled down his own political road.[4]

Wheeler remained neutral during the Fenton-Conkling war. However, he liked Woodford and looked forward to leading the upcoming Wheeler-Woodford campaign in the North Country. Before officially kicking off his reelection bid, Bill and his wife Mary threw open their home on Elm Street in Malone to celebrate their twenty-fifth wedding anniversary. Their friends and neighbors "thronged" their parlors. The friendly Wheeler press reported that people loved the Wheelers "not only for their kindness and urbanity, but as patterns and exemplars of social and domestic happiness."[5]

The Democrats in the Seventeenth Congressional District nominated a sixty-four-year-old farmer from Bangor, George Mott, to run against Wheeler. A trustee of the South Bangor Methodist Episcopal Church, Mott had been the last Democrat to represent Franklin County in the assembly, having won election in 1856.[6] On the state level, the Democrats renominated John T. Hoffman to run against Woodford for governor.[7] In their campaign, the Democrats praised Hoffman, attacked President Grant, criticized the tariff as "robbery," and opposed prohibition of the sale of alcohol. In response, the Republicans praised President Grant, attacked Hoffman, applauded the reduction in taxes and said towns and cities should have the right to prohibit the sale of liquor as long as they had the right to license its sale.[8]

Wheeler's campaign literature cried out that the Democrats had won control of the state in 1868 "illegally" through "penury and fraud." As proof, pointing to Boss William Marcy Tweed's influence in New York City, the GOP held up confessions of men who registered to vote more than one hundred times under different names and instances in 1868 where one man on the same day voted more than twenty times for Hoffman. Wheeler's election circulars boomed, "The Democratic Party is still what it always has been—the enemy of freedom, justice and equal rights."[9]

Wheeler also ran heavily on his pro-railroad, pro-Northern Pacific record in Congress. Advertisements in the local newspapers selling bonds for the Northern Pacific, extolling the virtues and richness of the land through which the Northern would run, helped enhance Wheeler's appeal and standing in the eyes of North Country voters. The great banking house of Jay Cooke & Company had been hired by the Northern to market its bonds and manage the finances of the line. Jay Cooke & Company had made an international reputation selling government bonds to finance the Civil War. In the summer of 1870, Cooke began a tremendous nationwide advertising campaign to sell Northern Pacific bonds, which continued through the fall election. As part of the campaign, the advertisements appeared in newspapers throughout Wheeler's congressional district. The advertisements pointed out that one of the local agents for the sale of the bonds was the National Bank of Malone.[10] From the election results, it appears that few voters were troubled by the fact that Congressman Wheeler also sat on the board of directors of the National Bank. In fact, many voters may have been favorably impressed by his position.

When the votes were counted on November 8, Wheeler won reelection by winning more than 69 percent of the vote defeating Mott 13,020 to 5,699. However, statewide the Democrats swept to victory. Hoffman defeated Woodford by more than 33,000 votes and the Democrats won control of both houses of the state legislature and sixteen of the state's thirty-one seats in Congress.[11]

Once the dust from the election had settled in the North Country, Bill and Mary Wheeler traveled back to Washington for the opening of the third session of the Forty-first Congress. Legislation enabling the construction of the nation's third transcontinental railroad, the Southern Pacific, weighed heavily on Bill's mind. This bill loomed as one of the most significant and controversial measures that Wheeler would sponsor during this session.

On February 21, Wheeler brought out a bill incorporating the Southern Pacific Railroad and granting it twenty alternate sections (square miles) of public land on each side of the road for every mile of track it laid—about thirteen million acres. The bill called for the construction of a southern trunk railroad from Marshall, Texas to San Diego, California. The Senate was considering adoption of a similar bill. Skillfully utilizing the House rules, Wheeler put strict time limits on discussion of his measure and kept it firmly under his control, much to the dismay of the bill's opponents.[12]

Wheeler began his remarks in support of the Southern by arguing that because the North and Central sections of the country had been given transcontinental railroad lines, "common justice" demanded that the South be given one also. In addition, Bill said that the new road would save the taxpayers' money because, according to the commanding general of the army, William T. Sherman, if the line

WHY

NORTHERN PACIFIC RAILROAD

7-30 GOLD BONDS

Are a GOOD INVESTMENT for

THE MECHANIC

Operative, Laborer and Farmer?

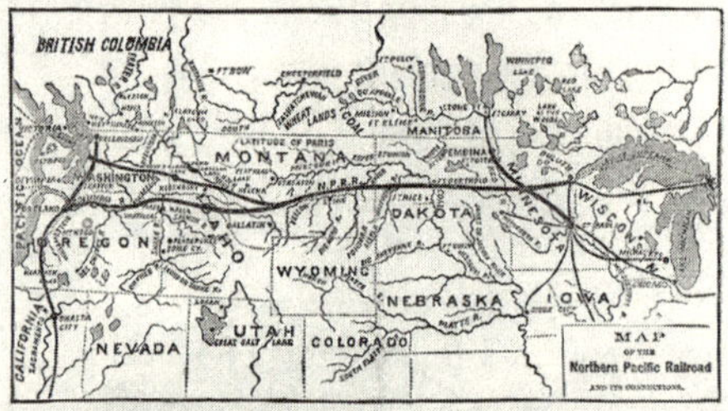

In any community, the class most interested in monied securities are those of small or moderate means. The Mechanic, the Farmer, and Workingman compose the majority of population, whether in town or country. The earnings of these classes should be safely secured by investments of a character beyond suspicion. The Capitalist can afford to make ventures, for, if a portion of a large income be lost, no serious inconvenience is felt. But the Workingman or person of moderate means cannot afford to risk his hard earned savings; hence this class of individuals wisely scrutinize, *first*, the security proposed, and next, the *income* to be realized—in other words, their great object is to place their surplus where it will be *perfectly safe*, and then as profitable as possible.

We unhesitatingly recommend the *First Mortgage Gold Bonds of the Northern Pacific Railroad Company* to persons of moderate means, as a security peculiarly adapted to meet their wants, for the following reasons:—

FIRST.—Because of their *entire safety*, being secured by a first and only Mortgage on the entire Road and all its equipments, and also on a Tract of Fifty Acres of Land for every **$100** Bond issued. They are emphatically *a Real Estate Security.*

SECOND.—Money invested in these Bonds yields an interest of $7\frac{3}{10}$ per cent. in Gold, or more than **8** per cent. currency, which is from two to three per cent. higher than can usually be obtained for money deposited in Banks.

THIRD.—These Bonds can always be disposed of at *ten per cent.* ABOVE PAR for the Company's Lands at their lowest cash price. Thus, any person proposing, at some future time, to secure a *Homestead* for himself or any of his family, can exchange his Bond for Land at ten per cent. premium, and in the meantime will have regularly received a yearly interest of $7\frac{3}{10}$ per cent. Gold.

FOURTH.—Much of the money invested in great enterprises like the Northern Pacific Railroad, comes back to the industrial classes, by creating a demand for the products of mechanics, operatives, &c.

FIFTH.—These bonds can be procured in sums of **$100** and upward, either "Coupon" or "Registered." A **COUPON** bond is payable principal and interest to *bearer.* A **REGISTERED** bond is payable principal and interest *only* to the party in whose name it is issued; and even should it be destroyed, mislaid or stolen, nothing is actually lost, as the bond is worthless to any one except the rightful owner, and will be at once replaced. Hence the money invested is always as secure as if deposited in the strongest bank.

Persons wishing to purchase **7-30's** or to exchange other bonds for them, can do so on application to any of the Banks or Bankers advertised to sell this loan, of whom information, maps, pamphlets, etc., may be obtained. Those living in localities remote from Banks, may send money or bonds directly to us by express, and we will send back Northern Pacific bonds at our own risk, and free of cost to the investor.

JAY COOKE & CO.

NEW YORK, PHILADELPHIA, AND WASHINGTON,

Financial Agents Northern Pacific Railroad Co.

Banks and Bankers generally throughout the Country are Agents for the sale of this Loan.

An advertisement placed by Jay Cooke & Company seeking buyers for Northern Pacific Railroad bonds. Library of Congress.

were built, half his infantry and cavalry could be dispensed with. Furthermore, Wheeler stated that the road would encourage trade and promote friendship with Mexico and also provide an outlet to the ocean for the vast mineral wealth of the New Mexico and Arizona Territories, thereby developing the nation's resources and increasing its taxable wealth and national power. Last, Bill said the Southern Pacific would help heal the "north-south division" in the nation by bringing "the South into direct contact with northern men, northern progress, northern ideas and capital." Wheeler predicted that construction of the Southern Pacific would cause sectional "antagonism" to "fade out" and accomplish what so far, the Reconstruction statutes had failed to do.[13]

When Wheeler yielded the floor, opposition to the new southern transcontinental line sprang into action. Congressmen from Pennsylvania, Indiana, and Delaware were the line's most caustic critics. Democrat Richard J. Haldeman from Harrisburg, Pennsylvania, argued that the size of the land grant undermined "republican virtue." Haldeman assailed railroad promoters by likening them to "the robber knights of the Middle Ages" who were using "unscrupulous cunning" instead of "the mailed hand." The Pennsylvania congressman had another problem with the bill. Because "myriads of cheap laborers" would be required to construct the line, Haldeman was alarmed that the Southern Pacific would "bring large numbers of Chinese into our midst." Horrified at that prospect, Haldeman warned that "we must consider what sort of people we want in this country."[14]

The ardent abolitionist and unsuccessful candidate for vice president on the Free Soil party ticket in 1852, Indiana Republican George W. Julian, launched a savage attack on the bill. He began by insinuating that Wheeler was acting as a tool of the railroad interests and declared that "commercial feudalism" was at the heart of the problem created by "the railway power in the United States." The congressman from Indiana contended that Wheeler's Southern Pacific bill posed the question of "whether we shall have a government owned and dominated by great corporations which never die, which band themselves together as a unit against the rights of the people, and will accept nothing short of imperial power over Congress, state legislatures and the courts." Julian concluded, "In theory ours is a government of the people but in practice, it is rapidly degenerating into an oligarchy of grasping capitalists."[15]

As the time for debate began to run out on the opposition, the former schoolteacher and railroad executive, Delaware Democrat Benjamin T. Biggs, assaulted Wheeler's bill. He asserted that it made "the rich richer and the poor poorer." But, he said, the most insidious thing about the measure was the impact the Southern Pacific would have on race relations. Biggs stated that blacks were not satisfied with the end of slavery, "they insist on attending white schools and churches, staying in the bedrooms of white hotels, and playing in white amusement parks." Biggs warned that building the Southern would enable GOP carpetbaggers and scalawags and other "vile adventurers and soldiers of fortune in the South" to continue their efforts "to debase and degrade the whites."[16]

Wheeler marshaled a powerful counterattack in support of his proposal. Republican George E. Harris of Mississippi, a former Confederate army officer and lawyer, said that the Democratic opposition "surpasses Satan for impudence and bears off the palm for stupidity."[17] Republican Richard C. McCormick, a New York native, former newspaperman and delegate to Congress from the Arizona Territory, described the arguments by opponents of the Southern Pacific bill as "the buncombe of the demagogue." For McCormick, one of the most persuasive reasons why the bill should pass was that the railroad would "forever settle the vexatious Indian question" and would protect the people in the Territories of Arizona and New Mexico from "vicious wild men" by sweeping away "the terrible Apaches and Comanches."[18]

When the time for debate was up, Wheeler quickly moved passage of his bill and it passed easily 135 to 70. He now had to wait for action on the measure in the Senate.[19] Bill did not have long to wait. The Senate passed a similar bill but there were some differences between the House and Senate versions that required the appointment of a Conference Committee that consisted of three members from each house. Wheeler was named the spokesman for the House version and Louisiana Republican William P. Kellogg was named the spokesman for the Senate version.[20]

Wheeler and Kellogg hammered out a compromise. The Conference Committee's bill extended the line to New Orleans on the eastern end and added a line from San Diego to San Francisco on the western end. On March 3, the last day of the session, Wheeler presented the compromise bill to the House urging that it be passed because "simple justice" demanded it. Bill turned back a feeble attempt by opponents to amend the measure and the House accepted the Conference Committee's report and passed the bill 125 to 64.[21] With this vote, a southern transcontinental railroad line was on its way to being built and the fifty-one-year-old congressman from Malone had added a second transcontinental railroad feather to his cap.

He had only one evening to celebrate his railroad victories because he had to prepare the next morning for the opening of a new Congress, the Forty-second. The new House contained 129 Republicans, 87 Democrats, 10 Conservatives, two Liberal Republicans and one Independent.[22]

Largely because of Wheeler's success in promoting the construction of two new transcontinental railroads, there was a groundswell of support among Republican congressmen to reward Wheeler by having him appointed chairman of the powerful Ways and Means Committee, the chief tax-writing committee in the House. However, Speaker Blaine disappointed Wheeler. Instead of naming Bill chairman of the Ways and Means Committee, he reappointed him chairman of the Pacific Railroad Committee. Blaine also named Wheeler to the Joint Committee on the Library, which was devoted to the administration of the Library of Congress.[23]

During the Forty-second Congress, Democrats laid the groundwork for a program known as the *New Departure*, which was designed to set the stage for them winning the presidency in 1872. They voted for measures guaranteeing Southerners home rule while at the same time bowing to the finality of Reconstruction, the permanence of black suffrage and the protection of black rights. In an effort to reanimate the spirit of Reconstruction, Republicans proposed an enforcement act aimed at suppressing the Ku Klux Klan (KKK). The GOP identified the KKK as an arm of the Democrats. The Democrats denied the bill was necessary and claimed the Klan was a figment of the GOP's imagination.[24]

Wheeler was in favor of the Ku Klux Klan Act of 1871, also known as the *Civil Rights Act of 1871*. He agreed that additional laws were necessary in order to enforce the Fourteenth Amendment, which had been ratified in 1868. However, Wheeler wanted a strong law with teeth. When the Ku Klux Klan Act came up for a vote in the House, Wheeler fought to strengthen the bill by voting for amendments to make it possible for people whose houses were burned down or destroyed, or who were whipped, wounded, or killed by people seeking to deny them their Fourteenth Amendment rights, to sue the county, parish, or city for full compensation in federal courts. The amendments were voted down 132 to 45. On April 19, the second to last day of the first session, Wheeler had to eventually settle for what he certainly felt was a watered-down version of the bill because it did not create liability for county and local governments and in fact, put a cap on damages. With Wheeler's vote, the final version of the Ku Klux Klan Act passed the House 93 to 74.[25]

Between sessions, Bill focused on political work designed to promote his renomination to run for a third straight term in the Forty-third Congress. The agreement between St. Lawrence and Franklin County Republicans only covered the Forty-first and Forty-second Congresses. There was no agreement in place concerning who should run for the Forty-third Congress. Bill argued that the district should follow the precedent set by Hulburd, his predecessor in office. He had served three straight terms before stepping down.

Bill instigated an undercover public relations and marketing campaign to promote his renomination. An anonymous letter "from Washington" began appearing in the North Country newspapers. It was a plea for the retention of incumbents and warned of the "evil effects of frequent changes." The letter writer complimented Wheeler as "an excellent representative," "fitted for any position by training and talent," "able and faithful in committee" work, and "equal to all contingencies of debate." The author predicted Wheeler would "demonstrate the wisdom of his district in retaining him."[26]

Wheeler also relied on the influence of the men for whom he had secured federal jobs. The Seventeenth Federal Collection District was a major source of patronage for Bill. Between the first and second sessions of the Forty-second Congress, Bill had a hand in the appointment of three assistant assessors from Franklin County and five more from St. Lawrence County.[27]

As the political pressure mounted on Republicans in the North Country to renominate Wheeler, the second session of Congress opened on December 4, 1871, in Washington. Wheeler's agenda was once again filled with proposed railroad legislation. One of the most controversial bills that Wheeler was successful in having passed was a proposal that granted one-half of Goat Island, which was located in San Francisco Bay, to the Central Pacific Railroad for its use as a western terminus.[28]

Closer to home in the North Country, he introduced a bill releasing twenty-five acres of federal land in Plattsburgh to the New York and Canada Railroad and managed to get the bill passed, without debate, by asking the House for "a favor."[29] Wheeler also introduced a bill to authorize construction of a railroad bridge across the St. Lawrence River from Ogdensburg to the Canadian shore.[30]

Wheeler's devotion to the success of U.S. railroads intersected with his love of nature when it came to a bill to create the Yellowstone National Park. After the Civil War, there was a surge of interest in the beauty of Yellowstone's geysers and the extraordinary rock formations surrounding them. Jay Cooke, the financier of the Northern Pacific Railroad, felt the line could make money from tourism if the public became attracted to the area. Cooke subsidized a national lecture tour about the beauty of Yellowstone and lobbied Congress to pass legislation creating a national park. A bill setting apart a tract of land near the headwaters of the Yellowstone River as a public park soon passed the Senate and came before the House. Wheeler lined up votes to support it. Given his affection for the Adirondack wilderness, it was not surprising that he was moved by the arguments that the Yellowstone area was a place of "beautiful decorations, a living museum and a geological sideshow." With Wheeler's vote, the bill passed 115 to 65.[31]

While the second session of the Forty-second Congress wound down, Wheeler kept his eyes on Albany where the New York legislature was busy redrawing congressional district lines using the results of the 1870 census. Bill's memory of being reapportioned out of office the last time district lines were redrawn was still fresh and he applied as much political pressure as he could muster to keep his congressional district intact. He was successful. Although the legislature changed the district's number from seventeen to eighteen, the lines of the district remained the same. For the next ten years, Franklin County and St. Lawrence County would continue to constitute a congressional district. It had a population of 114,000, about 22,000 less than the average population of the other congressional districts in the state.[32]

As the spring of 1872 approached the North Country, Wheeler's Republican party faced a crisis. It was being torn apart by dissidents, called Liberal Republicans, who challenged the party regulars on several issues including corruption in government, Grant's financial policies, and a Radical Southern policy. In addition, rumors of scandals involving the financing of the transcontinental railroads, kickbacks in the Post Office Department, and bribery in the War Department and Treasury Department were flying.[33]

In Washington, Wheeler was looking forward to the conclusion of the second session and he was very concerned about what the split in his party would mean to his bid to win renomination and election to a third straight term.

16

Returning the Salary Grab

☆

The unrest in the Republican Party had enormous implications for Bill Wheeler's political future. Edwin A. Merritt of Potsdam in St. Lawrence County was one of the leaders of the Liberal Republicans in the North Country. Six years previously, Merritt's attack on corruption in his county's Republican circles divided his party and opened the door for Wheeler to take the congressional nomination away from St. Lawrence County Republicans, even though they controlled two-thirds of the delegates to the nominating convention. Now, in 1872, Merritt was on the prowl again and divisions in the GOP were reopening. This time he was attacking President Grant and threatening to run for Wheeler's seat in Congress as a Liberal Republican. To make matters worse for Wheeler's reelection prospects, Democrats were discussing the possibility of endorsing Liberal Republican candidates.[1]

Bill was deeply concerned by this turn of events. He could see how an ambitious St. Lawrence County Republican might take advantage of the party factionalism in the county, as he himself had done, and use it to take the congressional nomination away from him and return it to St. Lawrence County. Even if Bill could sidestep that development, he worried about how many voters might desert him on election day and cast a ballot for a Liberal Republican-Democratic ticket. Wheeler had major political problems on his hands but he dealt with them confidently and aggressively.

In a move that appealed to the reformer-instincts of the North Country's Liberal Republicans, Wheeler boldly stepped forward to prevent the destruction of the forests of the Adirondacks, which dominated the southern landscape of both Franklin and St. Lawrence Counties. He was driven by his love for fishing and camping in the wild South Woods with his Saranac Navigation Company. However, his zeal was tempered by a firm religious belief in the Protestant work ethic and its financial rewards. Wheeler wanted to save the Adirondacks for nature lovers and at the same time protect the forests for entrepreneurs. A substantial number of Wheeler's supporters earned a living by harvesting wood from the Adirondack forests. Wood was needed for buildings, furniture, and fuel for homes and factories. In addition, wood was reduced by furnaces to produce charcoal and potash.[2] Iron and steel industries used charcoal for fuel. Potash was used in the manufacturing of fertilizer, glass, and soap.[3]

In addition to those making money from the wood industry, nascent tourism had begun to enrich resort owners in the Adirondacks. Ever since the Reverend William H. H. Murray published *Adventures in the Wilderness* shortly after the Civil War, a great flood of men, women, and children began to sweep into the Adirondacks.[4] From Wheeler's hometown perspective, there was "no better place than Malone from which to enter the woods."[5] The Adirondacks were becoming firmly established as one of the United States' popular resorts.[6] Hotels sprang up throughout Franklin and St. Lawrence Counties. Paul Smith on Lower St. Regis Lake in Franklin County built one of the most famous resorts in Wheeler's congressional district. Around a spacious hotel, Smith built a complex of buildings that included two dormitories for his staff, a sixty-horse stable, a casino that had a special wire to the New York Stock Exchange, a four-story warehouse, an office, and a sawmill.[7]

As the 1872 election approached, it was not difficult for Wheeler and others to see the threats to the future of the Adirondacks. Vast areas of the forests had been clear-cut by the charcoal industry. Lumbermen were harvesting all the wood they could get their hands on. One of the most respected voices to protest this exploitation was Verplanck Colvin who had been lobbying public officials for years to create a forest preserve and public park in the mountains.[8] Liberal Republicans supported Colvin's proposal to make a Wilderness Park out of the Adirondacks. Horace Greeley's *New York Tribune,* the most prominent voice for Liberal Republican positions, explained why a state park should be established. Doing so would preserve the timber, the game, and collect all the waters of the Adirondacks "into a vast reservoir that would supply water to Albany and New York as well as other main cities and large villages along the Hudson River."[9]

Paul Smith's Hotel in Franklin County on Lower St. Regis Lake.
Detroit Publishing Company Collection, Library of Congress.

Public and political pressure mounted to support the creation of a public park in the Adirondacks. On March 15, 1872, a bill was introduced in the New York legislature to appoint a seven-member commission to look into the expediency of the state taking title to timberland regions of the Adirondacks lying in seven different counties including the two counties that constituted Wheeler's newly numbered Eighteenth Congressional District, Franklin County and St. Lawrence County. Using his political influence and following his political instincts, Wheeler thrust his name forward and became one of the seven park commissioners who were appointed to two-year terms. Others who won appointment included surveyor and park advocate Verplanck Colvin of Albany, timber preservationist and scientific forester Franklin B. Hough of St. Lawrence County, and former Democratic governor and 1868 candidate for president Horatio Seymour.[10]

Several weeks before the Liberal Republicans met in Cincinnati to nominate a candidate to oppose Grant, Wheeler shifted gears away from issues that might attract Liberal Republicans and made a direct appeal for the backing of mainstream party members in his congressional district by lending his name to support a mass demonstration in favor of Grant at the Cooper Institute in New York City. In a telegram to William E. Dodge, one of the event's organizers, Wheeler praised Grant and the Republican Party for saving the Union, enfranchising black men, cutting taxes and shoring up the national credit.[11] These points became the core of Wheeler's 1872 campaign.

When the Liberal Republicans nominated Horace Greeley to run against Grant in May, Wheeler's backers went on the offensive. Having already described Greeley's criticism of the Republican Party as "the prattle of a sore-pated politician," they summed up his drawbacks by saying he was "wanting in sound judgment and statesmanlike sagacity," "unsafe and unreliable," "a man of inordinate ambition," and "a very Uriah Heep."[12]

In June, the Republicans nominated Grant for president and replaced Colfax with Henry Wilson of Massachusetts to be Grant's running mate. A month later, the Democrats adopted the Liberal Republican platform and endorsed Greeley for president. With Grant in place to run again for president,[13] Wheeler stepped up his campaign to run again for Congress. The Eighteenth Congressional District convention would be held at the Whitney House in Potsdam on August 19. Two days later, a GOP state convention would be held in Utica to nominate a candidate for governor.[14]

In the weeks running up to the conventions, a curious tug of war over Wheeler's political future broke out in the pages of North Country newspapers. The publicity heightened his desirability as a candidate. Some newspapers called for Bill to run for governor and others argued that he should return to Congress. The *Watertown Times* boomed Wheeler for governor citing his business experience, integrity, and intelligence. The paper said, "His fairness of character is proverbial. He is not in any way mixed up with our State party factions and stands aloof from all quarrels."[15] The *Potsdam Courier* acknowledged the Wheeler boom for governor but declared, "You can't have him!" The *Courier* stated that the people in the Eighteenth Congressional District wanted to reelect Wheeler to Congress. The *Utica Herald* agreed saying that his district could not "spare Mr. Wheeler from his seat in Congress and we know Congress can not afford to lose his wise and judicious counsels."[16]

Newspaper after newspaper waded in to fight for Wheeler's political future. The coverage was so extensive, it was hard not to believe that Bill had engineered the tug of war as a way to turn the spotlight on himself. In any case, he modestly declined to encourage a bid for governor by telling his allies that he felt he did not have enough money to become governor.[17]

In the second week of August, the GOP county convention named Wheeler to be a delegate to the upcoming state convention. A few days later, on August

19, Wheeler was unanimously nominated to run for a third term in Congress.[18] Commenting on his renomination and noting that he also had been mentioned as a probable convention choice to be president of the GOP state convention, the *New York Times* listed Wheeler as one of the "most distinguished Republicans in the State."[19]

The state convention was held in the "spacious and elegant" Opera House in Utica, which had just been built and could seat two thousand people.[20] All the luminaries of the regular party were present including its leader, U.S. Senator Roscoe Conkling. On the opening day, Wheeler was elected president of the convention. He worked hard on his acceptance speech, which set the tone for the convention. Bill praised the GOP as "the noblest political organization ever born to man." He described the campaigns of the Democrats and Liberal Republicans as "the new machinations of the old conspirators against the Union who have marshaled to their aid, for a new assault, every political camp follower, and every disappointed, starved and ravenous place-hunter in the land." He told the delegates that their election day opponents were once again spreading "the cloud of treason and disunion" across the nation as "a pall." Wheeler described the Liberal Republicans as "struggling malcontents" and their agreement with the Democrats to back the same candidates as "a hollow, hypocritical, huckstering alliance." Bill laced his praise for Grant's wartime record with contemporary poetry written by John Greenleaf Whittier, a man Wheeler described as a "liberty-loving" poet. Bill predicted that the Democrats and the Liberal Republicans would "meet their Appomattox" after the votes were counted in November. As his speech wound down, Wheeler urged the convention to nominate men "of unimpeachable personal integrity and unquestionable capacity for public office." He borrowed more poetry, this time from Oliver Wendell Holmes Sr., to conclude his speech by describing the Union as "One flag, one land, one heart, one hand, one nation evermore."[21] Many Republican patriotic hearts in the Utica Opera House beat a little faster as delegates applauded Wheeler's address.

Bill returned to Malone after the convention nominated a GOP state ticket headed by John A. Dix for governor.[22] In September, state Liberal Republicans and Democrats met in Syracuse and nominated Democrat Francis Kernan for governor and Liberal Republican Chauncey Depew for lieutenant governor.[23]

In the Eighteenth Congressional District, Bill was overjoyed to learn that his preconvention strategy of stroking the interests of Liberal Republicans had worked. State Liberal Republican leader Merritt had backed off from running against Wheeler for Congress. Because of Merritt's popularity in the district and his standing in the party, he would have been a formidable candidate for Bill to go up against. Instead, the Democrats and Liberal Republicans nominated the

Canadian-born lawyer, William P. Cantwell of Malone, to run for Wheeler's seat in Congress. Cantwell, a graduate of the University of Vermont, had practiced law and done newspaper work in Montreal before moving to Franklin County in 1853. Before the Civil War, Cantwell had been elected school commissioner and during the war had served as district attorney.[24]

There were few surprises during the campaign. Wheeler and the other Republican candidates tied themselves to Grant's coattails. Bill sparked the organization of Grant and Wilson Clubs throughout his congressional district and gave lengthy speeches denouncing the Democrats and Liberal Republicans while praising Grant.[25] One unusual campaign event was a joint Wheeler-Cantwell fundraiser run by Republican and Democratic women. Tickets were sold for each candidate and the man who had the most tickets sold for him was awarded a cane.[26]

Wheeler's campaign peaked on election eve at a raucous rally in King's Hall in Malone. He "thrilled" his listeners with a forty-five-minute speech that was continually interrupted by applause.[27] On November 5, when the votes were counted, Wheeler overwhelmingly won election to the Forty-third Congress by garnering 69 percent of the vote defeating Cantwell 14,725 to 6,565.[28] Statewide, Grant and Dix also were victorious but Wheeler ran ahead of them in Franklin County.[29] The Republicans won control of the legislature, enabling them to subsequently reelect Conkling to another six-year term in the U.S. Senate.[30]

In December, Bill and his wife returned to their apartment on 12th Street in Washington to prepare for the opening of the third session of the Forty-second Congress.[31] After they were settled in, he was shaken to learn what a Congressional inquiry had uncovered. It had unearthed information about a sensational scandal involving the construction of one of the transcontinental railroads that came within the purview of Wheeler's Pacific Railroad Committee, the Union Pacific Railroad. The charges of corruption concerned a construction corporation named the Credit Mobilier of America and its dealings with many prominent political figures including Vice President Colfax and Vice President-elect Wilson, as well as many of Wheeler's Republican colleagues in the House such as Speaker Blaine and future President Garfield. The Democratic leader of the House, James Brooks of New York City, was also implicated in the scandal.[32]

Credit Mobilier was a dummy corporation set up to divert the profits from building the Union Pacific to the bank accounts of the railroad's promoters. Before the investigative spotlight had been turned on the corruption, the Credit Mobilier had run off with as much as $23 million that Congress had earmarked for construction of the Union Pacific.[33] In 1868, before Wheeler had arrived back on the congressional scene in the House, Congressman Oakes Ames, a shovel manufacturer from Massachusetts and the chief organizer of Credit Mobilier, began doling out shares of stock in the dummy corporation to key congressional leaders to thwart a potentially damaging congressional investigation into the scheme.[34]

Four years later, in the 1872 campaign, the New York *Sun* began writing articles about the corruption that the Credit Mobilier was engaged in. As one of the leading railroad men in the House, Wheeler was alarmed by the *Sun*'s revelations but because he was not a member of the House when the stock had been distributed, it was easy for him to publicly dismiss the charges as "campaign oratory." However, they did not go away and a House committee was appointed to investigate the allegations.[35]

When the third session of the Forty-second Congress opened, the investigating committee was continuing its probe into the role of House members in the affair but its proceedings were being conducted behind closed doors. On January 6, 1873, anxious to avoid the possibility of being tainted by the investigation because of his position as chairman of the Pacific Railroad Committee, Wheeler endorsed a resolution that the investigatory committee open its doors and do its work out in the open so everyone could see what was going on. With Wheeler's vote, the resolution passed 130 to 7—a surprising 104 members did not cast a vote on the measure.[36]

By the end of February, the House investigating committee finished its work. Ames had incriminated many of his political associates. He told the committee how he had bribed selected House colleagues not to investigate Credit Mobilier's fraudulent activity. Ames testified that he had either given stock free to some congressmen, such as Garfield, or sold shares to others at cut-rate prices. The new owners of the stock were guaranteed an immediate, and extremely generous, dividend, with another one guaranteed to be paid within a year.[37] Shockingly, the House investigating committee whitewashed all the GOP congressmen, except Ames. It recommended that Ames, and Brooks, the only Democrat caught up in the scandal, be expelled from the House. Wheeler supported the resolution to expel them but, before a vote could be taken, it was amended to take the teeth out of the resolution. As amended, instead of calling for the expulsion of the two men, the measure merely "condemned" them and censured them for their corrupt involvement with Credit Mobilier. Seeking expulsion, Wheeler voted against the amendment calling for censure but it passed 115 to 110. Bill was left with no alternative but to vote for the resolution as amended and Ames and Brooks were censured.[38]

Many political observers in Washington would not shut their eyes to the House cover-up and prominent Republicans, such as Speaker Blaine and Garfield, had to answer prickly questions about their involvement with Credit Mobilier for the rest of their political lives. The Credit Mobilier scandal was only the first of a number of scandals that tarred the reputation of Grant's second term.[39] Wheeler's name was never mentioned in connection with any of them. Nevertheless, as a man who had deep religious pride in his own honesty, he must have had second thoughts about assuring the nation back when he was advocating the construction of the Northern Pacific Railroad, that it was "preposterous" to believe Congress could ever permit a "huge swindle" or fraud to be undertaken![40]

More sensitive to the venality of his Republican House colleagues than ever before, Bill was outraged by what the House did next in the final days of the third session. It passed a law that became known by historians as the *Salary Grab*.

Benjamin Butler, Republican from Massachusetts, was the Salary Grab's ringleader. On February 10, 1873, he offered an amendment to an appropriations bill, which raised the pay of the president and the justices of the Supreme Court. Butler's amendment also called for raising the salaries of congressmen and U. S. senators from $5,000 a year to $8,000 a year, retroactively from the beginning of the Forty-second Congress in 1871.[41] If it passed, Wheeler and all the other members of both houses of Congress would be paid a lump sum bonus of $3,000 when Congress adjourned on March 3. To allow the House to act on his proposal, Butler had to win a two-thirds vote to suspend the rules. Wheeler voted against suspending the rules and the salary increase was defeated 120 to 81.[42] But Butler and his Salary Grab were not to be denied.

On March 1, with two days of life left in the Forty-second Congress, Butler brought the Salary Grab amendment back before the House. This time, to sweeten the measure for some of its opponents, he cut the proposed raise by $500. The new version of the Salary Grab called for raising congressional salaries from $5,000 to $7,500, again retroactively. Wheeler was truly dismayed and disgusted by the gall of his colleagues to even consider voting themselves a retroactive bonus like this one. The prospect of enacting the Salary Grab so soon after the revelations of the Credit Mobilier investigation appalled Bill even more! Time after time, Wheeler voted to kill the measure but on three separate attempts, the Salary Grab was kept alive 105 to 66, 104 to 79 and 100 to 97.[43]

On March 3, the last day of the Forty-second Congress, the Salary Grab came before the House again. This time it was in the form of a report from a House-Senate conference committee. Wheeler opposed adopting the report along with Republican John Farnsworth, a lawyer from Chicago, who warned that it would "completely wreck" the GOP and "cover its history with dishonor." The Democratic House leader, Samuel J. Randall, taunted Wheeler and the other opponents of the Salary Grab by saying that if it passed, they should not take the money. The congressman from Malone thought to himself that Randall had made an excellent point and made plans to do that very thing! When the time came for the vote, Wheeler voted yet again against the measure but it passed 102 to 96.[44]

What happened next landed Wheeler on the front page of the *New York Times.* After Congress adjourned, Wheeler took his $2,500 bonus and bought U.S. bonds with it. He told the press he wanted to put the money to work immediately to help pay off a portion of the national debt. Next, he cancelled the bonds, which stopped the interest payments and assigned the bonds to the Secretary of the Treasury.[45]

The *Times* praised Wheeler for refusing to profit from the Salary Grab.[46] Because he was one of the first, if not *the* first congressman to return the pay raise, Wheeler's honor, integrity, and clean record were lauded by newspapers across the North Country, as well as by those in Albany, Saratoga, and Boston.[47] By the end of the year, nineteen of the seventy-four U.S. senators and 47 of the 252 U.S. representatives followed Wheeler's example and returned their back pay.[48]

Exhausted by the intensity of the last month of the Forty-second Congress, Bill and Mary Wheeler traveled south to Virginia and Tennessee for a few weeks to relax and visit friends and relatives when the third session adjourned.[49] There would be nine months to pass before the Forty-third Congress opened for business. As spring slowly began to arrive in the North Country, disturbing news came trickling in to Wheeler's office about another potential financial scandal. Charges were being leveled against Ezra Cornell for mishandling and pocketing money earmarked by the state for the founding of Cornell University. Governor Dix turned to Wheeler and two other prominent political figures to investigate the charges.

17

No "Unproductive and Useless Park"

Ezra Cornell had been a successful businessman building and managing telegraph lines before he made a fortune when his telegraphic company merged with others to form the Western Union Telegraph Company in 1856. He was a state senator at the time the federal Morrill Act made proceeds from the sale of federal lands available to the states to finance the teaching of agriculture and the mechanical arts. Cornell introduced a bill in the state senate to use the federal aid from the Morrill Act to establish a university on his three-hundred-acre farm in Ithaca.[1]

Charles C. Cooke, founder of the New York People's College in nearby Havana,[2] Schuyler County, also sought the Morrill Act money for his school. Jeremiah McGuire was his attorney. After months of wrangling and financial maneuvering, Cornell and his university won out over the rival claims of Cooke and his People's College. In 1865, the legislature passed a law creating Cornell University and scrip for 990,000 acres of federal land in the west, New York's allotment of land under the Morrill Act, was sold to Cornell. He founded a company to sell the land and turn over all profits from the sales to New York, for the benefit of Cornell University.[3] It opened in 1868 with 425 students.[4]

In May 1873, McGuire, now an assemblyman from Schuyler County, assailed Ezra Cornell from the floor of the assembly charging him with fraudulently using the profits from the sale of the federal lands to create a private $22 million fortune for himself.[5] McGuire demanded that Governor Dix appoint a commission to investigate Cornell's business activities. The next day, Cornell telegraphed Dix to deny the charges and also called for an investigation.[6]

In the last week of May while Wheeler was off on his annual fishing expedition with his Saranac Navigation Company in the Adirondacks, he received a telegram from Dix appointing him to the three-man Cornell Land Investigation Commission. He cut his fishing trip short to head down to Albany to meet with the other two men Dix had appointed. Bill was the only Republican. The other two men were Horatio Seymour, former Democratic governor from Oneida, and John D. Van Buren, a well-known Democratic lawyer from New York City.[7]

The commission scheduled public hearings to take testimony about the charges and set in motion a series of inquiries to the governors of other states about their management of Morrill Act aid.[8] It would be ten months before the commission would issue its report, which completely exonerated Ezra Cornell from any mismanagement of the funds.[9]

Work on the Cornell investigation was not the only matter demanding Wheeler's attention during the summer of 1873. In July, the Adirondack Park study commission issued its report. For more than a year, the commission had examined and analyzed environmental and economic information about the Adirondacks. Each of the body's seven members brought their own frame of reference to the discussion about what the commission's report should say but in the end, it primarily reflected the viewpoints of Verplanck Colvin, Franklin B. Hough, and Wheeler.[10]

Colvin, a twenty-five-year-old lawyer from Albany who was now serving as the superintendent of the state topographical survey of the Adirondacks, had been calling for the creation of an Adirondack Park since 1868. Colvin's primary concern was watershed protection. St. Lawrence County's Franklin B. Hough was a country doctor and a historian as well as one of the nation's first native-born scientific foresters. Hough was primarily concerned with timber preservation.[11] Wheeler loved the wild beauty of the Adirondacks and respected the concerns for protecting the watershed and preserving timber but his primary interest was economic. As a conservative businessman, Bill wanted to protect jobs and industry located in the Adirondacks.

The findings contained in the Adirondack Park study commission's report were highly significant. The report served as the first official government building block on which subsequent calls for the creation of a state Adirondack Park would rest.[12] For the first time in New York State history, a commission created by the state legislature endorsed the absolute and immediate need for state government protection of the Adirondack forests from "wanton destruction."[13]

The Adirondack Park study commission's report in 1873 described "little settlements," such as this one on Saranac Lake, as "indispensible" to the completeness of a park. Detroit Publishing Company Collection, Library of Congress.

Colvin's influence in the report was reflected in its emphasis on the importance of the watershed for both the Erie Canal and the state's mills and factories. In addition, the report highlighted the importance of the forests to hold back floodwaters of the Hudson and the Mohawk rivers from melting snow.[14]

Hough's influence was seen in the report's recommendation that the Adirondack forests be managed by professional foresters as they were in Germany, France, England and Ireland with trees being cut only when they reached a certain age and the area replanted to provide a harvest for future generations.[15]

Wheeler's influence could be found in the economic concerns expressed in the report. It refused to suggest modeling an Adirondack Park after Yellowstone Park, which the report said was created "simply in order to preserve it, as a pleasure ground for the people." The report condemned the "creation of an expensive and exclusive park for mere purposes of recreation" and "utterly and entirely" repudiated the idea of "an unproductive and useless park." The Adirondacks, according to the report, should be open to careful forestry and mining. The report added that the little settlements in the Adirondacks would be "indispensable" to

Raquette Lake from West Mountain in the Adirondacks.
Detroit Publishing Company Collection, Library of Congress.

the completeness of a park because they could provide for the needs of tourists and lumbermen. The local inhabitants could work as guides for tourists and hunters and "protect the game and timber from unlawful destruction." The report warned that it would be "improper" to think of enclosing or fencing in the park because "it should be a common unto the people of the state."[16]

The tension between Colvin and Hough's viewpoints, which emphasized the priority of preserving and protecting the forests of the Adirondacks from destructive forces, and Wheeler's viewpoint, which emphasized the priority of preserving and protecting private property rights and the economic benefits that flow from them, can be felt in the North Country to this day whenever issues concerning the Park arise.

Wheeler took two trips with his wife and friends following the completion of his work on the Adirondack Park study commission. On his first trip, he went to Duluth, Minnesota, to investigate how the construction of the Northern Pacific Railroad was progressing and to invest in some real estate. With the help of a Duluth real estate agent he did not know very well, he purchased several choice acres of land in the heart of the growing city. When the paperwork was signed, Bill and his traveling companions boarded a Northern Pacific train and rode it west, across the entire state of Minnesota, to Fargo, North Dakota, on the western bank of the Red River of the North.[17] His second trip took him to the White Mountains of New Hampshire where he and his wife vacationed for two weeks.[18]

Bill and Mary no sooner had returned home from their vacation than terrible national economic news greeted them. On September 18, Jay Cooke and Company, the highly respected bank that was financing the construction of the Northern Pacific, suddenly closed its doors and went out of business, triggering an uproar on Wall Street. Western Union stock dropped ten points in ten minutes and railroad securities began to fall. The following day, the stock market crashed. Western Union went from 92¼ to 45, with no takers. Banks across the country collapsed and investment houses suspended business. The next week, one thousand men were laid off at Rogers locomotive works in Patterson, New Jersey. The New York Stock Exchange closed for seven and a half days. Factories shut down and mortgages were foreclosed. There were strikes, lockouts, and boycotts.[19] The Panic of 1873 had begun. By the end of the year, five thousand businesses declared bankruptcy and a half-million workers were jobless. It was the worst economic disaster in U.S. history to that time.[20] Wages declined and agricultural prices dropped so low that many farmers, unable to pay their mortgages, had to sell their family farms.[21]

As this distressing news cascaded all around him, Wheeler traveled to Washington for the opening of the first session of the Forty-third Congress on December 1. Bill was one of two-hundred Republicans in the House, which also had eighty-three Democrats and nine men from other assorted parties.[22] He soon found himself enmeshed in the bitter feud that had developed between New York's U.S. Senator Roscoe Conkling and Congressman James G. Blaine of Maine.

The Conkling-Blaine feud had its origins shortly after the Civil War came to an end. Both men were serving their second terms in the House and began jousting with each other for legislative dominance and peer approval. They both wanted to be recognized as the alpha Congressman. As the rivalry intensified, it became more personal. During one speech, Blaine sarcastically attacked Conkling's style and appearance by referring to "his grandiloquent swell, his majestic, supereminent, overpowering, turkey-gobbler strut."[23] Extremely sensitive to his appearance, Conkling was deeply stung by Blaine's attack and never forgot it. In 1867, the New York legislature elected Conkling to the U.S. Senate and he happily left the House to Blaine. Two years later, with Wheeler's support, Blaine was elected Speaker. In the following year, Conkling won absolute control over the state GOP in New York and had become one of President Grant's strongest supporters in Washington.

Conkling and other leaders of the national Republican Party, men who were chieftains in various states in the Middle West and the Northeast, subsequently became known as the *Stalwarts*. They were supposed to have been stalwart in their support for Grant and the patronage system. In New York and Washington, the Stalwarts were led by Conkling who was Grant's most passionate advocate. Over time, the Stalwarts derisively began to call Blaine and his followers *Half-Breeds*, claiming that they were only half loyal to Grant and fully loyal to no one but themselves. Eventually, Blaine's followers wore the label proudly and adopted it as their own.[24]

Fiercely independent and religiously honest, Wheeler was determined to be his own man and tried to perform a balancing act between Conkling and the Stalwarts, and Blaine and the Half-Breeds. This was not easy. Wheeler was a New York Republican and Conkling was the leader of the New York Republican Party who wielded great power as the organization's absolute boss. Wheeler was also a House Republican and Blaine was the leader of the House who wielded great power as Speaker.

Several months before the opening of the Forty-third Congress, Wheeler was approached by Conkling and other friends of Grant. They asked Wheeler to challenge Blaine for Speaker. With their support, they said, Wheeler could win. The press picked up on the story and soon Wheeler began to read encouraging articles about his prospects for becoming the next Speaker. The *New York Times* reported that Bill was assured of strong support from Western congressmen if he ran against Blaine. The *Albany Journal* predicted that because of Wheeler's popularity in the House, he was the only man who had a chance of defeating Blaine.[25]

Blaine reacted to news of Wheeler's potential challenge by cozying up to Bill and reminding him how well they worked together in the House and how warm their friendship had become. To crush the growing anti-Blaine movement, Blaine asked Wheeler to write a letter denying his interest in becoming Speaker.[26] By this time, Bill must have known that he did not have the votes to defeat Blaine because he decided to make the most out of his threat to Blaine by cutting a deal with him instead of running against him. Wheeler said that he would agree to support Blaine if he would agree to appoint Bill chair of the Appropriations Committee in place of Garfield who had been tainted by the Credit Mobilier investigation.[27]

There were several reasons why Wheeler chose the Appropriations Committee. First, he desired to step down from the Pacific Railroad Committee to distance himself from the railroad corruption that the Credit Mobilier investigation had dredged up. Wheeler knew that his unblemished integrity was one of his political strengths and he wanted to avoid the slightest appearance of impropriety. Second, Bill was eager to assume more power and authority for himself. As chair of the

FRANK LESLIE'S ILLUSTRATED NEWSPAPER

No. 1,701.—Vol. LXVI.] NEW YORK—FOR THE WEEK ENDING APRIL 21, 1888. [Price, 10 Cents.

ROSCOE CONKLING.

SEE PAGE 151.

Roscoe Conkling. U.S. Senate Collection.

Appropriations Committee, his influence would extend to every corner of the federal government and into every House district because the committee controlled the power of the purse.

Blaine led Wheeler to believe that the Appropriations post was his if he supported Blaine for Speaker. Wheeler thought he had made a deal. After he announced that he was not a candidate for Speaker, Bill supported the reelection of Blaine who won the post 190 to 81. After the vote was announced, Bill was stunned when Blaine double-crossed him and told him that he was going to name Bill to chair the Pacific Railroad Committee again. After an angry altercation between the two men, Wheeler refused to accept Blaine's appointment. To appease the furious congressman from Malone and his many friends in the House, Blaine appointed Wheeler chair of the Commerce Committee and also named him to a seat on Garfield's Appropriations Committee. However, from that time on, Wheeler knew that Blaine was not a man he could trust and there always was a bitter feeling between them.[28] Given Wheeler's ethics, Blaine's treachery meant that Bill would never become a Half-Breed. His ethics also told him that he would never become a Stalwart, either. Wheeler spurned the idea of becoming a vassal-henchman for Conkling who, as one historian aptly put it, played the role of lord-boss, controlling New York as his fiefdom, using patronage and protection in return for fealty and support.[29] Wheeler steadfastly charted an independent course between Blaine and Conkling. There would be times when this position would work to his political advantage, but there would be other times when his refusal to join either faction harmed him and he had to pay a stiff political price for his independence.

Once the committee assignments had been agreed on, the first thing Wheeler did was appoint Frederick J. Seaver, assistant editor of the *Malone Palladium*, to assist him in Washington as clerk of the Commerce Committee.[30] The second thing Bill did was announce his legislative goals. Always a frugal man, Wheeler declared that he was determined to cut a substantial amount of fat out of the federal budget. As chairman of the Commerce Committee, he set goals to cut 75 percent to 80 percent of pork out of the river and harbor appropriations, to reduce the federal workforce in all departments within his purview, and to transfer the Bureau of Indian Affairs from the Department of the Interior to the War Department to save the Indians from "the rascality of sharpers."[31]

The most contentious issue involving Wheeler's goal to cut pork out of the rivers and harbors budget concerned a proposed bill to pay $1.25 million to the Louisville & Portland Canal Company[32] for its bonds and $114,000 for back taxes the company owed the city of Louisville.

During committee sessions, Wheeler was adamantly opposed to federally subsidizing the canal company but committee members outvoted him. They voted unanimously to bring the bill out to the House for action over Wheeler's objections. When the bill was before the House, Wheeler, to use the words of his opponents, devised an "ingenious attempt" to kill the measure. Knowing that the state of Kentucky took great pride in the canal and that the Kentucky legislature would not meet again for two years, Wheeler proposed an amendment that provided that no federal money be appropriated for the canal unless the state of Kentucky ceded jurisdiction over the canal to the federal government! Proponents of the federal subsidy were beside themselves with anger over Wheeler's tactic. He was attacked for being anti-business and anti–Ohio River valley. Wheeler stood his ground. He denied that he was opposed to commerce in the Ohio River valley and reiterated his position that no federal money should be spent to subsidize a business that the federal government had no control over. New York Republican Stewart L. Woodford, who had just won election as a freshman congressman from Brooklyn, raised legal questions about the ownership of the canal—a direct challenge to the heart of Wheeler's argument. Woodford joined others who contended that Kentucky had turned the canal over to the federal government before the Civil War. An angry Wheeler jumped to his feet and quoted canal company records, which showed that during the Civil War, the federal government had taxed the canal. Wheeler scathingly asked, "When before did the government of the United States ever tax its own property?" Briefly taken aback, proponents of the subsidy indignantly questioned where Wheeler had obtained the reports. He fired back that he had written the city of Louisville for them and sternly warned his colleagues that he did not take the floor to speak unless he knew what he was talking about. Wheeler remarked, "I do not intend to grope about in the dark and take things on assumption." When time ran out for debate about Wheeler's "ingenious" amendment, the House passed it 130 to 95, and then voted for the bill, as amended, by the same margin.[33]

The North Country press was ecstatic that Wheeler had saved the national treasury $1.25 million. In addition, the *Albany Journal* described Wheeler's work as a "brilliant success" and the *New York Times* praised Wheeler's "great skill."[34] The accolades were premature, however. The measure soon came back to the House in the form of a conference report from a House-Senate committee, without Wheeler's amendment.

Wheeler heatedly took the floor and tried to put his amendment back into the report. He likened his opponents to cuttlefish, which eject "an inky fluid by which it darkens the waters and conceals its purpose and object of attack." Bill said he knew he was in a fight against strong opponents who were supported by influential Western newspapers but added, "No disparity of odds ever deters me when I am conscious of the right." From his opponents, Wheeler demanded "facts, not arguments . . . not sophistries or theories or speculations." Challenged to explain how he, the chairman of the Commerce Committee, could possibly oppose support for business interests in the Ohio River valley, Wheeler thundered back, "I speak for the people of the United States and not for the people of the Ohio River solely." When the time came for the vote, the House rejected Wheeler's amendment 143 to 73 and then passed the conference report.[35]

Wheeler had more success cutting the budget working on the Appropriations Committee where he came up with a plan to slash military spending. His proposal generated fierce opposition. Garfield had put Bill in charge of the army's budget and Wheeler proposed cutting troop levels by almost 20 percent. He argued that national security should rest on a volunteer army because a large standing army went against U.S. policy and tradition. To reduce the need for the army to protect Western settlers, Wheeler called for a "contraction of population." He denounced "adventurous men" who moved "beyond the bounds of civilization" to purposely incite "Indian outrages" in order to justify an appeal for military protection.[36]

Wheeler's assault on the army's budget provoked sharp opposition. He met it with more pluck, confidence and humor than his House colleagues had ever heard from him before. Wheeler dismissed the testimony of a long string of generals who opposed the cuts, by arguing that it was only military "human nature" for generals to want to protect their "power and influence."[37] He answered critics of his bill who argued that settlers in Texas needed military protection from Indians and Mexican horse thieves, by asserting that during the Civil War, Texans sent their military forces away to serve in the Confederate army and yet were still able to successfully defend themselves from threats at home.[38] Other opponents cited the need for military protection from Indians in Arizona and the Dakotas, from Mormons in Utah, and from postelection day troublemakers in Louisiana.[39] Wheeler responded by declaring that if more men were needed, "I will tell you where there are plenty of missing ramrods!" He said they could be found working as "private servants" in the homes of "prominent officials in Washington."[40]

Wheeler added that in addition to troop reduction, the army budget could be cut by requiring the army to use $7 million of old-style uniforms that had not been issued after the new uniforms had been adopted in 1872. The House convulsed with laughter as Wheeler promised that warlike Kiowa and Modoc chiefs would "pardon our troops" if they did not wear the new uniforms in battle.[41] The House and Senate passed the army appropriations bill and Wheeler's reputation as a congressman who knew how to save the taxpayers' money soared.[42]

Exhausted and needing relief from the intense pressure he was working under, Wheeler and his wife took a short break from the Washington scene toward the end of the session. They went back up to Malone where Bill and members of the Saranac Navigation Company promptly went fishing for a week in the Adirondacks where they had "excellent success."[43] Rejuvenated, Bill returned to Congress for the final weeks of the session, during which he pushed bill after bill from his Commerce Committee through the House without discussion.[44]

Pleased with his overall legislative performance, Wheeler returned home to the North Country to ready himself to run for an unprecedented fourth straight term. The GOP nominating convention for the Nineteenth Congressional District was scheduled to be held on September 21 at the Whitney House in Potsdam Junction. The GOP state convention to nominate a governor would be held two days later in Utica.[45] Given Wheeler's popularity and name-recognition in St. Lawrence and Franklin Counties, together with the strength of his political organization in both counties, there was no organized opposition to his renomination.

Wheeler's reputation throughout the North Country had been further enhanced by press reports touting him for the U.S. Senate. Earlier in the year, some newspapers mentioned him as a potential successor to Reuben Fenton when his term expired. Other stories suggested Wheeler be named to take Conkling's place in the U.S. Senate should Grant appoint him to the U.S. Supreme Court.[46]

At the congressional district convention, Wheeler was unanimously renominated. At their congressional district convention, the Democrats nominated a lawyer from Canton in St. Lawrence County, William H. Sawyer, to oppose Wheeler.[47]

On the state level, the Republicans renominated Dix for governor. The Democrats chose Samuel J. Tilden to run against Dix. Tilden had been Democratic state chairman since 1866 and had managed Horatio Seymour's unsuccessful presidential campaign against Grant in 1868. Tilden's work battling the Tweed Ring in New York City and helping bring down William M. "Boss" Tweed made him a highly popular statewide figure.[48]

Wheeler's campaign tied the Democrats to the Ku Klux Klan. His Republican team told voters that the election of Democrats would "fire every Ku Klux heart with new passion." The Wheeler Republicans also borrowed words from civil service reformer and editor, George W. Curtis, to describe the Democrats as "very much the same persons who upheld slavery, opposed the war, opposed emancipation, and opposed civil and political equality as the basis of Reconstruction."[49]

Sawyer and the Democrats had more than enough ammunition to fire back at Wheeler and the Republicans. The Democrats were able to place blame on the Republicans for the Panic of 1873, the Salary Grab, and the corruption uncovered by the Credit Mobilier investigation.

On November 3, the voters had their chance to speak. Almost 69 percent of them voted to reelect Wheeler to the Forty-fourth Congress by giving him 12,323 votes to Sawyer's 5,553. No one representing Franklin and St. Lawrence

Counties had ever been elected to so many consecutive terms to Congress before. Bill Wheeler was humbled and thrilled by the results.[50] According to the press, Bill's victory proved that "the age is not all venal, for we have this proof that truth, honesty, integrity, and Christian patriotism have a high value in the minds of the people."[51]

However, beyond the borders of his congressional district, Bill was appalled by what he saw. The Democrats had won control of the House for the first time since the Thirty-fifth Congress opened in 1857. Tilden had swamped Dix by more than fifty thousand votes and the Democrats had carried the assembly by such a margin that they would be able to elect the next U.S. Senator from New York when Fenton's term expired.[52]

Privately, in the warmth of his parlor on Elm Street in Malone, Wheeler relished his own victory to a fourth straight term but he was not looking forward to serving as a member of the minority party in the Forty-fourth Congress. However, it would not open until December 6, 1875, more than a year away.[53] Until then, Bill had to prepare for the second session of the Forty-third Congress, which would open on December 7, 1874. He had no way of knowing that in the first six months of the coming year he would be successfully defusing a racial civil war in Louisiana or that his work in Louisiana would catapult him to the front of the national GOP stage where a president and vice president would be nominated in 1876.

18

An "Earnest Champion of the Right"

☆

News of intermittent racial civil warfare in Louisiana rocked Wheeler as he sat at his desk on the floor of the House listening to President Grant's annual message on opening day of the second session of the Forty-third Congress on December 7, 1874. Politically, Louisiana was equally divided into two opposing camps based on race. On one side were about 87,000 newly enfranchised black voters together with a handful of out-of-state whites who had moved into the state at the end of the Civil War. They constituted the state Republican Party. On the other side were about 87,000 white voters who made up the state Democratic Party. In his message, Grant stated that he had received reports that during the recent November state election, gangs of whites had terrorized blacks to prevent them from voting for Republican candidates. According to Grant's sources, blacks had been assaulted, shot, and murdered. The president asked Congress to investigate. In response, Speaker Blaine appointed Wheeler and six other congressmen to a Select Committee on Southern Affairs to delve into the charges. Bill's friend from Worcester, Massachusetts, George F. Hoar, was named committee chairman.[1]

Boiling racial animosity and rampant political corruption were at the root of the unrest in Louisiana but the immediate causes of the violence stemmed from a disputed election for governor two years previously in which Republican William Pitt Kellogg, a former U.S. Senator, was declared the winner despite the claims of

Democrat John McEnery that he had won the election by ten thousand votes. One of Kellogg's most influential supporters, James F. Casey, was Collector of the Port of New Orleans and President Grant's brother-in-law.[2]

Refusing to accept defeat, McEnery organized a private army and attacked the police stations in New Orleans in an unsuccessful attempt to win control of the city and foment civil unrest. His followers in many white, rural parishes refused to pay their taxes or follow state laws. Meanwhile, racial tension throughout the state heightened as Kellogg began enforcing new state civil rights laws concerning public accommodations and schools. On top of all this turmoil, the depression that swept the nation in 1873 added to Louisiana's woes. Unemployment skyrocketed, businesses failed, and people were unable to pay their taxes. As news of the crisis in Louisiana filtered North, Liberal Republicans and Democrats blamed Grant and the carpetbagger state government for all the bad news.[3]

In 1874, the emergence of the White League made the bad news in Louisiana even worse. Organized by white supremacists, the White League promised to restore white rule by any and all means possible including assassinating GOP government officials, terrorizing black workers, and shutting down the court system. Some Democrats hailed an upcoming "war of the races" and sounded the battle cry, "the niggers shall not rule over us." Words soon turned into action. In one parish, six local Republican officeholders were murdered. In New Orleans, the White League attempted a coup d'état to place McEnery in the governor's chair. After a battle with the city police and armed black citizens, 3,500 White Leaguers took control of city hall, the statehouse, and the arsenal. Governor Kellogg ran for safety to the custom house where federal troops protected him under orders from Grant in Washington. Outgunned, the White Leaguers retreated.[4]

The war for Louisiana moved to the ballot box in 1874. Emboldened by the popular support the White League had received in many areas of the state, Democrats campaigned with gusto. When the polls closed, they thought they had won enough seats to control the House of Representatives, 58 to 48. The GOP election return board thought otherwise. Citing violence and intimidation, the board took five seats away from the Democrats and gave them to Republicans, which created a 53 to 53 tie in the House and generated more heated hostility.[5]

It was against this backdrop of chaos and conflict that Wheeler and six other congressmen were appointed to the Select Committee on Southern Affairs and charged with investigating allegations of wrongdoing in Louisiana. On December 22, 1874, the full committee sent a three-man subcommittee to New Orleans to investigate and report back. Inexplicitly, all three members of the subcommittee were anti-Grant congressmen. New York Democrat Clarkson Potter was named subcommittee chairman. The other two subcommittee members were anti-Grant Liberal Republicans.[6]

While the Potter subcommittee interviewed witnesses in New Orleans, Louisiana Democrats tried to gain control of the House of Representatives by seating the five Democratic candidates that had been ousted by the GOP election return board. Responding to Republican pleas for help and acting under orders from Grant to keep the peace and maintain Kellogg in power, General Philip Sheridan ordered federal troops to physically remove the five Democrats from the House chamber. The next day, Sheridan wired Washington suggesting that the leaders of the White League be put on trial in military courts as "banditti." Opponents of Reconstruction howled that Sheridan's use of military force was proof of what could happen to democracy in the United States if the federal government continued to interfere in "local affairs." Many Americans were shocked to learn that federal troops had used bayonets to remove state legislators from their desks. In Boston, a mass meeting at Faneuil Hall heartily applauded the White Leaguers for fighting to preserve the republican form of government, as the founding fathers had done, and called on Grant to recall Sheridan to Washington.[7]

A week after Sheridan's "banditti" remark, the Potter subcommittee turned up the political heat on the Grant administration even higher. In its report to Congress, the subcommittee concluded that the 1874 election in Louisiana was free and fair, there was no evidence of terrorism by the White League, and the GOP election return board had unjustly and illegally deprived the Democrats of their rightful control of the House of Representatives. Washington Democratic leaders waved the Potter report as proof that Grant had been wrong to use troops to keep Kellogg and his allies in power and that the GOP carpetbaggers were the ones responsible for civil unrest in Louisiana. Liberal Republicans piled on and renewed their attacks on the Grant administration. Regular Republicans nervously saw the chaos in Louisiana as a serious threat to their prospects for winning the presidency in 1876. They turned to Wheeler and the remaining members of the Select Committee who had not participated in the writing of the Potter report, and implored them to go to New Orleans, undo the harm that had been done, and somehow bring an end to the chaos in Louisiana.[8]

Regular Republican leaders in Washington knew that when the Select Committee arrived in New Orleans, the success or failure of its mission would rest on the shoulders of the congressman from Malone because he had a congressional history of being able to reach compromises with Governor Kellogg. During the Forty-first Congress when Wheeler was chairman of the House Pacific Railroad Committee, Kellogg was a U.S. Senator and chairman of the Senate Pacific

Railroad Committee.[9] When their respective houses passed different versions of the same railroad legislation, Wheeler and Kellogg were designated to negotiate away the differences. The two men liked and respected each other and both valued the art of compromise. Before Wheeler and the committee left for Louisiana, he analyzed what he had to do in order to bring an end to the chaos and turmoil in Louisiana. His challenge was to convince both factions to agree to give something up. As Wheeler saw it, the possibility for a compromise lay in the willingness of Kellogg and the Republicans to give up control of the state House of Representatives, and the amenability of McEnery and the Democrats to give up claims to the governor's office and control of the state Senate.

Wheeler took the outline of his potential compromise to President Grant for his approval before presenting it to the warring parties in New Orleans. Grant listened to Bill, and perhaps wanting to think some more about the political ramifications of Wheeler's strategy or about its impact on future federal support for the protection of black civil rights, said nothing. Wheeler waited for some comment about his plan but Grant did not express interest or approval. Wheeler was furious and angrily stomped out of the White House vowing never to go back to see Grant again. Bill cooled off after a good night's sleep and in the morning, Grant sent for him. When Bill sat down with the president again, he told Bill that after thinking about Wheeler's plan, he liked it, thought it would work, and promised to lend Wheeler the entire support of his office to make it work. After a mollified and greatly relieved Wheeler left the White House, Grant ordered Sheridan in New Orleans to assign military bodyguards to protect Wheeler wherever he went during the course of his negotiations.[10]

When Wheeler and the committee arrived in New Orleans, they reviewed the testimony of the ninety-five witnesses that the Potter subcommittee had relied on for its findings and interviewed additional public officials to help the committee evaluate the evidence.[11] Simultaneously, at the special request of both factions, Wheeler began individual meetings with Republican and Democratic leaders.[12]

Bill proposed that the Kellogg and McEnery forces agree to allow Wheeler's congressional committee to act unofficially as an arbitration board with power to make decisions about the 1874 election results. As he explained how this would work, he let it be known to both sides that it appeared to him that the committee would award the GOP control of the Senate and the Democrats control of the House. Democrats liked what they had heard. It proved that they had been right to stand up for their rights in the House, and that Sheridan and the Republicans had been wrong to use military force against them. Because of this, Republicans balked at accepting Wheeler's proposal until Bill explained to them that in order for the Democrats to be granted control of the House, they would have to agree to

William Pitt Kellogg. Brady-Handy Collection, Library of Congress.

recognize Kellogg as governor and not use their power in the House to impeach him or remove him from office. This would mean that the Republicans would be entitled to remain in power until the end of their terms, unchallenged. Suddenly, the Republicans began to show more interest in Wheeler's plan and it was the Democrats who began to squirm and feel uneasy. To sweeten his proposed compromise, Wheeler told both factions that they could expect the committee's report to blame the unrest on both the Republicans and the Democrats because Bill would, in all likelihood, be asked to write it. As the discussions wore on, Wheeler saw leaders from both factions begin to nod their heads in agreement.[13]

Kellogg's Republicans immediately accepted Wheeler's compromise but the Democrats were divided. At first, the Democrats voted to accept it but then the White League got wind of it. They denounced the proposed compromise for recognizing Kellogg's "infamous usurpation" and condoning his "crimes." In the name of "the white people of Louisiana," "the fair minded people of the country," and "all we hold dear," the White League called for a mass meeting to demand that the Democrats repudiate their vote to accept Wheeler's compromise. The Leaguers declared that it put their "reputation and honor" at stake. Seven thousand people came to the meeting and fiery speeches rang out in the night excoriating Wheeler's compromise. After the meeting, the Democrats met again and voted to reconsider their vote to accept. They sent representatives to make counterproposals to Wheeler but they were rejected. Several days passed and Democrats began to have second doubts about having bowed to White League pressure. They approached Wheeler and asked him if it was too late to accept his original compromise offer. Wheeler stonewalled them and refused to answer right away, explaining that he and the committee were about leave New Orleans and return to Washington. The Democrats promptly organized their own committee to follow Wheeler to Washington, hoping to get better terms there.[14]

On the way back to Washington, Wheeler wrote a revised report about what the committee had learned from their investigation.[15] To undo the political harm that had been done to the Republican Party, Wheeler's report denounced the major finding of the Potter report and asserted, "the election of 1874 was neither full, free nor fair." Relying on "the indisputable facts of history" and using grisly details, Wheeler put the 1874 violence and unrest in historical perspective. He reminded the nation that there were "six bloody and terrible massacres" of blacks in the state during the 1868 presidential election campaign and, in the previous six years, two thousand blacks had been murdered for political reasons. All the murderers were still at large.[16]

Wheeler recounted how the 1874 campaign had begun with the Democratic party organizing itself into the "White Man's Party," which kicked off its campaign by circulating handbills signed by hundreds of planters calling for employers to discharge blacks who would not vote the "white man's ticket." The handbills read, "To save your country, do not employ the negro. Wild beasts can only be tamed by hunger." The distribution of handbills was followed by a statewide campaign of "lawless violence" to terrorize blacks. To prove his finding that the 1874 election was neither free nor fair, Wheeler used the testimony of prominent black preachers, legislators, judges, and businessmen who had been driven from their homes and the polls, fearing for their lives.

To lay the groundwork for negotiating an end to the ongoing chaos and violence in Louisiana, Bill's report then took a surprising turn. Wheeler wrote that even though the Potter report was completely wrong about whether the 1874 election was free and fair, it was correct about who should have been declared the winners in the election!

Using words that would come back to haunt him when the 1876 presidential and vice-presidential election returns in Louisiana were challenged by the national Republican party, Wheeler asserted that, on its own, the state election return board had no legal authority to go behind the returns and decide which ones were valid and which were not. According to Wheeler, the only legal power the board had was to compile the results that had been reported from the officials in the local election districts. It had no legal right to throw out votes from polling places where the board found violence and intimidation to exist. For this reason, Wheeler declared that the election return board's decision to deny five Democrats their seats in the state House of Representatives because of intimidation and violence at the polls was legally wrong.

The report's two major conclusions were carefully drafted by Wheeler to aid him in his negotiations to bring peace to Louisiana. First, to please the Republicans, Wheeler wrote that Congress and the Louisiana state legislature should recognize Kellogg as the lawful governor. Second, to please the Democrats, Wheeler wrote that the Louisiana House of Representatives should seat the Democrats whose election victories had been wrongly overturned by the GOP state election return board.[17]

Wheeler's report was a seminal document for the Republican Party. Bill's statesmanlike commentary provided a political road map for the party to follow in the upcoming 1876 federal election campaign. The report contained guidance to the party about how to answer thorny questions about the future of the South and Reconstruction.

Wheeler told his party that white racism in the South was despicable and white Democrats who were promising to grant Southern blacks their constitutional rights were hypocrites because they had no "understanding of what justice and equality really meant" for blacks. Wheeler explained what he meant by giving examples of white hypocrisy. Whites who kill blacks go unpunished, but blacks who "snap a cap" at whites are given "fearful vengeance." Whites who bodily throw Republican officials out of their offices are not punished, but blacks who defend public officers are massacred. Whites who band together to agree not to hire blacks who vote Republican are not censured, but those who try to organize blacks to refuse to work for Democratic planters are murdered.

Despite all the rampant racism and hypocrisy, Wheeler told his party that white Southern anger and frustration were understandable. In Louisiana, for example, the 90 percent illiteracy rate of black Republican voters enabled GOP officials to manipulate their electorate into supporting "great maladministration," wasteful spending, and heavy taxation. However, Wheeler wrote, "the ballot, not violence or assassination" should be the remedy for these "evils." If "the mob or the assassin" attempted to settle questions of law by bloodshed, the president and Congress have a constitutional duty to support the true government against all usurpers. Wheeler was adamant that "every power lodged in Congress or the President must be exercised if needed to secure national elections against violence."

Wheeler's next point drew support from Liberal Republicans and others who had become weary of Reconstruction and the never-ending federal intervention in the South. Wheeler argued, "You cannot change great currents of public sentiment, or habits of thought and feeling of great bodies of men by Act of Congress." He added that there would be no prosperity or peace in the South until "the great body of white people . . . learn to obey the law, to submit to the Constitution, to respect labor," and "base their institutions in liberty, equality and justice."

Independent-minded voters and Southern moderates were pleased by what Wheeler wrote next. He said that Northern politicians of both parties must share responsibility for the chaos and turmoil in the South. According to Wheeler, "the Southern problem" would have disappeared long ago if the Democratic Party of the North had refused to associate with "men who would commit, tolerate, extenuate or overlook murder" and if the Republican Party of the North had refused to affiliate with "men who would plunder the public for personal gain."

The last major point in Wheeler's report was the most farsighted. It was years ahead of his time and reflected one of his core beliefs that he personally acted on until his dying days. To Wheeler's way of thinking, Southern racism, violence, and corruption were only symptoms of the real disease, which was ignorance. For Bill, the cure for ignorance was public education. If the nation wished to cure the disease of ignorance in the South and prevent its evil symptoms from spreading, Wheeler recommended that the federal government should provide "efficient aid to the state to establish public education."[18]

In addition to a political road map Republicans could use in the 1876 campaign, Wheeler's report also contained a prophetic observation about how the civil unrest in Louisiana could affect the 1876 presidential election results. He accurately predicted that if the election were tainted by violence and fraud, both sides would claim victory and "the real expression of the will of the people" in the 1876 election would be "in doubt."[19]

Wheeler and the congressional committee arrived in Washington from New Orleans during the waning days of February 1875. The Louisiana Republicans had agreed to the terms of the Wheeler Compromise but the Democrats had not. The *Albany Journal* reported, "The country is approaching a very grave crisis." The contingent of Louisiana Democrats who had followed Wheeler north to Washington seeking modification of the proposed compromise arrived in the nation's capital hard on his heels. In a meeting with Wheeler, they argued that they could never in good conscience recognize the "great criminal" Kellogg as governor. Wheeler retorted that if they did not recognize Kellogg, they, and they alone, would be responsible for failing to bring peace to Louisiana. Dissatisfied, the Democrats attempted an end run around Wheeler and went to see Grant in the White House. Grant refused to negotiate with them and sent them back to Wheeler. Meanwhile, Wheeler's report was printed for national distribution and released to the press.[20]

The Louisiana Democrats in Washington buckled under the mounting pressure. They voted to accept the compromise and telegraphed their decision to their fellow Democrats back home in Louisiana. They also agreed to accept the Wheeler Compromise by a vote of 34 to 33 and sent a letter of acceptance to Wheeler in Washington. To firm up the agreement and keep the pressure on, Wheeler's colleagues in the House voted 163 to 89 to recognize Kellogg as governor of Louisiana and to recommend that the Louisiana House seat the rightfully elected winners of the state election. It was understood that Wheeler and his congressional committee would do the choosing of the "rightfully-elected winners."[21]

The press sang Wheeler's praises. *Harper's Weekly* said he was "one of the ablest, most experienced and purest men in public life" and the *New York Commercial Advertiser* described him as "the soul of truth and honor."[22] As soon as the forty-four leaders of the Democratic Party in Louisiana individually signed their names to the terms of the Wheeler Compromise and sent the document to Bill, he arranged to have Governor Kellogg ship the contested election materials to the business office of congressional committee member William W. Phelps in New York City. At 10 a.m. on March 15, Wheeler and the committee examined the contested returns and awarded the Democrats 12 seats in the state House of Representatives, which gave them control of the body, 63 to 47. The Republican control of the state Senate was undisturbed. When all seven members of the congressional committee signed the award and sent it to Kellogg, another wave of accolades swept over Wheeler. The *Albany Journal* lauded his "clear-headed wisdom" and the *Rochester Democrat and Chronicle* thanked him for "patriotic and self-sacrificing exertions in behalf of peace."[23]

Even though all the negotiating was over and the opposing factions had agreed to abide by the Wheeler Compromise, the Louisiana Republicans and Democrats in the state legislature had not actually voted to do so yet! Kellogg had called a special session of the legislature for that purpose and the congressman from Malone left for New Orleans on April 7 to personally oversee the voting and make sure no one got cold feet at the last minute.[24]

This was Wheeler's defining moment as a national political figure. If anyone had any doubts about who was responsible for bringing peace to Louisiana, they were dispelled. Bill stepped forward in New Orleans, all alone, to ensure that his compromise was carried out—the congressional committee did not go with him. The eyes of the nation were riveted on him when the Louisiana legislature convened on April 14. By a vote of 89 to 15, the House granted the contested seats to the Democrats, and then by another vote of 89 to 18, the House adopted a resolution recognizing Kellogg as governor and pledging not to impeach him for prior acts. When the state Senate confirmed the House action on April 17, the Wheeler Compromise was legally executed and Bill heaved a huge sigh of relief.[25]

From all corners of the nation, Democrats, Republicans, and Liberal Republicans applauded Wheeler for his accomplishment. The anti-Grant *Nation* praised him and the Republican press hailed him as an "earnest champion of the right" and a "sagacious statesman." The *New York Times* saluted Wheeler for his "remarkable tact and candor" and added that the adoption of the compromise was a sign that peace was finally coming to the South for all classes and races. The *North Louisiana Journal* gushed, "Honor and thanks to William A. Wheeler" for his compromise "by which we were led from our wanderings in the 'wilderness' to the verge of the promised land, and if we fail to achieve a successful future, it will be our own fault."[26]

Wheeler reveled in the national spotlight. It may have been at this time, in the late spring of 1875, that he first dared to seriously think about running for president in 1876. Bill seized the moment and wrote his first presidential opinion piece for the *New York Times*. In the form of a letter ostensibly about the Wheeler Compromise, Bill described his vision for the future of the South and Reconstruction. He proudly stated, "Riot, tumult and anarchy have given way to a government whose scepter is not the bayonet, but the voluntary adherence and support of the people." Wheeler went on to warn that peace in Louisiana may merely be "a lull in the storm" and that Northerners would be deluding themselves if they thought the South was about to transform itself "into model Northern communities." He said that kind of change would only come after "a long course of patient waiting" and "a good deal of unavoidable friction which will call for forbearance." Wheeler's formula to "diminish the friction" in the South called for creating "some system to aid in the education of the masses." Wheeler's formula also entailed guaranteeing the Southern people "equal and exact justice" while at the same time, holding them accountable "by every necessary means," for guaranteeing "manhood and citizenship" to "all within their borders."[27]

As soon as he returned to Malone from New York City, Bill took a break from government and politics by going on several vacations with his wife, Mary. In late May and June, they went south into the Adirondacks where they stayed at Martin's Hotel, a famous resort on Lower Saranac Lake. In early August and again in early September, Bill and Mary vacationed in the White Mountains.[28]

Rested and refreshed, the Wheelers returned to Washington for the opening of the first session of the Forty-fourth Congress on December 6. This promised to be a politically awkward and uncomfortable session for Bill because, for the first time since 1857, the Democrats controlled the House. Democrat Michael C. Kerr was elected Speaker in place of Blaine and named Wheeler to the Appropriations Committee. Because of Bill's interest in education and experience dealing with the army's budget, he was also appointed to the Board of Visitors of the U.S. Military Academy at West Point and to the board of trustees of the Institute for the Deaf and Dumb in the District of Columbia.[29]

From his position on the Appropriations Committee, Wheeler managed the passage of a bill that slashed $219,000 out of the army's budget for military fortifications. However, beyond that, Bill's legislative activity during the session was low key. There was a reason for this. With the presidential nominating conventions looming in the summer and the presidential elections in the fall, the House was reluctant to consider any major legislation.[30] This allowed Wheeler time to explore the feasibility of running for the Republican nomination for president at the upcoming national party convention in June.

19

The "New York Lincoln"

☆

The GOP national convention was scheduled to open in Cincinnati on June 14, 1876, the nation's centennial year. Ever the political realist, the fifty-six-year-old congressman from Malone knew that winning the presidential nomination would be a long shot. If he decided to run, Bill would not be considered a major candidate. He would be running as a compromise candidate—someone the convention might turn to in order to break a deadlock among the major candidates.

There were distinct political advantages to running for president, even if he lost. His bid could enhance his chances to win the nomination for other higher offices such as vice president, governor, or U.S. senator. The balloting for vice president would come directly after the voting for president. The state Republicans would nominate a governor about two months after the national convention adjourned. The state legislature would elect a man to the U.S. Senate a few months before Democrat Francis Kernan's term expired in March 1881. By running for president, Wheeler had everything to gain politically and nothing to lose—in fact, he had a safety net. Because of his popularity and the strength of his political organization, renomination to a fifth straight term in Congress would be his for the asking.

In Malone with his close political friends, Wheeler evaluated the reasons why national convention delegates might decide to vote for him. Bill had name recognition with men in almost every state delegation because of his ten years in

Congress. Fellow GOP congressmen and other Washington insiders from across the country knew Bill and respected his abilities. In Wheeler, they saw an intelligent man who paid attention to details and was a man of his word. Because of his recent work to bring peace to Louisiana, Bill had special appeal to both black and white Republicans in the South. He had a reputation for fairness. Wheeler had condemned white racism and given vigorous support to the Republican carpetbagger administration in Louisiana. He was adamant that blacks should be guaranteed their recently won constitutional rights. Democratic Congressman Lucius Q. C. Lamar of Mississippi felt Wheeler was so popular in the South, he predicted that Bill would carry Louisiana, Mississippi, Alabama, and North Carolina if he ran for president.[1]

Wheeler also was an attractive candidate to reformers and Liberal Republicans. He detested political corruption and had great personal integrity. Bill had not been tainted by any railroad scandals despite working as chairman of the House Pacific Railroad Committee for many years. The story about how he ran a crooked railroad lobbyist out of Washington was well known. Adding luster to his image as an honest politician was that Wheeler was one of the first congressmen to refuse his portion of the Salary Grab pay increase and return the money to the U.S. Treasury. Reformers and Liberal Republicans also liked Bill because of his conviction that there were limits to what Congress could do to reconstruct the South. They, like many average Americans, were getting weary of Reconstruction and constant federal intervention in the South.

Bill's strongest suit for delegate support lay in the fact that he came from the Empire State. It was expected that the Democrats would nominate New York Governor Samuel Tilden for president and Bill's supporters argued that Wheeler's presence at the top of the ticket would greatly help the Republicans capture New York's thirty-five electoral votes. Newspapers were talking about Wheeler as the "New York Lincoln."[2] They were also describing Wheeler's congressional district as the "Banner Republican District of the U.S." because of the large Republican majorities he had rolled up.[3]

Wheeler and his close associates also analyzed the reasons why Bill would have difficulty garnering delegate support. In the first place, he was not as wealthy as the other candidates and did not have the backing of any national factions—he was not a Blaine man or a Conkling man. Furthermore, Bill did not command the loyalty of a majority of the delegates from his own state as the other candidates did theirs. Another problem for Bill was that, compared to the other candidates, he did not come from an urban center that provided easy access to the national media. Wheeler's base of operations was in a relatively isolated, rural part of New York, near the Canadian border. Bill's reluctance to promote himself by writing and publicizing his positions also held him back in the eyes of many delegates who were more familiar with the views of other candidates. Another negative for Wheeler was that he had never won election to statewide office as had many of the other candidates. Last, Bill knew he would have problems winning the support of some delegates because he was not a politically glamorous candidate—he did not have a reputation as a great public speaker and he did not wear the latest fashions.

As Bill examined the pluses and minuses of his candidacy, he concluded that his strengths outweighed his weaknesses. After he analyzed the attributes of the four major candidates running for the GOP presidential nomination, he could see why the convention might deadlock on a choice, and if it did, he believed that he had as good a chance to win the nomination for president as any of the other compromise candidates.

Of the four major candidates, the clear front-runner was the Speaker of the House, James G. Blaine of Maine.[4] He was the leading candidate of the non-Grant Republicans. A popular congressman, he was an excellent speaker and because of his charisma, the press referred to him as *the magnetic man*. Blaine's major hurdle to winning the nomination was the ugly rumor that as Speaker he had been the beneficiary of corrupt financial transactions involving the railroads. He dismissed the rumors as lies but they kept resurfacing to tarnish his reputation and give hope to his opponents, especially New York's senior U.S. Senator Roscoe Conkling, the second major candidate.

Some observers said Conkling had become a candidate for president merely to deny Blaine the nomination. Their longtime political rivalry for leadership of the Republican Party had degenerated into a mutual vilification society—they hated each other! Conkling had the support of Grant Republicans and was one of the nation's premier political speakers. He had a national following. The Republicans needed to win New York to win the 1876 election and many political leaders felt Conkling's popularity in the Empire State as a two-term senator would be the key to such a victory. Others were not so sure. They yearned to bring an end to widespread political corruption in Washington by instituting civil service reform and abolishing the spoils system. Conkling controlled the nation's largest single source of federal patronage, the New York Custom House. He was certain that his continued control of the state GOP was dependent on continued control of New York's federal patronage. Consequently, civil service reform was anathema to Conkling. He once said, "When Dr. Johnson called patriotism the last refuge of a scoundrel, he forgot the possibilities contained in the word 'reform.'"[5] Another weakness in Conkling's candidacy was that he would have to share the pro-Grant delegates with the third major candidate, Oliver P. Morton, the former governor of Indiana and one of that state's current U.S. senators.[6]

Indiana was another key state the GOP had to win in order to win the election in November and many Republican leaders felt with Morton at the head of the ticket, the GOP would carry the Hoosier State. He had a reputation for honesty, which was a positive for his candidacy. However, he had several negatives with some delegates. Moderates did not like his radical positions on Reconstruction and anti-Grant reformers did not trust Morton because of his strong ties to the Grant administration. Having to share Grant Republican delegates with Conkling also hurt the Indiana senator's chances to win the nomination. One of Morton's biggest liabilities as a candidate was his health. He had suffered a paralytic stroke in 1865 and had never completely recovered from it.[7]

Benjamin H. Bristow of Kentucky was the fourth major candidate for the presidential nomination. As Grant's Secretary of the Treasury, he had prosecuted the Whiskey Ring and was the favorite of the reform wing of the GOP. Calling for honesty in government, he was hated by Grant Republicans and machine politicians. As honest and intelligent as he was, he did not have widespread support because he did not have a charismatic personality.[8]

Wheeler's plan to win the presidential nomination hinged on a convention deadlock. If the delegates were unable to deliver a majority vote to one of the major candidates, Bill counted on winning the nomination as a compromise candidate. In addition to Wheeler, there were three other men the convention might compromise on. One was Marshall Jewell, the former governor of Connecticut, who was Grant's postmaster general. He was expected to drop out of the balloting early and posed only a minor threat to Wheeler's chances to win. The second potential compromise candidate was John F. Hartranft, governor of Pennsylvania. He commanded that state's fifty-eight-man delegation and was expected to remain in the balloting as a candidate longer than Jewell. However, his biggest drawback as a possible compromise nominee was the fact that because Pennsylvania was so heavily Republican, he was not needed as a candidate to carry the Keystone State in the upcoming election.[9] The third possible compromise candidate, Governor Rutherford B. Hayes of Ohio, posed the most serious threat to Wheeler's hopes.

Hayes had won statewide election to be governor in Ohio three times and it was essential to carry Ohio if the GOP hoped to win the election. Because he had been governor, he had extensive executive experience and had demonstrated sound administrative ability and skills. Hayes had the united support of the entire forty-four-man delegation from Ohio. In addition, he had Civil War experience having risen to the rank of general and had been wounded in battle. On top of that, because the convention would be held in Cincinnati, it was expected that the city would be swarming with thousands of his supporters, giving delegates the impression that Hayes had more support than he actually had. The convention's location

Rutherford B. Hayes. Brady-Handy Collection, Library of Congress.

also meant that Hayes would be able to keep in close personal contact with the political situation from the executive mansion in Columbus. Last, Hayes had an experienced team of campaign managers led by the ex-governor of Ohio, Edwin F. Noyes, and U.S. Senator John Sherman. They had an excellent relationship with the national press corps and it was rumored that they would not hesitate to offer cabinet posts and possible U.S. Supreme Court nominations to Blaine's opponents to win delegate support.[10]

As compromise candidates, Wheeler and Hayes shared many strengths. The major candidates objected less to them than they did to each other. Both men were known as conciliators and were attractive alternatives to the hard-to-please, reform-minded Bristow delegates. Wheeler and Hayes both had long honest careers in government and were men of integrity. Both men had campaigned for Grant in 1868 and 1872 but neither man was known as a hard-line, dyed-in-the-wool pro-Grant supporter, nor had they turned into rabid anti-Grant partisans in 1876.[11]

In the eyes of some delegates, however, there were several things about Wheeler that made him more attractive to vote for than Hayes. Wheeler had greater name recognition by congressmen and Washington insiders from across the country. Many of them were delegates. His role in getting the Wheeler Compromise adopted in Louisiana and preventing a racial civil war in that state was well known by knowledgeable political figures in Cincinnati. In addition, Wheeler had more recent Washington experience than Hayes. During the last eight years, Bill had been in Washington as a congressman dealing with the nation's major issues. He was a man who knew what the contemporary nuts and bolts of Washington power politics were and how they worked. Wheeler was a practical political figure from the national scene, not an "insular" western governor with limited recent experience dealing with national affairs.[12] Wheeler's intelligence was respected by the men he worked with, whereas some newspapers reported that Hayes's enemies "thought him slow." In Boston, Henry Adams would describe Hayes as a "third rate non-entity."[13]

Once Wheeler made the decision to run as a compromise candidate for president, he assembled a three-man campaign team. From the North Country, he chose Wells S. Dickinson of Bangor in Franklin County and Henry R. James of Ogdensburg in St. Lawrence County. The owner of eight potato starch mills, Dickinson was Wheeler's chief political lieutenant.[14] James was editor and publisher of the *Ogdensburg Journal* and Wheeler's longtime friend and supporter.[15] The third member of the team was Massachusetts Congressman George F. Hoar of Worcester. Having worked with Wheeler in the House for the last eight years, Hoar had great respect for Wheeler's ability, intelligence, and moral character. Hoar agreed

George Frisbie Hoar. Brady-Handy Collection, Library of Congress.

to work on winning support for Wheeler from the nation's reformers and anti-Conkling Republicans. One of Hoar's strongest arguments to reformers was that Wheeler would make a more popular candidate for president than Bristow because of Wheeler's warm personality.[16]

Wheeler also cast his net into the political waters of two other neighboring states. In Vermont, he won support from former U.S. Senator and four-term Congressman Luke P. Poland, also a reformer and an opponent of Conkling. In

Pennsylvania, key political leaders were enthusiastic about Wheeler's candidacy and offered to help him after the early ballots at the convention.[17]

Next, Wheeler mounted a nationwide publicity campaign. It trumpeted the news that even though Wheeler was not seeking the presidency, he would make an excellent choice for the office![18] The publicity campaign's dual message illustrated a peculiar characteristic of nineteenth-century political behavior. In Wheeler's day, it was considered unseemly for a candidate to solicit votes—in fact, political self-seeking was thought to be discreditable and corrupting of character.[19] Wheeler's hometown paper touted Wheeler's candidacy on a regular basis but it also assured its readers that Wheeler "has never in any way entered the [presidential] contest, and the mention of his name has always been without his consent." The paper vowed, "If nominated, the office will seek the man and not the man the office."[20]

The publicity campaign generated immediate results. The early stories in the press about Wheeler's candidacy were encouraging to him. New York newspapers glowed with praise. The *Albany Express* said Bill would make an "admirable compromise candidate" for president. The *New York Tribune* reported that talk preferring Wheeler to other men for president was "becoming rife at Washington." The *Utica Herald* in Conkling's hometown declared that Wheeler was "the coming man" for president and that in the South, "he is there believed to be the most popular Republican."[21]

Newspapers in other states also began writing favorably about the congressman from Malone. In New Hampshire, the *Concord Monitor* stated that a Republican ticket with Wheeler on it would make a "strong team." In Iowa, the *Hamilton Freeman* described Wheeler as "a wise, pure and truly great statesman" and that his "character, record and fitness are absolutely unassailable." The *Iowa Commercial* in Dubuque said a ticket with Wheeler for president and Hayes for vice president would be "a tower of strength." The paper praised Wheeler because his "private and public record is without blemish," and he "has great ability and large experience, yet has no bitter personal enemies, and is obnoxious to no party."[22] The *Boston Record* said it liked Wheeler's chances to win the presidential nomination because "he is the one man who hasn't an enemy or rival in the Republican Party" and because he had won a "national reputation by his skill in arranging the Louisiana compromise."[23]

Just as the Wheeler for President boom was beginning to heat up in the newspapers across the country, Wheeler was dealt a devastating blow. His wife, Mary, died unexpectedly on March 3, 1876. She had been suffering from a cold and a slight fever for about a week. Bill thought she was on the road to recovery but one morning as she was getting dressed for the day, she fell to the floor and died within a few hours. The cause of death went unreported.[24] Wheeler was stunned and overwhelmed with grief. His friends said he seemed to lose all interest in the world and shut himself off from his campaign and all other activities.[25] Mary's body lay in state in Wheeler's parlor before Bill took her remains by train to Malone.[26] At their request, both U.S. Senators from New York, Conkling and Kernan, were among Mary's pallbearers.[27] Speaker Blaine's wife, Harriet, and the poet Gail Hamilton (Mary Abigail Dodge), helped Wheeler with Mary's personal effects.[28] In Malone, funeral services were held for her at Wheeler's Congregational Church. Political dignitaries from across the North Country filled the pews.[29]

Mary was only forty-eight years old when she died. She and Bill had been married for more than 30 years.[30] Mary was a popular woman in Washington. She was remembered for her work during the Civil War caring for sick soldiers and her subsequent "life of philanthropy."[31] The press admired her "republican style of dress," which avoided showy ornamentation.[32] Mary and Bill would often sing hymns together while they both worked around their apartment in Washington. Mary had a "rich voice" and Bill had a "deep, clear bass." Their friends described their duets as "an unconscious impression of domestic harmony."[33] Mary shared Bill's deep religious beliefs and when they were in Washington, they regularly attended church and weekly prayer meetings at the New York Avenue Presbyterian Church. In Malone, they were active members of the Congregational Church on Main Street.[34] She was buried in the Wheeler-King family plot in Malone's Morningside Cemetery.

Mary's death threw the Wheeler for President campaign into a tailspin. As Bill mourned the loss of his wife, the New York Republican Party was preparing to elect seventy delegates and alternates to the national convention. A GOP state convention to select the delegates was scheduled to meet in Syracuse on March 22. Bill expected that a solid Conkling delegation would be chosen but he counted on both Dickinson and James to be elected delegates. Wheeler thought he would be able to pry away at least twenty to thirty New York delegate votes from Conkling for himself if a deadlock developed. Conkling had his own plans. He plotted to have the state convention instruct the New York delegation to vote as a seventy-man unit for Conkling for president. However, things did not go smoothly for him. Opposition to sending a pledged delegation sprang up in New York City and in the North Country. In New York City, George W. Curtis organized opposition to adoption of the unit rule and a pledged delegation, and Wheeler and his supporters did the same in the North Country.[35]

Wheeler had originally planned to attend the state convention to work with Curtis against sending a delegation pledged to vote for Conkling but Bill could not summon the will or the physical energy to go—the state convention was being held less than three weeks after Mary had died. Instead, he passed the word to his friends at the state convention that he was against the unit rule and against sending a pledged delegation to Cincinnati. Wheeler's allies joined with Curtis and his supporters to oppose the proposals. In their place, the convention adopted a resolution that merely said, "We present Roscoe Conkling to the National Republican Convention as our choice for President." This was a huge victory for Wheeler and the other anti-Conkling Republicans. The "presentation" of Conkling was not an instruction to vote for Conkling. Delegates would be free to vote as they pleased when the time came.[36] Dickinson and James were elected national convention delegates and Alonzo B. Cornell was elected chairman of the New York delegation.[37]

It would be almost three months before the GOP national convention would open in Cincinnati on June 14 and the drumbeat in the newspapers about Wheeler for President continued. The strongest and most influential voice to encourage Wheeler's candidacy for president was that of the *New York Times.* It praised Wheeler citing his "large experience in public affairs," his "spotless public and private life," and the fact that he had "no enemies to punish and no friends to reward." The *Times* predicted that if the convention deadlocked, it was likely that the delegates would compromise on Wheeler for president if they wanted "an Eastern man" but if "a Western man" was desired, they would probably choose Hayes.[38]

News from Hayes's home state of Ohio gave the morale of the Wheeler for President campaign team a major boost. In a letter to the *Columbus State Journal,* General James M. Comly, one of Hayes's friends and political supporters, admitted that Wheeler made a "formidable candidate for president." Comly stated that Bill had the support of a majority of the GOP congressmen in Washington due to their "personal knowledge" of Wheeler's "undoubted integrity and great ability." Hayes's former comrade in arms continued by writing that because of the respect Blaine and Conkling had for Wheeler, their delegates could find their way to compromise and unite behind him.[39]

Political observers noted that after stalling soon after Mary Wheeler's death, the Wheeler for President campaign had regained momentum. A report from Vermont noted that Wheeler was "attracting much attention" because he was "not a politician but a statesman" who "had been entirely independent of the [Grant] administration."[40] The *Boston Globe* reported that Wheeler's "stock is rising" and the *New York Tribune* observed the "noticeable fact" that Wheeler was "developing strength" in an "increasing number of states." In Connecticut, the *Danbury News* praised Wheeler's "fearless honesty and integrity" by explaining to its readers that Wheeler "don't claw you and rub your left shoulder blade and invite you to ask him for favors he will never bestow."[41]

Encouraging political news was not confined to the pages of eastern newspapers. In Wisconsin, the *State Register* spotlighted Wheeler's role in bringing "order out of chaos" in Louisiana.[42] Several newspapers in Illinois emphasized the attractiveness of Wheeler's religious vigor. The *Chicago Inter-Ocean* described Wheeler as a "tower of moral and political strength" and as a man of "high Christian character."[43] The *Springfield Journal* touted Wheeler for president because he was "one of God's noblemen."[44]

As the month of May wound down, Bill prepared himself for the political drama that was about to unfold in June at the convention in Cincinnati. To clear his head and restore his mind and body, he went fishing in the Adirondacks with his Saranac Navigation Company. The expedition stayed at the Prospect House on the Upper Saranac Lake and fished for four days before returning to Malone.[45]

Refreshed, Bill headed south to Albany where he attended the first meeting of the Board of Commissioners of the State Survey on May 31. He had been appointed by the legislature to the seven-man commission whose task it was to make a trigonometric and topographical survey of the state to determine the state and county lines.[46]

After the commission meeting, Wheeler continued south down the Hudson River to West Point where, on June 8, he attended his first meeting as a member of the Board of Visitors of the U.S. Military Academy at West Point, the body in charge of overseeing the institution's financial and educational affairs.[47] Bill stayed in Garrison, across the river from West Point, at the home of his brother-in-law, Henry W. Belcher, and nervously waited for the political news about the convention to reach him by telegraph from Cincinnati.[48]

20

"God's Hand Is in This Work"

☆

As Wheeler was preparing to attend to his official duties in Albany and West Point, the odds that there would be a deadlocked convention improved considerably. A Hayes supporter had leaked information to the press that once again implicated the GOP frontrunner for the presidential nomination, James G. Blaine, in railroad corruption. Blaine managed to mute the attack with a dramatic speech from the floor of the House nine days before the Cincinnati convention opened, but the assault on his honesty weakened his drive for delegate votes and checked his political momentum.[1] In the midst of Blaine's difficulties, Congressman Charles B. Farwell of Chicago added spice to Wheeler's campaign by predicting a convention deadlock and a Wheeler victory. His prediction gave credence to political rumors that Blaine was about to transfer his strength to Wheeler as a way of paying Bill back for not challenging Blaine for Speaker during the Forty-third Congress.[2]

The Wheeler for President campaign was given another boost in Cincinnati two days before the convention opened on June 14, 1876. At a meeting of the New York delegates at their headquarters in the Grand Hotel, Conkling's supporters made a second attempt to adopt the unit rule and bind all seventy delegates to vote for him. Bill's spokesman in the delegation, Henry R. James, joined with reformer George W. Curtis to beat back the Conkling effort. James's demand for freedom of action was met with approval by a majority of the delegates and unit rule was rejected, once again.[3]

Trainloads of supporters of the major candidates had been pulling into Cincinnati every day during the week running up to June 14. Conkling had some fifteen hundred workers in Cincinnati, each wearing a blue badge bearing Conkling's name and a yellow silk hat. They paraded through the streets with a brass band carrying a huge sign that read, "Roscoe Conkling's Nomination Assures The 35 Electoral Votes Of New York." The Bristow Club of Cincinnati boasted about two thousand to three thousand backers of the Treasury Secretary. His pictures and banners seemed to be everywhere around the city. One of the busiest headquarters was that of Blaine's supporters. Seventeen train carloads of them arrived from western New York on June 13. Morton's supporters had their headquarters, flags, and banners as did those of Ohio Governor Hayes, who monitored the political activity from the governor's residence in Columbus.[4]

Former New York governor and GOP national chairman Edwin D. Morgan opened the sixth national Republican convention at noon on Wednesday, June 14, in Cincinnati's Exposition Hall.[5] He had hopes of his own that the convention would choose him for president or vice president but that did not happen. Instead, he had to wait until August and be satisfied with the GOP nomination for governor which he won at the GOP state convention.[6]

Ominously, from the point of view of Wheeler's supporters, former Ohio Governor Noyes, the leader of the Ohio delegation and Hayes's campaign manager, was selected to give one of the opening day speeches. With a nod toward Hayes's Ohio delegation, Noyes promised the convention that it could count on Ohio in November if the delegates nominated "a man who is honest," a man who knows "what is right and what is wrong," and a man "that is brave enough and strong enough to carry out his convictions."[7]

On Thursday, the candidates for president were nominated. Wheeler and his campaign team adopted an unorthodox strategy. They decided not to put Bill's name in nomination with a formal speech. Instead, they planned to put Wheeler's name in nomination by having a few delegates cast their votes for him, and keep his name in front of the convention delegates by continuing to cast their votes for him, ballot after ballot, until some delegates began to sense that the convention was deadlocked. When that happened, Wheeler's team counted on one or two states to change their votes from the major candidate they had been supporting, and cast their votes for Wheeler, thereby starting a chain reaction among the 756 delegates, which would result in Wheeler winning the necessary 379 votes to win the nomination. To avoid unnecessarily offending Conkling's men in the New York delegation, Massachusetts Congressman Hoar agreed he would arrange for the Wheeler votes to be cast by Massachusetts delegates. Hoar's ally in this plan was fellow Massachusetts delegate James Russell Lowell, poet, essayist and former editor of the *Atlantic Monthly.*[8]

All the other men seeking the presidential nomination, the major candidates and the compromise candidates followed an orthodox strategy and had their names placed in nomination by formal speeches. Stewart L. Woodford, the man who had edged Wheeler out for the nomination for lieutenant governor ten years earlier, nominated Conkling. A Civil War veteran and one of New York's finest orators, Woodford hailed Conkling "as true to the old Republican party as the needle to the pole" and a "faithful and true friend of Ulysses S. Grant."[9] Wheeler's friend and contact in the Vermont delegation, former Congressman and U.S. Senator Luke P. Poland, seconded Bristow's nomination. He reminded delegates that Vermont and Bristow's home state of Kentucky had entered the Union at the same time and that during the days of the "Great Compromiser," Henry Clay, the two states stood side by side.[10]

Robert G. Ingersoll of Illinois, arguably the nation's most famous agnostic, orator, and lecturer, nominated Blaine by giving one of the most celebrated political speeches in U.S. history. Ingersoll described Blaine as "an armed warrior" and a "plumed knight" who marched through the halls of Congress throwing his "shining lance" against "the brazen foreheads of the defamers of his country and the maligners of his honor." By the time he called for the nomination of "that prince of parliamentarians," Exposition Hall was in an uproar. The delegates loved the speech and cheered until their voices became hoarse. If the voting for president had begun that day, Wheeler's hope for a deadlocked convention would have been dashed and Blaine might have won the nomination right then and there. However, the gas lighting in the hall was found to be unsafe and the convention adjourned until Friday. Blaine's supporters were convinced they had been the victims of sabotage by his enemies.[11]

The nominating speeches provided talking points for Wheeler's campaign team to use when courting delegate support that evening. If Blaine was "the prince of parliamentarians," as Ingersoll had stated, delegates could also be told that Wheeler was the crown prince of parliamentarians. If Bristow and the "Great Compromiser," Henry Clay, were to be mentioned in the same breath as Poland had done, delegates could be urged not to forget that Wheeler was the architect of the compromise that brought peace to Louisiana. And if anti-Grant delegates had recoiled in disgust at hearing Woodford nominate Conkling as Grant's "true friend," they could be reminded of a revealing colloquy between New York's senior senator and Wheeler. Conkling told Wheeler that if he joined forces with Conkling, Wheeler might aspire to anything "in the gift of the State of New York."

Wheeler replied, "Mr. Conkling, there is nothing in the gift of the State of New York which will compensate me for the forfeiture of my self-respect."[12]

At 10:40 a.m. on Friday, June 16 the balloting for president began. On the first ballot, no one received the necessary 379 votes to win the nomination. Of the major candidates, Blaine came the closest with 285. The others fell far short of the mark. Morton had 124 and Bristow 113. Conkling's total stood at ninety-nine having won sixty-nine of New York's seventy votes—Curtis voted for Bristow. There were no surprises in the totals compiled by the four compromise candidates. As he had planned, Wheeler had a total of three, all from Massachusetts. Hayes won all of Ohio's forty-four votes plus a handful from other states for a total of sixty-one. All of Hartranft's fifty-eight votes came from his home state of Pennsylvania and ten of Jewell's eleven votes came from his home state of Connecticut.[13]

On the second ballot, Blaine crept up to 296 and as expected, Jewell withdrew from the race. Elihu B. Washburne of Illinois, a former congressman and present U.S. ambassador to France, jumped in as another compromise candidate by polling one vote from Minnesota. The total votes for all the other candidates remained about the same. They did not change significantly at the end of the third ballot either. When there was no major change in the totals at the conclusion of the fourth ballot, the spirits of Wheeler and the other compromise candidates rose—it appeared that none of the major candidates could win a majority and the convention had become deadlocked.[14] Delegates began looking for signs of a significant shift in the voting.

The break came during the fifth ballot but Wheeler's friends were disappointed because it was not a break for Bill, it was a break for Hayes. William A. Howard of Michigan, a former congressman and present land commissioner of the Northern Pacific Railroad, persuaded the six Blaine and eleven Bristow supporters in the Michigan delegation to switch their votes to Hayes, which gave him all of Michigan's twenty-two votes. Hayes's total jumped to one hundred and four.[15]

Delegates continued to switch their votes to Hayes during the sixth ballot and he gained nine more votes. Blaine gamely fought back and added twenty-two to his total but it was not enough to stem the rising tide for Hayes. Throughout all of this, Wheeler refused to concede defeat and withdraw his name from the balloting. After the second ballot, he lost one of his votes but his remaining two supporters from Massachusetts did not waver. By continuing to poll two votes on the third, fourth, fifth, and sixth ballots, Wheeler successfully carried out his strategy and kept his name in front of the convention.[16]

On the seventh ballot, both Morton and Bristow withdrew and their supporters started a stampede for Hayes who won the nomination with 384 votes. On this final ballot, New York cast sixty-one votes for Hayes and nine for Blaine.[17]

Because of the importance of winning New York's thirty-five electoral votes on election day in November, the Hayes men from Ohio and other national Republican leaders signaled that they wanted a New Yorker to run with Hayes for vice president.[18] Led by Massachusetts Congressman Hoar, Wheeler supporters fanned out around the convention floor to urge delegates to vote for Wheeler. Hoar concentrated on seeking votes for Wheeler from southern states.[19] Dickinson and James concentrated on the seventy-man New York delegation, which was divided between Woodford and Wheeler.[20] Delegates primarily from Connecticut, New Jersey, and Kentucky chose to ignore the appeal for a New Yorker to be chosen to run with Hayes and a five-man race developed for the vice presidential nomination. There were three major candidates and two compromise candidates.

Among the major candidates, Wheeler was the front-runner. Because he was from New York and had kept his name in front of the convention through six consecutive ballots for president, he was a popular choice. The prominent Bristow supporter, Luke Poland from Vermont, put Bill's name in nomination. To show New York support for Wheeler, Henry James seconded the nomination. Bill received another second from a delegate representing the Pennsylvania delegation.

New York's Stewart Woodford was the second major candidate. He had kept his name in front of the convention by nominating Conkling for president, chairing the convention as president pro tempore when the president was unavailable, and frequently speaking on issues from the convention floor. New York Congressman Thomas Platt, a well-known Conkling lieutenant, nominated Woodford who was expected to mount a strong challenge to Wheeler for the nomination. A delegate from Mississippi seconded Woodford's nomination, which indicated that he had support in the South.

Marshall Jewell was the third major candidate. He was a former four-term governor of Connecticut and was serving as U.S. ambassador to Russia when President Grant tapped him to become his postmaster general. In addition to solid support from the Nutmeg State, Jewell also had strength in a number of southern states as well. He was nominated by former Congressman Ebenezer R. Hoar of Massachusetts, brother of George F. Hoar, a key member of Wheeler's campaign team. Jewell's nomination was seconded by a delegate from Texas to show Jewell's southern support.

The compromise candidates were Frederick T. Frelinghuysen, U.S. senator from New Jersey, and Joseph R. Hawley of Connecticut. Frelinghuysen was nominated as the favorite son of a unanimous New Jersey delegation. Hawley, a former congressman and governor, was nominated by John Marshall Harlan of Kentucky, the same man who nominated Bristow for president.[21]

As soon as all the nominations had been made, the balloting for vice president began. After the votes from the first eight states were recorded, Jewell surprised Wheeler by jumping into the lead. Jewell had thirty-six votes, Wheeler thirty-five, and Woodford twenty-five. However, as the voting continued, it became clear that Wheeler's unorthodox campaign strategy that he used for his presidential bid was going to pay him handsome dividends. Large blocks of former Blaine, Bristow and Hayes delegates cast their votes for Wheeler. In New England, the states of Maine, Massachusetts, and New Hampshire cast forty-nine of their fifty votes for the congressman from Malone. The western states of Illinois, Iowa and Michigan voted their 86 votes unanimously for Wheeler. By the time the roll call of states reached New York, Bill had a very healthy lead with 206 votes, followed by Jewell with 80, Woodford 70, Frelinghuysen 29, and Hawley 25.

New York's seventy delegates caucused to decide how they were going to vote. The delegation was in turmoil because of competing factions and political ambitions. According to one political analyst on the scene in Cincinnati, the turmoil in the caucus was caused by intense rivalry between New York GOP state chairman and Conkling ally, Alonzo B. Cornell, and the anti-Conkling president pro tempore of the state senate from Westchester County, William H. Robertson. Both men wanted the GOP nomination for governor that would be up for grabs at the upcoming state convention in August. They knew that Wheeler and Woodford were also potential candidates for governor. Because Cornell reckoned that Wheeler would make a stronger candidate for the gubernatorial nomination than Woodford, Cornell supported Wheeler for vice president. Robertson saw matters differently. He reckoned that Woodford would make a stronger candidate for the gubernatorial nomination than Wheeler. Hence, Robertson supported Woodford for vice president.[22]

When Woodford analyzed what was going on inside his delegation, he was discouraged to learn that Wheeler would win at least 37 of New York's 70 votes, 28 of which would be delivered to him by Cornell allies. That left Woodford with only 33 votes, at most. He also examined how the states that had not yet been called on had voted for president. In these states, he anticipated that votes from Grant Republicans, the delegates who had voted for Conkling or Morton, would be his. However, there were only 15 of them. In contrast, Wheeler had been winning the Blaine-Bristow-Hayes delegates and 206 of them had not voted yet. It became obvious to Woodford, before New York had a chance to announce its vote for vice president to the convention, that Wheeler was going to sweep to victory. When the caucus was over and the New York votes were divided between the two men, Woodford stoically walked up the aisle to the convention platform and withdrew from the race. In his withdrawal speech, he admitted that he did not

Stewart L. Woodford. Brady-Handy Collection, Library of Congress.

have a majority of his delegation behind him but promised to do "all that lies in my power" to help the ticket win in November.[23] When Woodford was finished speaking, New York cast its 70 votes for Wheeler. As the balloting continued, every single delegate from North Carolina, Ohio, Oregon, and Rhode Island voted for Wheeler, as did 12 of South Carolina's 14 delegates. After South Carolina's votes were recorded, Wheeler had 366 of the 379 votes needed to win the nomination. Frelinghuysen had 89 votes, Jewell 80, Woodford 75, and Hawley 25.[24]

Before another state could be called, Marshall Jewell's name was withdrawn and a motion was made to suspend the rules and nominate Wheeler by acclamation. The convention roared its approval and the convention chairman could barely be heard above the din announcing that William Almon Wheeler had been nominated to run as the Republican candidate for vice president.[25]

News of Wheeler's victory immediately flashed along the telegraph wires throughout the nation and reached Bill at the home of his brother-in-law, Henry W. Belcher, in Garrison at 5 p.m. Wheeler was mobbed by a group of well-wishers from the Military Academy at West Point led by General James H. Hall. Prominent local Republicans also descended on the house to extend their hearty congratulations to the congressman from Malone. They included Assemblyman Hamilton Fish Jr. from Putnam County, the son of President Grant's former secretary of state, and representatives from the distinguished Livingston family, William Livingston and Frank Livingston. In the evening, Republican glee clubs from Garrison and Cold Springs arrived to serenade Wheeler. At 8 p.m. the Cold Spring Coronet Band led several hundred people in a torchlight parade from the Garrison railroad station to the Belcher residence where more music was played and fireworks were detonated in Bill's honor.

From the balcony of the house, he thanked the crowd, referred to the Republican Party as "the conscience of the country," and predicted a "splendid victory." He wasted no time in attacking the Democratic Party for being "false to its promises, false to its duties," and false to the opportunity it had while in control of the House of Representatives in Washington, to institute reforms. When he was finished speaking and came downstairs to shake everyone's hand, more cannons and Roman candles were discharged. The festivities lasted until 10 p.m.[26]

The North Country also celebrated Wheeler's nomination with bells, bonfires, bands, fireworks, and cannons firing salutes of thirty-eight guns—Colorado was set to become the thirty-eighth state to enter the Union on August 1. Triangular transparencies with the names of Hayes and Wheeler were raised and carried in front of processions that marched through the streets of Ogdensburg and Malone.[27]

Wheeler's game plan to win the presidential nomination had been sound. If a few key states had broken for him instead of for Hayes, Wheeler might have been the man chosen to head the national GOP ticket. When friends asked him how he felt about losing the presidential nomination to Hayes, Bill told them, "God's hand is in this work, and the choice for first place is better as it is."[28]

As he traveled on the train back north to Malone from Garrison, Wheeler had time to think about how far he had come in life since his poverty-stricken childhood. As the cars rocked back and forth, he began to prepare himself for the biggest political campaign that he had ever faced in his fifty-seven-year-old life, and the first one he had ever engaged in without his wife, Mary, by his side.

21

"Hayes the True and Wheeler, Too!"

☆

As the train carrying Wheeler pulled into the Malone railroad station on June 29, 1876, he could hear a band playing, cannons firing, and people cheering. A huge throng of well-wishers greeted him as he got off the train. With the band leading the way, they escorted Bill in a procession up Elm Street to Bill's home where he spoke to the crowd. Thoughts about the untimely death of his wife, Mary, and his "desolate home" flooded over him, tears filled his eyes, and his lips quivered as he spoke. He said that without Mary being part of it, his nomination felt "utterly empty and meaningless." Regaining his composure, he confessed that his nomination was as unpredictable and wondrous to him as any of the tales from *The Arabian Nights,* a book that had thrilled him when he was a boy.[1]

Outside of Malone and the North Country, the response to Wheeler's nomination was equally warm and enthusiastic. With the exception of Conkling who did not comment on it, the major Republican candidates for the GOP presidential nomination lauded the choice of Wheeler for vice president. Morton expressed "great satisfaction" with Bill's nomination. Blaine said it was "a splendid nomination" that completed a "good ticket to win with" and Bristow said he was pleased with the choice of Wheeler because it made the GOP ticket "impregnable at both ends."[2]

For the 1876 campaign, an artist for the *Daily Graphic* (NY) drew this view of Malone (center) surrounded by panels showing (from the bottom left, moving clockwise): Wheeler's law office, the house in which he was born, his current residence, Malone's railroad depot, his sitting room, the Wheeler family gravesite, the school where he taught, the Bank of Malone, and Main Street. Courtesy of the Franklin County Historical and Museum Society.

Newspapers praised Bill's intelligence, honesty, strength, and religious devotion. They portrayed him as a "far-seeing statesman" who had great "moral and intellectual force." Describing Wheeler as a "plain and fearless man" and a "manly man," the press hailed his congressional district as the "Gibraltar of Republicanism." In Wheeler, editors saw "a man of the people" who was "thoroughly and conspicuously honest" and who had a "heart imbued with Christian principles"—a "true Christian gentleman."[3]

The University of Vermont showed its pride in Wheeler's nomination by conferring a bachelor of arts degree on him, which officially made Bill a member of the Class of 1842, the class he would have graduated with if he had not dropped out of school after his sophomore year, thirty-six years previously.[4]

Meanwhile, the Democrats met in St. Louis to nominate a ticket to oppose Hayes and Wheeler. It was the first time a national convention was held west of the Mississippi River.[5] The principal contenders for the presidential nomination were two governors, Samuel J. Tilden of New York and Thomas A. Hendricks of Indiana. Their states were battleground states on the 1876 electoral map of the U.S., which showed a solid Democratic South and a nearly solid Republican North.[6] Tilden had a national reputation as a reformer having successfully battled the Tweed ring in New York City and defeated the upstate New York Canal ring.[7] Hendricks was a former congressman and U.S. senator known for his inflationist or soft money positions.[8]

Tilden was the favorite to win the nomination. One of the reasons he had an edge over Hendricks was because some delegates were concerned that Wheeler's popularity in New York might deliver the Empire State's thirty-five electoral votes to the GOP. Tilden won the presidential nomination on the second ballot and Hendricks was subsequently nominated to run against Wheeler for vice president.[9]

In July, Hayes and Wheeler began corresponding with each other. Because they had not met personally yet, they made plans to do so and exchanged photos of themselves.[10] By nineteenth-century standards, it was not unusual that the two men had not met. Lincoln did not meet his running mate, Hannibal Hamlin, until after their election in 1860, and the Whig team of Taylor and Fillmore did not meet each other until after their election in 1848.[11]

In his initial letters to Hayes, Bill shared his New York political intelligence. He warned Hayes that Tilden was "a wonderful organizer and manipulator" who would be "utterly unscrupulous" when it came to using his "large wealth." On the Republican side of the ledger, Bill said he feared Conkling would attempt to control the GOP National Committee by making Cornell its chairman and urged Hayes to oppose him.[12]

As far as Wheeler was concerned, the number one issue in the upcoming campaign concerned the resolution of the racial conflict in the South. He argued that civil and political rights for whites and blacks had to be guaranteed "as securely in the cane breaks of Louisiana as on the banks of the St. Lawrence." To do that, Bill proposed a "most potent" step for the federal government to take—one that had traditionally been reserved for state and local governments. Wheeler urged that the government in Washington create "some system to aid in the education of the masses." In addition, he stated that in exchange for being granted "equal and exact justice" from the federal government, the Southern people should be held "to an exact, rigid observance" of their duty to grant blacks all their newly won constitutional rights. To emphasize this point, Bill waved the bloody shirt of war. He reminded voters that it was the Republican Party that had preserved the Union, abolished slavery, and declared that all men, black and white, should be guaranteed equal rights under the law.[13]

On other campaign issues, Wheeler was an enthusiastic supporter of hard money and favored the redemption of the paper greenbacks that had been issued during the Civil War, with coins, or as Bill put it, with "true money." He opposed "every form of sectarian influence" in the public schools, as well as all wasteful government spending.[14]

Much to the dismay of the reformers in his own party who had supported his nomination, such as New York's George William Curtis, Wheeler gave only tepid support to civil service reform. Unlike Hayes who boldly called for "thorough, radical and complete" reform of the spoils system, Wheeler would only say that federal jobs should be given out "only upon the basis of high character and particular fitness" and that federal positions should be "administered only as public trusts, and not for private advantage."[15] Wheeler was wary of instituting a civil service system in which it would be difficult or nearly impossible to fire incompetent government workers. Bill told Hayes that "our American notions are opposed to life estates in offices."[16]

Aside from writing formal letters to accept their nominations and giving a handful of speeches, Hayes and Wheeler followed accepted nineteenth-century campaign practices and played no active role in the campaign.[17] Hayes tried to entice Wheeler into making more speeches in more places than he wanted to give but Bill put Hayes off by citing poor health as an excuse.[18] It was expected that each state's GOP party organization would be responsible for winning their state's electoral votes. In New York, the Conkling-dominated state organization was slow to organize and begin work. He was still bitter about Hayes having defeated him for the presidential nomination and about Wheeler having defeated his choice, Woodford, for the vice-presidential nomination. One of the nation's best political speakers, Conkling had promised to support the Hayes and Wheeler ticket in September but New York's senior senator gave only one speech during the entire campaign—and in it, he neglected to mention either Hayes or Wheeler by name! Conkling claimed poor health as his excuse for not doing more.[19]

Hayes and Wheeler Clubs were organized in towns and cities across the nation. Patterned after the Wide Awakes that marched and campaigned for Lincoln in 1860, the uniformed members of the Hayes and Wheeler Clubs carried six-foot-long torches and shot off fireworks to liven up campaign rallies. The local chapters of the Boys in Blue, a national Civil War veterans' organization, joined the Hayes and Wheeler campaign effort. General John A. Dix, former governor of New York, rallied the Boys in Blue to work for Hayes and Wheeler by urging the veterans to "say to Hayes and Wheeler as you said to Lincoln, 'We are coming Father Abraham, five hundred thousand more!'" In western states, the Hayes and Wheeler Clubs were called *Haymakers*. They had banners with a scythe and pitchfork crossed before a wheel, with the printed motto, "Make Hay(es) while the sun shines./Then Wheel(er) in."[20] Reflecting the growing women's rights movement,

Grand National Republican banner. Library of Congress.

Ladies Hayes and Wheeler Clubs organized. Breaking with tradition, newspapers identified the married women who were involved in club activity by using their own first names rather than by referring to them as a "Mrs." followed by their husband's first and last names.[21]

Portraits of Hayes and Wheeler adorned the sheet music for a multitude of campaign songs that were written for national consumption by professionals who had taken over the campaign song-writing business from the amateurs.[22] The Tin Pan Alley men produced music for the "Hayes and Wheeler Songbook," and wrote such tunes as the "Hayes and Wheeler Grand March," and the "Hayes and Wheeler Polka." The songwriters tried to raise the pulse of the electorate with song titles such as, "Hayes and Wheeler! Hurrah!" "Hold the Fort for Hayes and Wheeler," and "For Hayes and Wheeler, We Are Marching On."[23]

Some campaign songs were written to appeal to specific interest groups. For older voters, the song "Hayes the True and Wheeler, Too!" harkened back to the popular 1840 Whig song, "Tippecanoe and Tyler, Too!" and associated the Hayes and Wheeler ticket with the highly successful campaign of William Henry Harrison and John Tyler.[24] The song, "The Boys in Blue Will See It Through," appealed to Civil War veterans.[25] Some campaign songs entertained voters with puns and other plays on words. The tune, "We'll Go For Hayes! We'll Wheel'er In On Time," was illustrated by a drawing showing Wheeler pushing Hayes in a wheelbarrow toward the White House.[26] The words of another campaign ditty called on men to "Vote, brothers, vote with care,/Vote for the brave old Governaire,/Vote for Hayes and Bill Wheelaire."[27]

Wheeler generated publicity for his campaign by sending letters to newspaper editors. His letter accepting the vice-presidential nomination received widespread coverage. In it, he took a moderate position concerning race relations in the South. Bill told the nation that it would take ten or fifteen years of "patient waiting" before communities in the South could be transformed into something like "our model Northern communities." Along the way to that transformation, he predicted that there would be "a good deal of unavoidable friction which will call for forbearance, and which will have to be relieved by the temperate, fostering care of the [federal] government."[28]

The Democratic response to Wheeler's acceptance letter was predictable. The *Brooklyn Eagle* described the letter as "a document of painful feebleness" and "schoolboyish." The paper said Wheeler's letter had "the superiority of mediocrity to a dead level of flapdoodle." According to the *Eagle*, the phrases used by Wheeler smacked of "some crossroads lawyer's draft of a clodhopper's last will and testament." The paper concluded by stating that Wheeler's style was the work of "a densely ignorant man" writing "driveling flatness."[29]

Hayes-Wheeler campaign song. Library of Congress.

In addition to Bill's acceptance letter, other letters were distributed and published as part of his campaign. Utica's Ellis H. Roberts, a former congressman and the editor of the *Utica Herald*, praised Wheeler's honesty. Roberts wrote, "When it was the fashion for all men to dabble in railroad stocks and bonds," Wheeler "never bought or sold a share of stock or a single bond in any of the

Pacific railroads."[30] Another letter writer praised Wheeler's "Christian character" and recounted Bill's role in aiding the Irish farmers in Franklin County when their farms were destroyed by a great brush fire in 1849.[31] Wheeler's 1856 letter supporting the antislavery forces in Kansas was also republished as part of the campaign. In it, Bill praised Frederick Douglass and contributed $100 to "aid our hunted and oppressed brethren in Kansas."[32]

Democrats did not sit idly by watching Wheeler burnish his public image. They launched several well-publicized attacks on Bill. They attacked him for libeling the people of southern Illinois by writing in the appendix to *Webster's Unabridged Dictionary* that they "had the reputation of being extremely ignorant." Coming to Wheeler's defense, the *New York Times* explained that a "William A. Wheeler" had written those words but the Democrats had attacked the wrong man. The "William A. Wheeler" who had disparaged the people of Illinois was not the Wheeler who was the GOP candidate for vice president—the author was the deceased philologist, William A[dolphus] Wheeler, from Cambridge, Massachusetts.[33]

The *Nation,* a pro-Tilden weekly magazine, leveled a more serious charge against Wheeler in New York. In a front-page story, the magazine called Wheeler a "land grabber" for engineering passage of congressional legislation enabling the construction of the Northern Pacific Railroad (a "land grant scheme") and the sale of Goat Island in California (a "notorious" job). In addition, the *Nation* accused Wheeler of being a "railroad wrecker" and claimed that Wheeler had been sued by a railroad for using his position as railroad trustee to "abstract" money from the treasury of the railroad.[34]

From Malone, Wheeler fired back through the pen of one of his lawyers, Albert Hobbs, and asserted that the *Nation*'s charge was a "baseless fabrication." In a letter sent to several major newspapers, Hobbs explained that the railroad in question was the Northern New York Railroad Company and that Wheeler had brought it to court, acting as trustee for the railroad's second mortgage bondholders, in order to obtain a court order granting bondholders permission to surrender the railroad's property to a new corporation that had been formed to operate the railroad. Hobbs further explained that during the court proceedings, there were never any charges that Wheeler had abstracted any money from the railroad treasury. In fact, Hobbs noted, the only money paid over to Wheeler was $120.13, which had been given to Wheeler by the new corporation to balance Wheeler's accounts as trustee. Every other dollar received and paid by Wheeler as trustee had been audited and allowed by the New York Supreme Court.[35]

Not satisfied by Hobbs's explanation, the *Nation* repeated its charges that Wheeler was a "railroad wrecker" and a "tricky fellow" who was guilty of "a gross abuse of power" in his role as trustee. As far as the *Nation* was concerned, Wheeler's financial accounts had been settled by "some hocus pocus collusion with a judge" who was "probably a shyster."[36]

As the campaign heated up, Wheeler was optimistic about its progress. He wrote Hayes that in Bill's experience, he had seen more "foamy enthusiasm" in former campaigns but he had never seen more "intense earnestness" than he was seeing now.[37]

While campaigning in New England, Bill delivered a spirited speech to a large Republican rally in St. Albans, Vermont. Partisan chants, cheering, and applause repeatedly interrupted him. It was one of Bill's finest campaign hours—he had never waved the bloody shirt of war so well. He warned his listeners that on election day, they were once again facing a united South with the Democratic Party in the North as its "subservient and pliant ally." Referring to the Democratic Party as "the Confederate party," Bill challenged his audience to tell him the difference between the pre–Civil War actions of the border ruffians in Kansas and the recent massacre in Hamburg, South Carolina, where blacks had been "first disarmed and then murdered in cold blood in order that the white race might assert its superiority." Wheeler told the crowd that he had been sitting in Congress with Democrats who a few years previously had been actively working to break up the Union and who defended the "hellish atrocities of Libby, Andersonville, and Salisbury"—three notorious Confederate prisoner of war camps. To cries of "No, No," Bill asked his audience if they were ready to turn the nation over to these Southerners and their "pliant ally," the Democratic party of the North. Bill cried out to the cheering throng that the "conscience of the nation" must be awakened to "avert this great peril." In conclusion, Wheeler exhorted Vermont Republicans, "Let your ballots protect the work so efficiently done by your bayonets at Gettysburg."[38]

As election day approached, Bill began to view the campaign through a stark religious lens. He wrote Hayes that in New York, the Democrats were using "every evil agency" at their command with the "cunning, adroitness and energy of the devil himself." However, Bill said he hoped for "the success of the right" because he believed in "an overruling Providence."[39]

Almost 8,500,000 voters went to the polls on election day, November 7, 1876. The weather was clear and cool in the West but wet in the East. After the polls closed and the ballots were tallied, Bill was disappointed by the results. He had failed to deliver New York's thirty-five electoral votes to the Hayes and Wheeler team. Tilden and Hendricks carried New York State by more than 32,000 votes. They had won in New York City and in Brooklyn by 70,000.[40] Wheeler was equally distressed by the early returns from other states. They indicated an apparent Tilden-Hendricks victory was in the making. The returns showed that Hayes and Wheeler were likely to lose the election nationally by a plurality of more than

250,000 popular votes. When they were translated into electoral votes, it appeared that Tilden and Hendricks might win at least 203 electoral votes—and only 185 were needed for the Democrats to claim victory. The next morning, newspaper headlines across the country proclaimed a Democratic win. The *New York Herald*'s headlines screamed, "AVE! CENTENNIAL SAM! COMPLETE DEMOCRATIC VICTORY." Headlines in the Republican Chicago *Tribune* cried out, "LOST. THE COUNTRY GIVEN OVER TO DEMOCRATIC GREED AND PLUNDER. TILDEN, TAMMANY, AND THE SOLID SOUTH ARE TO RULE THE NATION."[41]

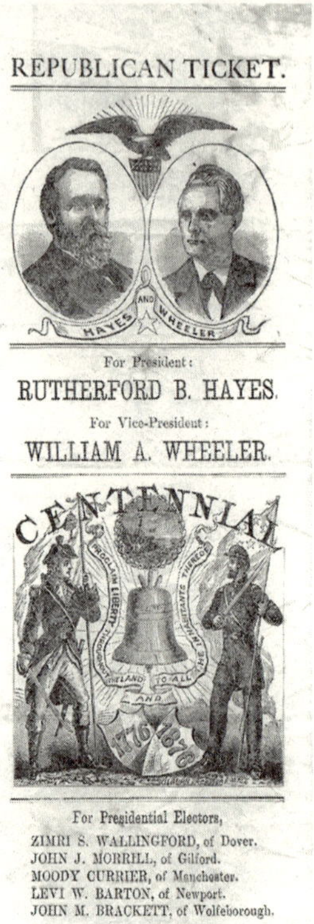

Ballot for Hayes and Wheeler.

However, on the basis of the returns compiled at Republican National Committee headquarters in New York City, the *New York Times* would not count Hayes and Wheeler out of the race yet and reported that the election outcome was "doubtful." Wheeler's friends in the North Country press echoed the doubt expressed by the *Times* but noted, "The result is uncomfortably close."[42]

Political leaders from both parties pored over the unofficial returns, which would not become official until each state's election return board certified the winners. Based on the early tallies, the party chieftains determined that Tilden and Hendricks were sure to win 184 electoral votes, Hayes and Wheeler were sure to win 165, and 20 votes were in dispute—both parties claimed them![43] Eight of the disputed votes were in Louisiana, seven in South Carolina, four in Florida, and one in Oregon. To win the election, Tilden and Hendricks needed only one of the twenty disputed votes but Hayes and Wheeler needed to win all twenty of them.

Republicans and Democrats in Oregon agreed that Hayes and Wheeler had carried the state by more than one thousand votes, but because of a fight over a legal technicality, one of Oregon's three electoral votes was in dispute. The argument in the three southern states was about who had won the most popular votes in each state thereby entitling the winners to cast the state's electoral votes. The Republicans and Democrats fought over the validity of the preliminary totals, which gave Louisiana to the Democrats by 6,300 votes, South Carolina to the GOP by about 1,000 votes, and Florida to the Democrats by 94 votes. The election return boards in all three states were controlled by Republican carpetbagger governments that were supported by federal troops. President Grant ordered the army to protect the return boards and alerted the war department to guard against fraud and violence.[44]

Northern Republican newspapers mocked the integrity of southern Democratic election officials with biting reports from "the clothes line telegraph." One "telegram" addressed to "S.J. Tilden" said, "There is no doubt about your election. Four thousand two hundred and eleven alligators voted the Democratic ticket in Swamp Parish, and unless scalawag Returning Board throws out these votes the result is assured." Another "telegram" read, "Our majority is increasing every hour. Twenty Negroes were shot yesterday, and we have smashed the ballot box and taken out the tickets which they cast last week. We rely on our friends in the North to prevent a carpet bag government from counting dead men's votes."[45]

As individuals, neither Hayes nor Wheeler took part in contesting the election results. Both men acted as observers while their Republican associates worked to influence the return boards in Florida, Louisiana, and South Carolina to certify Republican victory by invalidating Democratic votes because of the use of fraud, violence, and intimidation. It would have been particularly awkward and troubling for Wheeler to attempt to sway the decisions of the return boards in light of the legal position he had taken at the time of the Wheeler Compromise. In the report he had written for Congress about the 1874 election in Louisiana, Bill had declared that the state election return board had no legal right to go behind the returns filed by each local election district and throw out votes because of violence and intimidation—its only legal power was to compile the election results that had been reported to it by local officials. Other tough-minded Republican political operatives did not feel bound by Wheeler's interpretation of Louisiana election law and headed south to spearhead a struggle to win electoral votes for Hayes and Wheeler. They were spectacularly successful in all three states.[46]

In South Carolina, the return board invalidated the votes in two counties before certifying that the seven Hayes and Wheeler electors had carried the state. In Florida, citing instances of fraud and corruption by Democrats, the return board declared that the four Hayes and Wheeler electors had won Florida by nine hundred votes. In Louisiana, the return board cited fraud, violence, and intimidation as reasons to throw out fifteen thousand votes, thirteen thousand of them were Democratic. As a result, instead of losing Louisiana by sixty-three hundred votes, the eight Hayes and Wheeler electors were certified as winners by more than three thousand votes.[47]

On December 6, as provided by the Constitution and congressional law, the electoral college "met" in the thirty-eight state capitals. The electors cast their votes

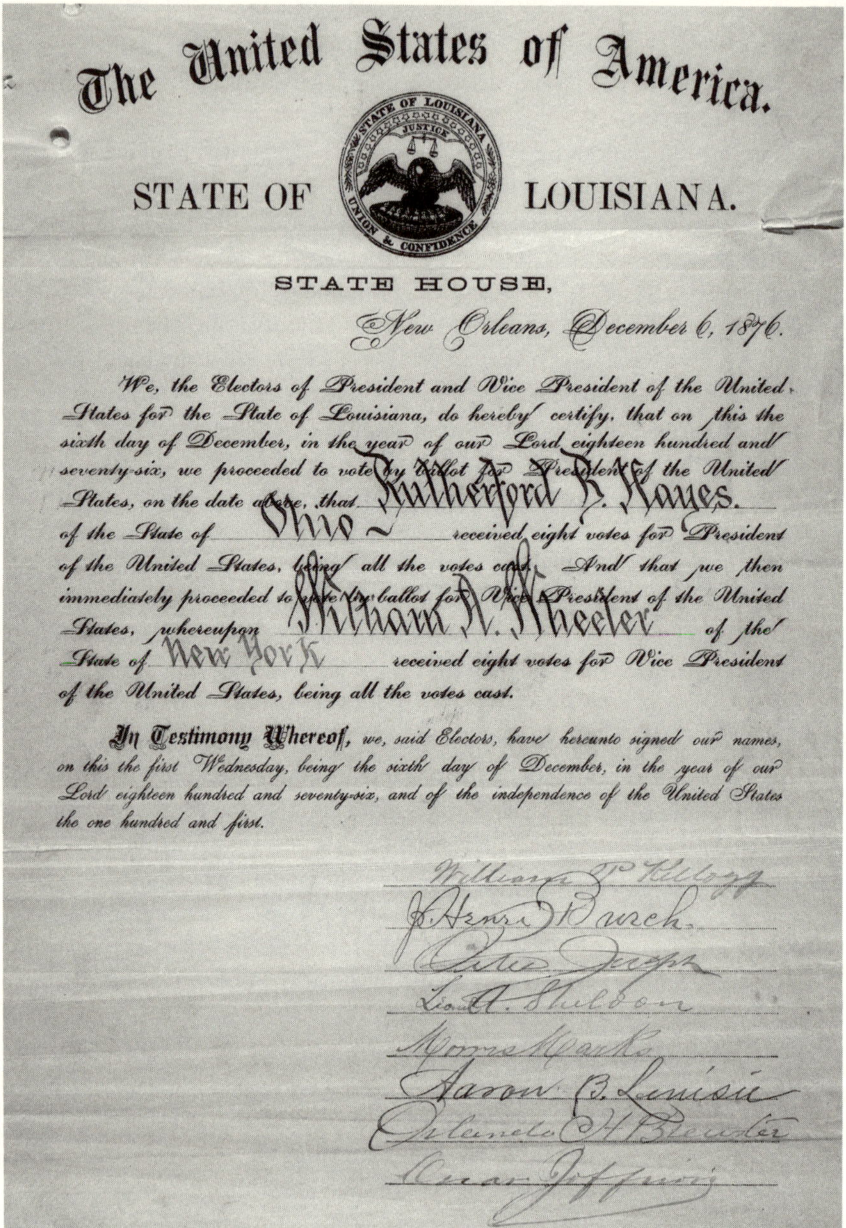

The United States of America.

STATE OF LOUISIANA.

STATE HOUSE,

New Orleans, December 6, 1876.

We, the Electors of President and Vice President of the United States for the State of Louisiana, do hereby certify, that on this the sixth day of December, in the year of our Lord eighteen hundred and seventy-six, we proceeded to vote by ballot for President of the United States, on the date above, that Rutherford B. Hayes of the State of Ohio received eight votes for President of the United States, being all the votes cast. And that we then immediately proceeded to vote by ballot for Vice President of the United States, whereupon William A. Wheeler of the State of New York received eight votes for Vice President of the United States, being all the votes cast.

In Testimony Whereof, we, said Electors, have hereunto signed our names, on this the first Wednesday, being the sixth day of December, in the year of our Lord eighteen hundred and seventy-six, and of the independence of the United States the one hundred and first.

William P. Kellogg
J. Henri Burch
Peter Joseph
Lionel A. Sheldon
Morris Marks
Aaron B. Levissee
Orlando H. Brewster
Oscar Joffrion

Louisiana's "official" certified eight electoral votes for Hayes and Wheeler. Library of Congress.

for president and vice president and sent the results to the president of the U.S. Senate. In thirty-four states, there were no surprises and the balloting took place as expected. However, in Louisiana, South Carolina, Florida, and Oregon, the Republican electors and the Democratic electors each met separately, voted, and sent their ballots to Washington. On a desk in the president of the Senate's office, there were 184 votes for Tilden and Hendricks, 165 for Hayes and Wheeler, and 20 claimed by both the Democratic and Republican candidates.[48]

Republicans claimed that the twenty votes cast by their electors in Louisiana, South Carolina, Florida, and Oregon were the "official" electoral votes and should be counted as such in Washington because they had been cast by electors whose election victory had been duly certified by their state's election return boards and high government officials. The Democrats heatedly disagreed. They argued that the twenty votes cast by their electors should be the ones that were counted because the official state certification was the product of fraud and intimidation.

Hayes and Wheeler supporters were confident that when the electoral votes were counted, their men would win the election with 185 votes because the math was simple—165 undisputed votes plus all 20 of the "official" votes from Louisiana, South Carolina, Florida, and Oregon, equaled a winning majority of 185. Tilden and Hendricks forces were equally confident that when the votes were counted, their men would win. For Democrats, the math was also simple. All they needed for victory was to win one of the twenty votes that in their view had not been cast as a result of fraud and intimidation.

Political observers across the nation were alarmed by the certainty of victory expressed by both sides. To them, it became readily apparent that the outcome would depend on who was going to do the counting—but who was legally entitled to count the electoral votes for president and vice president?

22

"As Righteous as an Edict of God"

★

According to the Twelfth Amendment of the Constitution, once the electoral votes have been sent to the president of the Senate, "The President of the Senate shall, in the presence of the Senate and House of Representatives, open all the certificates and the votes shall then be counted." However, if there is a dispute about *which* votes should be counted, the Constitution does not explain who should have the power to settle the disagreement—the president of the Senate or the combined House and Senate?

This was not a new question to veteran politicos, such as the congressman from Malone. He was familiar with the raging controversy that had broken out in Washington in 1857 concerning who had the legal authority to count disputed electoral votes cast in the 1856 election.[1] Wheeler also knew that in order to avoid a similar controversy that threatened to erupt after the 1864 election involving the counting of electoral votes sent to Washington by a number of southern states that had seceded from the Union, Congress had adopted the Twenty-second Joint Rule in 1865. It provided that a member of the House or the Senate could object to a decision by the president of the Senate to count a particular electoral vote. According to the rule, the electoral vote that had been objected to could not be counted unless both houses agreed to overrule the objection.[2]

Wheeler disagreed with the legal premise underlying the Twenty-second Joint Rule. Bill was adamant that the duty of electing the president and the vice president belonged "entirely to the States" and that "Congress could not go behind the returns beyond the mere question of the regularity of the certificates."[3] In this regard, Wheeler found himself in the same camp with Indiana's Senator Morton who objected strongly to the Twenty-second Joint Rule because it granted power to one house of Congress "to disfranchise any and all of the States."[4]

As a congressman serving in the Forty-second Congress, Wheeler had first-hand experience with the workings of the Twenty-second Joint Rule when it was used to count the electoral votes cast in the 1872 election. Sitting with the members of the House and Senate, Bill watched the president of the Senate, Vice President Schuyler Colfax, open the certificates and count the votes. Wheeler listened to lawmakers object to Colfax counting votes from Arkansas, Louisiana, Mississippi, and Texas. When the issue concerning the validity of those votes came before the House under the dictates of the Twenty-second Joint Rule, Wheeler demonstrated his objection to the rule by refusing to vote on whether the official returns from the four states should be counted.[5]

Following the 1874 election for the Forty-fourth Congress, which would convene on December 6, 1875, the Republicans maintained their control of the Senate but the Democrats seized control of the House. They secured enough seats to enable them, according to the Constitution, to elect the president in 1876 if no candidate received a majority of the electoral votes. Alarmed by the possibility that the Democrats in the House might use the Twenty-second Joint Rule to deny the Republican candidate for president a majority and throw the presidential election into the House, the Senate effectually repealed the Twenty-second Joint Rule by refusing to reenact it.[6]

The Senate repeal set the stage for the constitutional crisis, which developed between December 6, 1876, when the electors cast their ballots, and March 4, 1877, inauguration day. Those three months were some of the most tumultuous and tension-filled months in U.S. political history. Talk of revolution, fear of anarchy, threats of violence, and mass uncertainty swept the nation.

The GOP argued that according to the Constitution, the president of the Senate alone should decide which electoral votes should be counted. Because Vice President Henry Wilson had died in 1875, Republican Senator Thomas W. Ferry of Michigan was president of the Senate. If Ferry were permitted to count the votes, Hayes and Wheeler would win the election. The Democrats argued that according to Republican legal precedent, the Twenty-second Joint Rule was still in effect and that a disputed electoral vote could not be counted unless both houses agreed to count it.[7] If House Democrats were permitted to invalidate electoral votes by refusing to allow them to be counted, Tilden and Hendricks would win the election. As partisan political passions rose, Republicans became convinced that the Democrats were trying to steal the election from them, and Democrats became convinced that the Republicans were trying to steal the election from them.

While Wheeler was visiting his sister in New York at her residence on West 42nd Street, he reiterated his position that Congress had no legal authority to go behind the returns to investigate an individual state's conduct of the election. Wheeler said, "The action of the returning board on this point has been final and conclusive." As far as Bill was concerned, he and Hayes had been "legally, honestly and fairly elected by a majority of the electoral college." When the *New York Herald* pressed Bill to react to the possibility that the House might throw out the electoral votes of Louisiana and Florida, and the Senate might respond by throwing out the votes of Alabama and Mississippi, the newspaper reported that "Wheeler's face assumed an expression of contempt." Speaking in a "quick, sharp and rugged way," Bill once again denied "the right of either or both branches of Congress to canvass the votes" and stated, "the action by the state returning or canvassing board should be final and conclusive."[8]

Back in Malone, Wheeler read ominous newspaper stories about northern and western Democrats forming secret organizations of armed men who held "blood-and-thunder" meetings, which featured chants of "Tilden or war." Publically, Bill played down the threats of armed revolution and said they were "all talk, my friend." When asked by a reporter if he thought that a Democratic army could capture the government, Wheeler replied with "inimitably dry humor." He said, "I know very few men who would defray their own expenses or buy their own horses and guns to put Mr. Tilden into the presidential chair. I do know two or three men in my own town who want to go to Washington with their muskets to see that Mr. Tilden is inaugurated but they are generally men who do not go out after sundown—they'll fight valiantly for post offices, but that's about it."[9]

Newspapers also carried stories about rumored compromises for settling the electoral dispute. One rumor had it that Tilden would be chosen president by the House, Hendricks would accept appointment to be ambassador to England, and Wheeler would be chosen vice president by the Senate.[10] Bill described this rumor as "necessarily absurd" because he said he "did not believe that the suffrages of the American people can be made the subject of dicker or barter." However, he added that if Tilden were lawfully elected president by the House and he were elected vice president by the Senate, Bill would serve with Tilden and "yield to him ready and hasty allegiance."[11]

In mid-December, the House and Senate decided that the only way to settle the dispute was through compromise and the lawmakers established a joint congressional committee to resolve the crisis.[12] One solution initially bandied about called for the creation of an electoral commission with power to count the votes, which would be composed of an equal number of Republicans and Democrats. To break potential tie votes, one member of the commission would subsequently be eliminated by drawing a name. Wheeler's hometown newspaper promptly labeled the proposal "a childish proposition." The paper said a simpler way would be for the candidates to be blindfolded and draw straws, or toss a coin, to determine who would be president and vice president.[13]

Wheeler was extremely alarmed by the establishment of the congressional joint committee because Conkling was one of its members and Bill did not trust him. Wheeler had heard rumors that Conkling, disappointed by the candidacies of Hayes and Wheeler, was thinking he might be able to get a better deal to improve his power base in New York State from Tilden, than he could get from Hayes. Conkling wanted assurances from the new administration that he would be granted control over the patronage appointments at the New York Custom House.[14] Conkling had been heard to say that Tilden and Hendricks should win the election because the Democrats had carried Louisiana and Florida, and that the returns certified by the state boards were invalid.[15]

Because of his concern about being betrayed by Conkling, Bill decided that it was time for a face-to-face meeting with Hayes and a trip to Washington to personally investigate what was going on there. Wheeler decided to go to Washington by way of Hayes's home in Fremont, Ohio. Bill met his running mate for the first time on January 10, 1877, and spent several days with him discussing the electoral crisis, the potential threat posed by Conkling, and cabinet choices. After shaking hands with hundreds of well-wishers at a grand reception put on for him at the state capitol in Columbus by the leaders of the Republican and Democratic parties in the Ohio legislature, Bill took the afternoon train to Washington.[16]

After his arrival in Washington on January 12, Bill spent a week investigating the circumstances surrounding the appointment of the joint committee working to resolve the election dispute. He met with trusted colleagues and with President Grant. Wheeler wrote Hayes that according to their friends in Washington, Conkling was working to defeat them and that he had taken a stand against their election with "premeditated malice." Wheeler added that President Grant had told him that he had been shown a list of thirteen senators who planned to work with Conkling against the election of Hayes and Wheeler. Nevertheless, Bill closed his letter to Hayes with the hope that Conkling "will yet come to himself."[17]

While Bill was in Washington, he met with the Appropriations Committee and took his seat in the House for several hours where Democrats and Republicans warmly greeted him. The House Speaker and Democratic chairman of the House Appropriations Committee, Samuel J. Randall of Pennsylvania, and Vermont Senator Justin S. Morrill, Republican chairman of the Senate Committee on Public Buildings approached him. They told Wheeler that they wanted to reward him for his political achievements by including the erection of a new post office in Malone in the public buildings legislation that was currently before Congress. Bill surprised them by turning down their proffered going away present. Wheeler said he had always opposed such appropriations for small towns when they came before him for a vote and he could not accept one now for his hometown.[18]

As January came to an end, Wheeler returned to Malone to await the counting of the vote. The joint committee recommended to both houses that they pass a law creating an electoral commission to resolve the dispute. The committee proposed a commission of five representatives, five senators, and five justices of the Supreme Court. The members of the commission would be equally divided between the two parties with the exception of the fifth justice who would be chosen by the two Republican and two Democratic justices. The lawmakers expected the fifth justice to be David Davis of Illinois because he was a political independent. In fact, at the time he was being discussed as the probable fifth justice, Davis was seeking election to the U.S. Senate by the Illinois legislature running as the Greenback party candidate. For practical purposes, if Davis were named to the commission, he would be the man with the power to decide which electoral votes should be counted, rather than Ferry, because according to the proposed legislation, commission decisions about the validity of disputed electoral votes could not be overturned unless both houses agreed to do so—a highly improbable occurrence given the political make up of the two houses.[19]

Wheeler was very uncomfortable with the proposed legislation because Conkling had been instrumental in crafting it and strongly supported its passage. In addition, although Davis had been a Republican in prior years, Bill was extremely uneasy with the prospect that Davis would decide the election because, during the election campaign, he was rumored to have preferred Tilden to Hayes. To Bill, this explained why more Democrats than Republicans wanted Davis to be appointed to the election commission. To make matters even worse, Wheeler also had learned that Davis was courting Democratic support in the Illinois legislature to win his bid for the U.S. Senate. For all of these reasons, Wheeler had to agree with Morton who denounced the commission bill on the floor of the Senate because it doomed the Hayes and Wheeler ticket to defeat. Despite Morton's thunderous objections, Conkling's rhetoric and arm twisting in the Senate helped split the Republican opposition to the bill and it passed with solid Democratic backing—twenty-six of

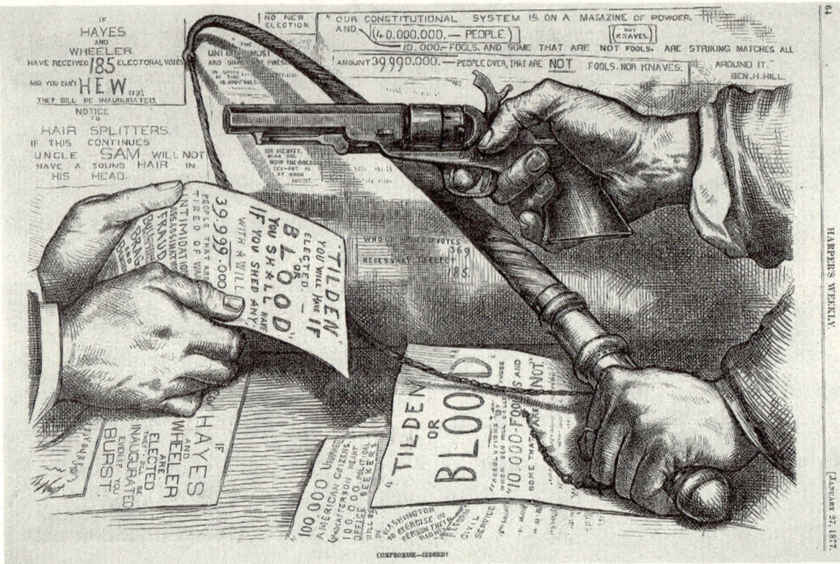

Cartoon by Thomas Nast reflecting the suspicion held by Wheeler that the electoral commission created by Congress to count the 1876 electoral votes doomed the Hayes and Wheeler ticket to defeat because it would allow Democratic violence and intimidation to triumph. The cartoon's caption reads, "Compromise—Indeed!" U.S. Senate Collection.

the forty-seven votes for the bill came from Democratic senators. The bill easily passed the House because of overwhelming Democratic support and President Grant quickly signed it into law.[20]

Wheeler's disappointment with the measure was expressed in a letter he may have written that appeared in the press alongside news that the commission bill had become law. Referring to the commission as a *National Returning Board*, the letter said, "As boys toss up coppers and cry 'heads' or 'tails,' the nation will toss up a Supreme Court Judge and cry 'Hayes' or 'Tilden.' Cotton was king once, Chance is king today."[21]

Bill's deep concerns about his electoral fate were suddenly lifted when he learned some shocking news that destroyed Democratic calculations and expectations. Davis had won election to the U.S. Senate thanks to the votes cast for him by Democrats in the Illinois legislature but he had refused to accept appointment to the election commission because he did not want to give any appearance of impropriety. All the other Supreme Court judges available to be chosen as the fifth, tie-breaking justice on the electoral commission were Republicans! When Justice Joseph P. Bradley of New Jersey was chosen as the fifth justice, the Republicans emerged with an eight to seven majority on the commission.[22] Additional good news raised Wheeler's spirits even higher. Fearing that Conkling's admitted dislike of Hayes and Wheeler might cause Conkling to favor Tilden and Hendricks, Senate Republicans had excluded Conkling from the commission and named one of his arch rivals, Morton, instead.[23] In addition, the House named Wheeler's political ally and confidant, George F. Hoar, to the commission.[24]

Despite the political makeup of the electoral commission, Bill would not feel confident about his election until it made its first ruling. He did not have long to wait. In the presence of the House and Senate, Ferry began to methodically count the electoral votes, state by state, and when he reached Florida's four votes, objections to his decision to count them for Hayes and Wheeler rang out. In accordance with the new law, the matter was referred to the electoral commission and on February 9, after days of debate and political posturing, the commission voted by an eight to seven party-line vote not to go behind the official returns and awarded the votes to Hayes and Wheeler.[25]

This ruling was the sign Bill had been anxiously waiting for. Given the party-line nature of the vote, he was confident that all future objections to the official returns would also go his way. Consequently, he began packing for Washington and seriously preparing to become vice president. One of the first things he did was meet with his chief political lieutenant in his congressional district, Wells S. Dickinson of Bangor, to firm up decisions about what political strategy should be employed in the district during Bill's absence. Next, Wheeler appointed Wells's twenty-four-year-old son, Edwin E. Dickinson, to be his private secretary in Washington. Edwin had graduated from Wheeler's alma mater, the University of Vermont, and was currently working in the Dickinson family mercantile business while he studied law in Malone.[26] Last, Wheeler wrote to Hayes about the new cabinet. Bill said that he had been "flooded with letters" concerning cabinet appointments and told Hayes that he should expect the same, especially from candidates who had been defeated in the last election for the U.S. Senate. Bill advised Hayes against appointing any of these men because the cabinet should not become "a political infirmary." Bill also urged Hayes to avoid picking men who had been in Grant's cabinet or who had competed with Hayes for the presidential nomination. Wheeler told Hayes that he should make his cabinet choices based on "personal character, recognized capacity and experience" and that the primary characteristic of the Hayes administration should be "the advancement of the material interests of the nation."[27]

As Bill was making his travel plans, Ferry resumed counting the electoral vote. When he announced that the votes from Louisiana and Oregon were for Hayes and Wheeler, Democrats objected, once again. And once again, the electoral commission voted eight to seven to award the votes to the Republican candidates. Each commission ruling enraged the Democrats and they became more and more desperate about what they should, or could, do. Sensing defeat, they threatened to filibuster in the House to delay the count from going forward. If the count were not completed before inauguration day, March 4, the U.S. would not have a president or a vice president! On February 27, after considering objections that had been made to South Carolina's seven votes being counted for Hayes and Wheeler, the electoral commission awarded them to the governor of Ohio and the congressman from Malone, following yet a fourth eight to seven party-line vote. Ferry had no more disputed votes left to count, only undisputed votes remained uncounted.[28]

On February 28, the Democrats adjourned the House to prevent Ferry from counting the remaining, undisputed votes. On March 1, the day Wheeler left Malone for Washington accompanied by his brother-in-law, Howard E. King, and Bill's new secretary, Edwin E. Dickinson, the Democrats reluctantly reopened the House for business and Ferry prepared to finish counting the votes. However, the Democrats would not let him begin. They mounted a filibuster by filing motion after motion and debating each one, endlessly. Some political observers worried that the filibuster might work and that there would be no president or vice president on March 4, the day the new terms were to begin. Suddenly, there was a pause in the filing of motions and ensuing debate. Congressmen from Louisiana and South Carolina reported in private conferences with their colleagues that they had heard from Hayes's representatives, that if Hayes were elected president, he would withdraw federal troops from Louisiana and South Carolina and grant home rule to southern states. In addition, the congressmen said that they understood that Hayes would support a federal subsidy for the construction of the Texas & Pacific Railroad and would appoint a southern Democrat to his cabinet who would have permission to hand out patronage to his friends.[29] Because of this information, the Democrats brought the filibuster in the House to an end, enabling Ferry to pick up the count where he had left off and to finish it by announcing the votes from the remaining states. At 4:10 a.m. on March 2, based on totals showing that Hayes and Wheeler had 185 electoral votes to 184 for Tilden and Hendricks, Ferry declared that Hayes had been elected president and Wheeler had been elected vice president.[30] For the first time in American history, candidates for president and vice president who had lost the nationwide popular vote, won the election in the electoral college.[31] Democratic newspaper headlines in Malone charged the electoral college with corruption and screamed, "The Fraud is Consummated." Wheeler issued a sharp rejoinder by stating that the decision by the commission was "as righteous as an edict of God."[32]

Because inauguration day, March 4, 1877, fell on a Sunday, Hayes took his oath of office on Saturday night, March 3, in a private ceremony in the White House. Plans were made for Wheeler to be sworn in on Monday, March 5, after which a public swearing in would be held for Hayes.[33] The day set for the public inauguration was a cool and cloudy day and a few snowflakes fell as Kentucky Senator Thomas McCreery, a member of the Senate Committee on Arrangements, picked Wheeler up in a carriage at his residence on 12th Street and drove him to the White House. Bill arrived there at about 10 a.m. and was ushered into the oval-shaped Blue Room where he was greeted by Grant, Hayes, and Ohio Senator John Sherman, the man Hayes would later name to be secretary of the treasury. When everyone was ready, the party departed for the Capitol for the swearing in ceremonies.

Wheeler's carriage lined up behind the open barouche that Hayes and Grant would ride in. Other carriages containing Grant's cabinet and other guests lined up behind Wheeler. In back of them, a military and political escort moved into place. The military escort consisted of three divisions of armed forces, including a black military unit from Washington, and five bands. The political escort consisted of several Republican clubs who chanted as they marched, "Seven Can't Beat Eight." Once everyone was in place, the procession moved down Pennsylvania Avenue to the Senate wing of the Capitol.[34]

When it arrived, Wheeler went with McCreery to the Vice President's Room. It was the only space in Washington assigned to the vice president for his exclusive use. John C. Breckinridge, President Buchanan's vice president, was the first vice president to occupy the room once it was ready following the 1850s remodeling of the Capitol. The room's most recent occupant, Grant's vice president, Henry Wilson, had died in the room in 1875 after suffering a stroke. The Vice President's Room would be Bill's new office where he would receive official calls and transact his private and public business—he had never had such an elegant office as this.

It had a marble mantle above a working fireplace, which was located between two windows. The fireplace was fueled by dry hickory wood. Colorful Minton tiles that had been manufactured in England dotted the floor. An ornate gilded mirror hung on one wall—legend had it that the mirror had belonged to Dolley Madison. Prominently displayed on another wall above a large, green leather sofa was the celebrated four-foot by six-foot portrait of George Washington, *Patriae Pater*, painted by Rembrandt Peale in 1824. An elaborately carved mahogany table that doubled as a desk was in the middle of the room, surrounded by several stuffed, green leather chairs. On the left, inside the doorway, was a large, carved bookcase. A magnificent chandelier with eight glass bulbs hung from the ceiling

Stereoscopic view of the Vice President's Room in the Capitol Building, just outside the U.S. Senate chamber. U.S. Senate Commission on Art.

and provided gas lighting for the twenty-five-foot square room. Located across a narrow corridor from the Senate chamber, the Vice President's Room was also within a short walk to the luxurious bathing rooms in the basement of the Capitol, which were there for the use of House and Senate members. As president of the Senate, Bill could look forward to use of the bathing facilities where he could soak in a large marble tub, enjoy a massage and have his hair cut.[35]

As Bill stood in his new office, he had to have been struck by the supreme irony of a comment that had been made to him in this very room by Hannibal Hamlin of Maine, President Lincoln's first vice president. Only a freshman congressman at the time, Bill had stopped by the room to see if Hamlin wanted to have lunch and found him tired out by Senate debate and asleep in one of the stuffed chairs. After Wheeler roused him, Hamlin complained about the nature of the vice president's constitutional duties telling Bill he felt like the "fifth wheel of a coach" and said he would have lunch with Wheeler only if Bill promised him he would never be vice president. History did not record Bill's answer.[36]

As Wheeler waited in the Vice President's Room, spectators who had lined up outside the Capitol for hours made a dash for seats in the Senate galleries as soon as the chamber's doors were opened at 11 a.m. In thirty minutes, all the seats were taken. The floor of the Senate was crowded with Republican senators and representatives—Democratic lawmakers, including House Speaker Randall, boycotted the event. Bill was pleased that his longtime friend and financial adviser, ex-Governor and ex-Senator Edwin D. Morgan, was present. He sat with several other prominent New York political figures including: the man who had made the legal arguments for the Republicans to the electoral commission and who would be named by Hayes to be secretary of state, William M. Evarts; Conkling lieutenant and collector of the Port of New York, Chester A. Arthur; and the man Wheeler had defeated for the GOP vice presidential nomination, Stewart L. Woodford.

Among the military officers who were dressed in full dress uniform and sat in chairs placed in the rear of the chamber, were the commanding general of the Army, William T. Sherman, and the future Democratic candidate for president in 1880, General Winfield S. Hancock. Seated nearby the military officers were the foreign ambassadors who were dressed in their diplomatic costumes, which glittered with gold and silver embroidery, medals, and jeweled decorations. Shortly after they were seated, the justices of the Supreme Court dressed in their judicial robes entered the chamber and took their seats.

At precisely noon, President Hayes appeared at the entrance to the chamber, arm in arm with Grant. To vigorous applause and handkerchief waving by the spectators, Hayes and Grant, followed by the members of Grant's cabinet, walked to their seats in the front of the chamber. As soon as Hayes and Grant were seated in their elegantly upholstered chairs, the man who had counted the electoral votes as the president of the Senate, Senator Ferry, assumed the chair of the vice president and signaled Wheeler and McCreery in the Vice President's Room that Bill's inauguration was ready to begin. On the arm of McCreery, Wheeler entered the chamber by the south door to applause from the galleries and sat in a chair on Ferry's right. As Bill sat down and saw Hayes's wife, Lucy, sitting in a front seat in the private gallery next to the diplomatic corps, a wave of melancholy must have swept over Bill as he thought of his deceased wife, Mary, who would have been sitting next to Lucy if Mary had still been alive.

When the applause subsided, Wheeler rose and gave a brief speech. He said he knew from his experience "how delicate and at times difficult and complex" the duties of the vice president could be but he promised that he would lift himself "entirely above the elements of partisanship" and would administer the Senate rules "with courteous firmness." After more applause died down, Wheeler said he was ready to take the oath of office, which was then administered by Ferry. Wheeler's first official act as vice president was to direct the sergeant-at-arms to proceed with the presidential inauguration ceremonies. Wheeler joined the procession, which formed and marched to the east portico of the Capitol where Hayes took his public oath of office. After the ceremony, Wheeler returned to the Senate wing of the Capitol with Hayes and Grant where they entered their carriages and rode back to the White House.[37]

THE DAILY GRAPHIC

AN ILLUSTRATED EVENING NEWSPAPER.

39 & 41 PARK PLACE.

VOL. XIII. All the News. Four Editions Daily. NEW YORK, MONDAY, MARCH 12, 1877. $12 Per Year in Advance. Single Copies, Five Cents. NO. 1243.

THE INAUGURATION---VICE-PRESIDENT WHEELER TAKING THE OATH OF OFFICE IN THE SENATE CHAMBER.

[FROM A SKETCH BY OUR SPECIAL ARTIST AND PHOTOGRAPHS BY BRADY.]

Wheeler taking the vice president's oath of office. U.S. Senate Collection.

News of Wheeler's inauguration was greeted by fireworks and bonfires in the North Country. In Malone, 185 guns, one for each electoral vote cast for Hayes and Wheeler, were fired as the Hayes and Wheeler Guards paraded through the streets to band music. In Ogdensburg, a national salute of thirteen guns introduced the city band, which played patriotic music under a large Republican banner. The Ogdensburg celebration continued throughout the day featuring yet another salute, this one of thirty-eight guns, one for each state in the Union, as well as more band music and songs by glee clubs, bonfires, and speeches by leading political figures in the North Country.[38]

Meanwhile, across Lake Champlain in Burlington, Vermont, the student body at the University of Vermont celebrated Wheeler's inauguration by lighting a candle in every pane of glass on the front of the college's main building and installing a calcium light, which blazed down from the top of the building's dome. A torchlight procession made its way to all the homes of the professors and set the stage for a speech by UVM's president, Matthew H. Buckham. He praised his students and rejoiced with them at the elevation of a UVM alumnus to the second highest office in the nation.[39]

Later that evening, in Washington, the vice president from Malone had a chance to reflect on the day's experiences after he had retired to his 12th Street residence following the postinauguration day activities.[40] Wheeler had come a long way since his threadbare childhood in Malone and must have humbly thanked his God for it all. In addition, Bill may have even dared to think about the three men who during his lifetime had succeeded to the presidency following the president's death: John Tyler when Bill was twenty-one; Millard Fillmore when Bill was thirty-one; and Andrew Johnson when Bill was forty-five. Now, at the age of fifty-seven, for the next four years, it was his turn to be one heartbeat away from the presidency.

23

"A Wild and Joyous Time"

☆

Wheeler's social life blossomed in new directions during his years of service as the nation's nineteenth vice president. Hayes's wife, Lucy, took an immediate liking to Bill but he declined an offer to make his home in the White House when he was in Washington because he preferred to maintain his independence by continuing to reside in his quarters on 12th Street where he had been living as a congressman for the last four years.[1] However, he became a regular visitor to the Hayes White House throughout his vice presidency.

Bill and Lucy were both very religious and went to church regularly. At times he would offer to pick Lucy up at the White House so that they might "worship together" at his church, the New York Avenue Presbyterian Church.[2] They also shared a love of music and singing. She had a beautiful contralto voice and he sang with a "sweet clear" bass.[3] On Sunday evenings, Wheeler could usually be found at the White House hymn sings, which were held in the upstairs library. That's where the Hayes family gathered to sing gospel and folk songs with their close friends and other members of the "presidential family," which often included Secretary of the Interior Carl Schurz, Treasury Secretary John Sherman, and his older brother, General William T. Sherman. Wheeler would often bring copies of "The Presbyterian Hymn and Tune Book" for use at these songfests.[4]

Because of the status of his office and his friendship with Lucy, as well as his warm personality and fine sense of humor, Wheeler became a member of the inner social circle at the White House. He was the second most frequent guest for dinner—only the future president and close friend of Hayes from Ohio, William McKinley, was present for dinner more often than Bill. Sometimes, Wheeler attended intimate, informal dinners with senators, generals, cabinet members, and Supreme Court justices. On other occasions, he attended White House state dinners, the most important social events held in Washington and one of the highest honors the U.S. government could bestow on a foreign nation. These multicourse dinners could last up to three hours.[5] Perhaps the most extensively decorated events Bill participated in at the White House were Hayes's New Year's Day receptions. The hallways were decorated with flags, evergreens, and blossoming plants, the chandeliers in all the parlors were adorned with lilies, and the tables and mantels were bedecked with cut flowers. At these receptions, Bill stood in line as a member of the presidential party to receive the visitors, which included the diplomatic corps, foreign ambassadors in uniform and court dress, members of the Supreme Court and District Courts, senators, representatives, army and navy officers, and later in the afternoon, a host of private citizens.[6]

At the Hayes White House, Wheeler had the social time of his life. Lucy Hayes made him feel so much at home there, he implored her to allow him to entertain her in the North Country by coming up to Malone and accompanying him on an expedition into the Adirondacks where he offered to show her "the wilderness" and "our grand forests." Bill promised her that the beauty of the Adirondacks would make "the splendor of a White House reception pale in the contrast."[7]

Lucy accepted the invitation and arrived by train in Malone with her nine-year-old daughter, Fanny, and a mutual friend, Mrs. John Woodworth, on Saturday, May 18, 1878. Bill arranged for them to be picked up by carriages at the railroad station and brought to his home on Elm Street where they would stay and prepare for their trip into the Adirondacks. That evening, the Malone Coronet Band and the Malone Glee Club serenaded Bill and his three guests. His brick house was brilliantly lighted and a large gathering of people came to catch a glimpse of the vice president and the first lady. When they strolled side by side onto the veranda, they were met with prolonged applause and heavy cheering. Bill thanked the crowd for coming and praised Lucy as "the true ideal of an American woman" who had won the admiration of the American people not "by the arts of society, so called, but by strong native common sense" and her consideration for others, which Bill said sprang from "a thoroughly good heart." When Wheeler finished, he and Lucy went back inside to the glee club's rendition of the popular hit song, "Home Again," and a sparkling display of fireworks. On Sunday morning, Bill took his guests to his church, the Malone Congregational Church, for services. On Tuesday, Wheeler led his party south, into the Adirondacks.[8]

They made their headquarters at the Prospect House on Upper Saranac Lake. Bill hired one of his favorite Adirondack guides, Lucius Evans of Saranac Lake, to help them find the best fishing spots. Soon the telegraph wires from the Prospect House to Hayes in the White House hummed with news about their exploits in the wilderness. Wheeler sent a large fish that had been caught to the president. When it arrived, Hayes jokingly telegraphed Wheeler that although the note accompanying the fish said it weighed thirteen pounds, Hayes thought it weighed more like thirteen ounces![9] Two days later, Bill wired Hayes that Lucy was the "Champion of the day" because she had captured a deer swimming in the water that afternoon.[10] On May 30, Bill telegraphed Hayes that Lucy had caught a fifteen-pound salmon trout and that he was sending it to the president. Calling Hayes "a doubting Thomas" because of his comment about the size of the last fish he had sent him, Bill urged Hayes to "summon a coroners jury" to weigh the fish. When it arrived, Hayes was duly impressed with Lucy's catch and served it as the main course at an informal dinner party he gave for four of his cabinet members and several Republican House leaders.[11] Wheeler and his party left the Prospect House for a short stay at Paul Smith's magnificent resort hotel on Lower St. Regis Lake before heading back to Malone. They carried with them fifty pounds of trout they had caught.[12]

At noon while they were traveling through Duane on their way back to Malone from Paul Smith's Hotel, a touching scene took place, which may or may not have been prearranged by Wheeler. As their four-horse coach approached a small schoolhouse, a dozen boys and girls poured out into the schoolyard waving American flags and making formal bows to Wheeler and Lucy. Bill ordered the coach to stop and he introduced the children and their teacher to Lucy who spoke a few words to each of them and gave them all a warm hug before leaving.[13]

Lucy's eleven-day expedition into the Adirondacks with Bill came to an end when she arrived in Malone on Friday, May 31. She and her daughter spent the weekend and most of the following week recovering from their adventure. Bill held an open house for Lucy on the night before they boarded the train for Washington. When she got back to the White House, she wrote to thank Bill for "a wild and joyous time." Bill never forgot Lucy's visit and repeatedly wrote to the Hayes family about it for the rest of his life.[14]

There was much more to Wheeler's new social life than hymn sings, dinners, and fishing expeditions. Bill made an effort to find another woman to love. He missed his wife, Mary, and described her passing to Lucy as a "terrible shadow" that crossed his path.[15] However, he got involved in two romantic relationships, which cast some light on this shadow. They sprang from his newfound social life at the White House. To his friends, neither relationship held much promise to

Lucy Hayes. Brady-Handy Collection, Library of Congress.

become serious because one involved a woman who was thirty-four years younger than Bill, and the other involved a woman who was married.

The younger woman was Emily Platt, Hayes's twenty-four-year-old niece. Bill met Emily at one of the informal dinners he attended at the White House shortly after being inaugurated vice president. Soon they were singing gospel and folk songs together on Sunday nights at the Hayes hymn sings in the library. Bill was charmed by Emily but he admitted to Lucy that he felt his relationship with Emily was "constrained"—probably by the large difference in age between them.[16] In the fall, a rival for Emily's attention arrived at the White House and swept her off her feet. He was Russell Hastings, the former U. S. marshal for the Northern District of Ohio. He was an old friend of Hayes from the days when Hastings served as Hayes's aide-de-camp during the Civil War. Like Bill, Hastings was a widower, but unlike Bill, he was only forty-two and much closer in age to Emily than the fifty-eight-year-old vice president. Her romance with Hastings heated up and the couple was married at a quiet ceremony in the Blue Room of the White House six months after they began dating.[17] A few days after the wedding, Bill pined for Emily in a letter to Lucy. He said, "And so Emily has gone, I wish . . . there were more like her. I shall greatly miss her."[18]

Bill's romantic interests fared better with another woman who also frequented the hymn sings at the White House. She was Mrs. John M. Woodworth, the wife of Dr. John Woodworth, the medical hero of Sherman's March to the Sea who had been appointed by Grant to be the first supervising surgeon of the Marine Hospital Service.[19] The Woodworths used to live in the same apartment house as Wheeler when he was a member of Congress. When Mary died, they helped and consoled Bill. Mrs. Woodworth was musically minded and knew how to play the piano. She was often present to accompany Bill, Lucy, and the other singers on the piano at the White House songfests. When Lucy and Fanny traveled to Malone for their Adirondack expedition, Mrs. Woodworth came with them and stayed over in Wheeler's house for several days after Lucy and Fanny returned to Washington. Later that summer, Bill went to Martha's Vineyard with Mrs. Woodworth, accompanied by two other married couples who were friends of Wheeler from Malone. In March of the following year, Dr. Woodworth died and Bill was able to help and console the widow Woodworth.[20] During the course of the next two years, if rumors in the newspapers were true, Bill and Mrs. Woodworth continued to see each other and soon a newspaper headline trumpeted, "Wm. A. Wheeler's Approaching Marriage." According to the story, the wedding was supposed to take place in mid-winter of 1882.[21] The marriage never did take place. Why it was called off is a mystery, although one published report suggested Wheeler's poor health may have been the reason.[22]

Bill had no children and when his sixty-three-year-old unmarried sister, Sarah Fidelia, died on May 28,1879, he wrote Lucy, "I am all alone now." Fidelia had been an invalid for several years and died in Wheeler's home where she had been residing and receiving medical care.[23] To alleviate the loneliness that he said had "intensified" with the death of Fidelia, the last remaining member of his immediate family, Bill reached out to two of his cousins.

One of them lived in Pennsylvania and the other in Tennessee. They were both sons of Bill's uncle, Salmon Wheeler. The oldest, Alfred Wheeler, was five years younger than Bill, married, and the father of seven children. Even though Bill had recently been awarded an honorary doctor of law degree from Union College that he proudly added to the other honorary degrees he had received from the University of Vermont and Dartmouth, he could not compete with the number of advanced degrees that his cousin Alfred had earned.[24] They included a master of arts, a doctor of divinity, a doctor of law, and a doctor of medicine. Alfred could work as a minister, a doctor, and a lawyer but at the time Bill and Alfred began visiting and getting to know each other, Alfred was working as the editor of the *Pittsburg Christian Advocate*, a Methodist newspaper.[25] When Alfred and his family visited Bill in Malone, Alfred preached from the pulpit in both the Methodist Church and Bill's Congregational Church.[26] When Bill visited Alfred in Pittsburg, Bill preached from his vice presidential pulpit to the newspaper reporters who mobbed him.[27]

The other cousin Bill reached out to, Xenophon Wheeler, was also married and had three children. A Yale graduate and a Union captain in the Civil War, he was fifteen years younger than Bill. Xenophon was a lawyer and one of the wealthiest and most prominent residents of Chattanooga. In 1879, he was appointed U.S. Attorney for the Eastern District of Tennessee.[28] It is not known whether his cousin, the vice president, had a hand in his appointment but it would seem likely he did. The three cousins spent the Christmas of 1879 together in Chattanooga at Xenophon's home.[29]

Bill's social life at the White House, his romantic interludes, and his growing relationship with his cousins and their families, helped center Bill psychologically and provide balance to his high-powered political career, which was rapidly approaching a new stage. After his election, he did some long-range political planning. Because Hayes had renounced a second term in his letter of acceptance of the GOP nomination, Bill thought he might have an outside chance to succeed Hayes as the Republican nominee for president in 1880.[30] However, he dismissed that possibility in favor of a much more likely goal—winning election to the U.S. Senate when the term of Democrat Francis Kernan expired on March 3, 1881.

To achieve that goal, Wheeler would have to negotiate a number of treacherous, political crosscurrents swirling in the political waters of New York State.

Election to the U.S. Senate, in the days before the Seventeenth Amendment was ratified in 1913, lay in the hands of state legislatures. Bill calculated that for him to win election to the U.S Senate in New York, he would have to win the votes of between forty-five and sixty assemblymen and state senators in a Republican legislative caucus—a majority of the Republican legislators in office at the time of the U.S. Senate election. To do that, he would have to contend with powerful pro-Conkling and anti-Conkling Republicans who were on edge about Hayes's plans for civil service reform.

24

The Frozen Snake and the "Greatest of Humbugs"

★

The first few weeks of Wheeler's vice presidency were heady ones for him. The *Chicago Journal* reminded its readers that a year previously, the name of Wheeler was more familiar to the American people than that of Hayes, and that the GOP nominating convention could have just as easily named Bill to be the party's presidential nominee as it did Hayes. The *Journal* concluded saying, "The truth is the two men are peers and we confidently believe that the vice president will be an important factor in the new administration." Other newspapers stressed a similar theme. Some predicted that Wheeler would be as good for the nation as Jefferson and Adams were when they were vice presidents. Others expected Bill to sit with Hayes at cabinet meetings.[1]

In a letter to Hayes, Bill explained how he saw his role as vice president. Wheeler said he would have "no advice to proffer, no position to seek, but always at your command."[2] The president sought Wheeler's suggestions for cabinet appointments and Bill urged him to appoint Charles Devens to be attorney general. He was the law partner of Bill's political ally from Massachusetts, George F. Hoar. Hayes agreed with Bill's recommendation and appointed Devens to the post.[3]

Given Wheeler's extensive knowledge of parliamentary law, it was not surprising that he received rave reviews for his first few weeks of work as presiding officer of the Senate. On its front page, the *New York Times* gushed that Bill was "the best presiding officer that has filled the chair in many administrations."[4]

In July, the *Boston Herald* published a sensational story that brought Wheeler's heady days as vice president to an end. The article charged Wheeler with self-dealing and obstruction of justice while he was a congressman during the Civil War. Claiming to rely on "official documents," the *Herald* stated that in 1861, Wheeler had written to Lincoln's secretary of war, Simon Cameron, offering to sell the federal government one hundred thousand muskets that had been manufactured by the Remington Arms Company in Ilion, New York, a village on the Erie Canal in Herkimer County. According to the story, the war department agreed to purchase fifty thousand muskets from Wheeler before a formal contract had been executed. The *Herald* went on to explain that Wheeler's offer violated a law forbidding congressmen from contracting with the federal government. In addition, the paper charged Wheeler with opposing a congressional investigation into Cameron's military contracts.[5]

Other papers, including the highly respected *Springfield Republican,* immediately picked up the story and printed it. One referred to the charges as "a blister Mr. Wheeler would have to bear." Another said the charges were evidence that Bill was not the "political and personal saint" his friends made him out to be.

Wheeler jumped to his own defense and declared that every statement in the story was "wholly untrue" and "wickedly libelous." Bill wrote Samuel Bowles, the editor of the *Springfield Republican,* demanding that he print proof of the charges from the *Congressional Globe.* Along with the letter, Bill sent Bowles selections from the *Congressional Globe,* which showed that Bill had voted in favor of censuring Cameron. Wheeler also pointed out to the editor of the *Republican* that there were three men besides himself who were named "William A. Wheeler." One lived in Cambridge, Massachusetts, another in New York City, and the third in Worcester, Massachusetts. Bill concluded, "Does not the golden rule require that you substantiate your charges or retract them?"

The *Republican* quickly retracted its story but in doing so, it complained of the "insulting tone" Wheeler had used in his letter of complaint to Bowles. In the meantime, the Remington Arms Company denied it had ever had any business dealings with Wheeler—in fact, the company said it had never met him. Within another week, the *Boston Herald* received a letter stating that its charges against Vice President Wheeler were wrong—it was signed "William Adams Wheeler, 176 Fulton Street, New York." The *Herald* promptly retracted its story.[6]

False newspaper charges of corruption were minor concerns for Bill compared to several important political differences of opinion that cropped up between himself and the president during the first two years of Wheeler's vice presidency. The first rough spot with Hayes appeared when he proposed to carry out his end of the bargain he had made with southern Democrats to end the controversy surrounding the counting of the 1876 election returns. Hayes planned to order the federal troops out of the South even though doing so would pull the rug out from under the Republican governors in Louisiana and South Carolina—the only two Republican governors left in the South. Without the presence of federal troops, the two governors would be forced from office leaving the newly freed blacks in the two states at the mercy of white Democrats, many of whom were itching to return to the days when the blacks were their slaves.

Hayes believed that the U.S. public was tired of using federal troops to prop up one state government (Republican) against a rival state government (Democratic). He wrote in his diary that if withdrawing the troops "leads to the overthrow of the de jure government in a State, the de facto government must be recognized." The president wanted Wheeler to help him smooth things over with the Republicans in Louisiana before he ordered the troops out. Given Wheeler's successful experience negotiating political differences in Louisiana, Hayes felt Bill would be the perfect man to lead a presidential commission to Louisiana whose ostensible purpose would be to reach an understanding with the contending factions in order to guarantee black rights and avoid outbursts of violence when the federal troops were gone. Probably not wanting to be part of a sham whose real purpose was to cover up the military abandonment of the Republican whites and blacks in Louisiana and South Carolina, Bill jolted Hayes by flatly refusing to serve on the commission.[7]

Given Wheeler's experience working with southern politicians, he thought that Hayes was naive when it came to southern politics. Hayes thought that if he withdrew the federal troops, he might be able to cultivate the good will of the southern whites and motivate them to protect black rights. The president believed that the time for conciliation had come—there could be no permanent protection of the southern blacks without the cooperation of the southern whites.[8]

Wheeler was convinced that white southern Democrats could not be trusted to keep their word.[9] Bill wrote Hayes, "I never had a particle of faith in their beguiling professions." Wheeler likened the ex-Confederates to the frozen snake in Aesop's fable, "The Farmer and the Snake," which mortally bit a compassionate farmer who had picked the frozen snake up off the ground and put it inside his shirt to revive it.[10]

The second rough spot between Hayes and Wheeler concerned civil service reform. When Hayes issued orders on June 22, 1877, directing competitive examinations for certain federal jobs and forbidding federal office holders to actively participate in political organizations or campaigns, Bill growled with dismay.[11] As a hardened politician, Bill had learned that jobs for friends and family were the lifeblood of a successful political organization. Conkling's phrase, *snivel service,* aptly described Wheeler's opinion of civil service reform. Furthermore, he had no faith that a test could accurately measure a job applicant's suitability for employment. Bill also believed that it was a mistake to adopt rules that would make it difficult to fire lazy or uncooperative government employees.

Newspapers pounced on Wheeler's opposition to civil service reform and tagged him as an "anti-Hayes" man on this issue. Hoping to stir up discord within the Republican ranks, the Democratic *New York World* went so far as to say that Bill was "at the bottom of all this anti-Hayes agitation."[12] When Hayes reinvigorated the Civil Service Commission by appointing a new director, the press in the North Country echoed Wheeler's sentiments by calling the commission "the greatest of humbugs" and crying out, "good Lord, deliver us" from it.[13]

Bill may have been opposed to a Civil Service Commission but when it came to the president's frontal attack on Conkling's control of the New York Custom House, he gave Hayes substantial support. Because it collected more revenue than all other U.S. ports of entry combined, the Custom House in New York City was a major source of patronage and campaign contributions for the state's ruling political party.[14] During the Grant administration, Conkling had convinced the president to appoint Conkling loyalists to the helm of the Custom House. They included Chester A. Arthur, George H. Sharpe, and Alonzo B. Cornell.

Chester A. Arthur, a Phi Beta Kappa graduate of Union College and a lawyer from New York City, ruled the Custom House as collector. During the Civil War, Arthur had served as New York's quartermaster general for Governor Morgan. Since 1870, Arthur had been Conkling's chief political lieutenant. George H. Sharpe of Kingston was second in command at the Custom House holding the position of surveyor, the man in charge of the inspectors and weighers. A lawyer, he had previously worked as a special agent for the U.S. State Department for Secretary Seward and had been U.S. marshal for the Southern District of New York. The third man in authority was Alonzo B. Cornell, the Custom House naval officer. He was in charge of a multitude of clerks who computed the customs duties. A highly successful businessman from Ithaca, Alonzo was the son of Ezra Cornell. At the same time he was serving as naval officer, Cornell was doing double duty as Conkling's chairman of the Republican state committee.[15]

In the fall of 1877, Hayes trained his sights on Arthur, Sharpe, and Cornell and prepared to replace them at the Custom House, in the name of civil service reform, with men who were not in Conkling's camp. Bill had never been a Conkling supporter and remembered well how little Conkling had campaigned for Bill's election in 1876. In addition, Wheeler suspected Conkling of working behind the scenes with Tilden supporters during the vote-counting controversy to deliver electoral victory to the Democrats. The vice president from Malone winced every time he heard Conkling snidely refer to Hayes as "His Fraudulency" and "Rutherfraud B. Hayes"—if Hayes's election was a fraud, so was Wheeler's.[16]

The president chose Theodore Roosevelt Sr., the father of the future president, to replace Arthur, and L. Bradford Prince, a lawyer from Queens County, to replace Cornell. Hayes leaned toward replacing Sharpe with Edwin A. Merritt of Potsdam but before doing so, the president decided to clear the former Liberal Republican with Wheeler because of their testy political history in the North Country.

In a letter responding to Hayes's inquiry about Merritt's suitability to be the Custom House surveyor, Wheeler urged Hayes to make the appointment because Merritt was a "thoroughly honest and capable man." Knowing that Merritt disdained Conkling almost as much as Wheeler did, Bill added in his letter to Hayes that "no more political appointment could be made."[17]

One week before the voters went to the polls in the 1877 election, Hayes sent the nominations of Roosevelt, Prince, and Merritt to the Senate for confirmation. Sharpe withdrew his application for reappointment but that did not stop Conkling from launching a ferocious battle to keep Arthur and Cornell in office.[18] Conkling's defense of his two lieutenants was impressive and in December, the Senate rejected the president's nomination of Roosevelt and Prince. However, given Sharpe's withdrawal and Wheeler's support for Merritt, the North Country Republican won confirmation easily.[19]

Conkling was elated by his triumph over the Republican president and Wheeler was equally pleased that Merritt had won. Hayes was shaken by his loss but refused to surrender to the senior senator from New York. As soon as Congress adjourned, Hayes rang the bell for the second round of his attack on Conkling's control of the New York Custom House by suspending Arthur and Cornell. On July 11, 1878, Hayes appointed Wheeler's man, Merritt, to replace Arthur as collector. To replace Cornell as naval officer, Hayes named Cornell's deputy, Silas W. Burt, a civil engineer and college classmate of Arthur's from Albany.[20]

Wheeler was delighted by Hayes's grit and, behind the scenes, encouraged support for Merritt. Conkling was outraged by the president's renewed attack and vowed to crush him again by blocking Merritt's and Burt's confirmation in the Senate and thereby put Arthur and Cornell back in office.[21]

Reform and anti-reform Republicans began to draw battle lines as the 1878 election approached. Hayes's appointments had roiled the political waters and Conkling's friends accused the president of trying to set up his own machine in New York State.[22] Even though the only statewide race in 1878 was for a vacancy on the Court of Appeals, other important offices were on the ballot. Control of the House and the Senate in Washington were at stake as was that of the assembly in Albany. The makeup of the new legislature was of significant interest to Conkling because his term would expire in March 1879 and he wanted to be reelected. Wheeler's political future was also bound up in Albany politics. When his term as vice president was over, he hoped to succeed Democrat Francis Kernan in the Senate when his term expired in March 1881. Because of this, it was vital to Wheeler that he have a trustworthy Franklin County man in the assembly who would be his eyes and ears and carry out his political strategy.

In the summer of 1878, the man Wheeler had been counting on to serve in that capacity, John I. Gilbert, a three-term incumbent assemblyman from Malone, decided not to run for reelection citing poor health as his reason.[23] Two candidates stepped forward to vie for Gilbert's place. One was Hiram Burns, the Fort Covington town supervisor. The other was William D. Brennan of Malone, the Franklin County treasurer.[24] Probably because Wheeler admired the way Brennan had overcome many of the same obstacles that Wheeler had faced when he was growing up, Bill developed a liking for the thirty-nine-year-old Civil War veteran and backed him for the assembly nomination.

Brennan had been born in Canada and had come to Malone at the age of twelve to take a job as a water carrier for a gang of men working to build the Northern Railroad. He worked his way through Franklin Academy and was a student at Middlebury College when the Civil War broke out. Brennan left college and enlisted in the army, where he rose to the rank of captain. During action in Virginia, he was severely wounded in the foot requiring his leg to be amputated above the ankle joint. After the war, he returned to Malone, became a lawyer, got involved in Republican politics, and married. With Wheeler's considerable clout behind him at the GOP county convention in September, Brennan defeated Burns for the assembly nomination, thirty to eighteen.[25]

Wheeler was confident that he had made the right decision by choosing Brennan over Burns. Brennan professed loyalty to the vice president and promised to give him accurate reports about assembly politics and to lay the groundwork for Wheeler's upcoming bid for the Senate in 1881. When the county convention adjourned, Bill embraced the general election campaign, which was in full swing.

The depression that had begun with the Panic of 1873 was in its fifth year. Although some businesses, such as those involving railroads, mining, and construction, had improved by 1877, prices and wages continued to drop.[26] In response to the poor economic conditions, the Greenback Party had made inroads in New York State. The Greenbackers had blamed the depression on the contraction of the money supply after the Civil War and had run a candidate for president in

1876. Their platform demanded an end to the resumption of specie payments and called for the public debt to be paid with greenbacks. The call for "cheap money" had gained support from farmers in the West and Midwest but in New York State, the Greenbackers became more a labor organization than a farmers party.[27] In the summer of 1878, discontented New York labor organizations formed a Labor Reform Party, which subsequently merged with the Greenbackers at a convention held in Syracuse in July. Additional local Greenback parties sprouted up across the Empire State. In Franklin County, they organized parties in Malone and Chateaugay and had called for meetings in Bellmont and Duane. In addition to currency matters, their platforms called for an eight-hour workday, government control of the railroads, and an end to the use of convict labor and the importation of Chinese laborers.[28]

Wheeler observed Democrats all over the state scurrying to take advantage of the sudden surge in the popularity of the Greenback cause by forming alliances with Greenback interests. In several counties, it was hard to tell whether a Democratic Party even existed because Greenbackers replaced Democrats as candidates for Congress and the legislature.[29] It was against this political backdrop that Vice President Wheeler made a major campaign appearance in Canton at the St. Lawrence County Fair in September.

He arrived at the railroad station at 10 a.m. and was greeted by a large crowd and three bands. They formed a procession and marched Wheeler to the fairgrounds where the leading politicians from St. Lawrence, Franklin, Clinton, and Jefferson Counties and fifteen thousand other people had assembled to listen to the vice president's speech, which received front-page coverage in the *New York Times.* He began by denouncing the Labor Reform wing of the Greenbackers for its charges that capital in the United States unfairly dominated labor and politics. Bill labeled such arguments "wild notions" that came from the "Nihilism of Russia, Socialism of Germany, and Communism that has no geographical limits."

To cheers from his largely rural audience, Wheeler moved on to lambaste the currency proposals that had been advanced by the Greenbackers. He warned his listeners to beware the "great many panaceas" being offered by the Greenback party. He said, "I was born in the old school and have no faith in the new nostrums." Calling for a return to "the old paths," he encouraged his audience to adopt a "soberer view of life." The vice president said the nation could not regain prosperity until a far larger proportion of the people became willing to earn every dollar they received. Wheeler mocked "speculating in fancy stocks and the invention of fancy schemes of plunder." Wheeler said the foundation for permanent prosperity was "manly occupation" and "manly independence." Bill said, "Brain must go with hard hands, mind must go with muscle, if you would reach the full result of your labor." He concluded by praising the farmers in his audience by saying, "the proprietors of the soil stand at the basis of all society" and "are the guiding and controlling influence on government."[30]

Wheeler's rhetoric was the highlight of the campaign in the North Country and when the ballots were counted, the Republicans were victorious. Brennan was easily elected to the assembly, which would be controlled by the Republicans 98 to 30. Conkling's reelection to the U.S. Senate was assured.[31] Nationally, the political picture for the GOP was much dimmer. The Democrats retained a majority in the House and won enough state legislatures to enable them to take control of the Senate away from the Republicans when the Forty-sixth Congress opened on March 18, 1879.[32]

However, before that day arrived, the second round of Hayes's attack on Conkling's control of the New York Custom House played out in the Senate. According to law, Merritt and Burt had to win confirmation or Arthur and Cornell would be returned to their positions at the Custom House. Wheeler's political position during round two was influenced by his strategy for winning his own election to the Senate in 1881. Wheeler anticipated that there would be a number of strong Conkling and anti-Conkling candidates for the office—Bill wanted to be the compromise candidate, the man who would be acceptable to both the Conkling and the anti-Conkling forces. Given Wheeler's history with the senior senator from New York, he would easily be acceptable to anti-Conkling men. However, if he became identified as a rabid or ultra anti-Conkling man, Bill risked becoming unacceptable to Conkling supporters.

The public was unable to tell from the newspapers exactly where Wheeler stood when it came to replacing Arthur and Cornell, which is exactly what Wheeler wanted. For example, the *Albany Journal* reported that Wheeler was the man behind the movement against Arthur and Cornell but Wheeler's own hometown paper condemned the president's action as "a blunder" and "an expression of indifference for party harmony."[33]

Behind the scenes, Bill was forthright about where he stood. He wrote Hayes that he had "great confidence" in the integrity of Merritt and that his appointment would be acceptable to the great mass of New York Republicans.[34] Through his man Brennan in Albany, Bill generated additional support for the president. Brennan was one of fifty Republicans in the assembly and four state senators to sign a memorial to Conkling, requesting that Merritt and Burt be confirmed in order to end a quarrel which the memorial said was "unpleasant and dangerous to party harmony."[35]

In Washington, it did not take long for the confirmation proceedings to get ugly. Conkling attacked Hayes's sincerity by reading letters that had been written by the president's secretary and members of the cabinet to Arthur when he was the collector asking for jobs for friends. One letter sought a position for the son of Justice Bradley, whose vote on the electoral commission was critical to Hayes's election. Conkling ridiculed Hayes, using exclamations of mock surprise followed by comical questions and loud laughter. Observers said such a scene had never been seen before in the Senate and described it as a "grotesque exhibition." When it came time for the vote, Conkling's tactics backfired on him. Twenty-five Democrats joined fifteen Republicans to confirm Merritt, forty to thirty. Burt was confirmed thirty-one to nineteen.[36]

New York Republicans were stunned. They had thought Conkling was invincible.[37] Wheeler applauded the outcome and began to mull its impact on his upcoming bid for the Senate. All of New York's chief elected state officers, seven in number, from governor on down to engineer, would be standing for election in 1879. Bill wondered how Conkling's loss of control of the Custom House would affect his control of the GOP in the Empire State. Wheeler asked himself, could Conkling be beaten at the 1879 Republican state nominating convention? Would this be the right time to challenge Conkling's political authority?

25

"The Machine Always Slaughters Its New Converts"

☆

THE YEAR 1879 was the high point of Wheeler's public career in New York State. During this year, he not only was instrumental in saving the natural beauty of Niagara Falls from commercial destruction, he was also acknowledged by state Republican leaders as the one man who might be able to break the stranglehold Conkling had on the New York Republican Party.

Wheeler's involvement with the movement to preserve the natural beauty of Niagara Falls was driven by his love of the great outdoors and linked to his appointment in 1876 to be an original member of the Board of Commissioners of the State Survey, which was created to make an accurate survey of the state and county lines.[1]

In January 1879, Democratic Governor Lucius Robinson observed in his annual message to the legislature that the shores of the Niagara River around Niagara Falls were swarming with "sharpers, hucksters, and peddlers who perpetually harass all visitors." He called for the appointment of a commission to consider the creation of an international park, in cooperation with Canada, that would exclude all "the annoyances and vexations" he had mentioned, on both sides of the river.[2]

Newspaper reporters painted an even uglier scene than the governor had. One article noted that "unsightly mill shacks and rickety drinking booths" had been built along the riverbank, signs of "quack medicine men" had been painted on the rocks, and every prominent outlook had been "crowned with the booth of some vagabond peddler."[3]

In June, the Republican legislature referred the idea of creating a park to protect Niagara Falls to the Board of Commissioners of the State Survey. The director of the Board, James F. Gardner of Albany, accompanied by Frederick Law Olmstead, a well-known landscape architect, toured the grounds around Niagara Falls and began work preparing a report for the commissioners' study and approval.[4]

The *New York Times* reported that the idea of turning Niagara Falls into a "grand free park" was in the hands of Wheeler and the other commissioners of the board who included former Governor Horatio Seymour of Utica and President Frederick A. P. Barnard of Columbia College. The *Times* urged Bill and his fellow commissioners to "obliterate the stain" on Niagara Falls that had been put there by "hackmen and vendors of photographs, stuffed monkeys and South American parrots."[5]

State Survey Director Gardner submitted his report to the Board of Commissioners at a meeting in Utica on November 20. Wheeler and the other six commissioners voted unanimously to adopt the Special Report on the Preservation of the Scenery of Niagara Falls and sent it on to the legislature for action.[6]

Prospect Point at Niagara Falls. Detroit Publishing Company Collection, Library of Congress.

Niagara Falls. Detroit Publishing Company Collection, Library of Congress.

In their report, Wheeler and the other commissioners said that Niagara Falls was "the crowning glory" of the state and that New York held the Falls "under a sacred obligation to mankind." Asserting that the defacement of the scenery around the Falls was an "evil" that could not cure itself, the report said that gifts of nature like the Falls were "entitled to reverential protection." Wheeler and the other commissioners recommended that the legislature create a state park along the bank of the Niagara River by purchasing the land around the Falls, tearing down the buildings, planting trees and bushes, and constructing a road and walkways along the river together with an extended platform that would overlook the Falls.[7]

A memorial addressed to the governor of New York and the governor-general of Canada urging preservation of the Falls was made part of the report when it was submitted to the legislature on March 31, 1880. The memorial was signed by hundreds of prominent people including: justices of the U.S. Supreme Court and the courts of Great Britain; U.S. senators, congressmen and members of the British Parliament; presidents of many colleges including Yale and Harvard; clergymen, professors, mayors, and army generals; as well as the famous writers Ralph Waldo Emerson, Henry Wadsworth Longfellow, and Oliver Wendell Holmes. At the top of the list of luminaries who had signed the memorial, by itself on the very first line, was the signature of "W. A. Wheeler, Vice President of the United States."[8]

While the vice president took pleasure in knowledge that he was helping to carry out New York State's "sacred obligation to mankind," rebellious Republicans were imploring him to take on another obligation. They pleaded with him to lead an attack on Conkling's control of the party at the GOP state nominating convention that would be held in Saratoga Springs in September. Whether to do so was one of the most difficult and most important political decisions Wheeler ever had to make.

As much as he loathed Conkling, Bill was also a political realist who respected Conkling's power. The senior senator from New York State was a formidable foe who had a brilliant political mind and a statewide network of loyal friends. Based on Wheeler's political experience, he believed that Conkling would probably have the votes to control the upcoming convention. In light of this, and Wheeler's decision to run for the U.S. Senate in 1881 after his vice-presidential term expired, Bill's political instincts told him that leading a forlorn hope on an assault against Conkling's political machine at the convention was not a good idea.

The 1879 state election would be the first time in New York history that the governor and the other six top state officers would run for election at the same time.[9] State senators would also be on the ballot in November. Because they had two-year terms, the state senators elected in 1879 would be entitled to cast ballots in the legislature for the next U.S. senator from New York in 1881. Wheeler wanted friendly Republicans elected to the state senate—men who would vote for him. The politicians who would wield influence and power at the state convention would be the same men who also controlled the GOP state senate conventions, which would be held after the state convention. Many of these men would also be sitting in the legislature as state senators in 1881. If Bill really wanted to win election to the U.S. senate in two years, he had to make friends at the state convention, not enemies.

In August, Republican county conventions chose 450 delegates to the state nominating convention. Still reeling from Hayes's removal of Cornell and Arthur from the helm of the New York Custom House, Conkling was determined to regain his balance and tighten his grip on the party by delivering the nomination for governor to Cornell. Anti-Conkling Republicans were aghast at the thought of Cornell being their party's nominee for governor. They resolutely set out to stop Cornell from being nominated and end Conkling's dominance of the party.

Conkling controlled many levers of power and he adroitly pulled them. He worked overtime to handpick as many delegates as he could. Many men owed their government jobs to him and he had provided speakers and money to a multitude of local GOP organizations. Conkling began to call in his political debts.[10] He demanded that anyone who wanted to continue to be his friend had to prove his loyalty by supporting Cornell.[11] Conkling also dangled the nominations for other state offices before the eyes of uncommitted delegates in exchange for support for Cornell—often promising the same state office to more than one man! Boss Conkling also exploited political divisions within state senate districts by promising state senate candidates that they would be nominated without a fight if they supported Cornell for governor.[12]

Of the four men who decided to challenge Cornell for the gubernatorial nomination, Wheeler felt William H. Robertson, a former assemblyman, congressman, and Westchester County judge from Katonah, would make the best candidate. The fifty-six-year-old Robertson was serving his third term in the state senate when he announced his bid for governor. For many years, he had been one of Conkling's most outspoken antagonists. Their feud went back to 1872 when Robertson blamed Conkling for denying him the GOP nomination for governor by promoting the candidacy of General John A. Dix.[13]

After the convention delegates had been selected, Conkling counted them. Of the 450 delegates, he needed a majority of 226 to win the nomination for Cornell. It became quickly apparent to Conkling that he was in a tight race and that one of the keys to Cornell's victory was going to be the twelve votes from St. Lawrence County, part of Wheeler's former congressional district. Conkling's point man in St. Lawrence County was Seth P. Remington, collector of the port of Ogdensburg and father of the future artist, Frederic Remington. The collector had done a convincing job of making local GOP leaders believe that Cornell's nomination was inevitable and that they should support him at the state convention if they ever wanted anything from the governor's office after Cornell won the election. In addition, promises were made that if St. Lawrence County's twelve delegates voted for Cornell, opposition to the renomination of incumbent State Senator Dolphus S. Lynde of Hermon would be silenced and after his election, he would have his choice of plum committee assignments. To sweeten the deal even further, St. Lawrence County leaders were told that in exchange for supporting Cornell, Conkling would deliver the secretary of state's nomination to a St. Lawrence County man, the bright and upcoming thirty-three-year-old lawyer and timber magnate from Colton, A. Barton Hepburn.[14]

Conkling was not the only politico at the convention who knew how to count delegates. His opponents also saw the significance of the votes from St. Lawrence County and begged Wheeler to lead a charge against Conkling by running for temporary chairman of the convention, a post Conkling had reserved for himself.[15] Their thinking was that if Bill ran as a candidate, he would win the St. Lawrence County votes and defeat Conkling, a sure sign to all the delegates that Conkling did not have the votes to control the convention and keep all the promises he had made to win votes for Cornell.

Wheeler was flattered by all the statewide attention he was receiving but Conkling was one step ahead of his opponents. Before Wheeler had been approached to run for temporary chairman, Conkling had offered Bill the post of permanent chairman of the convention and Wheeler had already accepted it. The vice president wanted to use the position to burnish his image before the U.S. Senate election in 1881. In fact, in anticipation of becoming permanent chairman, Wheeler had already written and printed up copies of his convention keynote speech.[16]

As the delegates began to pour into Saratoga, newspapers described the convention as "the most remarkable political gathering ever held in the State." The press predicted that because the delegates would include such men as Wheeler, Weed, Morgan, Fenton, Conkling, Curtis, Arthur, and dozens of congressmen, state senators, and assemblymen, there would be "more distinguished men and wise leaders" among the delegates than had ever attended a similar meeting. One newspaper said it would be worth the trip to Saratoga just to catch a glimpse of such "eminent men."[17]

Anti-Conkling newspapers reported that even though the race for governor was close and that there was widespread opposition to Cornell, Conkling's "well-oiled and obedient political organization" made Cornell the favorite to win. According to news stories, Cornell's four opponents were unable to work with each other. Political analysts predicted that because the opposition was "so scattered, divided and disorganized," they would lose unless they united behind a new statewide leader, for example, a man such as Vice President Wheeler. But would he lead an attack against Cornell and Conkling? Wheeler had not yet announced whom he was going to support. Tension mounted as the convention's opening day arrived.[18]

Bill made a dramatic arrival in Saratoga shortly after midnight on September 3. Anti-Conkling newspapermen and delegates who wanted to know who he was going to vote for besieged him. Wheeler's surprise announcement that he was going to vote for Robertson reenergized the anti-Conkling wing of the party. The vice president was opposing Cornell! As Wheeler made his way down Broadway to his room at the Grand Union Hotel, Cornell's opponents pleaded with him to make an appeal to the St. Lawrence County delegates who were also staying at the Grand Union, to vote against Cornell. Bill agreed to meet with them but when he did, he learned they were going to vote unanimously for Cornell. The deal Conkling had made with them about guaranteeing no opposition to Lynde's state senate nomination and promising to name Hepburn secretary of state, was too good for them to pass up.[19]

Anti-Conkling forces pleaded with the vice president from Malone to increase the pressure on St. Lawrence County delegates by throwing his hat into the gubernatorial ring and making a personal plea for St. Lawrence County's votes. In effect, Cornell's opponents were asking Wheeler to out-Conkling, Conkling. They wanted Bill to threaten his allies in St. Lawrence County with the loss of his friendship if they did not vote for him. Bill refused to do that. He would not make the vote a personal matter, a test of loyalty and friendship. The contest for governor was very close—it could go either way. Wheeler had no jobs or nominations to offer anyone. All he had at his disposal was the logic of his political thinking and the warmth of his continued political friendship. Most importantly, Bill had no interest in becoming governor of New York—he wanted to be the state's next U.S. Senator. To do that, Wheeler needed friends, such as State Senator Lynde from St. Lawrence County. And no one had to tell the vice president that threatening potential supporters was not the best way to win their votes—in fact, one of Wheeler's favorite expressions was that "molasses would catch more flies than vinegar."[20]

In the early hours of the morning, before the convention opened, Bill made a second attempt to convince the St. Lawrence County delegates to change their votes but once again, Bill was rebuffed. He could not match Conkling's offer to Lynde and Hepburn. Frustrated, Bill gave his St. Lawrence County neighbors something to think about as he went out the door. Wheeler warned them, "The machine always slaughters its new converts."[21]

The doors to the convention hall in Saratoga were thrown open at 10:40 a.m. on September 3 and in a few minutes, the hall was packed. When Wheeler entered, the delegates greeted him with applause and cheers. He sat strategically in one of the corners of the hall and was immediately surrounded by a cluster of delegates led by his friend, Henry James of Ogdensburg. Conkling was also met with applause when he came in and sat down conspicuously in one of the aisles making it easy for his men to make their way to him with the latest political intelligence. When the roll call of delegates was read, Wheeler's name brought another round of "lively cheering" and delegates stood on their chairs to get a look at the vice president. As chairman of the Republican state committee, Cornell called the convention to order and Conkling was elected temporary chairman, according to plan. He gave a brief speech before Wheeler was elected permanent chairman, also according to plan. As Bill walked to the podium, he was again met with warm and vigorous applause.[22]

Using no notes, Wheeler confined his keynote speech to national issues. He spent most of his time attacking the South for using "a carnival of rifles, shot guns, masks, red shirts, and tissue ballots" to take over the machinery of Southern state governments. Referring to Southerners as "rebel traitors," he reminded the delegates that control of the entire federal government would be at stake in the upcoming 1880 presidential election. Wheeler decried the "red-shirted mobocracy of the South" and demanded the election of a federal government, which he said should "protect the weak, the ignorant and the helpless, whom we have liberated." The vice president sounded very much like the future U.S. Senator he hoped he would be.[23] At the conclusion of Wheeler's speech, as the delegates were applauding him, Conkling hopped up on the stage and cordially shook Wheeler's hand to the "howling delight" of the audience.[24]

When the convention took up the business of nominating a governor, an ominous silence fell over the hall. Nominating speeches were abandoned. Tension mounted even higher when the voting began. Everyone wondered if Conkling would be able to deliver 226 votes for Cornell. One observer wrote that every vote cast "sounded like the night step of a watchful sentinel." Conkling voted for Cornell. Wheeler and the three other Franklin County delegates voted for Robertson. All twelve delegates from St. Lawrence County voted for Cornell. Dozens of men were keeping count. At the conclusion of the voting, Cornell won the nomination with 234 votes. Wheeler's instincts that Conkling would win had been correct. However, as anti-Conkling leaders pointed out, if only nine of the twelve delegates from St. Lawrence County had voted against Cornell, he would not have won a majority and Conkling would have been stopped cold in his tracks. The balloting would have had to begin again with everyone knowing that Conkling did not have the votes to deliver what he had promised.[25]

But, as Wheeler had suspected, Conkling did have the votes and every man nominated to run on the state ticket was a man endorsed by Conkling. When the convention finished making up the state ticket, St. Lawrence County delegates were horrified to learn that they should have heeded Wheeler's warning about the machine always slaughtering its new converts. Conkling had gone back on his promises to them and his real choice for secretary of state, Joseph B. Carr of Rensselaer County, had handily defeated Hepburn, St. Lawrence County's candidate.[26]

Anti-Conkling Republicans were distraught that they had failed to take the party back from Conkling. Political analysts highlighted Wheeler's role in Conkling's victory. The *New York Times* attributed it to Wheeler's failure to "specifically and directly" ask the St. Lawrence County delegates to vote against Cornell. The *Brooklyn Eagle* saw things differently and observed that Wheeler did ask the St. Lawrence County delegates to oppose Cornell but they refused because of promises that had been made to them by Conkling's man, Remington. The *Eagle* correctly pointed out that there was nothing more that Wheeler could have done to stop Cornell because Wheeler could not match what Conkling had to offer. George W. Curtis's *Harper's Weekly* stated that Wheeler deliberately chose not to fight Conkling and that if Bill had been "willing to lead" such a fight, Cornell would not have won.[27]

During the fall election campaign, Wheeler joined other members of the Hayes administration, including Secretary of State Evarts and Treasury Secretary Sherman, in an about face and endorsed Cornell for governor. Bill said Cornell was "a man of spotless integrity, of rare good judgment, and of high executive capacity."[28] The vice president worked hard for a Republican victory and was not disappointed. A split in the Democratic Party helped the Republicans win every state office except state engineer. The Republicans also won control of the state senate by a margin of twenty.[29] This meant that if the GOP could win the assembly in 1880, the next U.S. Senator from New York would be a Republican. On the local level, Assemblyman Brennan of Malone, the man Wheeler was counting on to manage his U.S. Senate election campaign on the ground in the halls of the legislature, won his second one-year term.[30]

When the dust from the election had settled, the sixty-year-old vice president from Malone turned the page of his political playbook and prepared for the upcoming presidential election. His bid for the Senate would occur shortly after the first of the year following the presidential election and he would have to deal with all the same Conkling and anti-Conkling personalities that he had just dealt with in Saratoga. He asked himself, had he made a mistake by not making his opposition to Cornell and Conkling, personal? Would the machine slaughter him next?

26

Delivering a "Paroxysm of Partisan Fury"

☆

Wheeler's last full year as vice president became a burden to him. He told his friends that he was tired of being a "mere puppet" presiding over the Senate, repeating certain words and phrases, over and over again. Dissatisfied with being what he called a *nonentity* during the great debates and seeking to avoid the warmer weather that was about to descend on Washington, Bill packed up and left town in May to go fishing in the Adirondacks with his tried and true Saranac Navigation Company. There were about seven weeks left to go in the first session of the Democratic-controlled Forty-sixth Congress and Bill promised he would return for the second session, which would begin in December. The *Brooklyn Eagle,* which enjoyed kidding Wheeler about his love of fishing, used Bill's departure as an excuse to give him a new name—the paper called him "the piscatorial Mr. Wheeler."[1]

Once Bill was back in Malone, he was able to devote himself full time to New York State politics, which had begun to boil over with questions about who should be the GOP nominee for president in 1880. A boomlet for Wheeler had begun. The *Watertown Times* said Wheeler would make a "first class President" and the *St. Lawrence Plaindealer* chimed in to agree. In Massachusetts, the *Springfield Republican* saw Wheeler as a possible president and the *Potsdam Courier* reported that Wheeler was Vermont's first choice for president. Referring to Wheeler as "the

Great Quiet Man," the *New London Telegram* in Connecticut said Wheeler should not be counted out in the GOP presidential calculations. Newspapers in Cleveland, New York City, and Cincinnati all touted Bill as a possible candidate. The most flattering story appeared in the *Brooklyn Eagle,* which quoted an Indiana state government official who described Bill as "the New York Lincoln" and predicted that the 1880 Republican ticket would be Wheeler for president and Benjamin Harrison of Indiana for vice president.[2]

President Hayes confided to his diary that if New York could present Wheeler's name "with a fair degree of unity" for president, he would probably be nominated.[3] Given the political reality in New York, that was not going to happen and Wheeler knew it. Nevertheless, he did not discourage speculation about his political future because his chances for election to the U.S. Senate were enhanced every time a newspaper story hailed him as a leading national political figure.

The Republican national convention was scheduled to open in Chicago on June 2, 1880. The major candidates for president included Grant, Blaine, and Treasury Secretary Sherman. In New York, Conkling was furiously promoting Grant to run for a third term, something unprecedented in U.S. history. It was at this time that Conkling and his pro-Grant supporters began to be widely referred to as *Stalwarts.* In turn, they derogatorily referred to anti-Grant and anti-Conkling men who were coalescing around Blaine's candidacy as Half-Breeds.[4]

Wheeler steered clear of both camps and sought to be recognized as an Independent. He had admired Grant as a general and as a former president but Bill despised Conkling. Wheeler also distrusted Blaine, having been double-crossed by him in 1873 when he had welshed on his promise to appoint Bill chairman of the House Appropriations Committee in exchange for Bill's promise not to challenge Blaine for Speaker.

The New York GOP nominating convention cycle to name national convention delegates got off to an unusually early start because of Conkling's plan to bind New York's delegates to Grant. Not wanting to lose the momentum that had been created by the public enthusiasm generated by Grant's return from a two-year world tour, which he had undertaken after Hayes succeeded him as president, Conkling and the Stalwarts called an early state convention to name national convention delegates. The convention was scheduled to be held in Utica on February 25, more than three months before the opening of the national convention.[5]

Bill told the *New York Tribune* that he doubted Grant would be nominated because the boom for the former president would subside. Wheeler stated that the enthusiasm for Grant had been fueled by the reaction of "farmers and other plain, loyal people" to the southern Democratic refusal to accept the results of the

Civil War. According to Wheeler, Grant supporters were telling America, "Grant whipped these fellows once, and if necessary, he will do it again."[6]

When the GOP state convention convened in Utica, Wheeler saw to it that his chief political lieutenant, Wells S. Dickinson of Bangor, and Wheeler's close political ally, Henry R. James of Ogdensburg, were elected national convention delegates from Bill's congressional district.[7] Dickinson and James and sixteen other New York national convention delegates defied Conkling and came out against Grant. State Senator William H. Robertson, the man Wheeler had supported for governor the previous year in Saratoga, and three other state senators announced that they were joining the Half-Breeds and would support Blaine for president.[8]

When the GOP national convention opened in Chicago on June 2, Conkling and the Stalwarts battled gallantly for Grant but anti-Grant forces outnumbered them. On a critical vote that sealed Grant's doom, the unit rule was voted down 449 to 306, thereby permitting Blaine and Sherman delegates from New York and other pro-Grant states to oppose Grant.[9] For thirty-five ballots, no candidate could muster a majority to win the nomination. On the thirty-sixth ballot, Dickinson and other Sherman delegates joined forces with James and other Blaine delegates to nominate a dark horse, Congressman James H. Garfield of Ohio. He defeated Grant 399 to 306.[10]

Garfield's managers wanted to strengthen the ticket by having a New Yorker run for vice president. Ohio delegates said they would support any candidate chosen by the New York delegation and the men from the Empire State caucused. As a way of showing that Wheeler had significant political support from the North Country and as a way to keep his name fresh in the minds of the New York Republican leaders who were delegates, James nominated Wheeler for vice president. Lieutenant Governor George G. Hoskins, Stewart Woodford, and Chester Arthur were also nominated. The sense of the caucus was plainly for Arthur and the names of Wheeler and the other two candidates were withdrawn. By a voice vote, the caucus decided to present Arthur's name to the convention, which subsequently nominated him vice president on the first ballot.[11]

Arthur's nomination revealed an internal division inside the Stalwart's machine. Wheeler could not have asked for anything better to improve his chances for election to the U.S. Senate. During the discussions that took place inside the New York delegation prior to its decision to back Arthur, it became known that Conkling had wanted Arthur to run for the Senate, not for vice president. This news rankled former Congressman Thomas C. Platt of Owego who thought he should be the GOP candidate for the Senate. Platt was one of Conkling's three top political deputies. Arthur and Cornell were the other two. Because Arthur only half-heartedly supported Cornell's 1876 bid to become the Republican nominee for governor, animosity had been building up between the two men and Cornell had begun plotting to help Platt win the Senate seat.[12] All of this infighting was music to Wheeler's ears.

The news of Garfield and Arthur's nomination reached Wheeler in Malone by telegraph on June 8 and he called a ratification meeting to be held in the Concert Hall that evening. To muffle grumbling he had heard in local GOP circles about Assemblyman Brennan's lack of ethics, Bill arranged to showcase the assemblyman by having him chair the meeting. Later that summer, Brennan would be seeking the nomination to run for a third term and Bill was counting on him to win and manage his bid for election to the Senate in the legislature. Wheeler also used the meeting to court the Stalwarts and the Half-Breeds by pouring on the praise for Garfield and Arthur in a speech to party loyalists. Referring to himself as "we of the silver hairs," Wheeler reviewed his personal political experiences with both of the nominees. Bill said Garfield's name was "the synonym of the highest type of patriotic devotion to country, of statesmanship and of intelligent, fruitful service to the Republican party." Of Arthur, Wheeler said, "no man in the organization surpasses him" in "unsullied character and devotion to the principles of the Republican Party."[13]

Later in June, the Democrats met in convention in Cincinnati. Many observers had expected that the Tilden-Hendricks ticket of 1876 would be nominated to run again but Tilden was tainted by charges that he had tried to bribe electors in the South to vote for him, and Hendricks wanted to run for president, not vice president.[14] On the second ballot, the badly divided Democrats compromised and nominated General Winfield Scott Hancock, a distinguished Union officer from Pennsylvania, for president. William H. English, a wealthy businessman from Indiana who had served four terms in Congress during the administrations of Presidents Pierce and Buchanan, was named to run for vice president.[15]

In August, a bruising battle unfolded at the GOP Franklin County convention. On one side stood Wheeler and his men who were supporting Brennan's nomination for a third term in the assembly. On the other side stood the independent-minded Henry A. Paddock of Malone and his supporters. A lawyer, real estate entrepreneur, and owner of several saw mills and flour mills, Paddock was also a former county judge and national bank examiner.[16] Paddock vigorously opposed Brennan's nomination on the grounds that he had failed to help farmers when he was in Albany during his last two terms. In addition, with a nod toward Wheeler, Paddock charged that a corrupt "ring" had rigged the convention to secure Brennan's nomination. Wheeler was outraged by the charges and he lined up speaker after speaker from Moira, Bombay, Dickinson, Bangor, and Fort Covington, to deny Paddock's allegations. When it came time for the vote, Wheeler carried the day for Brennan who was renominated.[17]

During the fall election campaign, the Republicans promoted Garfield as the former "canal tow-path boy." The Democrats touted Hancock as "The Superb" and used a rooster to symbolize his candidacy.[18] Wheeler campaigned vigorously for Garfield and Arthur, which pleased both the anti-Conkling Half-Breeds and Conkling's Stalwarts. Bill's most controversial campaign speech was delivered at a rally in St. Albans, Vermont, to more than five thousand people.

He opened his remarks by entertaining the crowd with humorous comments about his years as vice president, which he described as having been a *side show* to the Hayes administration. Warming to his subject, Bill told his listeners that in church, he would usually hear the minister pray for the president, his cabinet, both houses of Congress, the Supreme Court, the governors, the legislatures of all the states, and "every individual heathen from Greenland to India"—but never for the vice president![19]

Wheeler continued in this light vein peppering his speech with quotes from Shakespeare, Alexander Pope, and Jonathan Swift, and then he abruptly shifted into attack mode by asserting that the Democratic Party was "hostile to free popular government." To the roar of his partisan audience, Wheeler said that the Democrats were "bred in the hatred of New England and the Union" and had "defended to the last the barbarism of slavery." He asked his listeners which party they wanted to control the federal government—"an unregenerate southern Democratic party," which was "tainted with the aristocratic caste of slavery and states rights" or the Republican party, which stood for "freedom, progress, education and equality before the law."[20]

Democratic newspapers were incensed by Wheeler's speech. One said it was impossible for Wheeler to make a political speech without pouring out "vials of abuse." Another called Wheeler an "unscrupulous knave" who gave a speech that was a "colossal lie." The *New York Herald* described Bill's speech as a "paroxysm of partisan fury," which was "reprehensible" given Wheeler's position as vice president.[21]

Wheeler's other major campaign appearance was less controversial than the one in St. Albans but it had more pomp and circumstance. He had come to speak at the New England Fair in Worcester, Massachusetts, at the invitation of his longtime friend George F. Hoar, who was now one of the Bay State's U.S. Senators. Arriving from Malone on an early train the day before his scheduled speech, Bill stayed overnight at Hoar's home. At 9:30 a.m. the following day, the Worcester Brass Band, the City Guards Regiment, and a battalion of the Second Worcester Infantry arrived at the Hoar residence to escort Wheeler to the fairgrounds. The public schools were closed and the businesses had shut their doors. Bill got into an open carriage and led a procession to the fairgrounds through the major streets of Worcester, which were lined with people who were excited to get a glimpse of the vice president.

When Wheeler arrived at the fairgrounds, the Fifth Worcester Battery fired a national salute of thirteen guns. As Bill stepped to the podium, the crowd gave three cheers for Wheeler, the federal government, and the flag. Quoting from the Bible, Daniel Webster, James Russell Lowell, and Oliver Wendell Holmes, Wheeler talked to the crowd about his New England family roots and the bravery of New Englanders in the American Revolution, the War of 1812, and the Civil War. As was his custom during such events, Bill praised the critical role farmers played in making good government possible. In closing, he urged his audience to never forget "the distinction between merely getting a living and the higher life" and to remember that "manual labor and mental culture go hand in hand."[22]

Wheeler wound up his campaigning by presiding over an election eve mass meeting in Malone. Special trains brought thousands of people to the rally from the east and west. More than fifteen hundred men were fed dinner at the Malone skating rink. Before the political speeches began, a four-mile long parade passed by 250 well-lighted homes and businesses, which displayed Republican campaign emblems and tableaux. Thirty-eight ladies from Brushton, each representing a state, marched in the parade wearing the cap and sash of the Goddess of Liberty. Despite suffering from an ulcerated sore throat, Wheeler spoke to the crowd for two hours lambasting the Democrats and the South.[23]

After the polls closed and the ballots were counted, Garfield and Arthur easily defeated Hancock and English in the electoral college 214 to 155 despite the fact that their popular vote plurality nationally was less than ten thousand. They carried New York State by slightly more than 21,000 votes. To Wheeler's delight, the GOP won control of the assembly 81 to 47, which guaranteed that the next U.S. Senator elected from New York would be a Republican. The GOP majority on a joint ballot of assemblymen and state senators would be fifty-two.[24]

Wheeler was amused by a scene he saw on Main Street in Malone on the day following the election. A procession of about one hundred men led by the Malone Glee Club marched through the village chanting choruses of popular songs. Each man carried a broom representing the Republican "sweep" in the election. One man carried a dead cock on a pole with a hand pointing toward it—"Hancock." Later, the cock and the hand were hung out over a sidewalk together with a crow and a placard bearing the word "his" attached to a shoemaker's last, so that the symbols read, "Hancock has crowed his last."[25]

Still chuckling, Wheeler summoned Brennan and his other political lieutenants to his office to discuss U.S. Senate election strategy. The outgoing vice president would be running as an Independent between the heavy guns held by Conkling's Stalwarts and Blaine's Half-Breeds and Bill wanted to be ready for anything and everything. However, there was no way he could have known that Brennan, the man he had handpicked to manage his campaign in the halls of the legislature, would betray him.

27

U.S. Senate Election Round One

The Double-Cross

☆

Wheeler thought he had an excellent chance of becoming become the next U.S. Senator from New York. For him to win the election, two things had to happen. First, he needed Conkling's Stalwarts and Blaine's Half-Breeds in the legislature to become deadlocked over who the GOP candidate should be. Second, Wheeler needed a majority of the Republican legislators to recognize him as the ideal compromise choice to break the deadlock. By the time New Year's Day of 1881 arrived, Bill thought that both things would indeed occur.

Conkling's Stalwarts had split into two warring camps and each camp had its own candidate for the Senate.[1] Governor Cornell was at the head of one faction and it backed former Congressman Thomas C. Platt of Owego in Tioga County. Before entering politics full time, Platt was a druggist, newspaper editor and bank president. He had served in Congress for two terms and had become one of Conkling's chief political lieutenants. At the time of the Senate election, he was a wealthy man who was president of the Tioga National Bank, the United States Express Company, and the Southern Railroad.[2]

Vice President-elect Arthur and House Speaker Sharpe headed up a second faction of Stalwarts who backed Congressman Richard Crowley of Lockport in Niagara County. He, too, was one of Conkling's top deputies. Before Crowley became a congressman, he had been appointed U.S. attorney for the Northern

District of New York by Grant, at Conkling's suggestion. The Northern District ran from Albany in the east to Buffalo in the west, and from the Canadian border on the north to the Pennsylvania line on the south.[3]

Blaine's Half-Breeds backed Chauncey Depew of Peekskill in Westchester County. A Yale graduate, he had become a lawyer and lobbyist for Cornelius Vanderbilt's railroads, the largest of which was the giant New York Central Railroad.[4] Depew had entered the race for the Senate at the behest of Blaine who had recently been designated secretary of state by President-elect Garfield as a reward for Half-Breed support at the national convention. Blaine was determined to use his influential position with Garfield to politically undermine his arch foe, Conkling. Once Garfield was in office, Blaine planned to influence the president to name a Half-Breed to be collector at the New York Custom House. Blaine's immediate objective was to muddy the waters of the Senate election in New York by having his ally, Depew, run for the position as a Garfield man.[5]

A fourth candidate sought to compete with Wheeler for becoming the compromise choice for the Senate. He was reformer Sherman S. Rogers of Buffalo in Erie County. In 1876, he had fought successfully to win the nomination for lieutenant governor to run for office with gubernatorial candidate Edwin D. Morgan.[6] Rogers was not a strong compromise candidate. He was not as well-known as Wheeler and he lacked Wheeler's experience in government on the national level. In addition, Rogers was handicapped because he did not command the same kind of loyalty from his legislative supporters as Wheeler did from his. Political observers predicted that at the first sign of pressure from the Stalwarts or the Half Breeds, Rogers's support would melt away.[7]

By law, the Senate election would involve a two-step process. First, the assembly and the state senate would vote separately to elect a candidate. Next, both houses would meet in a joint session. If each house had elected the same man, the joint assembly would declare him to be the duly elected Senator. If both houses had elected different men, the task of electing a Senator would shift from the hands of the separate houses and devolve upon the joint assembly.[8]

However, since the GOP controlled both houses of the 1881 legislature and had a two to one majority in a joint session, the real election would take place in a joint Republican caucus, which would nominate the GOP candidate. There would be 104 Republican assemblymen and state senators voting in the joint caucus. The candidate who could win fifty-three votes in the caucus would be the Republican candidate to run in the subsequent Senate election in each house.[9] In a joint GOP caucus, Wheeler calculated that Platt would have about thirty-five votes; Crowley, twenty-five; Depew, nineteen; and Rogers, ten.[10] Wheeler's campaign managers,

Lynde in the state senate and Brennan in the assembly, reported that sixteen legislators from Franklin, St. Lawrence, Jefferson, Lewis, Clinton, and Warren Counties had promised they would vote for Bill and remain loyal to him to the end.[11]

After studying the numbers, Wheeler concluded that if his supporters remained solidly in his column, a deadlock was certain to occur. Neither Platt nor Crowley could win a majority because neither Stalwart would pull out of the contest and support the other.[12] Even if Platt or Crowley were able to take all ten votes away from Rogers, both Stalwarts would still fall short of a majority because the Half-Breeds would never vote for a Conkling Stalwart. By the same logic, Wheeler did not see how Depew could win a majority either, even if he picked up votes from Rogers, because the Stalwarts would not vote for a Blaine Half-Breed. Bill was convinced he could win if he was seen as the compromise choice to break the deadlock. With sixteen votes of his own, all Bill needed at a minimum to win a majority was half the Stalwart vote and half the Half-Breed vote.

Wheeler's strategy to win the Senate seat had three prongs. The first involved his image. He planned to project himself as a true Independent by appearing to be aloof from the rough and tumble political battle for votes. Bill wanted to be *the man* referred to in the classic U.S. political adage, "The office should seek the man, the man should not seek the office."

The second prong of Bill's strategy involved timing. He directed Brennan, his campaign manager in the assembly, to do everything within his power to *prevent* the GOP joint caucus from being held *before* the Speaker handed out the committee assignments for the upcoming legislative session. Wheeler believed that it was imperative that the caucus be delayed so that he could take full political advantage of the anger and resentment that disappointed assemblymen would feel when they failed to be granted the appointments they believed they were entitled to, or had been promised. If the caucus were held before the committee assignments were made, the Speaker, a Crowley manager, could dangle committee assignments in front of assemblymen in exchange for votes for Crowley.

The third prong of Wheeler's Senate strategy involved loyalty. It was vitally important that the legislators who had committed themselves to vote for Bill, remain true to their word to the end. If any of them wavered or gave an indication that they would vote for a Stalwart or a Half-Breed, it would be a sign that Wheeler's candidacy was weak and that a deadlock could be averted if enough pressure were exerted or enough promises were made. Furthermore, if word got out that any one of Wheeler's supporters had made a deal to vote for a Stalwart, the Half Breeds would have reason not to vote for Wheeler as a compromise choice, and vice versa.

In keeping with Bill's strategy concerning his image, he announced his candidacy for the Senate by denying he was campaigning for support! Bill sent to the press in the North Country and in New York City, a copy of a letter he claimed he had written to "a friend in the interior of the State" who had written him. According to Wheeler, his "friend" had heard Bill's name mentioned "in several quarters" as a candidate for the Senate and wanted to help him with his campaign. Bill's reply admitted that becoming a U.S. Senator would be "the crowning honor of any man's life" but added that in light of his own views of "propriety and justice," he would not approach state legislators in person or by letter to ask for their support and would not compete with anyone for the Senate seat. He stated that the only competition he would enter would be competition to be a good citizen, unless the competition "should be enlarged by agencies outside my own." In other words, Bill said he was not going to personally campaign for the Senate but he would not stop others who wanted to campaign for him.[13]

The reaction to Bill's nonannouncement was encouraging. The downstate newspapers reported that Wheeler continued "to be the candidate mentioned first" for the Senate by "anti-Conklingites" and that Bill's refusal to "sacrifice his self-respect" by personally campaigning for the Senate was a "manly stand." In the North Country, the Republican legislators from the Nineteenth Congressional District announced that they were solidly in favor of Wheeler for the Senate and would present his name to the legislative caucus. This endorsement referred to Bill as an "able, broad and comprehensive statesman."[14]

The 1881 legislature convened on January 4 following a fight in the GOP assembly caucus over who should be elected Speaker. The Stalwarts put up Sharpe for reelection and the Half-Breeds backed Charles R. Skinner, a former newspaper editor from Watertown, for the post. Through Brennan, Wheeler signaled that he would support Skinner. Sharpe easily snuffed out Skinner's challenge and was reelected Speaker. Skinner could only muster twenty-four of the eighty-one possible Republican votes in the assembly. After Sharpe's election, both houses adjourned to get ready for the Senate election, which was expected to be held sometime during the following week. Political observers predicted various scenarios in which either Platt, or Crowley, or Depew, or Wheeler, would win. One analyst described the contest by borrowing words from John Milton's *Paradise Lost:* "confusion worse confounded."[15]

Wheeler opened his Senate election headquarters in the Delevan House on Monday, January 10. The office was staffed by Brennan, Lynde, James, and Dickinson. They were soon joined by longtime Wheeler supporter, Congressman John Hammond from Crown Point in Essex County. A brigadier general in the Civil

War, Hammond was currently president of the Crown Point Iron Company. The other major candidates, Crowley, Platt, and Depew, also had headquarters at the Delevan. However, unlike Wheeler who had remained in Malone, they were all present in Albany lobbying legislators for their votes. Vice President-elect Arthur was also in Albany to work with Sharpe to win the election for Crowley. Depew had the popular State Senator Robertson working hard in his corner as one of the leading spokesmen for Blaine's Half Breeds.[16]

On January 11, as Wheeler had expected, Speaker Sharpe tried to have the legislative caucus committees from both houses call a joint caucus before he announced the assembly committee assignments. It was a good political move to help Crowley. Sharpe hoped to use promises of committee assignments to win votes for Crowley. Wheeler had been careful to warn Brennan and Lynde about this. When the legislative committees refused to meet to issue a call for a joint caucus, Bill was delighted. His strategy was working. However, it did not take long for his joy to turn into shock and doubt.[17]

Unfazed by uncooperative caucus committee members, Sharpe boldly abandoned precedent and set in motion machinery to call a joint caucus by a petition signed by a majority of the Republican legislators. One by one they were called into the Speaker's office and asked to sign the petition. In ten minutes, fifty legislators had signed the call for a joint caucus. It was obvious that the Stalwarts were working together to get the petition signed and the anti-Conkling legislators were furious and frustrated. The petition was taken from the Speaker's office and brought to the Delevan House where additional legislators were rounded up to sign it and soon, with the signatures of a clear majority of the GOP legislators on the petition, an early caucus was scheduled to be held on January 13 at 7:30 p.m. Wheeler was dealing with the ramifications of the call for an early caucus when he learned additional news that stunned him. Bill found out that he had been double-crossed by the man he had handpicked to be his assembly campaign manager. Brennan had signed the petition![18] Wheeler wondered what other mischief Brennan had been up to and could not help but think the worst. Sure enough, rumors about the extent of Brennan's betrayal were everywhere. One of them truly alarmed Wheeler. Some observers had heard that Brennan had not only signed the petition, but he also had promised to vote for Crowley on the second ballot and bring as many Wheeler supporters with him as he could![19]

Brennan denied that he had politically stabbed Wheeler in the back and said that the rumors were wrong. As far as signing the petition was concerned, he could not deny that his name was on it but he argued that a majority was going to sign it anyway, with or without his signature, and he said he did not want to unnecessarily antagonize the majority by opposing an early caucus. Wheeler took a deep breath, and decided to reserve judgment about Brennan until after the Senate election was over.[20]

On January 12, it became apparent to Depew that the Half-Breeds were in a distinct minority and he set up a meeting with supporters of Wheeler and Rogers. At the meeting, Wheeler's men stood firm for their man. Depew asked for their support and they refused. Wheeler's managers asked Depew's men if they would vote for Wheeler. They said they could not answer that question and no agreement was reached. At this point, Depew's managers knew he could not win and the question facing the Half-Breeds was: To whom were they going to throw their votes? The Wheeler-Depew-Rogers meeting broke up at 10:00 p.m.[21] When Wheeler went to bed that night, he had mixed feelings about what would happen on the next day when the Senate election was held. If the rumors about Brennan were true, Bill had been sold out by a man he had trusted, a man from Malone who would not be an assemblyman in the first place, if Wheeler had not given him his blessing. On the other hand, other signs pointed to the fact that Bill was very much still in the race. Depew and the Half-Breeds knew they could not win. If they endorsed Wheeler, he would be halfway home to winning the election as the compromise choice. Unfortunately for Wheeler, and unbeknown to him, Blaine's Half-Breeds had other plans for their votes and those plans did not include handing their votes to Bill.

After Depew's managers left the meeting with Wheeler's men, the Half-Breeds arranged a meeting with Arthur, Crowley's manager. Robertson, on behalf of Depew, met with the vice president-elect and offered Depew's votes to Crowley if he would promise, after winning the election, not to oppose Garfield's appointments of Half-Breeds to patronage posts and to support Blaine's friends if they were attacked by the Stalwarts, meaning, without saying so, Conkling and Cornell. Vigorously shaking his head, Arthur refused to betray Conkling and rejected the proposed deal.[22] After leaving Arthur, Blaine's Half-Breeds pulled another card out of their sleeves. A contingent of them, including Depew and Robertson, went to see Platt and made the same offer to him. They specifically asked Platt if he would support the appointments of the Garfield administration, even if Robertson turned out to be one of the prominent nominees. When Platt agreed, Depew promised to endorse Platt, dooming Wheeler to defeat. Bill would not know his fate until the votes were cast on the next day.[23]

The Republican members of the assembly and the state senate filed into the assembly chamber on the evening of January 13 to name the GOP candidate for the U.S. Senate. Platt was nominated first, followed by Crowley and Rogers. Wheeler's

Thomas C. Platt. Brady-Handy Collection, Library of Congress.

supporters were caught by surprise when Elbridge G. Lapham, a congressman from Canandaigua in Ontario County, was nominated next. They were concerned that Lapham might take some votes away from Wheeler. Brennan rose to nominate Bill saying that he would be a fit successor to a Seward or a Silas Wright. Describing Wheeler as a "pure, honorable and great" man, Brennan reminded the joint caucus that for ten years, Bill had represented the "banner Republican district of the Empire State" in Congress. Lynde seconded Wheeler's nomination extolling his "indefatigable exertions" on behalf of Republican candidates during previous election campaigns. When Lynde sat down, the roll call vote to choose the next U.S. Senator from New York began. In the next few minutes, Wheeler's Senate candidacy went up in flames. On the first ballot, Platt won the nomination by a single vote. He garnered 54 votes, Crowley 26, Wheeler 10, Rogers 10, Lapham 4, and Levi P. Morton 1. Wheeler's votes came from St. Lawrence, Franklin, Warren, Clinton, Lewis, Essex, and Oswego Counties.[24]

If Blaine's Half-Breeds had not voted for Platt on the first ballot, Wheeler might have eventually won as the compromise choice on subsequent ballots. He wondered why Blaine had made a deal with the Stalwarts. Perhaps he was trying to deepen the schism in their ranks by playing one side against the other. But why did Blaine prefer a Stalwart to an Independent, like Wheeler? The answer, according to one political observer, was that Blaine and the Half-Breeds disliked Wheeler's "selfish conservatism" and his "old fashioned notion about patronage."[25] It was more likely that Blaine did not support Wheeler because Bill was too independent for him. There had been bad blood between the two men since their early days together in the House where they dueled over who had the superior knowledge of parliamentary law and who could trust whom to make fair rulings from the Speaker's chair. There was no way Blaine could forget Wheeler's complaint that Blaine had double-crossed him by not naming him chairman of the Appropriations Committee after Wheeler had agreed to withdraw his bid to unseat Blaine as Speaker.

The vice president from Malone was devastated by his defeat for the Senate but he became incensed when he learned that Brennan had been named chairman of the Ways and Means Committee—the most powerful committee in the assembly. As committee chairman, Brennan would become the nominal Republican leader of the assembly. Wheeler's friends and supporters in Franklin County immediately pointed to the committee assignment as evidence that Brennan had been rewarded for selling Wheeler out to the Stalwarts by signing the petition for an early nominating caucus and promising them to abandon Wheeler after the first ballot. Before returning to Washington to finish up his duties as vice

William Almon Wheeler. Brady-Handy Collection, Library of Congress.

president, Wheeler wrote Brennan a savage letter expressing his rage about Brennan's disloyalty. Brennan described it to his friends as a "cruel letter" that broke his heart and deprived him of his sleep.[26]

In Washington at noon, February 9, Wheeler led a procession of U.S. Senators into the House chamber to perform one of his last duties as vice president, counting the electoral votes for president and vice president. With the help of his secretary, Edwin E. Dickinson, Bill opened the official election certificates that had been sent to his office by the electoral college and handed them to the tellers to be counted. When he was done, he announced that Garfield and Arthur had been elected.[27] While this proceeding was going on, political and social pressure continued to mount against Brennan in Franklin County for ruining Wheeler's chances to win the Senate election. Brennan was gradually being ostracized by the communities he had been elected to serve. As the climate of opinion turned against him, he became the victim of small town shunning and the constant object of backbiting. Brennan appealed to Frederick D. Kilburn, a young and up-and-coming lawyer from Malone, to make a fact-finding trip to Albany and then proceed to Washington to mediate a peace and effect reconciliation with Wheeler.[28]

Wheeler was unconvinced by Kilburn's research that Brennan was anything other than a disloyal, untrustworthy, ingrate. Kilburn's mission was a failure. As a result, Brennan became more and more nervous and depressed. On February 17, he took an indefinite leave from the assembly complaining of nervous prostration and insomnia. As a way to lift his depression, his doctors recommended that he should take frequent drives to different parts of Franklin County and remain outdoors as much as possible. People began whispering behind his back, loud enough so that he could hear them, that he was mentally unsound. As his depression deepened, Brennan began to believe that his mental condition was incurable.[29]

Meanwhile in Washington, Wheeler's vice presidency was about to come to an end. At 10 a.m. on March 4, 1881, Wheeler, Hayes, Garfield, and Arthur, drove in open carriages from the White House down Pennsylvania Avenue to the Capitol for the inauguration ceremonies. About an inch of snow had fallen the night before but the skies were clear on inauguration day. In the Senate chamber at noon, Wheeler administered the oath of office to Arthur and then spoke a few farewell words to the hundreds of dignitaries who were present. Bill said that the senators had always shown him good feelings and he thanked them for it. After adjourning the Senate of the Forty-sixth Congress *sine die,* his last official act as vice president, Wheeler walked side by side with Arthur, behind Garfield and Hayes, to the east portico of the Capitol, where Bill listened to Garfield's address and watched him sworn in as president. That evening, Wheeler attended the inaugural ball held at the National Museum Building with Garfield, Hayes, and Arthur. Bright electric lights illuminated ropes of garlands that stretched from girder to girder across the hall. Colored lights flashed back and forth across the decorations, which included a statue representing America rising up from a base banked with tropical plants. The figure held the American shield in her left hand and in her right she held a torch whose flame was lighted by electricity. Wheeler shook hands in the receiving line until midnight before he went home, a private citizen once again.[30]

In Malone, Brennan's depression deepened even further as he read about the final days of Wheeler's vice presidency and began anticipating Bill's return to Malone where it would be extremely difficult for Brennan to avoid coming in contact with him. On Saturday, March 5, the day after the inauguration, Brennan went to a drug store and purchased ten grams of strychnine. On Monday morning, he got in a sleigh with his brother-in-law, George Sabin, for a trip to Duane. Sabin drove and they stopped at Ayer's Hotel, about fifteen miles south of Malone around noon for dinner. After they had finished dining, Sabin went out to get the horses ready to proceed to Lake Meacham where they intended to spend the night. Brennan said he would walk ahead for the exercise and that Sabin could follow and pick him up later with the sleigh. Sabin agreed. After he had hitched up the team and traveled a short distance, he found Brennan lying face down in the road, dead. His hand still held the cane he was using, his hat was still on his head, and the snow on all sides of him was undisturbed. A subsequent coroner's inquest determined that Brennan had died "from the effects of strychnine administered by his own hand while in a deranged state of mind." A note was found in his diary to his wife that said, "I have committed the awful crime of self destruction."[31]

Wheeler was still in Washington when he heard the news about Brennan's suicide. Bill's reaction to the tragedy is not known. He had to have been still smarting from his loss to Platt but Wheeler was making plans to go south to Tennessee to visit his cousins in Chattanooga.[32] The former vice president had no idea at this time that a major political surprise would be in store for him after he returned to Malone later that spring. In May, Platt and Conkling would unexpectedly commit "senatorial suicide" by resigning from the Senate.[33] This unprecedented event would give Wheeler a second chance to win a seat in the U.S. Senate and this time, there would be two seats up for election, not just one.

28

U.S. Senate Election Round Two

Caught in a Crossfire

☆

Waving the gold-headed cane the secretary and clerks of the Senate had given him before he left Washington,[1] Wheeler stepped off the train in Malone to a tumultuous welcome home celebration on April 7, 1881. Greeted by the Malone band and cheering throngs who shouted, "William A. Wheeler! Citizen Wheeler!" he was escorted home by the Malone glee club and town dignitaries. They had arranged with a local volunteer committee to have Bill's Elm Street residence opened, warmed up, and cleaned, before he arrived. In a speech from his front porch, he told the crowd that if he had to single out any of his "brilliant achievements," he would happily point to the fact that despite being surrounded by greed, corruption, and venality in Washington, he had maintained his integrity. Now that he was home, Bill said all he wanted to do was play a role in helping Malone advance materially and intellectually. And then, borrowing words from the poet Oliver Goldsmith, he added that he also hoped to "husband out life's taper" in Malone.[2]

But events in Washington prompted Wheeler to postpone husbanding out life's taper in Malone and to jump back onto the state's political stage for the second time that year as a candidate for election to the U.S. Senate. This election would be the most bizarre Senate election in New York political history, if not the nation's.

In joint session, both houses of the legislature would vote six days a week for more than seven weeks, a total of fifty-six ballots would be taken, before the legislators would be able to break a deadlock and choose two U.S. Senators. The election, replete with charges of bribery and a juicy sex scandal, gave impetus to the movement promoting direct election of U.S. Senators.

In Washington, due to the influence of Secretary of State Blaine, President Garfield nominated Robertson, one of Conkling's fiercest enemies and New York's most prominent Half-Breed, to replace Merritt as collector of the New York Custom House.[3] In a letter to Hayes, Wheeler praised Garfield for working to overthrow Conkling's machine, "the most damnable political despotism that ever existed."[4]

To protest Garfield's move to put the New York Custom House under the control of Blaine's Half-Breeds, Conkling and Platt shocked the U.S. political establishment by resigning from the Senate on May 16. They assumed that the legislature, which had just elected Platt, would routinely reelect them both and they would return triumphantly to Washington, their positions vindicated.[5] Conkling and Platt were wrong. New York Republican voters liked Garfield and viewed the double resignation as "childish."[6] Conkling's machine was on the verge of coming apart. The Half-Breeds exploited the surge of pro-Garfield public opinion by employing a new slogan, "Stand by the Administration," to rally support for men such as Depew, Rogers, and Lapham who announced their candidacies for the vacant seats.[7] In the North Country, anti-Conkling indignation meetings were held in Gouverneur, Potsdam, Canton, and Ogdensburg. Newspapers proclaimed that if Conkling and Platt were reelected, it would be "a dark day for New York Republicanism." A boom for Wheeler to run again erupted and Bill began to marshal his forces.[8]

Once again, Bill found himself in the middle of a political free-for-all between two factions, the Half-Breeds and the Stalwarts. However, these factions were less disciplined than they were in January when Platt had defeated Wheeler. The Stalwarts continued to be divided into two camps. There were the ultra-Stalwarts who would back Conkling to the end and there were the Independent Stalwarts who were hesitant to openly vote for Conkling because their constituents did not like him, but who wanted to help Conkling by making it difficult for his opponents to win a majority vote. The Independent Stalwarts planned to do this by randomly distributing their votes to other Stalwart candidates. The Half-Breeds played to pro-Garfield public opinion by encouraging the press to refer to them as Garfield's *administration men*. Within the Half-Breed faction, there were legislators who looked to Blaine and Robertson for leadership, and others who looked elsewhere. The latter referred to themselves as *Independent Half-Breeds*. A large number of legislators were derisively known as *featherheads* because they would vote any way

PUCK.

A HARMLESS EXPLOSION.

Cartoon by Joseph Keppler expressing joy at the unexpected resignation in 1881 of Roscoe Conkling and Thomas C. Platt from the U.S. Senate. Conkling is portrayed by the large balloon and Platt by the small balloon attached to a string tied to Conkling's back pocket. Both balloons burst harmlessly. The caption reads, "A Harmless Explosion." U.S. Senate Collection.

the political wind blew the hardest. Wheeler belonged to none of these factions. He drew his strength from his untarnished reputation for having integrity and being fair. Bill counted once again on having loyal support from a core group of legislators from the North Country.

Remembering that he would have been elected in January if Blaine's Half-Breeds had voted for him when Depew withdrew, Wheeler made plans to treat Depew's renewed candidacy with kid gloves. Even though Blaine did not hold Bill in high regard because of their contentious political past together in Washington, Wheeler felt he had good rapport with Robertson. After all, Bill had voted for Robertson, not Cornell, for governor at the 1879 GOP state convention. However, some of the Half-Breeds agreed with the *Albany Argus* that pointed out that by not personally insisting that his North Country delegates also vote for Robertson, when Wheeler held the balance of power between Robertson and Cornell at the 1879 convention, Wheeler had "paired off with himself." He had voted for Robertson and through his district delegates, he had also voted for Cornell.[9]

Bill planned to play a more active role in his campaign in Albany than he had in January. He would continue to make it appear that the "office was seeking the man" by convincing the press to write that he would not "convene conferences, pass Sundays in political plotting, plead personally with legislators, and promise rewards for votes." However, what he did not tell the press was that he planned to go to Albany and oversee his noncampaign when the occasion warranted it. Bill also tightened up his lines of communication to legislators in Albany, relying exclusively on his trusted lieutenant Dickinson and State Senator Lynde. Wheeler did not assign any important duties to the man elected to fill the vacancy in the assembly caused by Brennan's suicide, Samuel A. Beman of Malone. He had been Brennan's former law partner and Bill was wary of him. To prepare himself and clear his head before the action heated up in Albany, Bill went fishing with his Saranac Navigation Company for a week in the Adirondacks. He returned home on May 26 to make some last minute adjustments to his strategy with Dickinson before dispatching him to Albany on May 28.[10]

In Albany, the Stalwarts attempted to hold a joint GOP caucus of assemblymen and state senators to select the Republican nominees. According to the caucus call proposed by the Stalwarts, a secret ballot would be used and the winners would be determined by a majority vote. However, the Half-Breeds opposed the call. They were fearful that the Independent Stalwarts, whose constituents had told them to vote against Conkling, would ignore the anti-Conkling sentiment opinion from home and vote for him anyway, if they were able to vote in secret. There were 106 Republican legislators and, according to party rules, 72 had to agree before a caucus could be called. Forty legislators refused to agree and the plan for a joint caucus failed. Because there was no joint caucus to bind them, Republican legislators were free to vote for whomever they wished. Each house met separately to vote on May 31. There were twenty candidates and none of them received a majority vote. When the ballots in the assembly and the state senate were added together, Wheeler was the number one candidate behind Conkling for his seat and Depew was the leading candidate behind Platt for his seat. Political analysts thought it was significant that Robertson had voted for both Wheeler and Depew but Bill had to have been skeptical of the significance given the pivotal role the Half-Breeds had played in Platt's victory in January.[11]

On June 1, the assembly and the state senate met together in the assembly chamber for the first joint ballot. Robertson, president pro tempore of the senate, called the joint session to order and the legislators voted again. The results were similar to the voting on May 31. No one received a majority and Wheeler and Depew were the leading candidates to replace Conkling and Platt. To succeed Conkling who received 35 votes, Wheeler won 22 votes, Rogers 15, Cornell 10, and a scattering of others received a handful of votes. To succeed Platt who received 29 votes, Depew won 25, Cornell followed with 11, and Lapham had 8. A newcomer to the Senate race, Warner Miller, a congressman whose district included Herkimer, Lewis, and Jefferson Counties, also received eight votes. Several other candidates got a few votes each. As he had done the day before, the Half-Breed leader, Robertson, voted for Wheeler and Depew. Special agent of the U.S. Treasury Department, General Newton Martin Curtis of Ogdensburg, and the outgoing collector of the New York Custom House, Edwin A. Merritt of Potsdam, worked actively to lobby legislators to vote for Wheeler.[12]

Despite voting once, and sometimes twice a day, for the next week, the legislators were unable to break the deadlock and give any candidate a majority vote. Wheeler maintained his position as the leading candidate to oppose Conkling for his seat and Depew moved ahead of Platt in the voting for his seat. In response to Depew's growing support, the Conkling Stalwarts mounted a counterattack. They began pounding away at Depew's ties with Vanderbilt and the New York Central Railroad, hoping to play on fears in farming districts that if elected to the U.S. Senate, Depew would be a spokesman for monopolists. Democratic newspapers took advantage of the intra-party war by observing, "The Republican party in New York is the property of Vanderbilt, Gould & Company" and asking, "Why should not a railroad legislature send railroad agents to the United States Senate?" In addition, the Conkling men also began spreading the word that Depew had hired private detectives to shadow key GOP legislators to make sure they did not join the Conkling team. Depew denied all the charges and stated that if he were elected, he would resign from his job at the New York Central Railroad.[13]

On June 9, shortly after midnight, Conkling men alerted the press that they would be dropping a bombshell on Depew's campaign before legislators cast their ninth joint ballot. In the assembly chamber, before the voting began, Assemblyman Samuel H. Bradley of Cattaraugus County rose and said he had been paid $2,000 to vote for Depew by Senator Loren B. Sessions of Chautauqua County. Bradley stated that he had given the money to Speaker Sharpe who had the roll of bills in his pocket at that very moment. Sharpe patted his pocket and confirmed Bradley's story and then, as the *Times* reported, a "death-like stillness fell upon the Assembly—not a man, not a page moved for about half a minute." Soon, "a long drawn sensational whisper went about the chamber." A motion was made to form a Committee on Bribery Investigations. Wheeler supporters jumped to their feet to speak in favor of the committee. A Wheeler man, Assemblyman Ebenezer S. Crapser of St. Lawrence County, said he wanted a thorough investigation because he had heard that Depew was walking around Albany with "a satchel full of greenbacks."[14]

The Half-Breeds described the charges against Depew as "very fishy" and "a fraud, a humbug." They said the only people who believed that Depew had attempted to bribe Bradley for his vote were Conkling supporters. The *Brooklyn Eagle* looked at the bribery charges differently and told its readers that they were additional evidence that legislators in Albany were nothing more than "political prostitutes" who could be "bought and sold like sheep."[15]

The bribery charges did not immediately harm Depew's lead over Platt nor did they help Wheeler win more votes against Conkling. The totals of the two anti-machine candidates remained about the same for another week. However, on June 16, when the votes were counted after the sixteenth joint ballot, Wheeler surged ahead of Conkling 38 to 32 thanks to Rogers's supporters who decided to vote for Bill. Depew maintained his lead over Platt 54 to 27.[16] Wheeler's move into the lead against Conkling was the moment Bill had been waiting for and he took the train to Albany with a plan to break the deadlock and win a seat in the U.S. Senate for himself.

When he arrived on the evening of June 17, he took rooms at the Delevan House where his headquarters was located. He held a continuous series of meetings with legislators and the press in which he recast himself as an *administration man*. Bill argued that the only way the deadlock could be broken was if the legislators compromised and elected one Stalwart and one administration man to replace Conkling and Platt. Under Bill's compromise plan, neither Conkling nor Platt would be reelected but the Stalwarts would get to choose their replacements—one from the Stalwart camp and one from the top two candidates running as administration men. Bill urged all anti-Conkling machine Republicans to

Chauncey M. Depew. Library of Congress.

concentrate their votes on one candidate running against Conkling and one candidate running against Platt. At the time Wheeler was promoting his plan, he and Depew were the top two vote-getting administration men. In a letter to the legislators, Bill wrote that he thought Depew was the administration man who deserved to be elected. What Wheeler did not say in his letter was that he was counting on the Stalwarts to reject Depew and vote for him.[17]

The *Times* liked Wheeler's plan and said it made "good sense." The *New York Tribune* also applauded Bill's plan and told its readers that "Mr. Wheeler enters Albany like a gentleman, not like a primate." As others analyzed the plan, they saw it for what it was, a shrewd way for Wheeler to get himself elected! Wheeler believed that he and Depew would continue to run ahead of all the other anti-Stalwart candidates. If Bill's plan to break the deadlock worked the way he thought it should, he would be the administration man chosen to be the next U.S. Senator from New York, not Depew. Wheeler's political instincts told him that Bradley's bribery charges had seriously damaged Depew's reputation. And what was even more important, Bill was convinced that he would be more acceptable to Conkling and the Stalwarts than Depew because of Depew's long standing ties to Blaine.[18]

The voting continued unchanged with Wheeler and Depew maintaining their leads through the next four joint ballots although alarms were sounded in the Wheeler camp when Bill's vote fell from 38 to 35 due to an ominous surge in Half-Breed votes going to Lapham.[19]

Wheeler nearly won the election to be Conkling's successor on the twenty-third ballot thanks to inadvertent help from the Democrats. In their joint caucus, they had selected State Senator John C. Jacobs of Brooklyn to be the Democratic candidate for Conkling's seat.[20] Even though the state constitution disqualified Jacobs from becoming elected to the U.S. Senate while serving as a legislator, the Democrats chose to nominate him anyway, to honor him for the work he had done for the party. Jacobs had been consistently receiving fifty-two Democratic votes to succeed Conkling on the previous twenty-two joint ballots. On June 22, there were 155 Republican and Democratic legislators ready to begin voting on the twenty-third joint ballot. To win a majority, a candidate needed seventy-eight votes and Democrats had no reason to believe any candidate would be able to do that and win because the Republicans remained deadlocked. As the voting began, two things happened that caused consternation in Democratic circles and elation in the Wheeler ranks. Word spread that the presiding officer of the joint assembly was prepared to declare all the votes for Jacobs, at the end of the voting, to be void and unconstitutional. If that happened and Jacobs received his usual 52 votes, the total voting would be reduced to 103 and the winning majority would become 52! As this concern was being discussed by legislators, Wheeler began to win some Independent Stalwart votes and his total began to surge into the upper forties and approached fifty. As it did, a Democrat jumped to his feet and sounded the alarm. He exclaimed that if Wheeler could win fifty-two votes, and the Democratic votes were declared void, Wheeler would win the election. Jacobs hurriedly requested that his name be withdrawn and that former Congressman Clarkson N. Potter of Westchester County, the president of the American Bar Association, become the

Democratic candidate instead of Jacobs. In the chaotic scene that followed, Democrats frantically moved to change their votes. When the voting was completed, the Democrats heaved a sigh of relief. They had narrowly avoided helping the Republicans break their deadlock. However, when all was said and done, it was not as dark as the Democrats had feared because Wheeler had been unable to win fifty-two votes anyway, he only got fifty.[21]

On June 23, two more ballots took place and suspicion and distrust began to build between Wheeler and Depew men. Neither group wanted to see the other group's candidate win. Wheeler polled fifty on each ballot for Conkling's seat and Depew polled fifty-three on the first ballot for Platt's seat and fifty-two on the second. Eighteen legislators voted for Depew but not for Wheeler, and fifteen voted for Wheeler but not Depew.[22] It was obvious that the anti-machine legislators were not concentrating their votes on two candidates and Wheeler's plan to break the deadlock was not working.

After six more days and six more joint ballots, Wheeler and Depew continued to be the leading anti-Conkling machine candidates. And then, salacious events behind closed doors at the Delevan House permanently changed GOP voting patterns.

To counter the Stalwart's use of New York City detectives to spy on the Half-Breeds, Blaine's allies hired Pinkerton detectives and hotel workers to keep their eyes on the Stalwarts. On Wednesday, June 29, the Half-Breeds hit pay dirt. At 7:00 p.m. a hall boy in their employ at the Delevan brought word to them that Platt had engaged the services of a prostitute who had just checked into the hotel and was eating supper at that moment in the hotel's restaurant. The Half-Breeds could not believe their good luck. Several of them went to the restaurant to identify her. They learned that her name was Mrs. Baldwin, and that she was staying in Room 113. According to the men who saw Mrs. Baldwin, she was about thirty years old, wore gold-bowed eyeglasses, and was extremely attractive. The Half-Breeds posted one of their hall boys to watch for her on the corridor where her room was located and at least eleven Half-Breeds occupied the two rooms across the hall from hers. The group included assemblymen, former generals, and an ex-police commissioner. They brought a stepladder into one of their rooms and armed themselves with some crackers, cheese, and cigars as they waited for developments. At 10:00 p.m., they got word that Mrs. Baldwin and Platt had entered her room.

The Half-Breeds quietly hauled their stepladder out into the corridor and took turns watching the couple through the transom to Room 113 where the light remained on until midnight. As word spread about what was going on, more and more Half-Breeds arrived to get a peek, some came in their nightclothes. Once the novelty of voyeurism wore off, the Half-Breeds discussed what they should do next to take political advantage of the situation. Some suggested sounding the fire alarm or breaking down the door, but those ideas were rejected because they were considered too dangerous. After more discussion, they decided to write a note addressed to "United States Senator Thomas C. Platt, in care of Mrs. Baldwin, Room 113, Delevan House." The note said, "You are caught. If within 10 minutes you are not in your room, Number 83, the door of 113 will be broken in." They signed the note, "A Friend," put it in an envelope and slipped it under the door. In a few moments, Platt furtively rushed out of the room to the catcalls and jeers of the waiting Half-Breeds who pursued him down the hall where he escaped into a room of one of his friends.[23]

News of Platt's adultery spread rapidly among Republicans and Democrats. When Platt learned that the *Albany Argus* planned to print all the lurid details of his tryst, he sent for his wife and son to come to him in Albany. The thirty-first ballot was held as usual on Thursday, June 30, and there were no major shifts in voting, Wheeler and Depew remained in the lead. On Friday, July 1, after a lengthy consultation with his campaign managers, Platt shocked his supporters and withdrew his name from the Senate race. His withdrawal gave Wheeler's plan to break the deadlock a second life. Independent Stalwarts were now free to vote for whomever they wished. Observers speculated that Crowley and Cornell would benefit from Platt's exit and they were initially correct. On Friday's thirty-second ballot, Crowley and Cornell's totals increased but they did not affect the leads held by Wheeler and Depew.[24]

On Saturday, July 2, an hour before voting was scheduled to begin on the thirty-third ballot, more shocking news rocked the legislators. Men ran wildly between the assembly and the state senate with news from fragmentary telegraphic dispatches that President Garfield had been shot.[25] As Garfield was walking arm in arm with Blaine in a Washington railroad station waiting for a train to take Garfield to the commencement exercises at his alma mater, Williams College, Charles J. Guiteau fired two bullets from a .44 British Bulldog pistol at Garfield's back. One shot grazed his arm and did little damage but the other entered his lower back, deflected off a rib, and lodged near his pancreas. Guiteau was immediately arrested and told the nation that he was a Stalwart and had shot Garfield in order to make Arthur president.[26]

The assassination attempt quickly became a public relations nightmare for Conkling and the Stalwarts in Albany. Unsubstantiated rumors spread that Conkling had hired Guiteau to murder Garfield to make Arthur president. A national outpouring of hatred began to build up against the Conkling machine as the Senate election continued for seven more joint ballots. Surprisingly, Wheeler and Depew were unable to take advantage of the hubbub and increase their leads.[27]

The Republican legislators worried that they all might be politically tainted by the fallout from the Garfield shooting if they delayed making a decision any longer, so they made plans to break the deadlock. On Thursday night, July 7, sixty-five of them voted to circulate a petition to call a joint caucus after the Senate vote was tabulated on Friday. Even though the Conkling men had not signed the petition and were refusing to attend the meeting, a caucus was called anyway. It was set to begin at 4 p.m. on July 8.[28]

Wheeler had high hopes for victory when the caucus began and a resolution was adopted that virtually endorsed his original plan for breaking the deadlock. The caucus agreed to nominate one Stalwart, other than Conkling, for his seat, and one administration man to fill Platt's seat. These two nominees would be the caucus's choice throughout the official balloting until a winner emerged. Before the caucus voting got underway, Depew made a surprising announcement. He was withdrawing his name from the race. As Wheeler had privately predicted, Depew pulled out because he knew he would never be able to garner enough votes from the Stalwarts to win a majority. The door to Wheeler's election to be the administration man who would succeed Platt swung wide open—and then Robertson and the Half-Breeds slammed it shut in Bill's face. Instead of voting for Wheeler, the only front-running candidate still in the race, Robertson signaled the Half-Breeds to vote for Congressman Warner Miller, the president of the American Paper and Pulp Association and wealthy owner of a wood pulp and paper manufacturing business in Herkimer County. Wheeler's men were outraged by Robertson's about face and criticized him for "driving a knife" into Wheeler. Bill's men fought Miller off by denying him a majority for four ballots but when Rogers's men switched over to Miller, Wheeler's floor manager, Lynde, withdrew Wheeler's name and Miller was unanimously endorsed by the caucus to succeed Platt. To take Conkling's seat, the caucus unanimously chose Congressman Elbridge G. Lapham on the second ballot.[29]

Wheeler's North Country supporters were extremely bitter about the caucus decision and angrily charged Robertson with "bad faith." Exclaiming that they were "enraged" and "disgusted," Bill's men refused to accept the action by the caucus. They momentarily flirted with an offer from Conkling's Stalwarts to make a deal whereby they would join forces to elect both Conkling and Wheeler but eventually rejected it. They did not trust Conkling nor did they believe he could deliver on his promise. When the official joint balloting began again on Saturday, July 9, neither Miller nor Lapham could win a majority because to do so, they needed all of Wheeler's votes and a few more additional votes from the Stalwarts. It took five more joint ballots before Wheeler conceded defeat by asking Lynde to hold his nose and plead with the Republicans to unite in favor of Miller and Lapham.

On Saturday, July 16, 1881, Miller was elected to succeed Platt on the forty-eighth ballot when the congressman from Herkimer County won all of Wheeler's votes and six additional votes from the Stalwarts. It took five more days of voting before Lapham was able to defeat Conkling for his seat on the fifty-sixth joint ballot.[30]

For the second time in six months, Wheeler had been defeated in an election for a seat in the U.S. Senate by the power of Blaine's Half-Breeds and Conkling's Stalwarts. Caught between these two potent factions, Bill paid a high political price for refusing to make unsavory deals to win votes from either camp. As *Harper's Weekly* said about Wheeler years later, even though "there was no purer man, no man of wider experience in public life, of more admirable equipment in character, intelligence, temperament, and training in public service," when it came time to elect a U.S. Senator, Wheeler simply "was not the kind of Republican who was acceptable to the ruling influences in the party."[31]

Now that the political battle in Albany was over, the sixty-two-year-old former vice president settled down to "husband out life's taper" in Malone and, as he had previously stated to the *Boston Journal*, be "as good a citizen as possible."[32]

29

"Distressing Malady of My Bladder"

☆

The siren call of Washington politics would not leave Wheeler alone in Malone. Twice since he had conceded defeat in his race for the Senate, the glamour of national politics beckoned. Twice he said no. One call came from the Republican state committee, which asked Bill to accept the GOP nomination to run for congressman-at-large in the 1882 fall election. Given the frustration and disappointment he still harbored following his recent battles in Albany, his friends understood why he declined the offer.[1]

The second call came from the White House asking Wheeler to help resolve one of the most heated controversies facing the nation in the late nineteenth century—tariff reform. Arthur, having succeeded to the presidency after Garfield's death,[2] appointed Wheeler chairman of a tariff revision commission and submitted his name to the Senate for confirmation on June 7, 1882. As soon as Bill learned of his appointment, which he said had been made without his knowledge, he telegraphed Arthur that he could not serve because of his poor health. However, Bill's hometown paper revealed his real reason for turning down the appointment. Wheeler's congressional experience dealing with tariffs told him that the commission's work would be futile. Congress "would tear the commission's report to pieces, and if it does not reject it altogether, it will adopt it after serious mutilation."[3] As it turned out, Wheeler was correct. After the commission made its report, Congress changed so many of the commission's recommendations that the resulting tariff revision law became cynically known as "the Mongrel Tariff."[4]

At this time in his career, Wheeler was content to focus his energy, wealth, and experience on improving life on the local level. Although he joined the Malone Engine Company Number One, one of the village's first fire companies, and was elected to the board of directors of the Malone Water Works Company, he invested the bulk of his time and money on improving local public education and helping his church.[5]

Public education had always been highly important to Bill. He had worked as a public school teacher before he became a lawyer and railroad executive. While he was vice president, he had donated money to the Malone village school board to enable it to offer prizes to students for academic achievement. During Bill's last year as vice president, he donated $500, or about $11,000 when adjusted for inflation,[6] to the school board for prizes. Bill drew up a schedule of prizes to be offered to students, boys and girls, from grades one through twelve, for academic achievement in public speaking, essay writing, mathematics, grammar, spelling, and geography. In addition, prize money was set aside for six teachers who had created the best lessons and whose students had scored the highest on exams.[7] Once Bill's vice-presidential term had expired and he had returned to Malone as a private citizen, he ran for the school board and was elected to a five-year term. Wheeler served on the board's finance committee and continued to donate money for what became known locally as "the Wheeler Prizes."[8]

The time and money Bill gave to improve local public education paled in comparison to what Bill contributed to his church, the First Congregational Church of Malone. Its brick church building sat on the corner of Clay and Main Streets, a short walk through a lovely park, from Bill's house. The building was constructed in 1851 to replace the original stone structure whose cornerstone was laid in 1826, a few weeks before Bill turned seven years old.[9]

In 1882, the trustees of the First Congregational Church and Society decided they should build yet a third building because the brick structure was in serious disrepair and church membership had increased from two hundred to four hundred.[10] However, the project stalled when the first cost estimates for a new building came in at $25,000, or about $550,000 when adjusted for inflation. The trustees questioned whether they could raise such a large amount of money. That is when Wheeler came to the rescue. In May, he offered to give the Society $10,000, or approximately $221,000 when adjusted for inflation, toward the construction costs. The project took on new life following Wheeler's pledge and on June 1, other trustees pledged a total of $13,000 more. The women in the church raised an additional $3,000 and by the end of the month, the Society reported that it expected to have $30,000 to build a new church building.[11]

In July, the trustees named Wheeler to a three-member building committee to adopt plans and erect a new church. In September, Tristram Griffin of Boston was selected to be the architect. He was a familiar figure in Malone because he had also drawn the plans for the new Franklin Academy building and for the Wead Library.[12] Within two months, Griffin presented his plans for the church to Wheeler's building committee. The architect had designed a Romanesque stone structure, which featured a fortress-like tower that had a twenty square foot base and was more than one hundred feet tall. He gave the building committee a choice of stone for the structure—either limestone from Norwood in St. Lawrence County or marble from Isle La Motte, a Vermont island in Lake Champlain. The committee chose the Norwood limestone and hired contractor Orville Moore of Malone to oversee construction of the building, which took about a year and a half to complete. Inside the church, Wheeler paid for a marble tablet that was installed in honor of the man who had been one of Bill's surrogate fathers, Ashbel Parmelee, the church's first pastor. The plans called for the tablet to stand on a black walnut support to the right of the pulpit.[13]

As the building reached completion in September 1884, the building costs skyrocketed to $46,000, or about $1,000,000 when adjusted for inflation. The trustees were alarmed to learn that the Society did not have enough money to pay the contractor and turned to Wheeler for help. He spearheaded a drive to erase the debt. In mid-September, Bill announced after a meeting he chaired following church services, that between funds pledged by the ladies aid society and by other church members, there would be sufficient funds to pay off the debt.[14]

The new church was formally dedicated at 2:00 p.m. on October 14, 1884. During the dedication ceremonies, Wheeler, representing the building committee, presented the keys to the building to businessman Hiram H. Thompson, who was representing the Society's trustees. Bill also gave a speech in honor of the occasion. He may have been thinking about his own mortality when he said in closing, "Long may the imposing tower which crowns our church home stand as a sentinel over the last resting place of our sainted dead, and long may it look down on future generations."[15]

During the first few years following his vice presidency, Wheeler did a fair amount of traveling. He threatened to go on a European tour but when the Hayes family declined to join him, his worries about encountering "icebergs, storms and fire," deterred him from making the trip.[16] Instead, he visited the Hayes family at their home in Fremont, Ohio.[17] Bill also visited his cousins for Christmas in

First Congregational Church of Malone. Courtesy of the Franklin County Historical and Museum Society.

Chattanooga, Tennessee, and then continued south to Jacksonville, Florida, where he went black bass fishing on the St. Johns River.[18]

Sadly, in the summer of 1882, Bill's health began to slowly deteriorate. Bill wrote Hayes that he was "suffering from a distressing malady of my bladder, which as age goes on, is aggravated by complications with the bowels."[19] Accompanied by his physician, Dr. Theodore Gay of Malone, Bill spent July and August in the White Mountains and on the ocean at Mount Desert, Maine, hoping to ease his pain. He began to feel better by the fall but when he visited his sister-in-law in Garrison, New York, in January of 1883, eye problems that had forced him to drop out of UVM reoccurred.[20] Bill's eyes became so inflamed from the glare of the sun and ice while taking daily drives, he was confined to the house for the next three months, unable to read or write. To make matters worse, he also began suffering from insomnia.[21]

In the fall of 1884, his declining health prompted him to reluctantly resign from the Malone school board but it did not keep him away from the presidential campaign.[22]

The Republicans had nominated Blaine to run against New York Democratic Governor Grover Cleveland for president, and former Civil War General John A. Logan, to run against Wheeler's 1876 Democratic opponent, Thomas A. Hendricks, for vice president. In September, Democrats attacked Logan by playing up his ties to the Democratic Party and pro-Southern views before the Civil War. Wheeler leapt to Logan's defense by giving him a ringing endorsement, which stated that Logan had "atoned" for "all that was bad in his earlier political record" by "25 years of splendid service in war and the cause of national liberty and human progress."[23]

As Blaine's integrity and involvement with the Credit Mobilier scandal came under heavy attack by Cleveland Democrats, Wheeler's Republican friends implored him to help the party by also endorsing Blaine. Because of Bill's vexing political history with Blaine, no endorsement was forthcoming until a few weeks before the election and even then, when it came, it was tepid. Wheeler said, "Mr. Blaine is a man of wonderful versatility and genius" who if elected to the presidency, would "rightly discharge his duties."[24] After Blaine and Logan narrowly lost the election to Cleveland and Hendricks, Bill's postmortem, which he shared with Hayes concluded with the hope that a "decent respect for morality" will "consign him [Blaine] to final, political burial."[25]

In 1885, Wheeler's health continued its downward slide. He began writing his memoirs but was able to complete only two installments that were entitled, "Recollections: Then and Now, 1831–1885." In the first installment, he wrote about his experiences as a congressman in Washington during the Civil War and his memories of Lincoln. In the second, he described what life in Malone had meant to him. In it, he confessed that his life was "declining" and that he was living "almost wholly in the past."[26] In July, he stopped writing and sought out the medicinal waters and quiet social life of Richfield Springs in Otsego County to lift his spirits and ease his discomfort. The waters temporarily rejuvenated him and he was soon looking for new ways he could contribute to the well-being of his community.

In August 1886, the sixty-seven-year-old ex-vice president worked on a local committee that was feverishly trying to convince the state to build a new mental health hospital in Malone. A new facility had been proposed because of serious overcrowding of existing hospitals in New York State. According to some estimates, there were as many as three thousand mentally ill people in the state with no place to go for care and shelter. The state mental health commission wanted to build the new hospital somewhere in the North Country. Despite the best efforts of Wheeler's committee to promote the abundance of "pure, sweet water" in Malone as the reason to locate the facility there, the mental health commission chose Plattsburgh instead.[27]

In November, Bill's health took a dramatic turn for the worst. He would not live to see his sixty-eighth birthday. The critical nature of Wheeler's poor health first leaked out into the public eye on the pages of Joseph Pulitzer's *New York World.* In a sensational article that Bill's friends described as "a little short of ghoulish," Wheeler was pictured as a physical and mental wreck, lying in bed under the influence of heavy doses of opium, and being kept secluded from callers by jealous relatives who wanted to keep his condition a secret. While acknowledging that Bill was seriously ill, his friends said that he only used morphine on the advice of his physician and would see visitors if they called at his home.[28]

During the winter, Bill tried to get his mind off his deteriorating health by writing to his friends and relatives. He wrote to Hayes and his family, including his niece, the former Emily Platt, the woman he had been smitten with after his wife died but who was now married and living with her husband in Bermuda. In his letters, Bill reminisced about the good times they all had spent with each other when he was vice president. He smiled when he opened a letter from Hayes's daughter, Fanny, now twenty years old, and saw photographs she had sent him of herself and her family. Bill signed a warm thank you letter to her by writing, "Affectionately, Your Uncle William."[29]

On March 3, 1887, Bill began experiencing a chill that was so severe, his doctor thought it would kill him. The chill lasted a week and Wheeler became more feeble and depressed.[30] He remained in bed in critical condition for the next three months. On May 30, he lost consciousness and at 10:10 a.m. on Saturday, June 4, 1887, with some of his friends and his pastor, the Reverend C. S. Richardson, at

Wheeler's gravesite in Morningside Cemetery in Malone. The epitaph on his tombstone in the center reads, "William A. Wheeler, born June 30, 1819, was thus honored: member of the N.Y. legislature, Rep. in Congress, five terms, Prest. of N.Y. Cons. Con. 1867, Vice Prest. U.S. 1876–80, died June 4, 1887. A faithful public servant." On the left is a monument for his parents, Almon and Eliza Wheeler. Wheeler's wife, Mary, is buried on the right. The two markers in the rear are for his sisters, Fidelia and Jane M. Wheeler.

his bedside, Wheeler passed away, a few weeks short of his sixty-eighth birthday. His doctor said the immediate cause of death was a stroke.[31]

Bill had planned his funeral arrangements ahead of time. He had ordered a marble receptacle for his casket be installed in a gravesite next to that of his wife in Morningside Cemetery in Malone, left instructions with his brother-in-law to order an oak casket, and named his six pallbearers.

President Cleveland, who was vacationing two hours away from Malone in the Adirondacks when he learned of Wheeler's death, ordered the flags in all public buildings in Washington, D.C. to be displayed at half-mast until the day after Bill's funeral. At 10 a.m. on Tuesday, June 7, a military detachment from the New York State National Guard moved Wheeler's remains from his home to the vestibule of his church where he lay in state, surrounded by a six-man guard of honor, for two hours. All businesses and schools in Malone closed for the day and hundreds of people came to take one last look at Bill. Every village schoolteacher brought their classes in a group from their schools to view Wheeler's remains.

The church was filled to capacity when the funeral service began at 1 p.m. There were many dignitaries present including ex-President Hayes and his son Webb; ex-governor of Vermont and railroad executive, J. Gregory Smith; and the directors of the Ogdensburg and Lake Champlain Railroad who had come from Albany in a special train. Also present were congressmen, generals, state legislators, editors of newspapers, mayors, district attorneys, representatives from the Grand Army of the Republic, and the Malone Board of Education. A few Republicans rolled their eyes when they learned that two prominent Democrats, President Cleveland and Governor David B. Hill, had sent telegrams saying they were sorry they would not be able to come because they had to attend to "official duties."

The auditorium of the church was draped with crepe, national flags, and wreaths of flowers. Wheeler's pew was banked with ferns and flowers, which formed the letters of his name. Six clergymen from different faiths participated in the ceremonies, which included prayers and a sermon that discussed Wheeler's character as a citizen, patriot, and Christian. A choir sang Wheeler's favorite hymns, "Jerusalem the Golden," to open the service, and "Rock of Ages" to close it.

When the ceremonies were over, a funeral cortege was formed. Escorted by a military honor guard, it wended its way down Main Street to Morningside Cemetery on Raymond Street where Wheeler was buried next to his wife, Mary.[32]

Bill's death and burial did not bring tranquillity to Wheeler's former household. Within a week after his casket was lowered into the ground, a bitter court battle broke out over who was legally entitled to inherit Wheeler's substantial estate and how much his doctor should be paid.

30

Negotiating "Simple Justice"

★

As soon as Wheeler's heirs-at-law learned that he had not left them any money in his will, twenty-three of them hired lawyers to convince Surrogate Horace A. Taylor, a former county district attorney and county judge since 1878, to invalidate the will. Almost every attorney in Malone was retained to either challenge or defend the document.[1]

Wheeler's estate included more than $80,000, or almost $2 million in inflation-adjusted dollars, in gilt-edged securities, and a home and its contents worth $10,000. In addition, Bill owned a one-third interest in several thousand acres of undeveloped land in Minnesota.[2] In his will, Bill left most of his estate to the Presbyterian Board of Home Missions whose headquarters were in New York City. The Board of Missions had been organized in 1816 to carry out missionary work on the U.S. frontier. The Board anticipated receiving an inheritance of $74,000, or more than $1.7 million in inflation-adjusted dollars. Bill also left $5,000 each, or almost $119,000 in inflation adjusted dollars, to the Massachusetts-based American Board of Commissioners for Foreign Missions, the New York City–based American Bible Society, and his cousin, the Reverend Alfred Wheeler of Pennsylvania.[3]

Wheeler's eighty-year-old uncle on his mother's side, George C. Woodward of Malone, led the charge to overturn the will. Because he was Bill's only next-of-kin under New York law, Woodward stood to inherit a lion's share of Bill's estate if the will were broken. The other relatives would divide up what was left.[4]

To invalidate the will, Wheeler's relatives planned to prove that Bill was incompetent at the time he signed the will.[5] Pulitzer's "ghoulish" story in the *New York World* that pictured Wheeler lying in bed under the influence of opium was published shortly after Bill executed his will on March 30, 1886. In addition, opponents of the will were counting on community pressure to aid them. Some people in Malone resented the fact that Wheeler had left most of his estate to out-of-town strangers. Ignoring the fact that Wheeler had given away about $50,000, or about $1.2 million when adjusted for inflation, to public and private charities during the last few years of his life, they were angry that he had left no money to establish a local hospital, or build a public hall, or fund educational scholarships. Local newspapers fanned community unrest about the will. They changed their original description of Woodward as a man who had lived in "moderate circumstances," to a man who was "destitute."[6]

The validity of the will hinged on the testimony of the two people who witnessed its execution. They were Betsy Chambers, Wheeler's housekeeper for more than twenty-six years, and Fanny H. Wood, one of Wheeler's cousins who worked for him as his secretary. Proponents of the will were concerned that Surrogate Taylor might not find Chambers to be a credible witness because she stood to inherit $500, or more than $10,000 in inflation-adjusted dollars, if Surrogate Taylor declared the will to be valid.[7]

To avoid a full trial contesting the validity of the will, the Presbyterian Board negotiated a settlement with Woodward, which the press promptly described as "simple justice." The Board paid Woodward $5,000, or almost $119,000 when adjusted for inflation, and he agreed to assign to the Board all his rights in Wheeler's estate. As expected, the other relatives followed Woodward's lead and also assigned their rights in the estate over to the Board, but on "more moderate terms."[8]

On May 17, 1888, with all contesting parties financially satisfied, and having received testimony from Chambers and Wood that Wheeler was of sound mind when he signed the will with his own hand, Surrogate Taylor ruled that Wheeler's will was valid. However, this did not bring an end to the controversy surrounding Wheeler's estate. When the executor of Wheeler's estate, Harry S. House, opened the estate's mail a week later, he was shocked by the size of the bill that had been sent in by Dr. Theodore Gay. He was making a claim against Wheeler's estate for taking care of Wheeler during the last two years of his life.[9]

Dr. Gay was seven years older than Bill. The son of a Vermont physician, Gay graduated from Middlebury College before receiving his medical degree and coming to Malone in 1842 to practice medicine. After Bill retired from the state and national political scene, a friendship developed between Gay and Wheeler. They had much in common. Both men loved literature, especially Shakespeare; both were highly intelligent and respected by their peers; and, perhaps most importantly, both were widowers. Gay's wife had been an invalid for many years before she died in 1871. Dr. Gay accompanied Wheeler on vacations to New Hampshire, Maine, and downstate New York. When Bill became seriously ill in the last few years of his life, Gay limited his practice to only caring for Wheeler.

Dr. Gay billed Wheeler $14,800, or over $352,000 in inflation-adjusted dollars, for medical services Gay said he had provided Wheeler from April 1, 1885, through the day of his death, June 4, 1887. Gay charged Wheeler $15 a day in 1885, $20 a day in 1886, and $25 a day in 1887. When adjusted for inflation, Gay's per diem charges were about $357 in 1885, $476 in 1886, and $595 in 1887. In addition, Gay billed Wheeler for keeping a horse and carriage for two years.[10]

Arguing that the bill was unreasonable and excessive, House refused to pay it. Gay threatened legal action and once again, as it did with Wheeler's relatives, the Presbyterian Board of Home Missions stepped forward to negotiate a settlement. The press waded in on Dr. Gay's side quoting "prominent legal authorities in Franklin County" as saying that Gay's bill was not excessive, and editorializing that he deserved "liberal compensation" because he had devoted himself almost exclusively to Wheeler. Gay argued that he had given up a good practice to be Wheeler's medical advisor and constant attendant for several years.[11]

After two months of negotiations, Dr. Gay agreed to accept $10,000, or about $238,000 in inflation-adjusted dollars, for his services.[12] The payment to Gay brought an end to the turmoil surrounding Bill's estate but the controversy was the first sign that as time passed, Wheeler's legacy would become tarnished.

Epilogue

From "Sterling Gold" to Neurotic Timidity

Wheeler's reputation was at its zenith in 1887, the year he died. Hayes described Wheeler's character as "sterling gold."[1] According to the *New York Times,* Wheeler was a "frank and fearless" man who was "animated by a profound sense of justice" and "active in nearly every important measure that came before Congress from 1869 until 1876."[2] *Harper's Weekly* lauded Bill's "sound judgment, coolness and courage" and said, "few men in the history of the state . . . more truly deserve long and grateful recollection."[3]

Wheeler may have deserved long and grateful recollection, but he did not get it. Two men drew a road map that was used to tarnish Wheeler's reputation. As time passed, writers who blindly followed this map maligned Bill by claiming that he was a timid neurotic, an overly cautious hypochondriac, and a paranoid with an inferiority complex.[4] Others went so far as to describe Wheeler's vice presidential nomination as a "joke" or "the product of low comedy."[5] Misinformation like this eventually found its way onto the Internet where it further damaged Wheeler's reputation around the globe.[6]

The first man to significantly undermine Wheeler's legacy was Frederick J. Seaver of Malone. The editor of a Republican weekly newspaper, the *Malone Palladium,* Seaver had political ambitions for himself, which were dashed after he

Marble bust of Vice President Wheeler by the sculptor Edward Clark Potter. The U.S. Senate authorized the acquisition of the bust in 1886 for display in the Senate Chamber alongside busts of all the other former vice presidents. Potter's most notable works are his two marble lions for the New York Public Library. U.S. Senate Collection.

and Wheeler had a falling out around the time Bill's wife died in 1876. Until then, the two men were friends. When Bill became chairman of the House Commerce Committee in 1873 and had patronage to hand out, he hired Seaver to join him in Washington and work for him as the clerk of the committee.[7]

After Bill was sworn in as vice president in 1877, he decided not to retain Seaver as his executive secretary. Instead, Wheeler hired Edwin E. Dickinson, the twenty-four-year-old son of his chief political advisor in Franklin County.[8] Seaver never recovered from this blow to his ambition and never forgot who delivered it to him.

Four years later, Wheeler frustrated the editor's ambition again. In 1881, Seaver sought the Republican nomination to run for the assembly in a special election that had been called to fill the vacancy created when the Franklin County assemblyman, William D. Brennan, committed suicide after a quarrel with Wheeler. Wheeler refused to back the editor and in a hotly contested district convention, Seaver lost the GOP nomination to Brennan's law partner, Samuel A. Beman, after three ballots, 26 to 16. By Seaver's own reckoning, he would have won the nomination if Wheeler had backed him.[9]

Seaver waited until Wheeler died before seeking revenge. In a mixed newspaper review of Bill's life published a few days after he died, Seaver emphasized how Wheeler was always gloomy, depressed, and despondent about his health, and intimated that if it were not for the "supreme" support of Wheeler's wife, Mary, Bill's political career would not have gone as far as it did.[10] Seaver renewed his attack on Wheeler's legacy in 1918 when Seaver published a history of Franklin County. In it, he savaged Wheeler's reputation by writing that Wheeler chose not to run for governor in 1879 because he was a "passive" and timid man who "lacked aggressiveness and courage." Seaver attributed these weaknesses to Wheeler's "morbid and persistent belief" that his "health was precarious."[11]

As time passed, historians and authors of books about the vice presidents repeated Seaver's vindictive observations. Citing Seaver, one historian wrote that Wheeler "suffered from hypochondria," was "becoming paranoid" over his loss of power, and had "an inferiority complex."[12] In its official history of the vice presidents, relying solely on Seaver's opinion of Wheeler, the U.S. Senate Historical Office claimed as fact that Wheeler was "neurotically obsessed with his own well-being" and was "an excessively cautious politician—to the point of timidity."[13] Seaver's revenge was complete.

The second man to significantly undermine Wheeler' legacy was Hamilton J. Eckenrode, an early twentieth-century Civil War historian from Virginia. In a 1930 biography of Hayes, Eckenrode claimed that Wheeler's vice presidential nomination was a farce. According to Eckenrode, following Hayes's nomination for president in 1876 at the GOP national convention, the New York delegation was told that it could pick the vice presidential nominee as a sop to Conkling. Relying on information obtained from Hayes's son, Webb Hayes, who was supposedly present when the New Yorkers met to make their choice, Eckenrode described a scene in which New York delegates had difficulty deciding who should be the vice presidential nominee. According to Eckenrode, "They bandied the office about among themselves in caucus" until finally, "some one proposed, 'Let's give it to Wheeler.' So, William A. Wheeler, a second-rate politician was nominated."[14]

Because of its sheer entertainment value, Eckenrode's fanciful tale took on a life of its own in future books about the vice presidents and in articles about Wheeler on the Internet. In them, the authors embellished Eckenrode's story by painting a surreal picture of giggling New York delegates, hilariously trying to convince one another to accept the vice presidential nomination, until finally, after all the laughing and joking died down, they agree to hand the nomination to Wheeler, because no one else would take it.[15]

These derisive accounts of Wheeler's vice presidential nomination not only ignore Wheeler's earnest campaign for higher office at the convention, which attracted widespread national support, and turn a blind eye to the vice presidential candidacy of a Conkling man, Stewart L. Woodford of Brooklyn, they also disregard the fact that Wheeler was no friend of Conkling's! Because of this, and also because it is uncertain that Webb Hayes was actually present at the alleged meeting, modern historians and biographers have dismissed Eckenrode's story as either "unlikely" or "largely fiction."[16]

Since his death, Wheeler's name has slipped into the dustbin of history. Wheeler had no siblings or children to keep his memory alive or to defend his legacy when it was disparaged. With the simple passage of time, average people easily forget the names of political figures from bygone eras—Wheeler's name was no exception to this general rule. He soon joined the ranks of what the U.S. author Thomas Wolfe called *the lost Americans*. Referring to men like Wheeler from the days of Hayes, Garfield, and Arthur, Wolfe wrote, "their gravely vacant and bewhiskered faces, mixed, melted, swam together in the sea-depths of a past intangible, immeasurable, and unknowable as the buried city of Persepolis. And they were lost. . . . Which had the whiskers, which the burnsides: which was which?"[17]

A second reason that Wheeler slipped into the dustbin of history was because of the nature of the office of vice president. Unless the president gives the vice president authority to do something, the vice president has little power. As a consequence of this, as one historian put it, "in the popular mind, the vice president is often a figure of fun, someone who has no meaningful role in life other than to check on the president's health each morning."[18] The nation's first vice president,

John Adams, was the first to lament his role in the new federal government. In 1793, he described the vice presidency as "the most insignificant office that was the invention of man."[19] As time passed, the nature of the office of vice president changed little. John Nance Garner, Franklin D. Roosevelt's vice president during his first two terms and a man one historian called "the most powerful vice president in the history of the United States," declared that the office of vice president was not "worth a pitcher of warm piss."[20]

There is a third reason why Wheeler fell into the dustbin of history. Because of a dearth of sources about his life and accomplishments, little has been written about Bill Wheeler. Aside from a few letters, historians have been unable to locate his papers. In addition, the national press during Wheeler's day chose not to write many stories about him. Unlike a Conkling or a Blaine, Wheeler did not have the kind of flair or charisma that attracted attention—and reporters. Because of this, they often decided that he would not make a good story. As the *New York Times* wrote in his obituary, Wheeler's "personality failed to impress itself upon the public. . . . little public interest ever attached to him."[21] Furthermore, the vice president from Malone did not court the press, as most successful politicians do. He was not a self-serving man and even if he had been, he had few public relations skills. On top of that, Bill was hesitant to trust the fourth estate. In addition, most of Wheeler's political and legislative work in New York State and in Washington was done out of the limelight, in committees, one-on-one, behind closed doors. And perhaps most importantly, Wheeler's relations with the national press suffered because he lived so far away from the large urban areas where the national press was located. It was extremely difficult for newspaper reporters to regularly interact with Wheeler, even if they wanted to.

Other reasons for Wheeler's obscurity are less easy to understand. Often, modern writers have simply ignored his existence. For some unknown reason, there has been a scholarly blind spot when it came to writing about the nineteenth-vice president and this blind spot pushed Wheeler deeper into history's dustbin. For example, William H. Rehnquist, former chief justice of the U.S. Supreme Court and a man who should have known better, inexplicably left Wheeler completely out of his otherwise scholarly book about the highly controversial election of 1876, in which Wheeler won election to be vice president, running with the GOP candidate for president, Rutherford B. Hayes. Rehnquist discussed Hayes, his Democratic opponent, Samuel J. Tilden, and Tilden's running mate, Thomas A. Hendricks—but not Wheeler![22]

Yes, Wheeler has been consigned to the dustbin of history—except in Malone, New York, where he is revered as a North Country treasure and his memory is kept alive. In Malone, several buildings still stand as a reminder of his life. His

Wheeler bedroom located in the Franklin County Historical and Museum Society's House of History. Courtesy of the Franklin County Historical and Museum Society.

brick home, owned and maintained by the Malone Lodge of Elks, sits proudly on Elm Street. The handsome railroad station with its twin octagonal towers, which Wheeler arranged for the Northern Railroad to build, is also on Elm Street where the structure currently serves as the Malone branch of the Community Bank. Bill's church, the First Congregational Church of Malone, whose construction was made possible by his substantial financial contributions and fund-raising ability, towers majestically over Main Street.

In addition to these buildings, two civic organizations work to keep Wheeler's memory alive. Around the corner from Bill's church, on Milwaukee Street, the Franklin County Historical & Museum Society maintains a "Wheeler bedroom" in the Society's House of History, a Victorian house museum. This room contains bedroom furnishings from Wheeler's day and also displays two books that had a significant impact on Wheeler's life. One of them is Bill's homemade, annotated version of the *Digest of Rules of the House of Representatives* that he used to make his mark as one of the House's most respected parliamentarians. The second book is the hymn songbook said to belong to Wheeler's parents and used by them to teach Bill how to read music and sing when he was a child.

The dignified staircase in Wheeler's home, now owned by the Malone Lodge of Elks.

Annually, the Society commemorates Wheeler's birthday at his gravesite with the Malone Lodge of Elks. Ceremonies include wreath laying, a gun salute, speeches, and often a reception, which includes a gaily-decorated Wheeler birthday cake. In addition to partnering with the Society to celebrate Bill's birthday, the

Elks open Wheeler's former home to the public. They have designated a parlor on the first floor to be the "Wheeler room" and it contains one of Wheeler's desks. Much of the room's original woodwork has been restored including several secret compartments behind the paneling. When wedding receptions are held at the Elks Lodge, the newlyweds and their bridal party often enjoy having their pictures taken standing on the polished, deep golden-brown wood of Wheeler's dignified upstairs staircase. Members of the Elks also put up signs to Wheeler's grave in Morningside Cemetery in Malone and keep his gravesite in a condition fitting that of a former five-term congressman and vice president.

While Wheeler's memory is being kept alive in Malone, his legacy, dim as it may be, can also be seen in many other locations. In New York State, it can be seen in the beauty of the Adirondack Park and the Niagara Falls State Park. Nationally, it can be seen in the bustling cities that sprang up along the route of the Northern Pacific Railroad, such as Brainerd, Minnesota; Fargo and Bismarck, North Dakota; Billings, Montana; and Tacoma, Washington. And Wheeler's legacy can be found in New Orleans where Bill negotiated an end to a racial civil war.

William Almon Wheeler's actions touched millions of Americans. He lived an honest life that was driven by a resolve to do good works and serve his community. Indeed, he is a treasure—he is the political star of the North Country.

Notes

Abbreviations

AR	*Albany Argus*
BE	*Brooklyn Eagle*
HW	*Harper's Weekly*
FG	Malone (NY) *Franklin Gazette*
FP	Malone (NY) *Frontier Palladium*
DMA	Manchester (NH) *Daily Mirror & American*
NYT	*New York Times*
NA	*Nation*
MP	Malone (NY) *Palladium*

Introduction

1. Beaman, "William Almon Wheeler," 59–60; *NYT*, 6/18/1876, p. 1; *MP*, 5/18/1876 and 7/6/1876.
2. *BE*, 1/3/1877, p. 3; *MP*, 5/30/1872, 3/27/1884, 5/7/1885.
3. Seaver, *Historical Sketches of Franklin County*, 713; *FG*, 7/26/1889; *MP*, 6/9/1887.
4. Wheeler Papers, Wheeler to Lucy Hayes, June 24, 1878 and June 10, 1879.
5. *MP*, 5/22/1873.
6. *BE*, 8/8/1879, p. 2.

7. *BE*, 6/14/1880, p. 2.
8. *NYT*, 7/9/1876, p. 2; Hoogenboom, *Rutherford B. Hayes*, 344–345; *MP*, 7/13/1876.
9. Nevins, *Abram S. Hewitt*, 305; Beaman, "William Almon Wheeler," 59–60.
10. Wheeler Papers, Wheeler to Lucy Hayes, Sept. 24, 1877, and Wheeler to Rutherford B. Hayes, Dec. 13, 1876; *NYT*, 8/22/1872, p. 1; *MP*, 7/6/1876, 9/29/1881, and 6/18/1885.
11. Conlin, *American Past*, 44–45; Wheeler, *Genealogical and Encyclopedic History*, 200.
12. Wheeler, *Genealogical and Encyclopedic History*, 200 and 205.
13. *MP*, 6/18/1885.

Chapter 1. Tragedy in Malone

1. Seaver, *Historical Sketches of Franklin County*, 412.
2. Wheeler, *Genealogical and Encyclopedic History*, 230 and 236. Fairfield, Vermont was also the birthplace of Vice President and President Chester Alan Arthur. Ibid., 230.
3. University of Vermont, *General Catalog*, 41. In 1818, the University of Vermont granted Almon an honorary A.M. degree. Ibid.
4. Wheeler, *Genealogical and Encyclopedic History*, 250.
5. *MP*, 7/16/1885.
6. Seaver, *Historical Sketches of Franklin County*, 16 and 398.
7. Ibid., 402.
8. Hurd, *History of Clinton and Franklin Counties*, 378.
9. U.S. Bureau of the Census, 1860 census.
10. University of Vermont, *General Catalog*, 41; Blum et al., *National Experience*, 172.
11. Blum et al., *National Experience*, 175.
12. Wheeler, *Genealogical and Encyclopedic History*, 250.
13. Seaver, *Historical Sketches of Franklin County*, 97–98; Hurd, *History of Clinton and Franklin Counties*, 383.
14. Seaver, *Historical Sketches of Franklin County*, 97–98; *MP*, 6/22/1876.
15. Seaver, *Historical Sketches of Franklin County*, 97–98.
16. Wheeler, *Genealogical and Encyclopedic History*, 265.
17. Hurd, *History of Clinton and Franklin Counties*, 403.
18. Seaver, *Historical Sketches of Franklin County*, 475.
19. Hurd, *History of Clinton and Franklin Counties*, 392 and 414.
20. Seaver, *Historical Sketches of Franklin County*, 476.

21. Louis M. King to Franklin County Historical Society, Jan. 30, 1947; *Village Harmony.*
22. Klein, *Empire State,* 316.
23. Landon, *North Country,* 290.
24. Ibid., 291.
25. Kirkland, *Men, Cities and Transportation,* 158–159.
26. *MP,* 6/9/1887.
27. Hurd, *History of Clinton and Franklin Counties,* 379; Beck, *Elements of Medical Jurisprudence,* 2:113–115.
28. Seaver, *Historical Sketches of Franklin County,* 342–343; Beck, *Elements of Medical Jurisprudence,* 2:113–115; Hough, *History of St. Lawrence and Franklin Counties,* 502–503; *Poe Collection of Early American Letters,* Archive Index 91.
29. Landon, *The North Country,* 327; Klein, *Empire State,* 374.
30. Seaver, *Historical Sketches of Franklin County,* 696–697.
31. *NYT,* 6/26/1876, p. 5.
32. *MP,* 6/9/1887; *FG,* 6/10/1887.

Chapter 2. The Making of a "Cultivated" Man

1. *MP,* 7/16/1885; *FG,* 6/10/1887.
2. Seaver, *Historical Sketches of Franklin County,* 767–768.
3. *MP,* 6/18/1885.
4. Hough, *History of Clinton and Franklin Counties,* 512–513, 529–530, and 548; Seaver, *Historical Sketches of Franklin County,* 97–98; *MP,* 6/22/1876.
5. *MP,* 6/9/1887.
6. *MP,* 6/18/1885.
7. Conwell, *Public Services of Gov. Rutherford B. Hayes,* 313.
8. Hough, *History of St. Lawrence and Franklin Counties,* 548; Seaver, *Historical Sketches of Franklin County,* 421.
9. *MP,* 6/9/1887.
10. Seaver, *Historical Sketches of Franklin County,* 705.
11. Klein, *Empire State,* 372 and 377.
12. Hurd, *History of Clinton and Franklin Counties,* 415.
13. Seaver, *Historical Sketches of Franklin County,* 493; Landon, *North Country,* 327.
14. Klein, *Empire State,* 376.
15. Landon, *North Country,* 336.
16. Klein, *Empire State,* 376; Rayback, *Millard Fillmore,* 31–32.

17. Klein, *Empire State,* 377–378.
18. Seaver, *Historical Sketches of Franklin County,* 98 and 698; Hurd, *History of Clinton and Franklin Counties,* 381.
19. Kirkland, *Men, Cities and Transportation,* 161.
20. Ibid., 164. Vicious rapids downstream on the St. Lawrence River precluded vessels from easily passing east to Montreal. Shaughnessy, *Rutland Railroad,* 53.
21. Shaughnessy, *Rutland Railroad,* 53.
22. Ibid., 3.
23. Ibid., 53.
24. Seaver, *Historical Sketches of Franklin County,* 658–659.
25. Blum et al., *National Experience,* 225.
26. *NYT,* 6/5/1887, p. 5; University of Vermont, *General Catalogue,* 72.
27. Menand, *Metaphysical Club,* 250.
28. Daniels, *University of Vermont,* 80–81.
29. Marshall, *Universitas Viridis Montis,* 33.
30. Menand, *Metaphysical Club,* 246–247.
31. Marshall, *Universitas Viridis Montis,* 33.
32. Menand, *Metaphysical Club,* 248–249.
33. Ibid., 250.
34. Daniels, *University of Vermont,* 82.
35. University of Vermont, *General Catalogue,* 65–76. Bill's Class of 1842 had 115 students in 1838 and 128 students in 1839.
36. Ibid., 68.
37. Ibid., 64.
38. *NYT,* 6/5/1887, p. 5; *MP,* 6/9/1887.
39. Conwell, *Public Services of Gov, Rutherford B. Hayes,* 314.
40. *MP,* 6/9/1887.

Chapter 3. Love and the New District Attorney

1. Boller, *Presidential Anecdotes,* 90.
2. Blum et al., *National Experience,* 226–227; Conlin, *American Past,* 292; Klein, *Empire State,* 384–385.
3. Boller, *Presidential Anecdotes,* 91; Weed, *Autobiography of Thurlow Weed,* 490; Seaver, *Historical Sketches of Franklin County,* 100.
4. Seaver, *Historical Sketches of Franklin County,* 101.
5. Ibid., 185.
6. *MP,* 7/6/1876.

7. Ibid.
8. *NYT*, 7/9/1876, p. 12.
9. *MP*, 8/6/1863; Seaver, *Historical Sketches of Franklin County*, 745–746.
10. *MP*, 3/9/1876 and 3/16/1876.
11. *MP*, 7/14/1870.
12. *Appletons' Annual Cyclopedia*, 804; *MP*, 6/9/1887.
13. *MP*, 6/9/1887.
14. Klein, *Empire State*, 388–389.
15. Potter, *Impending Crisis*, 20–22.
16. Ibid.
17. Hough, *History of St. Lawrence and Franklin Counties*, 518; Kivic, "Abolition's Early Roots," 19; Klein, *Empire State*, 248.
18. Hurd, *History of Clinton and Franklin Counties*, 429.
19. *MP*, 6/22/1876.
20. Klein, *Empire State*, 392.
21. Folts, "Courts, state," in Eisenstadt, *Encyclopedia of New York State*, 413.
22. Hurd, *History of Clinton and Franklin Counties*, 468–469.
23. Rayback, *Millard Fillmore*, 165–167.
24. Seaver, *Historical Sketches of Franklin County*, 730–731; *FG*, 1/28/1881 and 11/12/1886.
25. Seaver, *Historical Sketches of Franklin County*, 102.
26. Dubin, *United States Congressional Elections*, 146.
27. Jenkins, *Life of Silas Wright*, title page; Southwick, *Presidential Also-Rans and Running Mates*, 193.
28. Potter, *Impending Crisis*, 78; Silbey, "Barnburners," and Sampson, "Hunkers," in Eisenstadt, *Encyclopedia of New York State*, 151 and 750.
29. Landon, *North Country*, 350.
30. Klein, *Empire State*, 394.
31. Landon, *North Country*, 351–354.
32. Seaver, *Historical Sketches of Franklin County*, 103.
33. Ibid., 730–731.
34. *NYT*, 6/26/1876, p. 5; *MP*, 6/22/1876.
35. Hurd, *History of Clinton and Franklin Counties*, 385.
36. Seaver, *Historical Sketches of Franklin County*, 185.
37. Scarry, *Millard Fillmore*, 95.
38. Potter, *Impending Crisis*, 64.
39. Klein, *Empire State*, 395.
40. Taylor, *William Henry Seward*, 42.
41. Dubin, *United States Congressional Elections*, 152.

42. Taylor, *William Henry Seward,* 73.
43. Klein, *Empire State,* 396.
44. Dubin, *United States Congressional Elections,* 152.
45. Hurd, *History of Clinton and Franklin Counties,* 481.
46. Shaughnessy, *Rutland Railroad,* 53–54.
47. Landon, *North Country,* 384.
48. Lyman, *Rails Into Racquetteville.*
49. Shaughnessy, *Rutland Railroad,* 55.
50. Seaver, *Historical Sketches of Franklin County,* 746.
51. Kirkland, *Men, Cities and Transportation,* 172–173.
52. Ibid.
53. *FP,* 1/24/1850.

Chapter 4. "Here Lies an Honest Man"

1. *FP,* 12/20/1849.
2. *MP,* 8/17/1876, 9/7/1876, and 6/19/1887.
3. Scarry, *Millard Fillmore,* 162 and 164.
4. *FP,* 10/25/1849.
5. Potter, *Impending Crisis,* 64–66 and 71; Alexander, *Political History,* 2:257.
6. Nevins, *Abram S. Hewitt,* 26–27.
7. Seaver, *Historical Sketches of Franklin County,* 794; *FP,* 10/31/1850.
8. Klein, *Empire State,* 398.
9. *FP,* 10/25/1849.
10. Klein, *Empire State,* 398.
11. *FP,* 11/22/1849.
12. *FP,* 11/5/1849.
13. *MP,* 6/19/1887.
14. Alexander, *Political History,* 2:150.
15. *FP,* 12/6/1849.
16. *FP,* 12/27/1849.
17. *FP,* 1/3/1850.
18. *FP,* 4/11/1850.
19. *FP,* 1/24/1850.
20. *FP,* 2/14/1850.
21. *FP,* 1/24/1850.
22. *FP,* 2/14/1850.
23. *FP,* 1/24/1850.

24. *FP,* 2/14/1850.
25. *BE,* 1/26/1850, p. 2; *FP,* 1/31/1850.
26. *FP,* 1/10/1850.
27. Sterngass, "Field, David Dudley," in Eisenstadt, *Encyclopedia of New York State,* 555.
28. Virtual American Biographies, "David Dudley Field."
29. *FP,* 1/17/1850.
30. *BE,* 3/8/1850, p. 2.
31. Glaeser, *Corruption and Reform,* 109–110.
32. *FP,* 4/18/1850.
33. *FP,* 5/2/1850.
34. Seaver, *Historical Sketches of Franklin County,* 748.
35. *FP,* 8/29/1850.
36. Blum et al., *National Experience,* 272.
37. *FP,* 2/7/1850.
38. Emerson, *Doo-dah!,* 145.
39. Ibid., 146.
40. *FP,* 4/18/1850.
41. Blum et al., *National Experience,* 274.

Chapter 5. "Old Hunkerism" Is Dead

1. *FP,* 7/11/1850; Telegraphic service would not arrive in Malone until 1851. Seaver, *Historical Sketches of Franklin County,* 443.
2. Rayback, *Millard Fillmore,* 255.
3. Seaver, *Historical Sketches of Franklin County* 717.
4. Barnes, *Memoir of Thurlow Weed,* 186–187.
5. *FP,* 9/19/1850.
6. Barnes, *Memoir of Thurlow Weed,* 186–187.
7. Scarry, *Millard Fillmore,* 178.
8. *FP,* 10/24/1850.
9. State legislatures elected U.S. Senators until 1913 when the Seventeenth Amendment to the U.S. Constitution was ratified providing for direct election by the voters.
10. *FP,* 10/24/1850 and 10/31/1850.
11. *FG,* 10/31/1850.
12. Ibid.
13. *FP,* 11/7/1850.

14. *FP*, 12/19/1850. Winning statewide by one of the smallest margins in New York State history, Hunt was elected governor by 262 votes. Alexander, *Political History*, 2:158.
15. *FP*, 11/14/1850.
16. *FP*, 11/21/1850.
17. *FG*, 11/21/1850.
18. Seaver, *Historical Sketches of Franklin County*, 118.
19. *FP*, 11/28/1850.
20. Gould, *Grand Old Party*, 20–22.
21. *FP*, 6/5/1851.
22. *FP*, 6/6/1850.
23. *FP*, 9/26/1850.
24. Lyman, *Rails Into Racquetteville*.
25. *FP*, 6/6/1850.
26. *FP*, 8/1/1850.
27. *FP*, 8/15/1850.
28. Shaughnessy, *Rutland Railroad*, 58–59.
29. Lyman, *Rails Into Racquetteville*.
30. Landon, *North Country*, 385.
31. Seaver, *Historical Sketches of Franklin County*, 785–786.

Chapter 6. A "Mere Act of Justice"

1. *FP*, 1/1/1851.
2. *FP*, 11/28/1850.
3. *FP*, 12/12/1850.
4. *FP*, 6/5/1851.
5. Alexander, *Political History*, 2:161–162.
6. Ibid., 2:163
7. *FP*, 1/9/1851 and 1/23/1851.
8. *FP*, 2/6/1851 and 3/20/1851.
9. *FP*, 2/13/1851.
10. *FP*, 2/6/1851 and 2/13/1851.
11. Rawley, *Edwin D. Morgan*, 17.
12. *FP*, 3/27/1851; *MP*, 6/9/1887; Rawley, *Edwin D. Morgan*, 17.
13. *FP*, 4/10/1851.
14. *BE*, 4/14/1851, p. 2.
15. *FP*, 4/24/1851.
16. *FP*, 5/22/1851.

17. *FP,* 6/5/1851.
18. *FP,* 6/12/1851 and 7/10/1851; Rawley, *Edwin D. Morgan,* 18.
19. *FP,* 7/3/1851.
20. *FP,* 7/3/1851; *FG,* 7/5/1851.
21. Kirkland, *Men, Cities and Transportation,* 174–175.
22. Ibid.; *FP,* 7/10/1851.
23. *FP,* 7/3/1851.
24. *FG,* 7/5/1851.
25. *FP,* 7/10/1851.
26. *FP,* 10/23/1851.
27. *FP,* 9/4/1851 and 9/18/1851.
28. Mooney, "Raymond Henry J(arvis)," in Eisenstadt, *Encyclopedia of New York State,* 1286–1287.
29. Sterngass, "Morgan, Edwin D(enison)," in Eisenstadt, *Encyclopedia of New York State,* 1009.
30. Seaver, *Historical Sketches of Franklin County,* 731; *FG,* 11/12/1886.
31. Hurd, *History of Clinton and Franklin Counties,* 385.
32. *FP,* 1/8/1852.
33. *FP,* 7/31/1851; Hough, *History of St. Lawrence and Franklin Counties,* 530.
34. Hurd, *History of Clinton and Franklin Counties,* 412–413.
35. *FP,* 10/16/1851.
36. *FP,* 1/22/1852 and 4/22/1852.
37. Smith, Mortgage, Northern Rail Road Company to George Curtis, William A. Wheeler, and Jabez C. Howe; *MP,* 6/9/1887.
38. *FP,* 2/19/1852.
39. *FP,* 7/29/1852 and 2/3/1853.
40. Seaver, *Historical Sketches of Franklin County,* 452.
41. Shaughnessy, *Rutland Railroad,* 59
42. Hurd, *History of Clinton and Franklin Counties,* 417.
43. *FP,* 3/10/1853.
44. Smith, Assignment of Mortgages, George Curtis to William A. Wheeler, Jabez C. Howe and John S. Eldridge.
45. Wheeler, *Report of the Trustees,* 4.
46. Ibid.
47. Ibid.
48. Ibid., 6.
49. Ibid., 7.
50. Ibid., 9 and 20.
51. Ibid., 18.

CHAPTER 7. "GRINDING" IT OUT IN ALBANY

1. Scarry, *Millard Fillmore,* 232–233.
2. Potter, *Impending Crisis,* 245.
3. Ibid., 248.
4. Seaver, *Historical Sketches of Franklin County,* 171.
5. Rayback, *Millard Fillmore,* 392.
6. Potter, *Impending Crisis,* 250.
7. Ibid., 245.
8. Rayback, *Millard Fillmore,* 384.
9. Potter, *Impending Crisis,* 247–248.
10. Klein, *Empire State,* 401.
11. Potter, *Impending Crisis,* 247–248.
12. Rayback, *Millard Fillmore,* 384.
13. Landon, *North Country,* 400.
14. Alexander, *Political History,* 2:211–214.
15. Seaver, *Historical Sketches of Franklin County,* 107.
16. Ibid., 778–779; U.S. Bureau of the Census, Series M653, Roll 754, p. 74.
17. Klein, *Empire State,* 408.
18. Seaver, *Historical Sketches of Franklin County,* 104.
19. Klein, *Empire State,* 408.
20. Landon, *North Country,* 400–402.
21. Klein, *Empire State,* 408.
22. Ibid., 409.
23. *NYT,* 5/29/1856, p. 1.
24. *MP,* 7/14/1870; *MP,* 7/20/1876; *FG,* 2/15/1895.
25. Russotto, *National Party Conventions,* 32.
26. Sterngass, "Morgan, Edwin D(enison)," in Eisenstadt, *Encyclopedia of New York State,* 1009.
27. Russotto, *National Party Conventions,* 32.
28. *NYT,* 6/26/1876, p. 5.
29. Alexander, *Political History,* 2:241–242.
30. Blum et al., *National Experience,* 309.
31. Lyman, *Rails Into Racquetteville.*
32. *NYT,* 9/24/1857, p. 1.
33. Hurd, *History of Clinton and Franklin Counties,* 381.
34. Alexander, *Political History,* 2:245.
35. Morgan Papers, Wheeler to Edwin D. Morgan, 11/2/1857.
36. Alexander, *Political History,* 2:245; *MP,* 6/9/1887.

37. Seaver, *Historical Sketches of Franklin County,* 104–105.
38. *NYT,* 1/8/1858, p. 1 and 3/24/1858, p. 1.
39. *NYT,* 3/22/1858, p. 1.
40. *NYT,* 1/20/1858, p. 5.
41. *NYT,* 4/8/1858, p.1 and 4/12/1858, p. 1.
42. Morgan Papers, Wheeler to Edwin D. Morgan, 3/18/1858.
43. Alexander, *Political History,* 2:255.
44. *NYT,* 1/19/1859, p. 8.
45. *NYT,* 2/15/1859, p. 8.
46. *NYT,* 9/8/1859, p. 1.
47. Ibid.
48. Klein, *Empire State,* 413.
49. Emerson, *Doo-Dah!,* 227–228; Potter, *Impending Crisis,* 380.
50. Alexander, *Political Crisis,* 2:258–259; Seaver, *Historical Sketches of Franklin County,* 105.
51. U.S. Bureau of the Census, Series M653, Roll 754, p. 74.
52. *FP,* 1/12/1860.
53. *FP,* 12/13/1860.
54. *FP,* 1/5/1860; Seaver, *Historical Sketches of Franklin County,* 742.
55. Hurd, *History of Clinton and Franklin Counties,* 381.
56. *FP,* 9/20/1860. The two-term Republican incumbent was George William Palmer of Plattsburgh, one of the founders of the Republican Party in Clinton County. *NYT,* 3/3/1916, p. 11; Dubin, *United States Congressional Elections,* 177 and 182.

CHAPTER 8. A PEN "DIPPED IN GALL"

1. Klein, *Empire State,* 414.
2. *FP,* 2/16/1860.
3. Rawley, *Edwin D. Morgan,* 99.
4. Morgan Papers, Wheeler to Edwin D. Morgan, 4/3/1860. Morgan did veto the bill but the legislature passed it again, over his veto. Rawley, *Edwin D. Morgan,* 100.
5. *FP,* 5/24/1860.
6. Potter, *Impending Crisis,* 433–434.
7. *FP,* 7/5/1860.
8. Potter, *Impending Crisis,* 433; Seaver, *Historical Sketches of Franklin County,* 111; *FP,* 7/12/1860.
9. *FP,* 7/19/1860.

10. Seaver, *Historical Sketches of Franklin County,* 111; Potter, *Impending Crisis,* 433.
11. *FP,* 7/19/1860 and 7/26/1860.
12. *FP,* 8/23/1860.
13. Morgan Papers, Wheeler to Edwin D. Morgan, 8/30/1860.
14. *FP,* 9/6/1860 and 9/13/1860.
15. *FP,* 9/13/1860 and 9/20/1860.
16. *FP,* 9/27/1860.
17. *FP,* 9/27/1860 and 10/4/1860.
18. *Biographical Directory of the United States Congress.* He was the grandfather of the famous Federal Circuit Judge, B. Learned Hand.
19. *FP,* 10/18/1860.
20. *FP,* 10/25/1860.
21. *FP,* 11/1/1860.
22. Dubin, *United States Congressional Elections,* 191; *FP,* 11/8/1860 and 11/22/1860.
23. Klein, *Empire State,* 414.
24. Ibid.
25. Nevins, *Abram S. Hewitt,* 111–112.
26. *FP,* 2/14/1861.
27. *FP,* 1/31/1861.
28. *MP,* 5/7/1885.
29. Ibid.
30. Greenberg, "Lincoln's Crackdown."
31. *FP,* 4/25/1861.
32. Ibid.
33. Ibid.
34. Landon, *North Country,* 438–439; *FP,* 5/2/1861.
35. *FP,* 5/2/1861.
36. *FP,* 5/2/1861 and 6/20/1861.
37. *FP,* 4/25/1861.
38. *FP,* 5/2/1861.
39. *FP,* 6/27/1861.
40. Ibid.

Chapter 9. An Early-Morning Knock on the Door

1. Dubin, *United States Congressional Elections,* 191.
2. *Cong. Globe,* 37th Cong., 1st Sess. 2 (1861).

3. *Cong. Globe,* 37th Cong., 1st Sess. 5 (1861).
4. *FP,* 7/11/1861; Seaver, *Historical Sketches of Franklin County,* 230–231.
5. *Cong. Globe,* 37th Cong., 1st Sess. 13 (1861).
6. *Appendix to Cong. Globe,* 37th Cong., 1st Sess. 2 (1861). The preamble to Article One, Section Nine, where the authority to suspend habeas corpus is located, refers to "specified acts which the Constitution expressly prohibits **to Congress** [emphasis added]." Therefore, critics of Lincoln, including the Flanders brothers, could argue that a "plain reading" of Section Nine shows that suspension, if undertaken, is a power reserved for Congress, not the President. For an excellent discussion of Lincoln's suspension of the writ of habeas corpus in the context of New York State politics, see Frank J. Williams, "When Albany Challenged The President," *New York Archives,* Winter 2009, pp. 31–36.
7. *U.S. House Journal,* 37th Congress, 1st Sess. 40 and 81 (1861).
8. Vazzano, "William A. Wheeler," in Purcell, *Vice Presidents,* 171.
9. *Cong. Globe,* 37th Cong., 2nd Sess. 1342 (1862).
10. *Cong. Globe,* 37th Cong., 2nd Sess. 1365 (1862).
11. *FP,* 7/18/1861.
12. *FP,* 7/25/1861; Conlin, *American Past,* 405.
13. *FP,* 8/1/1861.
14. Vazzano, "Who Was William A. Wheeler?" 8.
15. *FP,* 8/29/1861.
16. *FP,* 9/19/1861.
17. *FP,* 8/22/1861.
18. *FP,* 10/17/1861; Marshall, *American Bastille,* 111–112.
19. Marshall, *American Bastille,* 112–114.
20. Ibid., 116; *FP,* 2/20/1862.
21. Seaver, *Historical Sketches of Franklin County,* 171.
22. Ibid., 462.
23. Greenberg, "Lincoln's Crackdown."
24. Seaver, *Historical Sketches of Franklin County,* 713.
25. *FP,* 11/28/1861.

CHAPTER 10. SUDDENLY, A "JUNIOR PARTNER"

1. Burlingame, *At Lincoln's Side,* 23 and 222; *MP,* 5/7/1885.
2. *FG,* 8/17/1894; *U.S. House Journal,* 37th Cong., 2nd Sess. 145 and 527 (1862).
3. *U.S. House Journal,* 37th Cong., 2nd Sess. 450 (1862); Jordan, *Roscoe Conkling,* 38.
4. *Cong. Globe,* 37th Cong., 2nd Sess. 1971 (1862).

5. *U.S. House Journal,* 37th Cong., 2nd Sess. 878–880 (1862); Conlin, *American Past,* 435.
6. *Cong. Globe,* 37th Cong., 2nd Sess. 2023–2030 (1862). Arizona did not become a state until fifty years later, the forty-eighth state in 1912.
7. Klein, *Empire State,* 430; Alexander, *Political History,* 3:33–35.
8. Mohr, *Radical Republicans,* 3–4.
9. *U.S. House Journal,* 37th Cong., 1st Sess. 53–56 (1861).
10. Ibid., 37th Cong., 2nd Sess. 421 (1862); *Cong. Globe,* 37th Cong., 2nd Sess. 1563 (1862).
11. Vazzano, "Who Was William A. Wheeler?" 8.
12. *U.S. House Journal,* 37th Cong., 2nd Sess. 877 (1862).
13. Ibid., 885–892 (1862).
14. Hough, *History of St. Lawrence and Franklin Counties,* 580; Alexander, *Political History,* 3:29; *FP,* 3/27/1862 and 5/1/1862.
15. *FP,* 9/25/1862.
16. *FP,* 3/27/1862 and 5/1/1862.
17. *FP,* 8/7/1862.
18. Morgan Papers, Wheeler to Edwin D. Morgan, 8/22/1862.
19. *FP,* 8/7/1862.
20. *FP,* 9/25/1862.
21. *FP,* 10/2/1862.
22. *FP,* 9/25/1862 and 10/2/1862.
23. Alexander, *Political History,* 3:42–44; Taylor, *William Henry Seward,* 206; Mohr, *Radical Republicans,* 3–4.
24. Alexander, *Political History,* 3:39–40.
25. *NYT,* 10/25/1862, p. 1; *FP,* 10/30/1862.
26. Dubin, *United States Congressional Elections,* 194; *FP,* 11/6/1862; Alexander, *Political History,* 3:51.
27. The Twentieth Amendment of the U.S. Constitution abolished the lame duck session in 1933 by changing Article I, Section 4, which created it.
28. Jewish Virtual Library, "General Grant's Infamy."
29. Ibid.
30. Ibid.; *Cong. Globe,* 37th Cong., 3rd Sess. 222 (1863).
31. *Cong. Globe,* 37th Cong., 3rd Sess. 222 (1863).
32. Jewish Virtual Library, "General Grant's Infamy."
33. *U.S. House Journal,* 37th Cong., 3rd Sess. 483–484 (1863).
34. *FP,* 7/16/1863.
35. Greenberg, "Lincoln's Crackdown."
36. *U.S. House Journal,* 37th Cong., 3rd Sess. 540 (1863).

Chapter 11. A Sporting Gentleman Gets the Itch

1. *MP,* 8/6/1863.
2. *MP,* 1/14/1864 and 6/16/1864.
3. *MP,* 3/23/1865. In the fiscal year of 1865, 182 other state banks transferred their wealth to the national system. Stebbins, *Political History,* 40.
4. Hurd, *History of Clinton and Franklin Counties,* 57.
5. *MP,* 6/16/1864.
6. Otten, *Grand Old Partyman,* 29; Seaver, *Historical Sketches of Franklin County,* 706–707.
7. *MP,* 7/13/1865 and 8/10/1865.
8. Hurd, *History of Clinton and Franklin Counties,* 57; *MP,* 11/2/1865 and 8/30/1866.
9. Dartmouth College, *Minutes,* 3:375.
10. *DMA,* 7/21/1865.
11. *MP,* 5/19/1864, 5/17/1866, and 6/4/1868.
12. Reeves, *Gentleman Boss,* 38; Alexander, *Political History,* 3:94–95; Morgan Papers, Wheeler to Edwin D. Morgan, 3/21/1868.
13. Mohr, *Radical Republicans,* 12; *MP,* 9/1/1864. At the last minute, Wheeler sent an alternate to take his place. *MP,* 9/8/1864.
14. *MP,* 9/29/1864.
15. *MP,* 10/6/1864; Mohr, *Radical Republicans,* 14.
16. *MP,* 10/27/1864 and 11/3/1864.
17. Mohr, *Radical Republicans,* 14–15; *MP,* 11/10/1864 and 12/29/1864.
18. *MP,* 4/6/1865.
19. *MP,* 4/20/1865.
20. Alexander, *Political History,* 3:127–128; Reeves, *Gentleman Boss,* 39.
21. Alexander, *Political History,* 3:132; Stebbins, *Political History,* 62.
22. *MP,* 9/21/1865 and 9/28/1865.
23. *MP,* 9/28/1865; Alexander, *Political History,* 3:132–133; Stebbins, *Political History,* 62–63.
24. *MP,* 9/5/1867 and 9/12/1867.
25. *MP,* 8/9/1866, 8/23/1866, and 8/30/1866.
26. Stebbins, *Political History,* 82–83; Blaine, *Twenty Years,* 2:220–222.
27. Morgan Papers, Wheeler to Edwin D. Morgan, 7/6/1866; Alexander, *Political History,* 3:162. Wheeler urged Morgan to support keeping Dunn on as Collector but he was replaced by Major Jacob Parmeter on August 10, 1866. Hurd, *History of Clinton and Franklin Counties,* 46.
28. Jordan, *Roscoe Conkling,* 96.

29. Rawley, *Edwin D. Morgan,* 223.
30. Stebbins, *Political History,* 93; Alexander, *Political History,* 3:151–152; Biographical Directory, "Stewart L. Woodford."

Chapter 12. "True to Our Trust, True to Ourselves, and True to Truth"

1. Mohr, *Radical Republicans,* 206; Morris, *Encyclopedia of American History,* 247.
2. Mohr, *Radical Republicans,* 115.
3. Ibid., 203–204.
4. Ibid., 202.
5. Ibid., 208–209. It was estimated that only three hundred black men could vote in New York City at this time. Ibid., 210n16.
6. *MP,* 10/4/1866, 10/18/1866, and 10/25/1866.
7. *MP,* 11/1/1866 and 11/8/1866.
8. Alexander, *Political History,* 3:165; Mohr, *Radical Republicans,* 204.
9. *MP,* 3/28/1867; Mohr, *Radical Republicans,* 211–217.
10. *MP,* 4/18/1867; Mohr, *Radical Republicans,* 218.
11. *MP,* 4/18/1867 and 4/27/1867.
12. Mohr, *Radical Republicans,* 219–220. Wheeler outpolled Greeley who won 152,952 votes. *MP,* 5/30/1867.
13. *MP,* 5/2/1867; *BE,* 6/3/1867, p. 11.
14. *Documents of the Convention,* Number 12, 1–9; *BE,* 6/3/1867, p. 11.
15. *Journal of the Convention,* 1262–1267; *MP,* 6/13/1867.
16. Mohr, *Radical Republicans,* 220.
17. *Journal of the Convention,* 1268.
18. *Proceeding and Debates,* 1:19.
19. Ibid., 1:19–20; *MP,* 6/6/1867.
20. *MP,* 6/13/1867; Mohr, *Radical Republicans,* 221. Cole pleaded insanity and his first trial ended with a hung jury. *MP,* 5/14/1868. At Cole's second trial, he was acquitted. *MP,* 12/3/1868.
21. Mohr, *Radical Republicans,* 222; *MP,* 6/20/1867 and 6/27/1867.
22. *Proceedings and Debates,* 1:20–21, 33, 53, 59, 61, 92, 93, and 95.
23. Mohr, *Radical Republicans,* 223–225.
24. Ibid., 225–226; Burrows, *Gotham,* 926.
25. Mohr, *Radical Republicans,* 227–229; Burrows, *Gotham,* 926.
26. *MP,* 8/8/1867.
27. Mohr, *Radical Republicans,* 236–238.

28. Ibid., 239–245.
29. Ibid., 243–245.
30. Ibid., 246–249.
31. Ibid., 263.
32. *MP,* 1/23/1868.
33. Klein, *Empire State,* 442; *MP,* 7/22/1869.
34. *MP,* 3/5/1868.
35. Ibid.
36. Ibid.
37. *MP,* 3/19/1868.
38. Burrows, *Gotham,* 926.
39. Mohr, *Radical Republicans,* 269. The judiciary amendment made changes to the structure of the Court of Appeals, gave the legislature power to appoint the Supreme Court justices, and lengthened their terms. Klein, *Empire State,* 442.
40. Klein, *Empire State,* 442.
41. *MP,* 3/5/1868.

Chapter 13. "Ho! For California"

1. Alexander, *Political History,* 3:192.
2. Conkling, *Life and Letters,* 305.
3. Morris, *Encyclopedia of American History,* 249.
4. Morgan Papers, Wheeler to Edwin D. Morgan, 3/21/1868.
5. Alexander, *Political History,* 3:192–193; Russotto, *National Party Conventions,* 40.
6. Russotto, *National Party Conventions,* 41; Alexander, *Political History,* 3:202–203.
7. *MP,* 2/13/1868.
8. *MP,* 6/4/1868.
9. *MP,* 6/18/1868.
10. *MP,* 6/25/1868.
11. *MP,* 8/27/1868.
12. Dubin, *United States Congressional Elections,* 212; U.S. Bureau of the Census.
13. *MP,* 8/20/1868; Seaver, *Historical Sketches of Franklin County,* 115.
14. *MP,* 9/10/1868, 10/8/1868, and 10/29/1868.
15. Blum et al., *National Experience,* 370.
16. Ibid.; *MP,* 12/26/1867.
17. *MP,* 11/5/1868.
18. Dubin, *United States Congressional Elections,* 212.

19. Alexander, *Political History,* 3:215. However, the Republicans won a majority in both houses of the legislature assuring the election of a Republican to the U.S. Senate when Morgan's term expired in March, 1869. Fenton defeated Morgan for the seat, 52 to 40. Ibid., 3:222.
20. Dubin, *United States Congressional Elections,* 214–215.
21. Ibid., 210–213.
22. *Cong. Globe,* 41st Cong., 1st Sess.4–5 (1869).
23. Blaine, *Twenty Years,* 2:431.
24. *Cong. Globe,* 41st Cong., 1st Sess.75–76 (1869).
25. Seaver, *Historical Sketches of Franklin County,* 41. Wheeler's annotated book of the House Rules is on display in the Franklin County Historical and Museum Society's House of History in Malone, New York.
26. Blum et al., *National Experience,* 420.
27. Ibid., 358.
28. *MP,* 4/1/1869.
29. Seaver, *Historical Sketches of Franklin County,* 709; *MP,* 6/9/1887.
30. *MP,* 5/20/1869.
31. *MP,* 5/27/1869.
32. *MP,* 6/3/1869.
33. *MP,* 6/10/1869.
34. *MP,* 1/23/1869.
35. Morgan Papers, Wheeler to Edwin D. Morgan, 12/7/1869, 12/9/1869, and 12/20/1869.
36. U.S. Bureau of the Census, Series M593, roll 937, p. 725.
37. Greene, *Yosemite,* 34–35.
38. Ibid., 53–54 and 59.
39. *MP,* 9/23/1869.
40. *MP,* 10/7/1869; Misch and Stone, "James Lick, the 'Generous Miser.'"
41. Smith, *Lost Landmarks,* 211–212.
42. *MP,* 10/7/1869.

Chapter 14. Spreading "Law, Order, Population, Industry and Wealth"

1. Wood, *Northern Pacific,* 15.
2. Smalley, *History of the Northern,* 120–122.
3. Wood, *Northern Pacific,* 15–17.
4. Smalley, *History of the Northern,* 138 and 140.
5. *U.S. House Journal,* 41st Cong., 2nd Sess. 200 (1870).

6. *Cong. Globe,* 41st Cong., 2nd Sess. 3263 (1870).
7. Ibid.
8. Ibid., 3264.
9. Ibid., 3264–3265.
10. Ibid., 3265–3271.
11. Ibid., 3786–3787.
12. *Appendix to Cong. Globe,* 41st Cong., 2nd Sess. 412–414 (1870).
13. Ibid., 391–392.
14. Ibid., 401–402.
15. Ibid., 396–397.
16. Ibid., 395–396. Ferry would become the presiding officer over the sixteen joint meetings of the House and Senate during the Hayes-Tilden/Wheeler-Hendricks electoral contest in 1877.
17. *Cong. Globe,* 41st Cong., 2nd Sess. 3793 (1870); *MP,* 6/9/1870.
18. *Cong. Globe,* 41st Cong., 2nd Sess. 3793 (1870).
19. Ibid., 3794.
20. Ibid.
21. Ibid., 3797–3853.
22. Cahill and Debolski, *North American Steam,* 176; Kagan, *American Heritage,* 128 and 254.
23. *Cong. Globe,* 41st Cong., 2nd Sess. 4512 (1870).
24. Johnson, *Oxford Companion,* 544.
25. *Cong. Globe,* 41st Cong., 2nd Sess. 4512 (1870).

CHAPTER 15. "COMMON JUSTICE" FOR THE SOUTH

1. *MP,* 8/30/1866.
2. Curtis, *Our Country,* 259.
3. *MP,* 9/8/1870.
4. Reeves, *Gentleman Boss,* 54; Alexander, *Political History,* 3:238.
5. *MP,* 9/22/1870.
6. Seaver, *Historical Sketches of Franklin County* 125, 171, and 793; U.S. Bureau of the Census.
7. Alexander, *Political History,* 3:230–231.
8. Ibid., 240.
9. Ibid., 242; *MP,* 8/11/1870.
10. Wood, *Northern Pacific,* 18–19; *MP,* 3/2/1871.
11. Dubin, *United States Congressional Elections,* 219; Alexander, *Political History,* 3:243–244.

12. *Cong. Globe,* 41st Cong., 3rd Sess. 1468–1470 (1871).
13. Ibid., 1472–1473.
14. Ibid., 1471–1472.
15. *Appendix to Cong. Globe,* 41st Cong., 3rd Sess. 193–194 (1871).
16. Ibid., 178–181.
17. Ibid., 238.
18. Ibid., 312–313.
19. *Cong. Globe,* 41st Cong., 3rd Sess. 1473 (1871).
20. Kellogg was a native of Vermont and he worked well with Wheeler on railroad matters.
21. *Cong. Globe,* 41st Cong., 3rd Sess. 1899–1900 (1871).
22. Dubin, *United States Congressional Elections,* 221.
23. *Cong. Globe,* 42nd Cong., 2nd Sess. 9–10 (1871).
24. Nevins, *Abram S. Hewitt,* 191.
25. *U.S. House Journal,* 42nd Cong., 1st Sess. 167–168, 191–192, and 196–198 (1871).
26. *MP,* 2/9/1871.
27. *MP,* 5/25/1871.
28. *Cong. Globe,* 42nd Cong., 2nd Sess. 1428–1432, 1606–1609, 2691–2703, and 2737–2739 (1872).
29. Ibid., 3748–3760.
30. *U.S. House Journal,* 42nd Cong., 3rd Sess. 29 (1872).
31. Ibid., 410; Graham, *Adirondack Park,* 61–63.
32. *MP,* 5/2/1872.
33. Blum et al., *National Experience,* 372–374; Conlin, *American Past,* 449–450.

Chapter 16. Returning the Salary Grab

1. *MP,* 6/6/1872.
2. After hardwood logs were burned, lye was leached from the ashes and then boiled down in large pots—"pot ash."
3. Graham, *Adirondack Park,* 10–11.
4. Ibid., 25.
5. *MP,* 6/1/1871.
6. Graham, *Adirondack Park,* 35.
7. Ibid., 33–34.
8. Ibid., 65–66 and 68–70.
9. *MP,* 4/25/1872.
10. *MP,* 6/27/1872; Graham, *Adirondack Park,* 74–75.

11. *NYT,* 4/18/1872, p. 1.
12. *MP,* 1/11/1872 and 5/16/1872.
13. Jordan, *Roscoe Conkling,* 180.
14. *MP,* 7/25/1872.
15. *NYT,* 7/9/1872, p. 5.
16. *MP,* 7/18/1872.
17. Seaver, *Historical Sketches of Franklin County,* 710.
18. *MP,* 8/22/1872.
19. *NYT,* 8/21/1872, p. 1.
20. *NYT,* 8/20/1872, p. 5.
21. *NYT,* 8/22/1872, p. 1.
22. *MP,* 8/29/1872.
23. Alexander, *Political History,* 3:296–297.
24. *MP,* 10/17/1872; Seaver, *Historical Sketches of Franklin County,* 724–725.
25. *MP,* 8/8/1872.
26. *MP,* 10/24/1872.
27. *MP,* 11/7/1872.
28. Dubin, *United States Congressional Elections,* 225.
29. *MP,* 11/14/1872.
30. Alexander, *Political History,* 3:305.
31. *MP,* 4/19/1877.
32. Jordan, *Roscoe Conkling,* 187–188.
33. Blum et al., *National Experience,* 371.
34. Jordan, *Roscoe Conkling,* 187.
35. Ibid.
36. *U.S. House Journal,* 42nd Cong., 3rd Sess. 122–123 (1873).
37. Jordan, *Roscoe Conkling,* 188.
38. *Cong. Globe,* 42nd Cong., 3rd Sess. 1831–1833 (1873).
39. Jordan, *Roscoe Conkling,* 189.
40. *Cong. Globe,* 41st Cong., 2nd Sess. 3793 (1870).
41. A law like this would have major problems passing constitutional muster today because of the Twenty-seventh Amendment, which was proposed in 1789 and ratified in 1992.
42. *Cong. Globe,* 42nd Cong., 3rd Sess. 1233–1234 (1873).
43. Ibid., 1976–1977 (1873).
44. Ibid., 2101–2105 (1873).
45. *MP,* 3/27/1873.
46. *NYT,* 3/26/1873, p. 1.
47. *MP,* 4/3/1873.

48. *MP,* 12/25/1873. With Wheeler's support in the next Congress, a bill to repeal the Salary Grab would pass the House 225 to 25. *U.S. House Journal,* 43rd Cong., 1st Sess. 232–233 (1874).
49. *MP,* 3/27/1873; *NYT,* 3/11/1873, p. 1.

CHAPTER 17. NO "UNPRODUCTIVE AND USELESS PARK"

1. Kammen, "Cornell, Ezra," in Eisenstadt, *Encyclopedia of New York State,* 396–397.
2. Today, Havana is named Montour Falls.
3. *NYT,* 5/23/1873, p. 1.
4. Kammen, "Cornell, Ezra," in Eisenstadt, *Encyclopedia of New York State,* 397.
5. Bishop, *History of Cornell,* 186.
6. *NYT,* 5/13/1873, p. 5 and 5/15/1873, p. 5.
7. *NYT,* 5/27/1873, p. 1; *MP,* 6/26/1873.
8. *NYT,* 6/14/1873, p. 5; *MP,* 6/12/1873.
9. *NYT,* 4/18/1874, p. 10; *MP,* 4/23/1874.
10. The other four members of the commission were: Horatio Seymour, Patrick H. Agan, William B. Taylor, and George Raynor.
11. Graham, *Adirondack Park,* 70–71 and 74–75; Terrie, "Adirondacks," in Eisenstadt, *Encyclopedia of New York State,* 14.
12. In 1885, the state legislature created a state Forest Preserve in the Adirondacks and declared that all the lands in the Preserve "shall be forever kept as wild forest lands." In 1892, the legislature carved an Adirondack Park out of more than 500,000 acres of state owned land. Graham, *Adirondack Park,* 106 and 124.
13. Ibid., 76; Schaefer, *Adirondack Explorations,* 99.
14. Graham, *Adirondack Park,* 76; Schaefer, *Adirondack Explorations,* 107–113.
15. Graham, *Adirondack Park,* 77; Schaefer, *Adirondack Explorations,* 113.
16. Graham, *Adirondack Park,* 77; *MP,* 7/17/1873; Schaefer, *Adirondack Explorations,* 9 and 113–115.
17. *MP,* 6/12/1873, 7/3/1873, 7/24/1873, and 6/7/1888.
18. *MP,* 8/21/1873 and 9/4/1873.
19. Chidsey, *Gentleman from New York,* 186–188.
20. Conlin, *American Past,* 487.
21. Blum et al., *National Experience,* 374.
22. Dubin, *United States Congressional Elections,* 228.
23. Jordan, *Roscoe Conkling,* 80.
24. Karabell, *Chester Alan Arthur,* 19; Welch, *George Frisbie Hoar,* 36.

25. Seaver, *Historical Sketches of Franklin County,* 709; *NYT,* 9/17/1873, p. 1; *MP,* 9/25/1873 and 11/20/1873.
26. Seaver, *Historical Sketches of Franklin County,* 709; *MP,* 9/25/1873.
27. Seaver, *Historical Sketches of Franklin County,* 709.
28. *Cong. Rec.*, 43rd Cong., 1st Sess. 74 (1873); Seaver, *Historical Sketches of Franklin County* 709; *MP,* 12/4/1873.
29. Welch, *George Frisbie Hoar,* 55.
30. *MP,* 1/1/1874. In 1918, Seaver published *Historical Sketches of Franklin County,* one of the most popular sources cited by historians writing about Wheeler. Seaver's account of Wheeler's life may have been colored by the committee clerk's failed dreams to climb the political ladder with Wheeler as his trusted advisor and right-hand man.
31. *MP,* 1/15/1874.
32. The canal had been built to bypass the falls in the Ohio River near Louisville, Kentucky.
33. *Cong. Rec.*, 43rd Cong., 1st Sess. 2654–2661 (1874); *BE,* 3/31/1874, p. 2.
34. *MP,* 4/9/1874.
35. *Cong. Rec.*, 43rd Cong., 1st Sess. 3498 and 3500–3506 (1874).
36. Ibid., 985–987 (1874).
37. Ibid., 1167–1168 (1874).
38. *MP,* 2/12/1874.
39. *Cong. Rec.*, 43rd Cong., 1st Sess. 989–990 (1874).
40. *BE,* 2/4/1874, p. 2.
41. *Cong. Rec.*, 43rd Cong., 1st Sess. 1240–1241 (1874).
42. *MP,* 2/19/1874 and 3/5/1874.
43. *MP,* 5/21/1874 and 5/28/1874.
44. *MP,* 6/11/1874.
45. *MP,* 8/6/1874 and 8/27/1874. Earlier in the year, the state legislature changed the number of Wheeler's district from eighteen to nineteen when the legislature redistricted the state a second time using the 1870 census in order to eliminate the congressman-at-large seat.
46. *MP,* 1/15/1874 and 1/22/1874. Grant did offer to appoint Conkling but he turned Grant down. Jordan, *Roscoe Conkling,* 200–201.
47. *MP,* 9/24/1874 and 10/22/1874.
48. *MP,* 10/1/1874; Sterngass, "Tilden, Samuel J(ones)," in Eisenstadt, *Encyclopedia of New York State,* 1558.
49. *MP,* 9/24/1874.
50. Dubin, *United States Congressional Elections,* 232.
51. *MP,* 11/26/1874.

52. Alexander, *Political History,* 3:319–321; Dubin, *United States Congressional Elections,* 180. The legislature elected Democrat Francis Kernan to replace Fenton in the U.S. Senate.
53. Before it was amended by the Twentieth Amendment in 1933, Article One of the U.S. Constitution provided that Congress should meet at least once in every year on the first Monday in December, unless Congress passed a law setting a different day. During the Civil War, Congress was in almost perpetual session because it had passed a law convening the new Congress immediately on the expiration of the old. In 1872, this law was repealed. Hence, the Forty-fourth Congress would not open until December 6, 1875. *MP,* 11/26/1874.

Chapter 18. An "Earnest Champion of the Right"

1. *Cong. Rec.*, 43rd Cong., 2nd Sess. 6 and 93 (1874); *NYT,* 2/24/1875, p. 2.
2. Otten, "Wheeler Adjustment," 351–352.
3. Ibid., 353–354; Foner, *Reconstruction,* 550.
4. Foner, *Reconstruction,* 550–551; Otten, "Wheeler Adjustment," 355.
5. Otten, "Wheeler Adjustment," 355–356.
6. Ibid., 357 and 359.
7. Foner, *Reconstruction,* 554.
8. Otten, "Wheeler Adjustment," 358–361.
9. Ibid., 361.
10. *MP,* 6/9/1887; Seaver, *Historical Sketches of Franklin County,* 709–710.
11. Otten, "Wheeler Adjustment," 358.
12. *MP,* 2/25/1875.
13. Ibid.; Otten, "Wheeler Adjustment," 362.
14. *MP,* 2/25/1875.
15. Otten, *Grand Old Partyman,* 102.
16. *Cong. Rec.*, 43rd Cong., 2nd Sess. 1647–1650 (1875); *NYT,* 2/24/1875, p. 2.
17. *Cong. Rec.*, 43rd Cong., 2nd Sess. 1647–1650 (1875).
18. Ibid., 1651–1652.
19. Ibid., 1647.
20. *MP,* 2/18/1875 and 2/25/1875; *BE,* 2/22/1875, p. 2, 2/23/1875, p. 2, and 2/24/1875, p. 2.
21. *BE,* 2/25/1875, p. 2; *MP,* 3/4/1875.
22. *MP,* 3/11/1875.
23. *BE,* 3/15/1875, p. 4; Otten, "Wheeler Adjustment," 363; *MP,* 3/18/1875 and 3/25/1875.
24. *MP,* 4/18/1875.

25. *MP,* 4/22/1875; Otten, "Wheeler Adjustment," 363.
26. Otten, "Wheeler Adjustment," 364; *NYT,* 4/19/1875, p. 4; *MP,* 4/22/1875 and 6/10/1875.
27. *NYT,* 5/10/1875, p. 5; *MP,* 5/13/1875.
28. *MP,* 5/27/1875, 8/15/1875, and 9/16/1875.
29. Dubin, *United States Congressional Elections,* 235; *MP,* 12/9/1875, 12/16/1875, 4/6/1876; *BE,* 12/20/1875, p. 4.
30. *MP,* 2/24/1876; Jordan, *Roscoe Conkling,* 227.

CHAPTER 19. THE "NEW YORK LINCOLN"

1. Beaman, "William Almon Wheeler," 35–36.
2. *NYT,* 6/12/1876, p. 10.
3. *NYT,* 4/3/1876, p. 1.
4. Jordan, *Roscoe Conkling,* 229–230.
5. Bergamini, *Hundredth Year,* 110.
6. Hoogenboom, *Rutherford B. Hayes,* 261
7. Jordan, *Roscoe Conkling,* 230; Hoogenboom, *Rutherford B. Hayes,* 261.
8. Jordan, *Roscoe Conkling,* 231; Hoogenboom, *Rutherford B. Hayes,* 261.
9. Hoogenboom, *Rutherford B. Hayes,* 261.
10. Hoogenboom, *Rutherford B. Hayes,* 262; Bergamini, *Hundredth Year,* 110, 158, and 160; DeGregorio, *Complete Book,* 283; Jordan, *Roscoe Conkling,* 235.
11. Hoogenboom, *Rutherford B. Hayes,* 261–262; DeGregorio, *Complete Book,* 284.
12. Before the convention opened, Hayes revealed some of his insularity to his wife when he wrote her that he was ashamed not to know who Wheeler was after General Sheridan had written Hayes touting a Hayes and Wheeler ticket. When the Ohio governor's name was mentioned in Washington, political observers were heard to ask, "Who is Hayes?" Williams, *Diary and Letters,* 3:301; Black, *King of Fifth Avenue,* 468.
13. Bergamini, *Hundredth Year,* 160; Black, *King of Fifth Avenue,* 468.
14. Seaver, *Historical Sketches of Franklin County,* 727.
15. *BE,* 6/13/1876, p. 2.
16. Welch, *George Frisbie Hoar,* 55–57.
17. *Proceedings,* 110–111.
18. *MP,* 2/17/1876; *NYT,* 4/3/1876, p. 1.
19. Welch, *George Frisbie Hoar,* 20; Chidsey, *Gentleman from New York,* 131; Seigenthaler, *James K. Polk,* 90–91.
20. *MP,* 4/13/1876. During the 1874 campaign for governor in New York, the

Democratic candidate, Samuel Tilden, was unmercifully criticized for standing "pauper-like, with hat in hand, at the door of [the Democratic] state convention begging delegates to vote" for him. Tilden's subsequent use of a direct mail campaign to solicit votes during the campaign was described as "repugnant to every right-minded man" because he had sunk to the level of a "mere canvasser." *MP,* 9/24/1874.

21. *MP,* 1/20/1876.
22. *MP,* 2/17/1876.
23. *MP,* 3/2/1876.
24. *MP,* 3/9/1876.
25. Hoar, *Autobiography,* 1:244.
26. *NYT,* 7/9/1876, p. 12; Dunlap, *Our Vice-Presidents,* 120.
27. Conwell, *Life and Public Services,* 320.
28. *MP,* 4/13/1876.
29. *MP,* 3/9/1876.
30. Ibid.
31. *MP,* 3/16/1876.
32. *MP,* 2/26/1880.
33. Conwell, *Life and Public Services,* 321; *MP,* 7/13/1876.
34. *NYT,* 7/9/1876, p. 12; *MP,* 3/9/1876.
35. *BE,* 6/19/1876, p. 1; Jordan, *Roscoe Conkling,* 232–233.
36. Jordan, *Roscoe Conkling,* 233; *MP,* 3/30/1876.
37. Jordan, *Roscoe Conkling,* 233; *Proceedings,* AO21–22.
38. *NYT,* 4/3/1876, p. 1.
39. *NYT,* 4/9/1876, p. 7.
40. *MP,* 4/20/1876.
41. *MP,* 5/11/1876 and 5/18/1876.
42. *MP,* 5/25/1876.
43. *MP,* 6/1/1876.
44. *NYT,* 6/12/1876, p. 10.
45. *MP,* 5/25/1876.
46. *NYT,* 6/1/1876, p. 7; New York, *Journal of the Senate.* There had been no survey of the state since the pioneer surveyors ran compass lines through the woods. Because of this, maps of the state were filled with errors. For example, Buffalo and Elmira were located on maps of the time three miles from their true locations and Syracuse was a mile and a half off. Lake Champlain had been laid out from a survey made before the Revolutionary War and maps of locations on the lake were off by as much as three miles. *NYT,* 1/24/1877, p. 2.

47. *MP,* 6/11/1876.
48. *BE,* 6/19/1876, p. 2; *NYT,* 6/18/1876, p. 1.

CHAPTER 20. "GOD'S HAND IS IN THIS WORK"

1. Jordan, *Roscoe Conkling,* 235–237.
2. *MP,* 6/15/1876.
3. *BE,* 6/13/1876, p. 2.
4. Reeves, *Gentleman Boss,* 91–93; Bergamini, *Hundredth Year,* 158.
5. *Proceedings,* 4.
6. Rawley, *Edwin D. Morgan,* 250; *BE,* 6/19/1876, p. 1; Alexander, *Political History,* 3:338.
7. Proceedings, 23–24; Hoogenboom, *Rutherford B. Hayes,* 262.
8. Welch, *George Frisbie Hoar,* 56–57; Alexander, *Political History,* 3:335–336.
9. *Proceedings,* 76–77.
10. Ibid., 70.
11. Ibid., 73–75; Bergamini, *Hundredth Year,* 159; Jordan, *Roscoe Conkling,* 239–240.
12. Hoar, *Autobiography,* 1:243.
13. *Proceedings,* 83–84; Jordan, *Roscoe Conkling,* 240.
14. *Proceedings,* 87 and 100–102.
15. Ibid., 103–104; Hoogenboom, *Rutherford B. Hayes,* 263. Hayes rewarded Howard for his support by subsequently appointing him governor of the Dakota Territory. Ibid., 576n22.
16. *Proceedings,* 105–106.
17. Ibid., 107–109.
18. Jordan, *Roscoe Conkling,* 241.
19. Hoar, *Autobiography,* 1:244.
20. *BE,* 6/19/1876, p. 1.
21. *Proceedings,* 110–111.
22. *BE,* 6/19/1876, p.1.
23. *Proceedings,* 111.
24. Ibid., 112. South Carolina's two other votes and Pennsylvania's fifty-eight votes were cast for Frelinghuysen.
25. *NYT,* 6/17/1876, p. 1; *MP,* 6/22/1876; *Proceedings,* 112.
26. *NYT,* 6/18/1876, p. 1.
27. *NYT,* 6/19/1876, p. 1; *MP,* 6/22/1876.
28. *MP,* 6/29/1876.

Chapter 21. "Hayes the True and Wheeler, Too!"

1. *MP*, 7/6/1876.
2. *NYT*, 6/17/1876, p. 1.
3. *NYT*, 6/17/1876, p. 4 and 6/19/1876, p. 4; *MP*, 6/22/1876, 6/29/1876, and 7/6/1876.
4. University of Vermont, Minutes, 6/28/1876.
5. Russotto, *National Party Conventions*, 45.
6. Karabell, *Chester Alan Arthur*, 37.
7. Sterngass, "Tilden, Samuel J(ones)," in Eisenstadt, *Encyclopedia of New York State*, 1558.
8. Colbert, Thomas Burnell, "Thomas Andrews Hendricks," in Purcell, *Vice Presidents*, 190–191.
9. Alexander, *Political History*, 3:341; Sterngass, "Tilden, Samuel J(ones)," in Eisenstadt, *Encyclopedia of New York State*, 1558.
10. Wheeler Papers, Wheeler to Rutherford B. Hayes, 7/1/1876.
11. DeGregorio, *Complete Book*, 190–191; Emerson, *Doo-dah!*, 281–282.
12. Wheeler Papers, Wheeler to Rutherford B. Hayes, 7/1/1876. Hayes pushed for his lieutenant, Edward F. Noyes, to be named chairman but the Grant and Blaine committee members named Grant's Secretary of the Interior, Zachariah Chandler, instead. Hoogenboom, *Rutherford B. Hayes*, 267.
13. *Proceedings*, 119.
14. Ibid.
15. Hoogenboom, *Rutherford B. Hayes*, 266; *Proceedings*, 119.
16. Wheeler Papers, Wheeler to Rutherford B. Hayes, 7/1/1876.
17. Hoogenboom, *Rutherford B. Hayes*, 266.
18. Wheeler Papers, Wheeler to Rutherford B. Hayes, 7/25/1876.
19. Chidsey, *Gentleman from New York*, 207–208; Alexander, *Political History*, 3:347.
20. Seaver, *Historical Sketches of Franklin County*, 115; *MP*, 7/6/1876 and 7/27/1876.
21. *MP*, 8/17/1876.
22. Hatfield, *Vice Presidents*, 245.
23. Hayes, "Sheet Music Collection."
24. Library of Congress, "Voices, Votes, Victory."
25. Duke University, "Historic American Sheet Music."
26. Hatfield, *Vice Presidents*, 245.
27. *MP*, 7/13/1876.
28. *Proceedings*, 118–119.
29. *BE*, 7/20/1876, p. 2.

30. *MP,* 7/27/1876.
31. *MP,* 8/17/1876.
32. *MP,* 7/20/1876.
33. *NYT,* 8/22/1876, p. 4.
34. *NA*, 10/5/1876, p. 203.
35. *NYT,* 10/12/1876, p. 4.
36. *NA*, 10/19/1876, p. 234.
37. Wheeler Papers, Wheeler to Rutherford B. Hayes, 9/8/1876.
38. *NYT,* 8/26/1876, p. 1; *MP,* 8/31/1876.
39. Wheeler Papers, Wheeler to Rutherford B. Hayes, 10/16/1876.
40. Alexander, *Political History,* 3:350; Bergamini, *Hundredth Year,* 300.
41. Hoogenboom, *Rutherford B. Hayes,* 274; Bergamini, *Hundredth Year,* 300 and 302.
42. *MP,* 11/9/1876; Hoogenboom, *Rutherford B. Hayes,* 274.
43. Hoogenboom, *Rutherford B. Hayes,* 279.
44. Ibid., 277 and 279; Bergamini, *Hundredth Year,* 307.
45. *MP,* 12/7/1876.
46. Hoogenboom, *Rutherford B. Hayes,* 276–277.
47. Ibid., 277–279.
48. Ibid., 279; *Proceedings,* 322.

Chapter 22. "As Righteous as an Edict of God"

1. U.S. House, *Proceedings,* 88–125.
2. Ibid., 147–149.
3. *BE,* 1/3/1877, p. 3; *MP,* 1/11/1877.
4. *NYT,* 10/29/1876, p. 2.
5. *Cong. Globe,* 42nd Congress, 3rd Sess. 1297–1305 (1873). Wheeler did vote to invalidate three votes from Georgia, which had been cast for Horace Greeley because their certificates were irregular on their face—Greeley had died before the electors had cast their votes. In the end, both houses agreed that the votes from Texas and Mississippi should be counted, and those from Georgia, Louisiana, and Arkansas should not be counted. Ibid., 1298 and 1305–1306.
6. U.S. House, *Proceedings,* 519; Jordan, *Roscoe Conkling,* 227.
7. Jordan, *Roscoe Conkling,* 251.
8. *BE,* 1/3/1877, p. 3; *MP,* 1/11/1877.
9. *BE,* 1/3/1877, p. 3; *MP,* 1/11/1877.
10. *MP,* 1/4/1877.
11. *BE,* 1/3/1877, p. 3; *MP,* 1/1/1877.

12. Hoogenboom, *Rutherford B. Hayes,* 285.
13. *MP,* 1/18/1877.
14. Hoogenboom, *Rutherford B. Hayes,* 280.
15. Jordan, *Roscoe Conkling,* 253; Hoogenboom, *Rutherford B. Hayes,* 285.
16. *NYT,* 1/9/1877, p. 5 and 1/12/1877, p. 1.
17. Wheeler Papers, Wheeler to Rutherford B. Hayes, 1/15/1877.
18. Seaver, *Historical Sketches of Franklin County,* 712.
19. Hoogenboom, *Rutherford B. Hayes,* 285–286; Jordan, *Roscoe Conkling,* 255–256.
20. Alexander, *Political History,* 3:355–356; Jordan, *Roscoe Conkling,* 259–260; Hoogenboom, *Rutherford B. Hayes,* 286.
21. *MP,* 2/1/1877.
22. Alexander, *Political History,* 3:356; Hoogenboom, *Rutherford B. Hayes,* 286; Jordan, *Roscoe Conkling,* 260.
23. Alexander, *Political History,* 3:357n51.
24. Jordan, *Roscoe Conkling,* 261n25.
25. Hoogenboom, *Rutherford B. Hayes,* 287; Jordan, *Roscoe Conkling,* 261.
26. Seaver, *Historical Sketches of Franklin County,* 727; *MP,* 3/8/1877.
27. Wheeler Papers, Wheeler to Rutherford B. Hayes, 2/8/1877 and 2/17/1877.
28. Hoogenboom, *Rutherford B. Hayes,* 287–288, 290–293.
29. Called "The Compromise of 1877" by some historians, the "understanding" has also been called "The Great Betrayal" by other historians because of the devastating impact it had on blacks in the South. Blum et al., *National Experience,* 382–383; *MP,* 3/8/1877.
30. Hoogenboom, *Rutherford B. Hayes,* 293–294; Jordan, *Roscoe Conkling,* 262–263.
31. To date, this has occurred two more times. In 1888, Republicans Benjamin Harrison and Levi P. Morton lost the popular vote to Democrats Grover Cleveland and Allen G. Thurman by more than 100,000 votes but were elected by the electoral college 233 to 168. In 2000, Republicans George W. Bush and Richard B. Cheney lost the popular vote to Democrats Albert A. Gore and Joseph Lieberman by more than 540,000 votes but won the election in the electoral college 271 to 266. DeGregorio, *Complete Book,* 286, 337, and 772.
32. *FG,* 3/9/1877; Seaver, *Historical Sketches of Franklin County,* 710.
33. Hoogenboom, *Rutherford B. Hayes,* 295; Kane, *Presidential Fact Book,* 124.
34. *NYT,* 3/6/1877, p. 1; *BE,* 3/6/1877, p. 4; *MP,* 3/8/1877 and 4/19/1877; Bergamini, *Hundredth Year,* 330.
35. U.S. Senate Commission, *Vice President's Room; NYT,* 11/23/1875, p. 1; Hatfield, *Vice Presidents,* 238–239; *MP,* 12/26/1878.
36. Hunt, *Hannibal Hamlin,* 155–156. The Constitution designates the vice

president to serve as president of the Senate and to cast the tie-breaking vote in the case of a deadlock. During Wheeler's vice presidency, this was the only constitutional duty assigned to the vice president in addition to the duty to receive and open the certificates containing the electoral votes.

37. *NYT*, 3/6/1877, p. 1; *BE*, 3/6/1877, p. 4; *MP*, 3/8/1877; Bergamini, *Hundredth Year*, 330.
38. *NYT*, 3/6/1877, p. 1.
39. Lindsay, *Tradition Looks Forward*, 242.
40. There would be no official residence for the vice president until Congress refurbished the Admiral's House at the U.S. Naval Observatory as a home for the vice president in 1974. Kane, *Presidential Fact Book*, 416.

Chapter 23. "A Wild and Joyous Time"

1. *MP*, 3/15/1877 and 4/19/1877.
2. Wheeler Papers, Wheeler to Lucy Hayes, undated. Lucy was a devout Methodist and usually attended the Foundry Methodist Church in Washington with the president. He was not a confirmed Christian but attended church to please Lucy. In his words, he was a "non-church member, a non-professor of religion," and a "worshipper of Ralph Waldo Emerson." Hoogenboom, *Rutherford B. Hayes*, 384 and 527.
3. *NYT*, 7/9/1876, p. 12; Whitcomb and Whitcomb, *Real Life*, 166.
4. Whitcomb and Whitcomb, *Real Life*, 166; Hoogenboom, *Rutherford B. Hayes*, 344–345.
5. Hayes, "Dining at the White House During the Hayes Administration."
6. *NYT*, 1/2/1880, p. 1.
7. Wheeler Papers, Wheeler to Lucy Hayes, 4/30/1878 and 6/24/1878.
8. *NYT*, 5/20/1878, p. 1; *MP*, 5/23/1878; *FG*, 5/24/1878.
9. Wheeler Papers, Rutherford B. Hayes to Wheeler, 5/25/1878.
10. Ibid., Wheeler to Rutherford B. Hayes, 5/27/1878.
11. Williams, *Diary and Letters*, 6/3/1878, 3:386.
12. Wheeler Papers, Wheeler to Rutherford B. Hayes, 5/30/1878; *NYT*, 5/31/1878, p. 5.
13. *NYT*, 6/30/1878, p. 8.
14. *MP*, 6/6/1878; Wheeler Papers, Lucy Hayes to Wheeler, undated.
15. Wheeler Papers, Wheeler to Lucy Hayes, 6/24/1878.
16. Hayes, "Rutherford Hayes Platt."; Wheeler Papers, Wheeler to Lucy Hayes, 6/24/1878.
17. Hayes, "Russell Hastings."
18. Wheeler Papers, Wheeler to Lucy Hayes, 6/24/1878. Emily subsequently gave

birth to three children and the couple moved to Bermuda where Russell established a business raising Easter lilies for export to the U.S. Hayes, "Russell Hastings."

19. This position evolved into Surgeon General of the U.S. Public Health Service. History of Medicine, "Origins of the National Institute of Health."
20. Williams, *Diary and Letters,* 12/16/1878, 3:514; *MP,* 6/6/1878 and 8/15/1878.
21. *FG,* 1/17/1882.
22. *BE,* 6/6/1887, p. 4.
23. Wheeler Papers, Wheeler to Lucy Hayes, 6/10/1879; *MP,* 6/5/1879; *NYT,* 5/29/1879, p. 5. Bill's mother, Eliza, had died on November 14, 1858, and his other unmarried sister, Jane, had died on November 23, 1866. Headstones, 2011, Morningside Cemetery, Malone, NY.
24. Bill was awarded honorary doctor of law degrees from UVM in 1867 and Union in 1877. *MP,* 8/15/1867; *NYT,* 6/28/1877, p. 2.
25. Wheeler, *Genealogical and Encyclopedic,* 250 and 266.
26. *MP,* 7/26/1877.
27. *NYT,* 3/3/1878, p. 6.
28. *NYT,* 2/1/1914, p. C5; Armstrong, *History of Hamilton,* 1:470.
29. *MP,* 12/25/1879.
30. DeGregorio, *Complete Book,* 289.

Chapter 24. The Frozen Snake and the "Greatest of Humbugs"

1. *MP,* 3/15/1877.
2. Wheeler Papers, Wheeler to Rutherford B. Hayes, 3/10/1877.
3. Wheeler Papers, Charles Devens to Wheeler, 3/6/1877; Hoogenboom, *Rutherford B. Hayes,* 297.
4. *NYT,* 3/15/1877, p. 1.
5. *MP,* 7/26/1877.
6. Ibid.
7. *MP,* 3/29/1877; Williams, *Diary and Letters,* 3/20/1877, 3:428.
8. Hoogenboom, *Rutherford B. Hayes,* 304–307, 309, and 311; Welch, *George Frisbie Hoar,* 77–79.
9. *MP,* 8/30/1877.
10. Wheeler Papers, Wheeler to Rutherford B. Hayes, 11/21/1878.
11. Alexander, *Political History,* 3:360.
12. *FG,* 1/18/1878.
13. *MP,* 12/6/1877.
14. Jordan, *Roscoe Conkling,* 93.

15. Ibid., 133, 146–150; *NYT,* 1/15/1900, p. 7.
16. Jordan, *Roscoe Conkling,* 280.
17. Wheeler Papers, Wheeler to Rutherford B. Hayes, 9/4/1877.
18. Alexander, *Political History,* 3:399; Jordan, *Roscoe Conkling,* 281–282.
19. Jordan, *Roscoe Conkling,* 286.
20. Alexander, *Political History,* 3:406; Jordan, *Roscoe Conkling,* 293; *NYT,* 12/1/1912, p. 15.
21. Under federal law, if Congress was not in session, a federal officer could be suspended and a replacement named to take his place, but if the replacement did not win Senate confirmation in the next session, the suspended officer could have his job back. Jordan, *Roscoe Conkling,* 283.
22. Alexander, *Political History,* 3:406–407.
23. *MP,* 8/22/1878; Hurd, *History of Clinton and Franklin Counties,* 382.
24. *MP,* 9/12/1878; Seaver, *Historical Sketches of Franklin County,* 721 and 808.
25. *MP,* 11/3/1864, 10/18/1866, 6/11/1868, 6/16/1870, 9/12/1878; *NYT,* 3/8/1881, p. 1; Seaver, *Historical Sketches of Franklin County,* 720.
26. Alexander, *Political History,* 3:446.
27. Klein, *Empire State,* 454; Alexander, *Political History,* 3:389.
28. Alexander, *Political History,* 3:389; Klein, *Empire State,* 454; Seaver, *Historical Sketches of Franklin County,* 117; *MP,* 9/26/1878.
29. Klein, *Empire State,* 455; Alexander, *Political History* 3:390 and 393.
30. *NYT,* 9/20/1878, p. 1; *MP,* 9/26/1878.
31. Alexander, *Political History,* 3:397.
32. Jordan, *Roscoe Conkling,* 296; Dubin, *United States Congressional Elections,* 249.
33. *MP,* 7/18/1878.
34. Wheeler Papers, Wheeler to Rutherford B. Hayes, 7/8/1878.
35. *MP,* 2/6/1879.
36. Alexander, *Political History,* 3:409; Jordan, *Roscoe Conkling,* 300–301.
37. Alexander, *Political History,* 3:410.

CHAPTER 25. "THE MACHINE ALWAYS SLAUGHTERS ITS NEW CONVERTS"

1. New York, *Journal of the Senate.*
2. *NYT,* 1/10/1879, p. 2.
3. *NYT,* 10/3/1879, p. 4.
4. *NYT,* 6/9/1879, p. 5.
5. *NYT,* 6/29/1879, p. 1. In addition to Wheeler, Seymour, and Barnard, the other commissioners were: Robert S. Hale, a lawyer and former Republican

Congressman from Elizabethtown; William Dorsheimer, Democratic Lieutenant Governor from Buffalo; Francis A. Stout and George Geddes. New York Commissioners, *Special Report.*

6. *NYT,* 11/21/1879, p.1.
7. New York Commissioners, *Special Report,* 9–16.
8. Ibid., 33–40. A bill appropriating money to create the Niagara Reservation was passed in 1885.
9. Alexander, *Political History,* 3:416. In addition to the governor, the other state officers up for election were lieutenant governor, secretary of state, comptroller, treasurer, attorney general, and engineer.
10. *NYT,* 9/1/1879, p. 1.
11. *NYT,* 9/3/1879, p. 1.
12. *NYT,* 10/21/1879, p. 1.
13. Alexander, *Political History,* 3:294; *NYT,* 12/7/1898, p. 7.
14. *NYT,* 9/3/1879, p. 1; *NYT,* 1/26/1922, p. 15; *BE,* 9/15/1879, p. 2; *NYT,* 9/5/1879, p. 1.
15. Alexander, *Political History,* 3:413.
16. *FG,* 9/5/1879.
17. *NYT,* 9/1/1879, p. 1; *MP,* 8/28/1879.
18. *NYT,* 9/1/1879, p. 1.
19. *BE,* 9/15/1879, p. 2; *NYT,* 9/3/1879, p. 1 and 9/5/1879, p. 1.
20. Seaver, *Historical Sketches of Franklin County,* 713.
21. *BE,* 9/15/1879, p. 2; *NYT,* 9/3/1879, p. 1 and 9/5/1879, p. 1.
22. *NYT,* 9/4/1879, p. 1; *MP,* 9/11/1879; *BE,* 9/4/1879, p. 2.
23. *NYT,* 9/4/1879, p. 1; *MP,* 9/4/1879.
24. *BE,* 9/4/1879, p. 2.
25. *NYT,* 9/4/1879, p. 1; *MP,* 9/11/1879. Robertson received 106 votes, Starin 40, Pomeroy 35, Hiscock 34, and Sloan l. Alexander, *Political History,* 3:416–417.
26. *NYT,* 9/5/1879, p. 1; Alexander, *Political History,* 3:416.
27. *NYT,* 10/21/1879, p. 1; *BE,* 9/15/1879, p. 2; *HW,* 3/26/1881.
28. *NYT,* 10/24/1879, p. 1; Reeves, *Gentleman Boss,* 155–156.
29. *MP,* 11/6/1879; Alexander, *Political History,* 3:426–427.
30. *MP,* 1/22/1880.

Chapter 26. Delivering a "Paroxysm of Partisan Fury"

1. *NYT,* 5/9/1880, p. 10; *MP,* 5/13/1880; *BE,* 6/14/1880, p. 2.
2. *NYT,* 4/10/1879 and 1/26/1880, p. 1; *BE,* 1/5/1879, p. 4; *MP,* 12/5/1878, 1/16/1879, 12/4/1879, 1/8/1880, 1/29/1880, and 2/5/1880.

3. Williams, *Diary and Letters,* 12/18/1879, 3:582.
4. Peskin, "Who Were the Stalwarts?," 705–706; Blum et al., *National Experience,* 470.
5. Jordan, *Roscoe Conkling,* 321–323; *MP,* 2/5/1880.
6. *MP,* 12/4/1879.
7. *MP,* 3/4/1880. Their alternates were E. D. Brooks and Assemblyman Daniel Peck, both from St. Lawrence County.
8. *MP,* 6/3/1880; Alexander, *Political History,* 3:436–437; Jordan, *Roscoe Conkling,* 327; Reeves, *Gentleman Boss,* 167.
9. Jordan, *Roscoe Conkling,* 332.
10. *MP,* 6/10/1880; New York voted 50 for Grant and 20 for Garfield. Alexander, *Political History,* 3:441.
11. *NYT,* 6/9/1880, p. 1; Reeves, *Gentleman Boss,* 181; Alexander, *Political History,* 3:442–445.
12. Jordan, *Roscoe Conkling,* 150 and 365; Reeves, *Gentleman Boss,* 167.
13. *MP,* 6/10/1880.
14. Jordan, *Roscoe Conkling,* 345–346; Alexander, *Political History,* 3:447–450.
15. Jordan, *Roscoe Conkling,* 346; Alexander, *Political History,* 3:457.
16. Seaver, *Historical Sketches of Franklin County,* 770.
17. *MP*, 8/12/1880.
18. *America Goes to the Polls.*
19. *NYT,* 8/16/1880, p. 3.
20. *NYT,* 8/13/1880, p. 5.
21. *FG,* 8/20/1880.
22. *NYT,* 9/10/1880, p. 5; *MP*, 9/16/1880.
23. *MP,* 11/4/1880.
24. *America Goes to the Polls; MP,* 11/18/1880; Alexander, *Political History,* 3:463.
25. *MP,* 11/4/1880.

CHAPTER 27. U.S. SENATE ELECTION ROUND ONE: THE DOUBLE-CROSS

1. *BE,* 1/4/1881, p. 3.
2. Sterngass, "Platt, Thomas C(ollier)," in Eisenstadt, *Encyclopedia of New York State,* 1212; *BE,* 1/14/1881, p. 2.
3. Alexander, *Political History,* 3:252 and 466; Jordan, *Roscoe Conkling,* 146 and 152.
4. Odom, "Depew, Chauncey M(itchell)," in Eisenstadt, *Encyclopedia of New*

York State, 457. Depew would become president of the New York Central in 1895.

5. Reeves, *Gentleman Boss,* 207; Jordan, *Roscoe Conkling,* 365.
6. Alexander, *Political History,* 3:338–339; Jordan, *Roscoe Conkling,* 246. Morgan and Rogers lost the election to Democrats Lucius Robinson and William Dorsheimer. Alexander, *Political History,* 3:350.
7. *BE,* 1/5/1881, p. 4.
8. Haynes, *Election of Senators,* 34–35.
9. Alexander, *Political History,* 3:468.
10. *BE,* 1/5/1881, p. 4; *NYT,* 1/13/1881, p. 1.
11. *MP,* 1/13/1881.
12. *BE,* 1/16/1881, p. 4.
13. *MP,* 11/18/1880; *NYT,* 11/22/1880, p. 5.
14. *BE,* 12/2/1880, p. 2; *MP,* 12/9/1880 and 12/23/1880.
15. *BE,* 1/4/1881, p. 3; *MP,* 12/30/1880 and 1/6/1881.
16. *NYT,* 1/11/1881, p. 1; *Biographical Directory.*
17. *BE,* 1/11/1881 and 1/12/1881, p. 4.
18. *NYT,* 1/12/1881, p. 1.
19. *BE,* 3/10/1881, p. 1.
20. Seaver, *Historical Sketches of Franklin County,* 117.
21. *NYT,* 1/13/1881, p. 1.
22. Reeves, *Gentleman Boss,* 210–211.
23. Alexander, *Political History,* 3:468; Jordan, *Roscoe Conkling,* 367.
24. *NYT,* 1/14/1881, p. 1; *MP,* 1/20/1881. The official election took place on January 18. In the Senate, Platt defeated the incumbent Democrat Kernan, 25 to 6, and in the Assembly, Platt defeated Kernan 79–44. Alexander, *Political History,* 3:468.
25. *BE,* 1/4/1881, p. 3.
26. Seaver, *Historical Sketches of Franklin County,* 117–118.
27. *NYT,* 2/10/1881, p. 1.
28. Seaver, *Historical Sketches of Franklin County,* 750. Kilburn would become the father of the thirteen-term Congressman from Malone, Clarence E. Kilburn, who served from 1949 to 1965. *Biographical Directory.*
29. *BE,* 3/10/1881, p. 1; *MP,* 2/24/1881 and 3/10/1881; Seaver, *Historical Sketches of Franklin County,* 118.
30. Reeves, *Gentleman Boss,* 220–221; *BE,* 3/4/1881, p. 4; Balch, *Life of James,* 556–558; *NYT,* 3/5/1881, pp. 1–2.
31. *NYT,* 3/8/1881, p. 1; *MP,* 3/10/1881 and 3/17/1881. Brennan left a wife and two children. He had been married to Laura C. Smith for eleven years. *MP,* 6/16/1870.

32. *NYT,* 3/15/1881, p. 2.
33. Klein, *Empire State,* 483.

CHAPTER 28. U.S. SENATE ELECTION ROUND TWO: CAUGHT IN A CROSSFIRE

1. *MP,* 3/10/1881.
2. *MP,* 4/14/1881.
3. Reeves, *Gentleman Boss* 223. Merritt was nominated to become consul general at London.
4. Wheeler Papers, Wheeler to Rutherford B. Hayes, 5/12/1881.
5. Reeves, *Gentleman Boss,* 231.
6. Jordan, *Roscoe Conkling,* 395.
7. *NYT,* 5/21/1881, p. 1.
8. *MP,* 5/19/1881 and 5/26/1881.
9. *AR,* 6/2/1881.
10. *MP,* 6/2/1881.
11. *NYT,* 6/1/1881, p. 1; Reeves, *Gentleman Boss,* 234–235.
12. *NYT,* 6/2/1881, p. 1.
13. *NYT,* 6/3, 6/4, 6/5, 6/7, 6/8, and 6/9/1881, p. 1; *BE,* 6/9/1881, p. 2.
14. *NYT,* 6/10/1881, p. 1.
15. *BE,* 6/9/1881, p. 4 and 6/10/1881, p. 2. Subsequently, Sessions was indicted and after a trial on the bribery charges, he was acquitted. Alexander, *Political History,* 3:480.
16. *NYT,* 6/17/1881, p. 1.
17. *NYT,* 6/20 and 6/21/1881, p. 1; *MP,* 6/23/1881.
18. *BE,* 6/19/1881, p. 6; *NYT,* 6/21/1881, p. 1; *MP,* 6/23/1881.
19. *NYT,* 6/22/1881, p. 1.
20. Former U.S. Senator Francis Kernan, the Democrat Platt had defeated in January, was the Democratic candidate running for Platt's seat. *MP,* 6/2/1881.
21. *NYT,* 6/23/1881, p. 1; *BE,* 6/23/1881, pp. 2 and p. 4; *Biographical Directory.*
22. *NYT,* 6/24/1881, p. 1.
23. *AR,* 7/1/1881.
24. *NYT,* 7/2/1881, p. 1; *BE,* 7/2/1881, p. 2; *MP,* 7/7/1881.
25. *NYT,* 7/3/1881, p. 5.
26. Reeves, *Gentleman Boss,* 237; Jordan, *Roscoe Conkling,* 405; DeGregorio, *Complete Book,* 302. Garfield lived for more than two and a half months after being shot. He underwent three operations, developed blood poisoning from having his wound probed by doctors using their bare fingers and unsterilized instruments, rallied briefly but died on September 19, 1881. Ibid., 303.

27. Reeves, *Gentleman Boss,* 243; Jordan, *Roscoe Conkling,* 406; *NYT,* 7/5/1881, p. 8, 7/6/1881, p. 5, and 7/7/1881, p. 2.
28. *NYT,* 7/8/1881, p. 5.
29. *NYT,* 7/9/1881, p. 1; *MP,* 7/14/1881.
30. *NYT,* 7/10, 7/14, 7/17, 7/23/1881, p. 1; *BE,* 7/10/1881, p. 6 and 7/14/1881, p. 4; *MP,* 7/21/1881 and 7/28/1881.
31. *HW,* 6/18/1887.
32. *NYT,* 11/14/1880, p. 2; *MP,* 11/18/1880.

CHAPTER 29. "DISTRESSING MALADY OF MY BLADDER"

1. *MP,* 10/12/1882.
2. Wheeler presided over a town-wide Protestant memorial service for Garfield held at the Congregational Church in Malone. *MP,* 9/29/1881.
3. *MP,* 6/15/1881.
4. Reeves, *Gentleman Boss,* 334; Karabell, *Chester Alan Arthur,* 116.
5. *MP,* 4/28/1881, 5/12/1881, and 5/4/1882.
6. Federal Reserve, "Consumer Price Index."
7. *MP,* 6/19/1879 and 7/1/1880.
8. *MP,* 8/12/1880, 2/24/1881, 6/30/1881, 9/22/1881, 10/13/1881, 11/24/1881, and 10/12/1882.
9. Seaver, *Historical Sketches of Franklin County,* 478.
10. Ibid., 479.
11. *MP,* 5/11/1882, 5/25/1882, 6/1/1882; Federal Reserve, "Consumer Price Index."
12. *MP,* 7/13/1882, 9/7/1882, and 9/14/1882.
13. *MP,* 11/9/1882, 4/12/1883, 8/7/1884, and 9/11/1884.
14. *MP,* 9/18/1884; Federal Reserve, "Consumer Price Index."
15. *MP,* 10/9/1884 and 10/16/1884.
16. Wheeler Papers, 4/10/1881, Wheeler to Lucy Hayes; *FG,* 4/1/1881.
17. *MP,* 10/13/1881 and 10/27/1881.
18. *MP,* 12/20/1881, 2/23/1882, and 3/16/1882.
19. Wheeler Papers, 12/12/1886, Wheeler to Rutherford B. Hayes.
20. *MP,* 7/20/1882, 8/31/1882, and 9/7/1882.
21. *MP,* 3/22/1883 and 4/19/1883; *NYT,* 4/22/1883, p. 13.
22. *MP,* 9/4/1884.
23. *MP,* 9/11/1884; Southwick, *Presidential Also-Rans,* 392. After the war, Logan had been elected president of the politically active fraternal organization of Civil War veterans, the Grand Army of the Republic, and in that position he

had successfully promoted the national observance of Decoration Day, which subsequently became the national holiday, Memorial Day. Ibid., 394.

24. *MP,* 10/23/1884.
25. Wheeler Papers, 12/12/1886, Wheeler to Rutherford B. Hayes.
26. *MP,* 5/7/1885 and 6/18/1885.
27. *MP,* 8/5, 9/2, 9/9, and 12/23/1886.
28. *MP,* 12/2/1886; *FG,* 12/3/1886.
29. Wheeler Papers, 12/12/1886, Wheeler to Rutherford B. Hayes; 1/7/1887, Wheeler to Fanny Hayes.
30. *NYT,* 3/12/1887, p. 1.
31. *MP,* 6/2/1887 and 6/9/1887; *NYT,* 3/12/1887, p. 1 and 6/5/1887, p. 5.
32. *MP,* 6/9/1887; *NYT,* 6/7/1887, p. 1 and 6/8/1887, p. 5.

Chapter 30. Negotiating "Simple Justice"

1. Seaver, *Historical Sketches of Franklin County,* 783; *MP,* 12/8/1887.
2. *MP,* 6/9/1887 and 6/7/1888; Federal Reserve, "Consumer Price Index."
3. Wheeler, Last Will and Testament; *Eighteenth Annual Report,* 140, 146, and 151.
4. *MP,* 8/4/1887, 12/8/1887, 4/26/1888, and 5/17/1888; Seaver, *Historical Sketches of Franklin County,* 738–739.
5. *MP,* 9/23/1887 and 12/8/1887.
6. *MP,* 12/8/1887, 6/9/1887, and 5/17/1888; Seaver, *Historical Sketches of Franklin County,* 712.
7. Wheeler, Last Will and Testament; *MP,* 12/8/1887.
8. *MP,* 4/26/1888 and 5/17/1888; *FG,* 4/11/1890.
9. Wheeler, Last Will and Testament; *MP,* 3/29/1888 and 5/31/1888.
10. *FG,* 6/1/1888; *MP,* 5/31/1888; Federal Reserve, "Consumer Price Index."
11. *NYT,* 6/16/1888, p. 3; *MP,* 8/16/1888.
12. *FG,* 8/17/1888.

Epilogue. From "Sterling Gold" to Neurotic Timidity

1. Williams, *Diary and Letters,* 4:327.
2. *NYT,* 6/5/1887, pp. 4–5.
3. *HW,* 6/18/1887.
4. Otten, *Grand Old Partyman,* 189, 265, 287; Hatfield, *Vice Presidents,* 243–244.
5. Tally, *Bland Ambition,* 153; Barzman, *Madmen and Geniuses,* 130.

6. *Wikipedia,* "William Almon Wheeler."
7. *MP,* 1/1/1874.
8. *MP,* 3/8/1877.
9. *MP,* 3/31/1881 and 4/7/1881; Seaver, *Historical Sketches of Franklin County,* 713.
10. *MP,* 6/9/1887.
11. Seaver, *Historical Sketches of Franklin County,* 713.
12. Otten, *Grand Old Partyman,* 189n39; 265, and 287.
13. Hatfield, *Vice Presidents,* 243–244.
14. Eckenrode, *Rutherford B. Hayes,* 135.
15. Tally, *Bland Ambition,* 153; Barzman, *Madmen and Geniuses,* 130; *Wikipedia,* "William Almon Wheeler."
16. Jordan, *Roscoe Conkling,* 241; Otten, *Grand Old Partyman,* 135–136.
17. Wolfe, "Four Lost Men," in *From Death to Morning,* 121.
18. Purcell, *Vice Presidents,* v.
19. Warren, "John Adams," in Purcell, *Vice Presidents,* 11.
20. Calder, "John Nance Gardner," in Purcell, *Vice Presidents,* 296.
21. *NYT,* 6/5/1887, p. 5.
22. Rehnquist, *Centennial Crisis,* 51–57 and 79–83.

Bibliography

Alexander, DeAlva Stanwood. *A Political History of the State of New York.* 3 vols. New York: Henry Holt, 1906–1909.

America Goes to the Polls. Hartford, CT: Travelers Insurance Companies, 1964.

American Bible Society. "About ABS." http://www.americanbible.org (accessed June 21, 2012).

Appendix to the Congressional Globe. 1870–1873.

Appletons' Annual Cyclopedia and Register of Important Events of the Year 1887. New York: D. Appleton, 1888.

Armstrong, Zella. *The History of Hamilton County and Chattanooga Tennessee.* Chattanooga: Lookout Publishing, 1931.

Balch, William Ralston. *The Life of James Abram Garfield.* Philadelphia: C. McCurdy, 1881.

Barnes, Thurlow Weed. *Memoir of Thurlow Weed.* Boston: Houghton Mifflin, 1884.

Barzman, Sol. *Madmen and Geniuses.* Chicago: Follett, 1974.

Beaman, Donald R. "William Almon Wheeler." Unpublished honors thesis, St. Lawrence University, Canton, New York, 1949.

Beck, Theodric Romeyn. *Elements of Medical Jurisprudence.* Philadelphia: J. B. Lippincott, 1863.

Bergamini, John D. *The Hundredth Year.* New York: G. P. Putnam's Sons, 1976.

Biographical Directory of the United States Congress. http://bioguide.congress.gov (accessed April 6, 2012).

Bishop, Morris. *A History of Cornell.* Ithaca, NY: Cornell University Press, 1962.

Black, David. *The King of Fifth Avenue: The Fortunes of August Belmont.* New York: Dial Press, 1981.

Blaine, James G. *Twenty Years of Congress.* 2 vols. Norwich, CT: Henry Bill, 1884–1886.

Blum, John M., Edmund S. Morgan, Willie Lee Rose, Arthur M. Schlesinger Jr., Kenneth M. Stampp, and C. Vann Woodward. *The National Experience.* New York: Harcourt Brace Jovanovich, 1977.

Boller, Paul F. Jr. *Presidential Anecdotes.* New York: Oxford University Press, 1981.

Burlingame, Michael, ed. *At Lincoln's Side.* Carbondale: Southern Illinois University Press, 2000.

Burrows, Edwin C., and Mike Wallace. *Gotham.* New York: Oxford University Press, 1999.

Cahill, Marie, and Tom Debolski. *North American Steam.* New York: Crescent Books, 1991.

Calder, J. Kent. "John Nance Garner." In *Vice Presidents,* edited by L. Edward Purcell, 289–296. New York: Checkmark, 2001.

Chidsey, Donald Barr. *The Gentleman from New York: A Life of Roscoe Conkling.* New Haven, CT: Yale University Press, 1935.

Colbert, Thomas Burnell. "Thomas Andrews Hendricks." In *Vice Presidents,* edited by L. Edward Purcell, 186–193. New York: Checkmark, 2001.

Congressional Globe. 1861–1873.

Congressional Record. 1873–1875.

Conkling, Alfred R. *The Life and Letters of Roscoe Conkling.* New York: Charles L. Webster, 1889.

Conlin, Joseph R. *The American Past.* Fort Worth, TX: Harcourt Brace, 1997.

Conwell, Russell H. *Life and Public Services of Gov. Rutherford B. Hayes.* Boston: B. B. Russell, 1877.

Curtis, Gates, ed. *Our County and Its People: A Memorial Record of St. Lawrence County New York.* Syracuse, NY: D. Mason, 1894.

Daniels, Robert V., ed. *The University of Vermont: The First Two Hundred Years.* Hanover, NH: University Press of New England, 1991.

Dartmouth College. *Minutes of Board of Trustees.* Hanover, New Hampshire, 1865.

DeGregorio, William. *The Complete Book of U. S. Presidents.* New York: Random House, 2001.

Documents of the Convention of the State of New York 1867–'68. Vol. 1. Albany, NY: Weed, Parsons, 1868.

Dubin, Michael J. *United States Congressional Elections, 1788–1997.* Jefferson, NC: McFarland, 1998.

Duke University Libraries. "Historic American Sheet Music." http://library.duke.edu (accessed June 21, 2012).

Dunlap, Leslie W. *Our Vice-Presidents and Second Ladies.* Metuchen, NJ: Scarecrow Press, 1988.

Eckenrode, H. J. *Rutherford B. Hayes.* Port Washington, NY: Kennikat Press, 1963.

Eighteenth Annual Report of the Board of Home Missions of the Presbyterian Church in the United States of America. New York: No. 53 Fifth Avenue, 1888.

Eisenstadt, Peter, ed. *The Encyclopedia of New York State.* Syracuse, NY: Syracuse University Press, 2005.

Emerson, Ken. *Doo-dah!.* New York: Simon & Schuster, 1997.

Federal Reserve Bank of Minneapolis. "Consumer Price Index (Estimate)." http://www.minneapolisfed.org/community_education/teacher/calc/hist1800.cfm (accessed February, 8, 2012).

Folts, James D. "Courts, state." In *The Encyclopedia of New York State,* edited by Peter Eisenstadt, 411–416. Syracuse, NY: Syracuse University Press, 2005.

Foner, Eric. *Reconstruction: America's Unfinished Revolution, 1863–1867.* New York: HarperCollins, 2002.

Frank, Sid, and Arden Davis Melick. *The Presidents Tidbits & Trivia.* New York: Greenwich House, 1984.

Glaeser, Edward Ludwig, and Claudia Dale Goldin. *Corruption and Reform.* Chicago: University of Chicago Press, 2006.

Gosnell, Harold F. *Boss Platt and His New York Machine.* New York: Russell & Russell, 1924, reprinted 1969.

Gould, Lewis L. *Grand Old Party.* New York: Random House, 2003.

Graham, Frank Jr. *The Adirondack Park.* New York: Alfred A. Knopf, 1978.

Greenberg, David. "Lincoln's Crackdown." *Slate Magazine,* November 30, 2001. http://www.slate.com (accessed February 2, 2012).

Greene, Linda Wedel. *Yosemite: The Park and Its Resources.* Washington, DC: U.S. Department of the Interior/National Park Service, 1987. http://www.nps.gov/yose/historyculture (accessed June 21, 2012).

Hatfield, Mark O. *Vice Presidents of the United States, 1789–1993.* Washington, DC: U.S. Government Printing Office, 1997.

Hayes, Rutherford B., Presidential Center, "Russell Hastings." http://www.rbhayes.org/hayes/mssfind/274/hastingsr.htm (accessed June 21, 2012).

Hayes, Rutherford B., Presidential Center, "Rutherford Hayes Platt." http://www.rbhayes.org/hayes/mssfind/274/platthayes.htm (accessed June 21, 2012).

Hayes, Rutherford B., Presidential Center. "Dining at the White House During the Hayes Administration." http://www.rbhayes.org/hayes/onlinetexts (accessed February 7, 2012).

Hayes, Rutherford B., Presidential Center. "Sheet Music Collection." http://www.rbhayes.org/hayes/materials (accessed May 19, 2012).

Haynes, George H. *The Election of Senators.* New York: Henry Holt, 1912.

Hewett, Waterman Thomas. *Cornell University: A History.* New York: University Publishing Society, 1905.

History of Medicine, "Origins of the National Institute of Health." http://www.nlm.nih.gov/exhibition/nih_origins/civilwar.html (accessed June 20, 2012).

Hoar, George F. *Autobiography of Seventy Years.* 2 vols. New York: Charles Scribner's Sons, 1905.

Hoogenboom, Ari. *Rutherford B. Hayes.* Lawrence: University Press of Kansas, 1995.

Holt, Michael F. *The Rise and Fall of the American Whig Party.* New York: Oxford University Press, 1999.

Hough, Franklin B. *A History of St. Lawrence and Franklin Counties, New York.* Albany, NY: Little, 1853.

Hunt, H. Draper. *Hannibal Hamlin of Maine.* Syracuse, NY: Syracuse University Press, 1969.

Hurd, Duane Hamilton. *History of Clinton and Franklin Counties, New York.* Philadelphia: J. H. Lewis, 1880.

Jenkins, John S. *The Life of Silas Wright.* Auburn, NY: Alden & Markham, 1847.

Jewish Virtual Library. "General Grant's Infamy." http://www.jewishvirtuallibrary.org (accessed March 16, 2012).

Johnson, Thomas H., ed. *The Oxford Companion to American History.* New York: Oxford University Press, 1966.

Jordan, David M. *Roscoe Conkling of New York.* Ithaca, NY: Cornell University Press, 1971.

Journal of the Convention of the State of New York. 2 vols. Albany, NY: Weed, Parsons, 1867.

Kagan, Hilde Heun, ed. *The American Heritage Pictorial Atlas of United States History.* New York: American Heritage, 1966.

Kammen, Carol. "Cornell, Ezra." In *The Encyclopedia of New York State,* edited by Peter Eisenstadt, 396–397. Syracuse, NY: Syracuse University Press, 2005.

Kane, Joseph Nathan. *Presidential Fact Book.* New York: Random House, 1999.

Karabell, Zachary. *Chester Alan Arthur.* New York: Henry Holt, 2004.

King, Louis M. Correspondence, January 30, 1947. Franklin County Historical Society, Malone, New York.

Kirkland, Edward Chase. *Men, Cities and Transportation.* Cambridge, MA: Harvard University Press, 1948.

Kivic, Peter. "Abolition's Early Roots in Franklin County." *Franklin Historical Review 41* (2006): 16–30.

Klein, Milton M., ed. *The Empire State.* Ithaca, NY: Cornell University Press, 2001.

Landon, Harry F. *The North Country: A History Embracing Jefferson, St. Lawrence, Oswego, Lewis and Franklin Counties, New York.* Indianapolis, IN: Historical, 1932.

Library of Congress. "Voices, Votes, Victory." http://myloc.gov/exhibitions/presidentialsongs (accessed November 19, 2011).

Lindsay, Julian Ira. *Tradition Looks Forward: The University of Vermont.* Burlington: University of Vermont and State Agricultural College, 1954.

Lyman, Susan. *Rails Into Racquetteville.* Massena, NY: Massena Printing, 1976. http://russnelson.com/RWnO/www.northnet.org/norwood/railroads.html (accessed June 15, 2012).

Marshall, Jeffrey D. *Universitas Viridis Montis.* Burlington, VT: University of Vermont, 1991.

Marshall, John A. *American Bastille.* Philadelphia: Thomas W. Hartley, 1881.

Menand, Louis. *The Metaphysical Club.* New York: Farrar, Straus and Giroux, 2001.

Misch, Tony, and Remington Stone. "James Lick, the 'Generous Miser.'" http://collections.ucolick.org/archives_on_line/James_Lick.html (accessed June 21, 2012).

Mohr, James C. *The Radical Republicans and Reform in New York during Reconstruction.* Ithaca, NY: Cornell University Press, 1973.

Mooney, Richard E. "Raymond, Henry J(arvis)." In *The Encyclopedia of New York State,* edited by Peter Eisenstadt, 1286–1287. Syracuse, NY: Syracuse University Press, 2005.

Morgan, Edwin D. Papers. Manuscripts and Special Collections, New York State Library, Albany.

Morris, Richard B., ed. *Encyclopedia of American History.* New York: Harper & Brothers, 1961.

Muzzey, David Saville. *James G. Blaine.* Port Washington, NY: Kenniket, 1963.

Nevins, Allan. *Abram S. Hewitt.* New York: Harper & Brothers, 1935.

New York. *Journal of the Senate.* 1876.

New York Civil Service Commission. *Fourth Report of the Civil Service Commission of the State of New York* (New York, 1887).

New York Commissioners of the State Survey. *Special Report of New York State Survey on the Preservation of the Scenery of Niagara Falls.* Albany, NY: Charles Van Benthuysen & Sons, 1880.

Odom, E. Dale. "Depew, Chauncey M(itchell)." In *The Encyclopedia of New York State,* edited by Peter Eisenstadt, 457. Syracuse, NY: Syracuse University Press, 2005.

Otten, James T. "The Wheeler Adjustment in Louisiana: National Republicans Begin to Reappraise Their Reconstruction Policy." *Louisiana History 12,* No. 4 (Fall 1972): 349–367.

Otten, James T. *Grand Old Partyman: William A. Wheeler and the Republican Party, 1850–1880* (unpublished PhD dissertation). University of South Carolina, 1976.

Peskin, Allan. "Who Were The Stalwarts? Who Were Their Rivals? Republican Factions in the Gilded Age." *Political Science Quarterly,* Vol. 99, No. 4 (Winter 1984–85), pp. 703–716.

Poe Collection of Early American Letters. http://www.poearchive.com/index.php (accessed June 21, 2012).

Potter, David M. *The Impending Crisis, 1848–1861.* New York: Harper & Row Publishers, 1976.

Proceedings and Debates of the Convention for the Revision of the Constitution of the State of New York 1867–'68; reported by E. F. Underhill, official stenographer to the convention. 3 vols. Albany, NY: Weed, Parsons and Co., 1868. [vol. 1, pp. 17–1032; vol. 2, pp. 1033–1968; vol. 3, pp. 1969-end].

Proceedings of the Republican National Convention, 1876. Concord, NH: Republican Press Association, 1876.

Purcell, L. Edward, ed. *Vice Presidents.* New York: Checkmark Books, 2001.

Rawley, James A. *Edwin D. Morgan 1811–1883: Merchant in Politics.* New York: Columbia University Press, 1955.

Rayback, Robert J. *Millard Fillmore.* Newtown, CT: American Political Biography Press, 1959.

Reeves, Thomas C. *Gentleman Boss.* Newtown, CT: American Political Biography Press, 1991.

Rehnquist, William H. *Centennial Crisis.* New York: Alfred A. Knopf, 2004.

Russotto, Patricia M., ed. *National Party Conventions 1831–1980.* Congressional Quarterly, 1983.

Sampson, Robert D. "Hunkers." In *The Encyclopedia of New York State,* edited by Peter Eisenstadt, 750. Syracuse, NY: Syracuse University Press, 2005.

Saturno, James V. "Procedural Distinctions between the House and the Committee of the Whole." *Congressional Research Service.* http://democrats.rules.house.gov/archives/98–143.pdf (accessed June 23, 2012)

Scarry, Robert J. *Millard Fillmore.* Jefferson, NC: McFarland, 2001.

Schaefer, Paul, ed. *Adirondack Explorations: Nature Writings of Verplanck Colvin.* Syracuse, NY: Syracuse University Press, 1997.

Seaver, Frederick J. *Historical Sketches of Franklin County.* Albany: J. B. Lyon, 1918.

Seigenthaler, John. *James K. Polk.* New York: Henry Holt, 2004.

Shaughnessy, Jim. *The Rutland Railroad.* Syracuse, NY: Syracuse University Press, 1997.

Silbey, Joel H. "Barnburners." In *The Encyclopedia of New York State,* edited by Peter Eisenstadt, 151. Syracuse, NY: Syracuse University Press, 2005.

Smalley, Eugene V. *History of the Northern Pacific Railroad.* New York: G. P. Putnam's Sons, 1883.

Smith, J. Gregory. Papers. Manuscript collection, Leahy Library, Vermont Historical Society, Barre.

Smith, James R. *San Francisco's Lost Landmarks.* Sanger, CA: Quill Driver Books/ Word Dancer Press, 2005.

Southwick, Leslie H., ed. *Presidential Also-Rans and Running Mates, 1788 through 1996.* Jefferson, NC: McFarland, 1998.

Stebbins, Homer Adolph. *A Political History of the State of New York.* New York: AMS Press, 1967.

Sterngass, Jon. "Field, David Dudley." In *The Encyclopedia of New York State,* edited by Peter Eisenstadt, 555. Syracuse, NY: Syracuse University Press, 2005.

Sterngass, Jon. "Morgan, Edwin D(enison)." In *The Encyclopedia of New York State,* edited by Peter Eisenstadt, 1009. Syracuse, NY: Syracuse University Press, 2005.

Sterngass, Jon. "Platt, Thomas C(ollier)." In *The Encyclopedia of New York State,* edited by Peter Eisenstadt, 1212. Syracuse, NY: Syracuse University Press, 2005.

Sterngass, Jon. "Tilden, Samuel J(ones)." In *The Encyclopedia of New York State,* edited by Peter Eisenstadt, 1558. Syracuse, NY: Syracuse University Press, 2005.

Tally, Steve. *Bland Ambition.* San Diego, CA: Harcourt Brace Jovanovich, 1992.

Taylor, John M. *William Henry Seward: Lincoln's Right Hand.* Washington, DC: Brassey's, 1911.

Terrie, Philip G. "Adirondacks." In *The Encyclopedia of New York State,* edited by Peter Eisenstadt, 11–16. Syracuse, NY: Syracuse University Press, 2005.

University of Vermont. *Catalogue of the Corporation.* Burlington, VT: 1844.

University of Vermont. *General Catalogue.* Burlington, VT: Free Press Association, 1901.

University of Vermont. *Minutes of Board of Trustees.* Burlington, VT: 1876.

U.S. Bureau of the Census. Heritage Quest Online. http://persi.heritagequestonline.com/hqoweb/library/do/census/results/hitlist?surname=wheeler (accessed January 30, 2008).

U.S. House of Representatives. *Proceedings and Debates of Congress Relating to Counting the Electoral Votes for President and Vice-President of the United States.* Washington, DC: Government Printing Office, 1877.

U.S. House Journal. 1861–1875.

U.S. House, H. R. 3004. *A Bill to Authorize the Construction of a Bridge Across the Saint Lawrence River.* 42nd Congress, 3rd Session, 1872.

U.S. Senate Commission on Art, Office of Senate Curator. *Vice President's Room.* S. Pub. 106–107. http://www.senate.gov/artandhistory/art/resources/pdf/Vice_President_s_Room.pdf (accessed June 23, 2012).

Vazzano, Frank P. "William A. Wheeler." In *Vice Presidents,* edited by L. Edward Purcell, 170–177. New York: Checkmark, 2001.

Vazzano, Frank. P. "Who Was William A. Wheeler?" *Hayes Historical Journal 9,* No. 4 (Summer 1990): 5–23.

The Village Harmony: or Youth's Assistant To Sacred Musick. Newburyport, MA: E. Little & Co., 1813.

Virtual American Biographies. "David Dudley Field." http://www.famousamericans.net/daviddudleyfield (accessed June 23, 2012).

Warren, Jack D. "John Adams." In *Vice Presidents,* edited by L. Edward Purcell, 1–13. New York: Checkmark, 2001.

Weed, Harriet A., ed. *Autobiography of Thurlow Weed.* Boston: Houghton, Mifflin and Company, 1884.

Welch, Richard E. Jr. *George Frisbie Hoar and the Half-Breed Republicans.* Cambridge, MA: Harvard University Press, 1971.

Wheeler, Albert Gallatin Jr. *The Genealogical and Encyclopedic History of the Wheeler Family in America.* Binghampton and New York: Vail-Ballou Co., 1914.

Wheeler, William A. Last Will and Testament dated May 17, 1888.

Wheeler, William A. *Report of the Trustees of the Second Mortgage Bond Holders of the Northern Rail Road Company.* Ogdensburgh, NY: Hitchcock, Tillotson & Stilwell, Printers, 1857.

Wheeler, William A. Papers. Rutherford B. Hayes Presidential Center, Fremont, Ohio.

Whitcomb, John, and Claire Whitcomb. *Real Life at the White House.* New York: Routledge, 2000.

White, Andrew Dickson. *Autobiography of Andrew Dickson White.* Seattle: World Wide School, 1999.

Wikipedia: The Free Encyclopedia. "William A. Wheeler." http://en.wikipedia.org/wiki/William_A._Wheeler (accessed May 17, 2012).

Williams, Charles Richard. *The Diary and Letters of Rutherford B. Hayes, Nineteenth President of the United States.* 5 vols. Columbus: Ohio State Archeological and Historical Society, 1922.

Williams, Frank J. "When Albany Challenged the President." *New York Archives* 8, No. 3 (Winter, 2009).

Wolfe, Thomas. "The Four Lost Men" in *From Death to Morning.* New York: Charles Scribner's Sons, 1935.

Wood, Charles R. *The Northern Pacific.* Seattle, WA: Superior Publishing, 1968.

Young, Klyde, and Lamar Middleton. *Heirs Apparent.* New York: Prentice-Hall, 1948.

INDEX